Crispin and Gill,

  With deep gratitude to
God and to you for all we did
together in those far-off days

  And with much love

       Mike

Christmas 2012

# ENDGAME

Secret talks and the end of apartheid

Willie Esterhuyse

TAFELBERG

Tafelberg
An imprint of NB Publishers
40 Heerengracht, Cape Town, 8000
www.tafelberg.com
© 2012 Willie Esterhuyse

Set in Bembo 11 on 13 pt
Translated from the Afrikaans by Linde Dietrich
Cover design by Michiel Botha
Book design by Nazli Jacobs
Front cover photograph of Thabo Mbeki: Africa Media Online
Index by Sanet le Roux
Printed and bound by Paarl Media Paarl
15 Jan van Riebeeck Drive, Paarl, South Africa
First edition, first printing 2012

ISBN 0-624-05427-6
e-ISBN 978-0-624-05812-0

To Annemarie:

What is told in this book was made possible by you. You not
only inspired me, but were ahead of me politically. Thank you for
accompanying me critically, and for tolerating and putting up with me.
And for always being there.

# Contents

# Acronyms and abbreviations

| | |
|---|---|
| AAI | Africa–America Institute |
| AB | Afrikaner Broederbond |
| ANC | African National Congress |
| Azapo | Azanian People's Organisation |
| BAT | British American Tobacco |
| Codesa | Convention for a Democratic South Africa |
| Consgold | Consolidated Goldfields |
| Contralesa | Congress of Traditional Leaders of South Africa |
| Cosatu | Congress of South African Trade Unions |
| CP | Conservative Party |
| EPG | Eminent Persons Group |
| Idasa | Institute for a Democratic Alternative for South Africa |
| MDM | Mass Democratic Movement |
| MK | UmKhonto weSizwe |
| Nactu | National Council of Trade Unions |
| NEC | National Executive Committee of the ANC |
| NIS | National Intelligence Service |
| NP | National Party |
| OAU | Organisation of African Unity |
| PAC | Pan-Africanist Congress of Azania |
| PFP | Progressive Federal Party |
| PLO | Palestine Liberation Organisation |
| RAU | Rand Afrikaans University |
| Sabra | South African Bureau for Racial Affairs |

| | |
|---|---|
| SACP | South African Communist Party |
| SADF | South African Defence Force |
| SSC | State Security Council |
| SU | Stellenbosch University |
| Swapo | South West Africa People's Organisation |
| TRC | Truth and Reconciliation Commission |
| UDF | United Democratic Front |

# Timeline

| | | |
|---|---|---|
| 1983 | | Formation of United Democratic Front (UDF) |
| 1985 | 16 – 22 June | Kabwe conference |
| 1985 | 19 June | Repeal of the Mixed Marriages Act and the Immorality Act |
| 1985 | July | First state of emergency declared in South Africa |
| 1985 | 15 August | PW Botha's Rubicon speech |
| 1985 | August | US Chase Manhattan Bank withdraws all its short-term loans to South Africa |
| 1985 | October | Formation of Discussion Group '85 |
| 1986 | 21 January | US Congress passes the Comprehensive Anti-Apartheid Act of 1986 |
| 1986 | February | Van Zyl Slabbert and Alex Boraine resign from parliament |
| 1986 | 2 March – 19 May | The Commonwealth's Eminent Persons Group visits South Africa |
| 1986 | 19 May | The SADF invades neighbouring states |
| 1986 | June | Second state of emergency declared in South Africa |
| 1986 | 1 July | Influx-control measures scrapped |
| 1987 | 20 February | Discussion Group '85 meets PW Botha at Tuynhuys |
| 1987 | March | First Newick Park talks |
| 1987 | May | Formation of the Independent Movement |
| 1987 | 6 May | General election |
| 1987 | 24 June | British business leaders meet ANC leaders in London |
| 1987 | 9 – 12 July | Dakar conference, organised by Idasa |

| | | |
|---|---|---|
| 1987 | September | Prisoner exchange between South Africa and Angola–Swapo |
| 1987 | 9 October | ANC issues a public statement in favour of negotiations |
| **1987** | **1 – 3 November** | **First Consgold meeting – Compleat Angler Hotel, Marlow** |
| 1987 | 5 November | Govan Mbeki is released |
| **1988** | **21 – 24 February** | **Second Consgold meeting – Eastwell Manor, Kent** |
| 1988 | 24 February | Government bans UDF and 16 other organisations |
| 1988 | 28 March | First discussion between Mandela and committee in Pollsmoor |
| **1988** | **21 – 24 August** | **Third Consgold meeting – Mells Park** |
| 1988 | 1 September | South Africa, Cuba and Angola sign the Geneva Protocol that ushers in the ceasefire in Namibia |
| 1988 | October | Leverkusen conference, organised by Idasa |
| 1988 | December | Mandela is moved to a house at the Victor Verster Prison |
| **1988** | **17 – 19 December** | **Fourth Consgold meeting – Flittwick, Bedfordshire** |
| 1988 | 22 December | Trilateral agreement signed between South Africa, Cuba and Angola |
| 1989 | January | PW Botha suffers a stroke |
| 1989 | 2 February | FW de Klerk takes over the national leadership of the NP |
| 1989 | 27 March – 1 April | Bermuda conference between Americans, the ANC and South Africans |
| **1989** | **21 – 24 April** | **Fifth Consgold meeting – Mells Park** |
| 1989 | 31 May | Esterhuyse meets Mbeki in London at the request of the National Intelligence Service (NIS) |
| 1989 | 5 July | Botha meets Mandela at Tuynhuys |

| 1989 | 14 August | PW Botha resigns as president after a confrontation with his cabinet |
| 1989 | 15 August | FW de Klerk appointed acting president |
| 1989 | 16 Augustus | State Security Council meeting: the NIS's motion is adopted |
| 1989 | 21 August | Harare Declaration |
| 1989 | 6 September | General election |
| 1989 | 12 September | The NIS meets the ANC in Lucerne |
| 1989 | 17 September | The NIS briefs De Klerk |
| 1989 | 20 September | FW de Klerk inaugurated as president |
| 1989 | 15 October | Walter Sisulu and six other political prisoners released |
| 1989 | 13 December | FW de Klerk meets Mandela |
| 1990 | 2 February | FW de Klerk unbans the ANC and other organisations |
| **1990** | **9 –11 February** | **Sixth Consgold meeting – Mells Park** |
| 1990 | 11 February | Mandela is released |
| 1990 | 11 April | First dialogue between the government and the ANC |
| 1990 | 28 April | Thabo Mbeki arrives in South Africa |
| 1990 | 2 – 4 May | The government and the ANC meet at Groote Schuur: Groote Schuur Minute signed |
| 1990 | June | State of emergency lifted |
| **1990** | **29 June – 1 July** | **Seventh Consgold meeting – Mells Park** |
| 1990 | 6 August | The government and the ANC meet in Pretoria: Pretoria Minute signed |
| 1991 | 12 February | The government and the ANC meet at DF Malan Airport: DF Malan Accord signed |
| **1991** | **10 – 11 August** | **Meeting of contact group at Hartebeespoort Dam** |
| 1991 | 29 November | The first Codesa negotiations begin |
| 1992 | 17 March | Referendum for white voters |

| | | |
|---|---|---|
| 1992 | 17/18 June | The Boipatong massacre; negotiations in jeopardy |
| 1992 | 26 September | Record of Understanding |
| 1992 | November | "Sunset clauses" |
| 1993 | 1 April | Resumption of formal negotiations |
| 1994 | 27 April | First inclusive general election |

# Prologue

I am often asked why I became involved in confidential talks with the banned African National Congress (ANC) from 1987 onwards. Various factors played a role in my decision, but two stand out: my participation in the activities of the Urban Foundation under the leadership of Jan Steyn since 1985, and later, a theatre performance that I witnessed in London in May 1989.

Steyn's passion for justice and equity and a South Africa of which we need not be ashamed was particularly inspiring. The Urban Foundation also exposed me to the realities of South Africa. One incident in which I became involved via the Foundation changed me irrevocably: allegations of harsh police action against squatters at Roodekrans, north of Johannesburg, and a statement about these events. Some people's shacks had been bulldozed and others' set alight. Sollie Masilela was one of those whose homes burned down, and he lost all his possessions. On 14 March 1987, a relative of Masilela's spoke about these events in Afrikaans. A translated excerpt from his statement reads as follows:

> If the government treats the people like this, what's going to happen in the country? The police fall under the government, and if the police behave so badly, then the government is to blame, isn't it? I don't want to see what the place looks like. My brother, too – we were halfway there when our knees became weak because of this thing, so we turned back.
>
> When I think of this thing, I just feel my scalp tighten. Why is it that when the children in the townships burn houses, they are guilty and they get shot, but the police are allowed to burn down houses? The children here look at what the police do, don't they, and when they act in the same way, what then?

A thing like this can break a man. Such a hardship is too much. He won't think twice about putting the rope around his neck and strangling himself, and then people will say he's mad, but how can you handle such a blow? You've got nothing left – all the years of collecting things bit by bit, money and furniture and stuff, and everything burns up in one night. Surely you will tell God: no, there are wrong things happening in this country, it's better for me to die.

I don't want trouble with the police. Like that day when we had Hendrik's braai for his birthday, I went to see the sergeant at Erasmia and told him on that day we're having a party, it's not a shebeen, and he gave me a letter and told me it was okay. If anybody wants to cause trouble, bring him, we'll lock him up and beat him a few times. So I filled up my bakkie in case I needed to drive there, but it turned out that it wasn't necessary.

And that Portuguese who owns the garage across the road, he lived near Renosterspruit and one day the black people's cattle got into his mealies. Then he took petrol and poured it over their houses and everything burned down – even the corrugated iron was burned, there was nothing left. Some other white people saw the people had nothing, so they brought them clothes and food and blankets. They went to court about this thing, but that white man got off scot-free.

And now we can't get a new pass. The queue at that office stretches up to the gate, and it never gets shorter. I went in October, and they told me next month. I went there in December, and January, and February and March, but I still don't have the pass. Having to go there every month costs a lot of money. Now we hear that if we don't have a pass by June and they catch you, you'll get three months in jail. If they catch you again, it's six months, the third time you get one year and then 18 months with no option of a fine, you just have to go to jail. So what do I do now to get the pass?

It was not hard for me to decide in 1987 to participate in dialogue with the ANC. This decision was justified anew in my mind by what I experienced in London in 1989.

"My last performance was at the Comedy Theatre in May 1989," relates the immortal actor Sir Alec Guinness in his book *A Positively Final Appearance*. "It was a two-hander, with Ed Herrmann, with whom I became great friends, and me playing USA and USSR diplomats."

I was there. The play was Lee Blessing's *A Walk in the Woods*: Herrmann played the young character, the American negotiator John Honeyman, and Guinness the older, more experienced character, the Russian negotiator Andrey Botvinnik. The play throws light on the protracted negotiations on nuclear disarmament that took place between the great powers in Vienna, Austria. Botvinnik and Honeyman, archenemies around the negotiating table, meet by chance in the woods and sit down on the same wooden bench. The two men talk and talk. On the bench in the woods they are simply two people who gradually start respecting and understanding each other. It becomes a moving tale of how trust and confidence can be created between political enemies: the coming into being of an "impossible friendship" that changes the course of history.

I was able to attend Sir Alec's last performance in May 1989 because I was in London to convey a message of historic importance to Thabo Mbeki on behalf of the National Intelligence Service. This message opened the path to official negotiations in South Africa.

*A Walk in the Woods* played a huge part in the story told in this book. Even before I saw the play I had read everything about the Vienna negotiations on nuclear disarmament I could lay my hands on; in my view, these were among the most crucial negotiations since the Second World War. I was immensely gripped by what I read, and by the play itself. In a certain respect it became my "model" of how trust can be built between political enemies.

Many years later, in 2006, I attended a conference on peace at the University of Notre Dame in the US. I referred to the play *A Walk in the Woods* that had influenced me so decisively. Ollie Williams, professor in business ethics at Notre Dame, asked me: "Do you want to hear the real story? Do you see that tower block? Father Theodore Hesburgh's office is on the top floor. He can tell you exactly what happened in Vienna."

As accredited representative of the Vatican, Father Hesburgh, an authority on nuclear physics, had been involved in the negotiation process in Vienna from the outset. In the end he was instrumental in bringing the negotiations to a successful conclusion through the personal, unofficial contact he brought about between the hostile negotiators.

In his office at Notre Dame I met a friendly, relaxed and talkative person. The smoke from his cigars aggravated my sinus problem, but I was glued to my seat. He told me the full story, puffing on one cigar after the other, and inspired me afresh. Hesburgh, a priest, is a peacemaker. A bridge-builder. He firmly believes that committed individuals can make a difference. The informal contact he established between individual negotiators as a go-between ultimately led to a breakthrough, and to disarmament. Building trust between "enemies" was decisive.

As we said goodbye, he stressed once again: "Hope is the key to the future."

# I
# Two telephone calls

My involvement started in 1987 with two telephone calls. One from London and the other, from Pretoria, a few weeks later. At the time of the first call it was already winter in Stellenbosch – rainy and cold, typical winter weather for this Boland town. It was shortly before the much-publicised Dakar conference that was held in Senegal between 9 and 12 July 1987, and I was at my home in the suburb of Mostertsdrift when the phone rang. After we had greeted each other, Fleur de Villiers asked: "Would you like to talk to the ANC outside South Africa?"

Not long afterwards, I received another call. The male caller was businesslike and to the point: "Professor, my name is Koos. My colleague and I work for the state. I'm phoning from Pretoria, and we would like to discuss an important matter with you. We want to arrange a meeting at your house. What does your diary look like for the next week or two?" We arranged a date and time without my having asked who exactly "Koos" and his "colleague" were.

I accepted that the discussion had to take place in private. "Koos" had said specifically: "We don't want to meet you at your office." Stellenbosch, I knew only too well, was like a sieve. Everybody knew everything about each other. Besides the jostling for public attention among the academics, political differences were increasingly emerging in what Willem de Klerk, FW de Kerk's brother, referred to as the battle between the *verligtes* and the *verkramptes* within the ruling National Party. Stellenbosch was at that time an intellectual and cultural mecca of Afrikanerdom, with the Afrikaner Broederbond (AB) setting the tone in the town. The Rembrandt empire of Dr Anton Rupert, South Africa's leading Afrikaner entrepreneur, also had its headquarters there. I understood Koos Kruger's insistence on privacy, and even more so when he later explained the nature of his connection to the state.

My family and I had been friends with Fleur de Villiers and her mother Edna since 1974. Before leaving for London, Fleur had been the assistant editor of the South African *Sunday Times*. She was one of South Africa's top political journalists, and had been the first female member of the parliamentary press gallery. Her value system had always been consistently liberal-democratic.

De Villiers was at that time less than impressed with the politically progressive Afrikaners, the so-called *verligtes,* who were firmly convinced that reform had to happen incrementally from within, and that the National Party was the only vehicle in this regard. In order to progagate their ideas and get them accepted in Afrikaner circles, the *verligtes* distinguished themselves very sharply from Afrikaners who had already positioned themselves outside the Afrikaner-nationalist fold as *liberals.*[1]

The liberals or *moralists* – and I use this term in a positive sense – were liberal-democratic in a dogmatic way. Some even advocated public moral outrage as a mode of resistance against apartheid. This stance excluded any form of cooperation with apartheid structures, as well as strategic compromises. The *verligtes,* in contrast, opted for strategies that played into the reformist possibilities offered by the system. They were sometimes seduced by the excitement they derived from brinkmanship, and enjoyed the benefit of good access to both the Afrikaans and English media and of delivering many opinion-forming addresses at business, cultural, political and ecclesiastical gatherings. Over time, these activities played a part in stimulating change processes and mental shifts.[2]

De Villiers had castigated the *verligtes* relentlessly in her influential columns, even referring to them mockingly as "chocolate soldiers": when politics became too hot, they melted. From 1968 to 1974 I was senior lecturer in philosophy at the Rand Afrikaans University (RAU), now the University of Johannesburg. RAU's first rector, Professor Gerrit Viljoen, liked to say that the university was founded in 1967 "by the Afrikaners for the Afrikaners in the city". Viljoen later became administrator-general in the former South West Africa (Namibia) and subsequently the minister of constitutional affairs in President FW de Klerk's cabinet who had to manage the political transition to a unitary state. During his term as rector, he was also chairman of the influential AB. At one stage he was chairman of the conservative but influential South African Bureau for Racial Affairs (Sabra); I served as chairman of the organisation's *Jeugaksie* (Youth Action) under Viljoen, but was kicked out and replaced by Professor Carel Boshoff.

Viljoen had a great influence on us, the young and enthusiastic corps of RAU lecturers. We were all Afrikaner idealists, inspired by the idea of a worthy place for the Afrikaner and the Afrikaans language in the City of Gold. Most of us were also motivated by the notion of reform from within. We addressed numerous meetings of predominantly working-class Afrikaners in and around Johannesburg, and wrote columns for Afrikaans papers such as the now defunct *Transvaler* and *Vaderland*.

As Afrikaner idealist, I was immensely annoyed by Fleur de Villiers's castigation of the *verligtes*. I turned up at her office one day in 1974 without an appointment. I said: "Are you the journalist who constantly criticises us progressive Afrikaners who are trying to do something positive for the country? And you with the venerable Afrikaans surname De Villiers!" This was the start of a lifelong and enriching friendship that not only influenced the formation of many of my political ideas and convictions, but left a footprint on the political development of South Africa itself. It was mainly Fleur who gave me a better understanding of the importance and functioning of unofficial and personal networks. Her own networks were excellent, and later extended across continents and among a variety of role players. Up to the mid-1980s she also had very good access to NP cabinet ministers and senior politicians because of their respect for her journalistic integrity.

In 1986, Fleur de Villiers had left South Africa and settled in London, partly because of her concern about the country's future after PW Botha's Rubicon speech in August 1985. In that hard-hitting speech, he had swept all hope for a negotiated settlement in South Africa off the table. In London, De Villiers had made a name for herself as a columnist for leading newspapers and journals, as well as a consultant for various international companies, including De Beers and Consolidated Goldfields (Consgold).

She explained over the phone: "I'm involved in talks with the management of Consolidated Goldfields here in London. We're very worried about the political impasse in which PW Botha and his government have landed

South Africa. The conflict will intensify. There's an urgent need to talk about the possibility of negotiations. I've spoken to Humphrey Woods of Consgold and he and the chairman, Rudolph Agnew, agree that an informal and confidential dialogue between Afrikaner opinion leaders with close ties to the government and ANC leaders in exile might help. Could you assist with a list of possible participants? What about Pieter de Lange and Johan Heyns? What do you say? Would you like to talk to ANC leaders outside the country on a confidential basis?"

At that stage there had already been contact between British business leaders and ANC leaders. The journalist Anthony Sampson, who had close ties with the ANC and would later write a biography of Nelson Mandela, had been instrumental in this. On 24 October 1986, for instance, Sampson received Oliver Tambo at his home in London. Tambo had been invited to London by David Astor, the former owner and editor of *The Observer*. During Tambo's visit Astor, a fierce critic of apartheid, introduced the ANC leader to top British businessmen. Tambo also met the editor of *The Economist*, Andrew Knight, and the chairman, the influential banker Evelyn de Rothschild. This was the start of a diplomatic coup for the ANC in Britain.

De Villiers later told me that the Consgold project, as we came to call it, had been proposed as a last resort because of a mounting sense of despondency. The British mining house Consgold, with a long history and profitable gold interests in South Africa, had participated in several meetings between ANC leaders and British businesspeople, including a fairly decisive gathering in London on 24 June 1987, where 23 prominent British and other business leaders held talks with senior ANC leaders such as Oliver Tambo, Thabo Mbeki, Mac Maharaj, Aziz Pahad and Jacob Zuma. Among the business leaders were Standard Bank chairman Lord Barber, Rio Tinto's Sir Alistair Frame, George Soros of the Soros Fund and Evelyn de Rothschild. Michael Young, the public relations director of Consgold who would play a key role in the unofficial ANC-Afrikaner contact group (the Consgold project), was also present. While the meeting in the upscale Connaught Rooms, hosted by David Astor, failed to give the participants much hope, it nonetheless created a strong sense of the need for urgent action.

The idea of informal and unofficial talks between ANC leaders and politically influential Afrikaners arose from this. De Villiers would initiate the initial contact with the Afrikaners, and Young would liaise with ANC leaders. The initiative took place in the same time slot as the Dakar conference, but in a totally different manner. The Consgold project was initiated from the ranks of the business sector.

The role played by business leaders in reform initiatives and transition processes in South Africa should not be underestimated. Naturally, they had a vested interest in developments in this regard. Once the Afrikaner business elite realised that apartheid did not make economic sense, they began to change their political tune. They put a great amount of pressure on the Botha regime, albeit mainly for strategic rather than moral reasons. The process of transition to an inclusive democratic dispensation was also inspired by economic forces and realities, even in the ranks of the ANC.

Johan Heyns, a well-known theologian from the Dutch Reformed Church who had been approached to participate in the project, declined the invitation. He later admitted to me: "The church would have crucified me." Pieter de Lange, a former colleague of mine at RAU and a kindred spirit, also turned down the invitation. So did Tjaart van der Walt, rector of the University of Potchefstroom. De Lange was the chairman of the AB at the time. Their positions within institutionalised Afrikanerdom, which was not only strongly hierarchical but also known for its scant sympathy for dissidents, made it impossible for them to participate. A choice in favour of working from within the system places severe restrictions on people with institutional positions who may nevertheless want to do something outside of the fold to stimulate transition processes.

In the end, Willie Breytenbach, Sampie Terreblanche and I were the only Afrikaner participants who attended the first dialogue session with four ANC leaders in November 1987. We were all from Stellenbosch University, knew each other well, and had gained a reputation as *verligtes*. Furthermore, as academics we were relatively independent, occupying professional positions where we could not be dictated to by politicians. A phenomenon that has as yet failed to receive due recognition is that academics at traditionally Afrikaans universities enjoyed a high level of academic autonomy and freedom. In the desert of apartheid, English-language universities were, of course, oases of freedom. But so, too, were Afrikaans universities in certain respects, albeit perhaps more in the form of bubbling fountains that were trying to break through the hard crust of apartheid. They were home to many people who practised loyal resistance and open dialogue in spite of the activities of the state's security services on university campuses, even Afrikaans ones. [3] It was a great shock to me, for instance, when someone from the NIS warned me against a high-profile student leader, Mark Behr. He paraded as a leftist political activist and was even chairman of the Stellenbosch branch of the anti-apartheid National Union of South African Students (Nusas). According to my source, Behr was in reality an informant of another, very militant state security service. He visited me at home sometimes, ostensibly to seek advice on sensitive political issues. It was also Behr who organised a visit of a group of student leaders to Lusaka for talks with the ANC in the 1980s.

I went to a lot of trouble to try and understand how these "services" operated and who the key players were. This effort, while not particularly successful as far as detail was concerned, was to good purpose nonetheless: I did not allow myself to be sucked into an atmosphere of mistrust ruled by conspiracy theories. My resolute discipline in this regard was strengthened when I read Ronald W Clark's book *Benjamin Franklin: A Biography in His Own Words* in 1988. When Franklin was warned about spies who were watching him, his reply was that he subscribed to a single rule in his life: not to become involved in political matters of which he would have to be ashamed if they were revealed. Honourable conduct at all times and under all circumstances, no matter how difficult it might be, he said, was crucial in this. In an environment where confidentiality and secrecy prevail, honourableness naturally makes heavy moral demands. You have to be prepared to admit failures in this regard very swiftly and honestly. My wife Annemarie was my active conscience as far as this was concerned. Her support and co-operation were never unconditional and uncritical.

Besides the three participants from Stellenbosch, the first meeting of the contact group was attended by Aziz Pahad, Tony Trew, Wally Serote and Harold Wolpe from the ranks of the ANC. It was a blessing in disguise that the numbers were limited, as unknown territory had to be explored and leaks avoided. It was decided that I would act as contact person on the domestic side and, in consultation with Thabo Mbeki and Michael Young, invite other Afrikaner opinion leaders as the talks progressed and the issues that had to be discussed required new entrants. Young would coordinate the whole project from within Consgold, liaise with the ANC leaders and make all logistical arrangements. Consgold would bear the costs associated with the project. While Young would act as independent chair of the scheduled discussion sessions, sufficient opportunity would also be allowed for the South Africans to confer with each other without Young's presence.

Young handled the scheduled sessions extremely well. His political links in Britain, for example with Lynda Chalker who was the British Conservative Party's African expert, were also very good. It was Young, in fact, who, in contravention of British premier Margaret Thatcher's guidelines, arranged a meeting between Lynda Chalker and Oliver Tambo in June 1987. I had the opportunity to meet Chalker personally, and gained great respect for her.

Young navigated our discussions with the ANC carefully without being intrusive. The value of a chair who is impartial yet has a good grasp of the political sensitivities and issues cannot be underestimated in exploratory talks of this kind.

The Dakar conference between a group of mostly dissident Afrikaners and the ANC, which elicited a good deal of negative reaction in the Afrikaans media, brought home an important lesson which we took due cognisance of in the planning of our dialogue project. This conference was unquestionably an important public demonstration of the necessity for a negotiated settlement. The negative reaction it provoked from the ranks of Afrikaners and the ruling elite, however, emphasised that exploratory talks about a negotiated settlement for the South African conflict were too delicate to be conducted in public and at conference level. Public conferences promote public awareness and debate, even support and mobilisation for some or other action. But that is not enough, and something else is required as well: clarification and understanding of the positions of key players; the building of trust and a good dose of confidence between contending parties and people who regard each other as enemies; an unformalised *compact* between traditional enemies to chart a route to peace.

To achieve these aims, dialogue and small-group meetings are more appropriate. These methods help one to tread footpaths out of cul-de-sacs. In fact, I already realised early in 1987 that a clear distinction has to be made between sustainable settlement processes and sensational public events. The one can, of course, promote the other, but that is not necessarily always the case. Process politics, as Wynand Malan, first a National Party politician and later a leader of the Independents, liked to call it, is never merely event-oriented. Instead, it focuses strategically and tactically on creating drivers and energies that propel developments in a certain direction. Naturally, this may have unintended consequences.

★ ★ ★

Something else needs to be said about 1987. On 26 January 1987 I received a letter from the Afrikaner Broederbond with reference to an earlier letter about a "brainstorming session regarding constitutional development" that would take place on 7 February. When I looked at the programme, which included the names of the speakers and most of the papers, I realised: Watch this space! Among the themes were: the process of constitutional development; confederation, federation and other constitutional systems/models; South Africa is one country with different fatherlands; the positive and negative features of the 1983 constitution; the constitutional implications of group characteristics other than ethnicity; group formation and coercion; freedom of association in the context of the dynamics of residential settlement patterns; merit and good governance; whether or not a bill of rights is advisable; political alliances; parliamentary and extraparliamentary politics; the ANC, PAC and other radical groups; the role of a government in respect of a negotiated settlement. I had to speak about "The identification of leaders". And I told myself that the writing was on the wall. *How* a settlement would take place, *what* would be settled and *who* would settle, was the crux of the matter. The big question, though, was how and by whom the preparation for the settlement process had to be done. And when.

That was my last appearance as speaker at a big Afrikaner Broederbond meeting. Over time, serious friction had arisen between me and the Brothers of the Stellenbosch division of the AB to which I belonged. It had had a long run-up, starting in 1979 after the publication of my book *Apartheid Must Die.*

Many Brothers were aggrieved by my views, and a delegation visited me at home. Carel Boshoff, then a heavyweight in the Broederbond, at least defended my right to freedom of expression. The existing tension changed into open conflict in March 1987, with the NP member of parliament for Stellenbosch, Piet Marais, the leading figure. Our good relationship crumbled one evening during a divisional meeting where I pronounced myself for a one-person-one-vote election in a unitary state. [4]

Those were turbulent times in white politics. Many *verligtes* were fed up with the ineffectual political pottering of President PW Botha's National Party. Many of them accepted that chiselling and hammering from within was no longer enough. But they did not want to join the "Progs" (Progressive Federal Party), whose leader, Dr Frederik van Zyl Slabbert, had resigned and left parliament the year before (1986). The political discomfort of the *verligtes* was the start of the Independent Movement that participated in the general election in May 1987. Advocate "Lang" Dawid de Villiers, who had distinguished himself at the International Court of Justice in The Hague on behalf of South Africa with regard to the status of South West Africa (Namibia) and eventually became managing director of the influential Nasionale Pers, even resigned from the board of Naspers to help with the Independent Movement.

These developments caused Piet Cillié, the doyen of Afrikaans journalism, editor of *Die Burger* and subsequently chairman of Naspers and professor in journalism at Stellenbosch University (SU), to say as he prodded my chest with his finger: "I'll keep a candle burning so that you people will be able to find your way back out of your political darkness." Cillié was a *verligte*, and later at his university office in Crozier Street also the leading light in the Protea discussion group where a number of Stellenbosch academics met to talk about the political road ahead. But he was a committed from-within-the-system person, and deeply loyal to Afrikaner institutions. Esther Lategan, Wynand Malan and Denis Worrall were the Independents' candidates in Stellenbosch, Randburg and Helderberg respectively. Malan won in Randburg. Worrall lost in Helderberg by a very narrow margin to Chris Heunis, an important cabinet minister. Heunis never recovered politically from this blow. Lategan lost to Piet Marais, but rocked the Afrikaner-nationalist establishment in the process. Another long nail had been driven into the monolith of Afrikaner power and Afrikaner hegemony.

A few weeks after the election I received a call from President PW Botha's office. He wanted to see me. We made an appointment, and I spoke to him in private. It was a very friendly, heart-to-heart conversation. Botha wanted to know why I had supported Lategan, Worrall and Malan. He suspected that it might be for a personal reason because Minister Pik Botha, so he had been told, had withdrawn my appointment as a special government envoy to Washington at short notice at the insistence of Heunis. He wanted me to know that he had had no hand in the decision. I assured him that that was not the reason, and that the cancellation of the appointment was a blessing in disguise. I explained to him what had motivated me to support the Independents, and that a from-within strategy had had its day. We spoke very frankly. When I got up to leave, Botha said : "It can sometimes get very lonely behind this desk of mine. People come and tell me what they think I would like to hear."

★ ★ ★

Against this background, the telephone call from Pretoria had me worried. Pretoria was the symbol of government power. I wondered almost automatically whether I had done something wrong in Pretoria's view. On the day of our appointment, Koos Kruger and his colleague Möller Dippenaar arrived at my house before me. Annemarie received them, and they waited for me in the lounge. At the front door, Annemarie told me: "They look like security policemen. Be careful with what you say," mindful of the fact that I sometimes failed to set a watch before my mouth. Koos Kruger and his "colleague Möller" informed me that they were from the National Intelligence Service (NIS). The country was faced with all sorts of serious security risks that might undermine the constitution and threaten the survival of the state. The NIS had a special division that had to attend to these risks. They had taken note of what I had said and written, and reckoned that I would be able to help them with the project. The contacts and networks I had at my disposal, and the documents they assumed I had collected and studied, might also be useful in this regard.

At this first meeting we did not talk about the possibility of talks and negotiations with the ANC, the unbanning of organisations and the release of, say, Nelson Mandela. Nor did I ask whether they were aware of Fleur de Villiers's call from London. I kept mum about that. Because of my interest in informal mediation, I learnt very early in my life to refrain from asking unnecessary questions, to listen and to give the interlocutor space and freedom. In our subsequent interaction I soon developed an excellent rapport with "Oom Koos", as I later called him out of respect, and Möller Dippenaar. We understood and trusted each other.

Annemarie and I did not find it hard to decide in favour of cooperating with the NIS. At that stage I already knew about Consgold's project and saw it as a golden opportunity. Before making our decision, however, we thrashed out the pros and cons, the likely impact on our family life and the consequences of an association with the NIS. In decisions of this kind there is always a tension between moral and strategic considerations. The NIS was, after all, one of the most untransparent and even fate-determining arms of the state. To us, it all boiled down to a central question: "Can cooperation with this influential arm of the apartheid state contribute towards advancing a process of peace and democratisation?" We also told ourselves that this was unknown territory, and that there might be many unintended consequences in store for us. It is impossible to know beforehand what the limits are of the compromises one would inevitably have to make in a process of this nature. We informed our children in very general terms about the matter.

My acceptance of the request led to an intensive briefing session with Koos Kruger and Möller Dippenaar. They were later joined by other members of the NIS team. The sessions generally took place in safe houses (flats, in certain cases), some of which belonged to private owners. One such safe house that I visited frequently was in a block of flats in the Strand, close to Stellenbosch. I was told that it belonged to a prominent cleric. Koos Kruger, who had come from the Bureau of State Security of General Hendrik van den Bergh and his friend Prime Minister John Vorster (the forerunner of the NIS), was very security conscious. He emphasised repeatedly that I should not breathe a word about the project, not even to my best friends. "It's a lonely road. Might even be dangerous. We'll train you in security measures and take good care of you." They also provided me with a codename: *Gert.* And with things like an anonymous postbox, a briefcase that resembled Kruger's, a tape recorder and a camera that I could not make head or tail of. In the event, it never proved necessary to use any of these accessories.

I did inform a few people of my activities, in order to have some kind of "record" with "witnesses" if anything had to go wrong. Besides Fleur de Villiers, whom I told at a later stage, I confided in Dawie de Villiers, a minister in Botha's cabinet and a man of the highest integrity. Years later he participated in the Consgold dialogue group on two occasions, and subsequently also played an important role in the negotiation process. Botha respected De Villiers because he did not fear Botha and always gave him his honest views about thorny political issues. Another person I took into my confidence was Professor Mike de Vries, the then rector of Stellenbosch University. We were very good friends, and I trusted him. I had to do a lot of travelling, mainly over weekends, also to overseas countries, and needed to obtain leave of absence for such trips. For reasons of secrecy and security, I could not use the normal channels in this regard. De Vries gave me the necessary permission and also respected the confidential nature of the project. He was very supportive, and often expressed the hope that Stellenbosch University would get credit someday for what was done for the sake of a negotiated settlement. I also gave a few close friends, such as Anton van Niekerk of su's department of philosophy, a broad outline of what I was involved in. One cannot take on a project like this without supportive family members and friends of incorruptible integrity.

The security training sessions were instructive in that they gave me a better grasp of the high-level thinking about security and political issues at the time. The State Security Council (ssc) and the cabinet were briefed regularly by the NIS and other security services. Later I heard about President PW Botha's situation room, where a screen allowed him to watch everything that had happened and who had said what. The "everything" had of course been selected and sifted by someone else beforehand. As time went on, I gained a clearer understanding of the magnitude and the explosiveness of South Africa's crisis. And also of the nature of the fool's paradise in which Afrikaners, in particular, were living. One such session on security left me shell-shocked. It had focused on how one should observe security measures in foreign countries, for example in hotels. Half-despairing because I could not remember or understand everything, I exclaimed: "But the ANC won't kill me! They have an interest in my survival." Someone remarked drily: "We're not trying to protect you from the ANC. The guys who'll be out to get you are the 'brown shirts'," in other words, the military.

Möller Dippenaar, who had studied to become a clergyman at one stage, was an exceptional individual. We had many and sometimes tough in-depth conversations. The NIS had well-educated and highly trained people among their ranks. Hanna Langenhoven, the only female member of the team, with whom I worked closely and whose intellectual abilities and sense of humour I came to value highly, told me recently that they had nearly suspended the project because I had no notion of security measures. Koos Kruger, on the other hand, was a policeman to the marrow, devoted and loyal to the state he served. He told me on several occasions: "I follow Paul in Romans 13. I am a part of the sword power of the state." Years later, Eugene de Kock said more or less the same to me when I visited him in prison. Kruger said more than once: "How do we know that we are using the sword power correctly?" And he also said: "Good intelligence helps us to use the sword power correctly." I told myself: "Intelligence is about information that can advance strategic objectives and planning. What is of prime importance, though, is the nature of the objectives." How and by whom the information can be verified, and especially the issue of accountability and oversight, are of course very material questions in a democratic state.

At the time I also accepted that if I could not develop a certain relationship of trust with people like Kruger and Dippenaar, the project I had let myself in for would flop. It was Kruger and Dippenaar who helped me to understand that moral considerations without strategic considerations are "blind", and that strategic considerations without moral considerations are "empty", if I may paraphrase the great German philosopher Immanuel Kant. It is a brute fact, however, that one should not be overly idealistic and romantically naive about a workable balance between the two. Something that helped me not to overrate my possible contribution and role was a remark by Eddie Orsmond, a postgraduate student who assisted me in the project and saw to it that minutes and appointments were kept. He once told me in a friendly yet firm tone:"Prof, you have to remember that Oom Koos and Dippenaar are privy to a bigger picture and plan. The two of us don't have access to that. We only know our picture, which is smaller, and which hopefully fits into a meaningful bigger picture."

The information sessions on how threats to the South African state were interpreted by the authorities were in one respect a learning experience. The model of the Total Onslaught featured prominently in most of these sessions. I referred to it ironically as the "spider web theory", with the ANC as the big, black and dangerous spider which, in cooperation with the communists, was manipulating just about everything that threatened South Africa. I was astounded at how strong the "belief" in this theory was. When one uses the myth of the "enemy" to justify actions and policies, it is apparently necessary to represent one's enemy as being more powerful than he really is. President PW Botha and his ministers believed their own propaganda. The idea of a Total Onslaught was exceptionally effective. Those who were sceptical of this propaganda were themselves part of the Total Onslaught. Hence a Total Strategy justified more or less any means whatsoever that would serve the end of state security. General Joep Joubert of the Special Forces was in my view completely honest when he stated before the Truth and Reconciliation Commission (TRC) on 8 October 1997 that he had simply done his "duty" in support of the survival of the government of the day. People who were a serious threat to the state were therefore eliminated. He had accepted that the country was involved in a "full-scale war". He was the product of the propaganda of the Total Onslaught.

As time went on, I got to know several staff members of the NIS. One of them was the top dog himself, Niel Barnard, a former academic from the then University of the Orange Free State who had taken over the leadership of the NIS at a young age. Barnard is an excellent poker player. Someone who does not reveal his strategy and tactics through body language or words. And brutally direct in his views when one crosses swords with him. Our personalities could not be more different. He once rebuked me half-jokingly for operating with a "Karoo decency". But from the outset I gained a respect for him that I have to this day. He had been instrumental in saving South Africa from a bloody and devastating civil war. I found out later that negotiation had been looked at as a strategic option in the NIS as early as 1984. A certain Swanepoel, who was apparently the chief director of strategic and operational evaluations of the NIS at the time, expressed the view in a report that the government had to start talking to Mandela. He developed a scenario in which Nelson Mandela would bring together millions of people in Johannesburg on his release. The idea of a gradual, well-controlled and incremental process that could lead to Mandela's release was born in the NIS. The point at issue was control over a process that was seen as inevitable, but which nobody wanted to discuss too loudly at the time.

Barnard's other senior colleague, Mike Louw, also deserves mention. Louw, whom I did not get to know as well as I knew Barnard, had an exceptional personality and acumen. He was, in a manner of speaking, not a card player. Rather a fly half in a rugby team. He could both read and direct a game pattern. It was Louw and Maritz Spaarwater, another person who deserves credit, who in talks with the ANC in Lucerne, Switzerland, on 12 September 1989 and thereafter, "freed up" the negotiations ball together with Barnard so that Codesa (the Convention for a Democratic South Africa) could kick off. Spaarwater was blessed with an extraordinary sense of humour. I, for one, don't believe one can participate in intensive "practice sessions" and "warm-up matches" with a view to averting a blood bath and playing a meaningful "final match" unless one has a supersize sense of humour. Humor, I learnt in the course of the whole process, is a defusing mechanism. It is like disarming a hand grenade. Spaarwater had this gift.

★ ★ ★

It was purely coincidental, but significant nonetheless: the calls from London and Pretoria, and what ensued from them, occurred against the backdrop of a dramatic event. On 3 and 4 July 1987, roughly a year after the PW Botha government had declared a state of emergency in South Africa, a sensational story dominated the headlines: Idasa, led by Frederik van Zyl Slabbert and Alex Boraine, with a delegation of 60 mostly Afrikaner participants from

South Africa, would hold a conference in Dakar, Senegal, with the banned ANC. This conference took place between 9 and 12 July 1987. About 20 members of the ANC took part, with Thabo Mbeki the leading light. The gifted writer and poet Breyten Breytenbach was also a major driving force. Among others, the themes that were discussed included what strategies should be followed to bring about change in South Africa, how national unity could be built, what the structures of a free South Africa should look like, and what form the economy should take. It became a media event. The Botha government was incensed, as were many Afrikaner journalists and their readers. Koos Kruger told me later: "The president wanted to have the Dakar conferees arrested on their return. Dr Barnard didn't deem it advisable. Looking back on it, what's your view?"

I didn't quite know what to say, but replied nonetheless: "Well, I wasn't invited. Can't say I know what I would have done if I'd been invited. And I don't really know what happened there. There were many people from South Africa at the conference. But not exactly scores of ANC exiles. Some of the participants from South Africa might have enjoyed being arrested. It would have had great news value. Many of them were publicity seekers. I think Barnard was right." In my opinion, the Dakar conference was important. It raised public consciousness for a negotiated settlement, and brought Thabo Mbeki to the fore as the driving force for a negotiated settlement among the exiles.

After Dakar, Idasa was world-famous, yet Dakar also sank Idasa as a possible mediator and negotiating partner. The organisation's public profile was too high and it was too geared to publicity. Both the NP government and the ANC, through their representatives, told me: Idasa is an outsider as far as the process itself is concerned. It is an open question whether the brainstorming session of the Afrikaner Broederbond on 7 February 1987, the formation of the Independent Movement in May 1987, and especially the confrontation between PW Botha and Discussion Group '85 on 20 February 1987 and the group's subsequent public statement, did not have a greater influence on settlement processes than Dakar.

From a remark Thabo Mbeki once made about Idasa, I concluded that this initiative and Slabbert's and Boraine's resignation from parliament had related to Slabbert's 1985 visit to the ANC in Lusaka when he was still the leader of the Progressive Federal Party (PFP). Idasa was seen as an alternative and better route towards influence on the ANC and especially involvement in a direct negotiating process. If my interpretation is correct, it was a strategic miscalculation. After all, direct bilateral negotiations between the NP government and the ANC were inevitable. This possible miscalculation most likely also played a role in the breakdown of the relationship between Mbeki and Slabbert at a later stage, and the reproach that Mbeki had not given Slabbert due recognition.

The NIS itself never had a dismissive attitude towards Slabbert. He was not regarded as a "sellout", at least not in my presence. From what I have been told, he was even approached for his views on a few occasions. There was, rather, reserve on their part because, according to my NIS source, he was too focused on political power and influence. That was why he opted for the public forum, it was said. Unfortunately, this view was shared by key figures in the ANC. They did not want him as a member of the unofficial Afrikaner contact group. What counted against Slabbert in the thinking of some ANC leaders at that stage was that he was not part of the Afrikaner inner circle, and that he was a committed liberal democrat rather than a social democrat. The ANC leaders who favoured a negotiated settlement did not just view Afrikaners as the ruling power elite. They were also of the opinion that Afrikaners who were part of the establishment were more attuned to social democracy than, for instance, English-speaking liberals. Hence they were rather prepared to negotiate with "racist nationalists" than with the "liberalists". That said, they didn't really have much of a choice, since the negotiations took place between parties with power and not between individuals with personal prestige and influence.

Against the NIS's recommendations, I once gave Van Zyl Slabbert a very brief account of what I was involved in. This happened after we had adjourned for lunch at a seminar meeting in Johannesburg, with the Dakar conference still fresh in people's minds. I was probably too vague, because he failed to react to my communication and simply said he was going to have lunch. I never raised the matter with him again. He spoke about it subsequently to Richard Rosenthal, to whom I will refer later, as well as to Thabo Mbeki. It was probably a gain that there had been no formal and direct contact between Idasa and the Afrikaner-ANC dialogue group. This left room for multiple dimensions and various simultaneous dialogues.

There were also other contacts with the ANC in exile. While the ANC under the leadership of Tambo and Mbeki were defeating the South African government hands down in the diplomatic battle in the international arena, impressive headway was also made in respect of contact with key figures from the ranks of white South Africa. It started as far back as 1984 with people like Professor HW van der Merwe of the University of Cape Town, Piet Muller of *Beeld* and Hugh Murray of *Leadership*. In 1985 Van Zyl Slabbert and Colin Eglin, both of the PFP, visited Lusaka. The ice was broken when a delegation of prominent business leaders, including Gavin Relly of Anglo American, travelled to Lusaka in September 1985 to hold talks with the ANC. Tambo, Mbeki, Chris Hani, Pallo Jordan and Aziz Pahad were among the ANC leaders they spoke to. President Kenneth Kaunda of Zambia was highly supportive of this meeting with the "capitalists". Though the initiative created a stir in some political and business circles in South Africa, it contributed significantly to the de-demonisation of the ANC, especially when word got around that Tambo had opened the meeting with a prayer.

In 1986 there were also a few "chance" meetings, notably the one in June that took place between Thabo Mbeki and Professor Pieter de Lange, leader of the Afrikaner Broederbond. It made a "huge impression" on Mbeki, as he told me later. The AB itself was at that time going through a phase of serious reflection in which people like De Lange and Willem de Klerk played an important role. And in 1988 there was of course the meeting of Louis Luyt, president of the South African Rugby Board, with the ANC. The political dykes against contact had cracked.[5]

In the chapters that follow, more will be told about the people and processes that were instrumental in establishing a climate that was conducive to negotiations as well as the agenda for the negotiating process. I give special credit to the NIS and Barnard in this regard. It should be mentioned that the NIS did not keep President PW Botha fully informed about the dialogue process, as was also admitted by Mike Louw in an interview with Geoffrey Heald. (2006: 89) Louw, who believed that human thought paradigms had to be "elastic" for one to understand and accept dramatic changes, was of the view that PW Botha, given his history and age, lacked this capacity.

The golden thread that runs through my narrative is the relationship between unofficial, private and confidential talks (referred to as "track two" in the literature on conflict resolution) and official, formal talks ("track one"). The Epilogue provides more detail on the theory behind this. [6]

# 2
## Between the iron fist and dialogue: the political context

On 15 August 1985 President PW Botha delivered his infamous Rubicon speech. Few political speeches in the history of the country dashed the hope and expectations of a negotiated settlement among the majority of South Africans to the extent that this one did. It had two consequences: on the one hand, the paradigm shift in international circles and among many *verligte* Afrikaners that the from-within strategy was no longer adequate or even tenable; on the other hand, the view among those associated with the United Democratic Front (UDF), founded in 1983, that pressure on the Botha government had to be intensified, and also *could* be intensified in light of the international reaction to the Rubicon debacle. Waves of revolt and protest had already been sweeping across the country, especially as of September 1984. In December 1985, as was later revealed, the Vlakplaas unit under the command of Colonel Eugene de Kock even thought it fit to shoot six MK cadres dead in Lesotho. Shortly after this incident, De Kock and the members of his unit were awarded medals by Louis le Grange, the minister of law and order.

For many years, *verligte* Afrikaners believed that a from-within strategy would bear political fruit in the form of more fundamental reform initiatives. In 1985 the Botha regime repealed the morally draconian Mixed Marriages Act and the notorious Section 16 of the Immorality Act that prohibited interracial sexual relations. Among *verligte* Afrikaners, this move ignited the hope that further reforms were on the cards. PW Botha was seen as a reformer who favoured an incremental approach. During a conference at the South African embassy in London in the 1980s, a black leader, John Mavuso, even declared that PW Botha was the Abraham Lincoln of South Africa. But as time went on, disappointment and disillusionment set in. Among the intellectuals of the new generation of Afrikaners in particular,

Botha was regarded as part of the problem of apartheid and not as a partner in its dismantling. A paradigm shift was waiting to be born. Once it happened, it gradually caused an expanding chain reaction that ultimately had an impact on PW Botha himself. Important role players inside and close to the Botha government began to realise that a military solution to the South African civil war and the other conflicts in which South Africa was embroiled in the region, was neither financially nor strategically an option. A political solution had to be found.

The UDF was also making things difficult for the Botha government. The banned organisations in exile, such as the ANC and the PAC, could easily be condemned as "terroristic". But how could one tag the UDF with that label? With respected church leaders such as Archbishop Desmond Tutu and Dr Allan Boesak in their ranks? In the end, the Botha government reacted to this conundrum in the only way they knew: a state of emergency, bannings and arrests! The clampdown restored a measure of order in some areas, but not peace and justice. Matters had already come to a head in March 1985, shortly before the Rubicon speech. The police fired on a crowd of about 4 000 people in Port Elizabeth in the Eastern Cape. Twenty people died, and Tutu was even arrested. Political activism was rampant in that region of the country at the time. ANC leaders such as Nelson Mandela, Govan Mbeki, Thabo Mbeki and Chris Hani hailed from the Eastern Cape, as well as the renowned Black Consciousness leader Steve Biko, who had been tortured to death by the security police in 1977. And then there were also Matthew Goniwe and his three comrades who had been murdered by the security police in 1985. The state's notorious hit squad the Civil Cooperation Bureau (CCB), funded with taxpayers' money, was born in this period as "counter-revolutionary strategy", a slippery slope to a moral-political quagmire.

Internationally, too, the Botha government faced more opposition than ever before. The speech was watched by an international audience of ±200 million television viewers, in a context where sky-high expectations of a dramatic breakthrough had been created beforehand, mainly by Minister Pik Botha and his department of foreign affairs. Any measure of credibility the so-called Total Onslaught by the communists against South Africa might still have enjoyed in any corner of the world was shredded by Botha in his Rubicon speech. The British prime minister, Margaret Thatcher, who was personally on reasonably good terms with Botha, also found herself increasingly under pressure, albeit that she slated the ANC as "terroristic". The Commonwealth was opposed to her "soft" approach and wanted to impose severe economic and other sanctions, which was done in August 1986. According to Thabo Mbeki, Thatcher's spokesman Bernard Ingham still referred to the ANC as a typical terrorist organisation in 1987. Mbeki claimed he had even said that anyone who believed the ANC would ever rule South Africa was living in "cloud-cuckooland". While there is doubt about the correct contextualisation of this remark by Ingham, Mbeki's reference to it nonetheless illustrated what his impression was of Thatcher and her spokesman.

Thatcher's firm stance against comprehensive sanctions was a big political consolation for apartheid South Africa, even though it did not protect the country from economic and financial erosion. She was not only the leader of the British Conservative Party, but also conservative in her personal views and thus strongly opposed to contact with the ANC, which she considered a violent and lawless organisation. On one occasion she was extremely upset about the prospect that the then South West Africa and South Africa were in danger of being taken over violently by Swapo, the ANC and the communists. Among others, she summoned Patrick Fairweather, assistant undersecretary of State, Foreign and Commonwealth Office, to draw attention to her alarm. It turned out that her source was a report by a well-known conservative US institution, whose views resonated with her own conservative value system.

Thatcher was told by her friend, US president Ronald Reagan, that he could no longer support her subtly in her resistance to more stringent economic sanctions and her cautious attitude towards South Africa. It should be remembered that shortly before the Rubicon speech, and following bloody clashes between police and protesters in black and coloured townships (for example, in Port Elizabeth in March 1985, as mentioned earlier), the Botha government had declared a state of emergency in July 1985 – the first in South Africa since the one declared in the wake of the Sharpeville incident in 1960. It was lifted briefly, but then reimposed in June 1986. The state of emergency continued for years and was extended every now and again. The political impasse in which South Africa already found itself became more and more stifling.

A technical term to describe this impasse would be "stasis" or "equilibrium" – a stalemate between two destructive forces (revolutionary and counterrevolutionary), with an inevitable end result: a sociopolitical implosion and a failed state. I never bought the story about a state that was in control and would have been able to maintain control for a long time with more and stronger instruments of power. The notion of a "hurting stalemate" made sense in this context. By 1986, the South African state was rapidly heading for a failed state whose elite would have had to be protected by totalitarian means. This prospect did not excite the moderate ANC leaders. A failed state propped up by draconian means destroys virtually all developmental possibilities in the medium to long term. PW Botha's Rubicon speech had cost South Africa millions of rands per word. The moderate ANC leaders, who included Tambo and Mandela, did not want to inherit a wasteland. Neither did the new generation of Afrikaners who had to fight in Angola.

How bleak the outlook was for this impasse, was made clear by events in the US in particular. On 21 January 1986, the Comprehensive Anti-Apartheid Act of 1986 (CAAA) was passed at a joint session of the House of Representatives and the Senate (the 99th Congress). It was "comprehensive" in all respects. With that, the argument that sanctions would hurt the oppressed and the disadvantaged more than the privileged whites was wiped off the table for good. Sanctions were called for as the only remaining nonviolent means to end apartheid. The legislation also spelled out the US policy in respect of a negotiated settlement, which included, among others, the following conditions: an end to the state of emergency; the release of political prisoners such as Nelson Mandela; the unbanning of the ANC and other political movements; a revocation of the Group Areas Act and the Population Registration Act and the granting of universal citizenship to all South Africans, including residents of the "homelands", namely the nominally independent and self-governing black states like Transkei and KwaZulu.

An international consensus, as expressed in the CAAA, had started to take root. It was this consensus that the De Klerk government had to comply with in February 1990. It is interesting to note that the US committed itself in the 1986 legislation to an effort to help bring about an agreement "to suspend violence and begin negotiations through co-ordinated actions with the major Western allies and with the governments of the countries in the region". Elsewhere in the legislation it was stated that unbanning had to apply to all groups "willing to suspend terrorism and to participate in negotiations and a democratic process". The issue of whether violence merely had to be "suspended" before a negotiation process could start or whether it should first be "renounced", would for a long time be a hot potato. So, too, would the question as to whether foreign governments should be involved in the settlement process.

In the West, the US was a major player in the sanctions campaign and more than a hundred companies withdrew from South Africa. Then came the sharpest and longest nail in the coffin: financial sanctions, with the US Chase Manhattan Bank delivering the first hammer blow in August 1985, following the Rubicon speech. Sanctions began to have an impact. A lifelong friend of mine, Howard Wolpe, a prominent Congressman and an activist in the Democratic Party, was at the forefront in this regard. While our sharp differences never threatened our friendship, they did help me to get a better grasp of South Africa's crisis. For my part, I have never believed that full credit for the success of the sanctions campaign had to go to the ANC and Thabo Mbeki's influence on the anti-apartheid movement. Another important contributing factor was the inept way in which the South African government had dealt with the crisis in the country since the 1980s and especially the disastrous Rubicon speech. It had stripped apartheid of all its moral-political embellishments, and left the emperor stark naked in the Western public arena.

A little more than a year after Botha's visit to Thatcher in 1984, the ANC got the opportunity to reply to questions and give evidence before the Foreign Affairs Committee of the British parliament on Tuesday, 29 October 1985. Oliver Tambo, Thabo Mbeki and Aziz Pahad represented the ANC. The focus of the discussion was mainly on violence and its use against "soft targets", as well as the issue of sanctions. Robert Harvey, author of *The Fall of Apartheid: The Inside Story from Smuts to Mbeki,* was also present in his capacity as MP. As Mbeki put it to me, the discussion turned into "a grilling". But it was also a "breakthrough" for the ANC's diplomatic initiative. Tambo passed the test as a moderate advocate of negotiations. Internationally, the South African government's myth of a bloodthirsty enemy was shown to lack credibility.

In the mid-1980s the West gave up hope that Afrikaner leaders would somehow still get a negotiation process going. Even Margaret Thatcher was no longer prepared to put in a good word for South Africa in the hope of a negotiated settlement. Botha was fully informed about her attitude. A number of influential business leaders, such as Dr Anton Rupert of the Rembrandt Group, were called on to help save the pieces, especially on account of Rupert's Swiss contacts. Rupert ultimately wrote Botha a long letter (24 January 1986) in which he stated in no uncertain terms that South Africa's real problem was apartheid. It had no effect.[1] Thabo Mbeki, who was not exactly a fan of Margaret Thatcher's, told me something very interesting in 1988. Margaret Thatcher had become annoyed with PW Botha. And the reason? He had insulted Geoffrey Howe, her secretary for foreign affairs. Thatcher might not have been very fond of Howe, but he was, after all, the "British" foreign secretary and a member of her team. Earlier, when Thatcher had received Botha at Chequers in June 1984, she had already told him fairly bluntly that he had to release Mandela. She was opposed to full-scale sanctions, and also said, to Botha's delight, that a cessation of violence was a precondition for negotiations with the ANC. This issue was to remain a stumbling block for a long time.

Howe visited South Africa in July 1986. Neither members of the ANC, including Nelson Mandela, nor Archbishop Tutu wanted to see him. Botha, who met Howe on 23 July and again on 29 July, was in one of his foul moods at the time. He dismissed Tutu's views as worthless and said that foreigners had to stop interfering in South Africa's affairs. After this, substantial and effective political pressure was undoubtedly applied by the West and particularly by Britain, which was a major trading partner with a significant cultural and demographic legacy in South Africa. Patrick Fairweather, who was in the inner circle of the Thatcher government – at one stage ambassador in

Luanda, Angola, and subsequently a British official in London – put it to me forcefully in London towards the end of 1988: "The cracks in the Botha government can no longer be plastered over. They will get bigger." This was indeed the case. The cracks did grow bigger, and could no longer be managed by way of parsimonious piecemeal reforms. There were simply too many sharp chisels that had got their tips lodged into cracks and crevices. It is doubtful, though, whether one can point to just *one* prominent chisel as having been the most decisive. It was rather a case of multiple chisels, that is to say, drivers and processes, that collectively created an energy and made change initiatives possible. These drivers made a political tipping point inevitable.

One can talk about primary and secondary drivers. Accordingly, to give excessive credit for the historic process of fundamental change or political shift that occurred to only a few individuals who are now being lauded as "heroic figures", demonstrates an overly superficial understanding of how historical processes of radical political and social change operate. I call it retrospective mythologising. Repressive systems such as apartheid are of a systemic nature. Hence, system changes require process-driven systemic transformation and not merely public leadership initiatives and even changes in leadership. Also not just public conferences, seminars and workshops. In a significant respect, the year 1986 was of crucial importance for the political processes that would take shape over the subsequent four to five years, albeit that South Africa already had six nuclear bombs at that stage. The notorious influx-control measures that had attempted to block black people's migration to urban areas and their ownership rights, were consigned to the scrap heap. And by PW Botha, of all people! This step had been preceded by intense lobbying, notably on the part of Jan Steyn and his Urban Foundation.[2] The law in question had been a cornerstone of the race-driven apartheid system.

Botha informed his caucus about this sensitive issue by using the analogy of an infestation of black ants that he had to deal with at his holiday home in the Knysna area. He spent many hours and emptied many spraycans of insecticide in his efforts to eliminate them. But they came back time and again. And he also realised: "I'm poisoning the soil." He told his caucus:

Black people are here to stay. We cart them away in buses; they come back. And we are poisoning our environment with legislation and measures aimed at keeping them out. The law must be scrapped.

The acknowledgement of black people's permanence in urban areas was a fatal blow to apartheid, even though its death was slow and the corpse would stink to high heaven for a long time to come. After this, there was no turning back on the road to a political settlement that required black people's participation and approval. The subsequent political machinations and the obstacles that were deliberately placed in the way were a futile attempt to control the outcome of the process. Yet they could neither reverse nor stop the process. Although Botha knew this, he could not, or would not, recognise the full political consequences of the step he had taken. The implications of the reforms he allowed had not been explored either strategically or morally within a greater vision. Instead, his reforms were haphazard and had unintended consequences, a criticism that was also levelled at him by FW de Klerk.

Botha's intention to control the process unilaterally was reflected by the combination of piecemeal reforms and draconian security measures. This combination caused the anti-apartheid fighters to intensify their efforts, created scores of martyrs, and destroyed the credibility of all incremental reform efforts. Though it may be argued that Botha's reform initiatives (unintentionally) undermined the apartheid system from within, his will and capacity to provide leadership in a more comprehensive peace process came under suspicion. Apart from the Western world that had intensified pressure on the Botha regime, there was also another factor: the world itself had changed. The Cold War was losing its aggressive heat and motivating ideological sentiments. The end of the rivalry between the superpowers was in sight. With his *glasnost* and *perestroika,* Mikhail Gorbachev had set in motion processes that would radically change his country. His party's Central Committee meeting in April 1985, and the 27th party congress, signalled unequivocally that a new order in the Soviet Union was imminent.

Oliver Tambo and Thabo Mbeki picked up these signals swiftly and clearly; for example, that Gorbachev was no longer in the mood for costly campaigns in other countries while the Soviet people themselves were unable to enjoy or even hope for a "better life for all". Tambo visited Moscow regularly in that period and was briefed fully by Gorbachev on the new developments. The centralist British Communist Party had never held much appeal for Tambo. To Tambo and Mbeki, Gorbachev's free-market sympathies were not bad news. To the amazement of all and the disappointment of the communists and socialists in the ANC, Gorbachev threw the Marxist-inspired notion of a world revolution on the intellectual and political scrap heap. And, as Thabo Mbeki more or less put it to me in 1989: when Gorbachev also dumped the Brezhnev doctrine of an Eastern Europe that would permanently be under the communist central control of Moscow, the ANC, with its idea of a revolutionary military takeover of South Africa, was in deep trouble. A negotiation route, Mbeki told me, was inevitable. The real problem, though, was how and on what terms. Another problem, he added, was to convince the majority of the ANC leaders of this. Among the exiles, Tambo and Mbeki had been the first leaders to read correctly the signs of a changing world without East-West rivalry. That was why, with Tambo's knowledge and cooperation, Mbeki began to work for a negotiated settlement in the 1980s.

The impact of the thawing of the Cold War was disillusioning to ANC leaders who firmly believed that they were winning the armed struggle. In a frank and private conversation, a senior ANC leader told me in 1989 about an ANC visit to President Gorbachev on an earlier occasion. Joe Slovo of the South African Communist Party, who was wholeheartedly involved in the armed struggle, had been among those present. Gorbachev had informed the delegation that ways had to be explored to enter into a negotiating process with the "Afrikaner government" with a view to a settlement. Apparently he had said/ordered: "The killings must stop. Start talking." The president of the Soviet Union also told Joe Slovo that he (Slovo) could make a start in this regard by discarding his Stalinist convictions. According to my source, Slovo, who had come looking for money and weapons for the armed struggle, had to be content with a signed photo of the Soviet president.

It is important to keep the following in mind: while there was mounting resistance to and even a loathing for the Botha regime in government circles in the US and Britain, this was certainly not the case when people talked about South Africa itself, its potential and its people – white, coloured, black and Asian. In countries such as the US, Britain, the Netherlands and Germany there was always a remarkable and sometimes incomprehensible affinity for the country and its people; it was the political leadership and system that elicited revulsion. This was also what I experienced in the course of my extensive contact with ANC exiles. Racism was not seen as "white nature", something with which white people identified purely because they were white. On 3 June 1986, for instance, almost a year after the notorious Rubicon speech and with states of emergency in force in South Africa, I made a presentation to the US secretary of state's Advisory Committee on South Africa. Among the committee members were Vernon Jordan, Leon Sullivan, Frank Thomas, Lawrence Eagleburger and John Dellenback, a good friend with whom I had become acquainted through the American Fellowship Movement , a non-ecclesiastical organisation that focused on personal networks. Herbert Beukes, South Africa's ambassador in Washington, had given some committee members my book *Apartheid Must Die*. He also advised me beforehand: "Be honest. You don't represent the South African government. The committee members would like to hear your views as an Afrikaner." I followed his advice.

At that stage I was already convinced that the ANC had established a right of veto in respect of everything proposed or initiated by the South African government, business sector, opinion leaders and academics to get reform off the ground. This right of veto, I argued, could only be revoked if the ANC were able to participate as a full and equal discussion partner in the deliberations about South Africa's future. The discussion in the committee was one of the most positive and enriching events in which I participated during 1985 and 1986. Since I relate strongly to symbolism, the date on which C William Kontos, the executive director of the committee, wrote me an exceptionally friendly thank-you note, was all the more meaningful: 16 June 1986. Thereafter I was more conscious of the political impasse in which South Africa found itself.

Both internationally and domestically things became more and more difficult for the PW Botha government. And likewise for those Afrikaners who not only hoped for reconciliation and peace, but were keen to actively do something about it "from within". This dilemma intensified as the civil war inside the country's borders escalated and the international pools of good-will started to run dry. In 1987 Pauline Baker of the Carnegie Endowment, but with her eye on a future important political position, wrote an article in *Foreign Policy* entitled "South Africa: Afrikaner Angst". Baker, whom I had met several times and whose political influence was growing, gave an inci-sive analysis of what was happening in South Africa. Her analysis was done after the election of 6 May 1987 in which the Independent Movement had participated. Baker contended that class differences among Afrikaners had ushered in a process of "fragmentation" and that the "disintegration of white solidarity" had major implications for the "racial struggle" in South Africa. She was of the view that the National Party's waning prestige cre-ated opportunities for the anti-apartheid movement to come up with pro-negotiation initiatives for a transition to a "true non-racial democracy". And that the West had to use these opportunities. This was exactly what happened. Botha's Rubicon speech had been instrumental in this!

Four other events, two in 1986, one in 1987 and another in 1988, also played a role in advancing the process of settlement. One was the sudden resigna-tion of Dr Frederik van Zyl Slabbert as leader of the Progressive Federal Party (PFP) on 7 February 1986. He resigned from parliament as well, a month before the visit of the Commonwealth Eminent Persons Group (EPG) to South Africa. His resignation and that of his colleague Dr Alex Boraine, an esteemed PFP parliamentarian, sent shock waves through government and opposition circles. In my view, no other event at that time cast doubt on the relevance of the (white) parliament as an institution in such a dramatic fashion. But their exit from parliamentary politics also scuttled the possi-bility of Boraine's and Slabbert's participation in the subsequent and in-evitable institutionalised negotiating process.

In the course of time it was rumoured in political and intelligence cir-cles that their resignations had been aimed at preparing them for key roles in the unavoidable settlement process, preferably at the request of the ANC. But neither the parliamentary parties nor the ANC gave serious consider-ation to this possibility. Thabo Mbeki once told me that it might be con-sidered to use them as consultants, to which he added: "It is clear, though, that the actual bargaining and negotiating would have to take place between the NP and the ANC ." In a certain respect Slabbert's book *The Last White Parliament* (1985) had set the stage for his decision. It is doubtful that the parliamentarians of the time, including the members of his own party, understood his book properly. The "white parliament" ultimately played a decisive role in the settlement process. It is a fact that it is hard to exercise political leadership without strong supporting institutions and solid networks. Idasa, the organisation founded by Slabbert and Boraine, could not really be such an institution or network.

Another event in 1986, however, proved more decisive in tipping the scales: the abortive visit of the Commonwealth's Eminent Persons Group to South Africa between 2 March and 19 May. The mission was supported by the 49 member countries. Former Australian prime minister Malcolm Fraser and General Olusegun Obasanjo, a former Nigerian military head of state who had voluntarily ceded power to a civilian government, were the co-chairmen. I had the privilege of meeting some of the members and having discussions with, among others, General Obasanjo. He also talked to Nelson Mandela in Pollsmoor Prison. Some other members were later granted permission to do so as well. The EPG's visit once again raised high expectations of the possibility of a negotiated-settlement process. The group formulated a working document in this regard that contained the elements of an international consensus, which had been orchestrated thoroughly and with unstinting zeal by Thabo Mbeki in particular. Margaret Thatcher, who had tried for a long time to ward off the sword of stringent sanctions, eventually had to yield to this consensus as well. Among others, criteria that were set for the start of negotiations according to this consensus included the unconditional release of Mandela and other political prisoners, and the abandonment of the condition that Mandela and the ANC first had to renounce the use of violence in pursuit of political aims. Thatcher had been a strong proponent of the latter condition because she equated the ANC with the Irish Republican Army and the Palestine Liberation Organisation.

Initially, the Botha cabinet had given the EPG delegation hope. In a cabinet-sanctioned document that was made available during a meeting between the cabinet and the EPG, it was stated: "It is the conviction of the

Government that any future constitutional dispensation providing for participation by all South African citizens should be the result of negotiations with the leaders of all communities . . . The only condition is that those who participate in the discussions and negotiations should foreswear violence as a means of achieving political objectives" (*Mission to South Africa* 1986:80). PW Botha had probably assumed that the ANC would never agree to that.

On 19 May 1986, an event occurred that spelled out with bullets and bombs who still ruled the roost politically in South Africa: the South African Defence Force (SADF), under Minister Magnus Malan, abruptly "targeted the enemy" (the ANC) in Botswana, Zimbabwe and Zambia. And that while the EPG was in the country, in the process of compiling their report! These three sovereign countries were, of course, members of the Commonwealth. To add insult to injury, it turned out that PW Botha had authorised the raids. His minister of foreign affairs, Pik Botha, who had been assisting the EPG and also helping to fan the flame of hope, had not been told of the invasion beforehand. This was political cynicism at its crudest and most brutal, albeit that Botha and Malan might have intended to highlight the sovereignty of South Africa in a possible settlement process. Maybe it was not so strange, either. The close cooperation between South Africa and Israel, also militarily, probably fostered this cynicism. There was something else as well: the infighting between factions within the government. Pik Botha and his senior officials hoped for a political breakthrough towards a negotiated settlement. The securocrats, and notably Military Intelligence that had PW Botha's ear at that stage, were not enthusiastic about this prospect. In addition, there was a power struggle between Pik Botha and some of the other cabinet ministers, such as Chris Heunis (constitutional affairs) and Magnus Malan (defence). Heunis, in particular, had leadership aspirations of his own and tried to stay close to PW Botha.

The EPG packed their bags and hurried off without having accomplished anything. Once again the "iron fist" ruled instead of dialogue. A good acquaintance who was close to the cabinet assured me: "We first need to soften up the enemy before we can talk. The SADF is our major trump card. And we can't allow foreign interference." But the EPG's initiative was not a totally lost cause. While Margaret Thatcher had been fairly unrelenting in her stance against mandatory sanctions at the Commonwealth conference in Nassau in October 1985, Britain joined the other Commonwealth countries in adopting sanctions resolutions in August 1986. To put it somewhat cynically: PW Botha and Magnus Malan had left her with no alternative. In fact, Thabo Mbeki told me that "Magnus's invasion" was tragic, but also political manna from heaven. At the Commonwealth conference (in August 1986) Thatcher even referred to Botha's "obstinacy" and the fact that Nelson Mandela was still in prison, and said that in light of the "fiasco" with the EPG, there was no prospect of a peaceful political dialogue between the South African government and representatives of the black population. She was at her wits' end. As Robin Renwick, the British ambassador in South Africa and someone who had Thatcher's ear, once put it to me: "Thatcher doesn't like unpleasant surprises. The Botha government specialises in them."

In August 1986, when Thatcher expressed her personal frustration and despair regarding the situation in South Africa in public for the first time, PW Botha was in one of his trademark belligerent and defiant moods at a meeting of his party members and supporters. In the words of someone who had been present, he was "pissed off". He was, after all, addressing a meeting of his own party. Vehemently opposed to foreign interference in South Africa's domestic affairs, an issue on which he had always been adamant, he warned the world: "Don't underestimate us." True to the military facet of his personality, he proclaimed dramatically and to the cheers of his party members: "We're not a nation of jellyfishes!" He could not have used a better metaphor in addressing his supporters. In fact, this was the one trait of Botha's that I came to know very quickly: he hated what he regarded as signs of weakness. That was why he simply could not react to foreign pressure with more understanding. It would have been a sign of weakness. This trait also explains his Rubicon speech. The road map proposed by the EPG (1986) did, indeed, influence the growing international consensus about a settlement. In fact, during the unofficial talks between the Afrikaner contact group and exiled ANC leaders in England the EPG's initiative cropped up repeatedly.

The third event that deserves mention occurred in 1987: the launch of the Independent Movement. The run-up to this step had consequences for the ruling power elite and its supporting organisations such as the Afrikaner Broederbond and the Afrikaans churches that have not yet been rated at their true value. Politically, this breakaway was as significant as the Dakar conference (July 1987), if not more so, as it was a rebellion from within the heart of Afrikanerdom and its institutions. A revolt against the leadership. This rebellion was also reflected in the article by Pauline Baker to which I referred earlier. It is a fact of life that rebels from within generally carry more political weight than critics on the outside. The internal rebellion had had a long genesis. At first it was mainly a Stellenbosch rebellion. That in itself had a political and opinion-forming benefit. The image and position of Stellenbosch University (SU) was a talking point within South Africa as well as in certain Western countries, albeit sometimes in dismissive and also ambivalent terms. What happened in Stellenbosch might not always have made sensational academic and scientific news. But invariably it was sensational political news. International journalists flocked to Stellenbosch.

As far back as February 1985, Sampie Terreblanche and I had had a meeting with Botha at his request. Professor HW van der Merwe of the University of Cape Town, who had close ties with Winnie Mandela and the ANC, had invited us to meet Thabo Mbeki in Lusaka as a result of an article of Terreblanche's that had appeared in the *Sunday Times*. Botha did not tell us how he had got wind of the invitation. He requested us kindly yet urgently to turn it down: "We don't talk to murderers," he said. We acceded to his request. As we left the building, Terreblanche remarked: "If we'd refused, PW would surely have thrown us from the window on the eighteenth floor." I realised then how much Botha, as someone who had started his advance to the highest political position as Cape leader of the NP, valued his "Stellenbosch connection", and that it might become a bargaining chip at some stage. That was why he treated even the outspoken Terreblanche more cautiously than he behaved towards other critics. The so-called *verligtes* of Stellenbosch had a political influence of which they themselves were unaware. In my opinion, they were better placed than the liberal moralists to exercise a material influence on the political course of events.

Matters rapidly came to a head. In October 1985, following Botha's Rubicon speech and shortly before Mandela was admitted to the Volks Hospital,

Terreblanche and several colleagues from SU, including me, formed Discussion Group '85. It became a chisel that struck a blow to the heart of the Botha regime. It was during this time, after Mandela's hospitalisation, that Kobie Coetsee, minister of justice, police and prisons, started talking to Mandela. There is little doubt in my mind that the possibility of Mandela dying in imprisonment had suddenly become a worrying problem for Kobie Coetsee and others. A memorandum by the discussion group about the deteriorating conditions in the country, drafted by Stellenbosch philosopher Anton van Niekerk, was submitted to Terreblanche's close friend Minister Chris Heunis on 28 January 1986. It dealt with four "conceptual obstacles" to a meaningful reform and negotiation process. "Power-sharing", it has to be said, was still the keyword at that stage. The first obstacle was that the international world had left us in the lurch. Without the international world, it was tickets for South Africa. Second, a negotiated settlement with black people in South Africa could not exclude the ANC. Not all black people were in favour of violence. Third, the South African government's problems could be traced back directly to its story about the Moscow-orchestrated "total onslaught". And fourth, the Group Areas Act and other measures had to go. The memorandum stated bluntly: "Within the next six months there has to be clarity about the government's intent to do away with apartheid in all its manifestations ... otherwise violence, riots and economic pressure are going to reach proportions that will threaten our existence beyond what can be anticipated." The political die was cast.

Heunis sat on the memorandum for many months. Eventually he informed Terreblanche that he had discussed the document with Botha. On 20 February 1987, Botha, together with Heunis, had a meeting with 28 of the rebels in Tuynhuys, his official residence. Six of the rebels acted as spokespersons. Afterwards Botha addressed the group for more than an hour. After his speech, he tried to end the meeting with his "final words". Chaos erupted as Terreblanche and Botha started yelling at each other. I intervened, and said I was taking over as chairman. Taken aback, Botha said: "This is my office. I'm the boss here." The great schism that had been threatening for so long, happened on that day. Terreblanche resigned from the National Party. Other resignations followed. On 8 March the discussion group issued a statement that disclosed the contents of the memorandum. It had reper-cussions internationally. NP hegemony had begun to crumble. In Lusaka, more notice was taken of this than of anything else. Hope of a negotiated settlement was kindled. Also in Pollsmoor, where Mandela was in conver-sation with Kobie Coetsee by that time.

At the time of the EPG's hasty departure the writing was already on the wall, scrawled in blood: Angola and South West Africa (Namibia). Here, Swapo and the Cubans were "the enemy". There were also ANC camps based in Angola. South Africa supported Unita, which was the opposition to the Angolan resistance movement, the MPLA, and Swapo, the resistance move-ment in South West Africa (Namibia). The Unita leader Jonas Savimbi was a personal friend of PW Botha's. In fact, Savimbi had been a guest of hon-our at Botha's presidential inauguration in Cape Town's Dutch Reformed Groote Kerk (on 14 September 1984). The Total Onslaught, and the SADF's Total Strategy, were visible in Angola and Namibia from South Africa's doorstep. And also in the kitchens, lounges and bedrooms of those whose young sons had been conscripted to implement the Total Strategy. Or, as an NP parliamentarian and a good friend told me heatedly: "To keep the communists away from our borders." Most Afrikaners believed this, too. Few issues had such an impact on South Africa's internal politics as the Angola-Namibia question, especially from 1988 onwards.

At the invitation of the SADF I had the opportunity to visit the "opera-tional area" with a group of friends from the Stellenbosch area. We were mainly in the north of Namibia, where we met the dynamic General Jannie Geldenhuys, among others. We visited the Omega base – to see "what the Defence Force is doing for the Bushmen" – and a few other places. All of us returned to Stellenbosch convinced that "the SADF is fighting for a good cause." Today I believe that the struggle for the preservation of the apartheid state was lost, in part, through the war in Angola. In conjunc-tion, of course, with the support South Africa gave to the Democratic Turnhalle Alliance (DTA) during the Namibian election in 1989, to Renamo in Mozambique and to Bishop Abel Muzorewa in Zimbabwe. These actions and others undertaken to keep "the enemy" (the ANC) outside the borders of the country and to restrain and even murder "the enemies" who were already inside, damaged the "old" South Africa financially and morally. There are bound to be sharp differences about this issue within Afrikaner ranks for a long time to come. Many Afrikaners still firmly believe that the war in Angola bought time for a negotiated settlement in South Africa, which is in my opinion an instance of after-the-fact justification and a form of retrospective mythologising.

* * *

I first met Chester Crocker at Washington's Georgetown University where he lectured and did research. He was a friend of the former *Sunday Times* editor Tertius Myburgh. Myburgh and I worked together on many issues, also because of our involvement in the United States South Africa Leadership Programme (Ussalep), which had an office in Washington. Crocker visited South Africa prior to his appointment as assistant secretary of state for African affairs in the Reagan administration. Together with Myburgh, we had a long and incisive discussion about his (Crocker's) policy position on South Africa and also the rest of Africa: constructive engagement. Myburgh and I were excited about this concept. Crocker eventually became intensively involved in the conflict between South Africa and Namibia-Angola, especially once the Cubans started featuring prominently. Occasional murmurs even came from mainly Citizen Force circles that Angola might become South Africa's Vietnam if South African forces were to penetrate too far and too deeply into that country. Contrary to what is often claimed, there was not always harmony and unanimity between Citizen Force and Permanent Force members.

Crocker was in favour of a negotiated settlement in Namibia-Angola. He was also convinced that such a settlement would pave the way for a negotiated settlement in South Africa. Botha's Rubicon speech and the successful anti-South African sanctions campaign in the US had in any case caused the Reagan administration a big political headache. In the US, with its sizeable African-American population and well-disposed Democratic Party, ANC leaders were welcome guest speakers at numerous meetings. Following Botha's Rubicon speech the ANC, with Tambo and Mbeki leading the way, won the diplomatic war against the South African government hands down in the US. Early in 1987, for instance, Tambo visited the US where he held discussions with many people, including former secretary of state Henry Kissinger. Rightists in the US were up in arms about Crocker's stance and "befriended" South Africa. On Friday, 7 December 1984 the National Coalition Of Americans Committed To Rescuing Africa From The Grip Of Soviet Tyranny lashed out at Crocker through a kind of open letter to him: "Why is Chester Crocker trying to sell 20 million black Africans into communist slavery?" This suited the myth of the Total Onslaught to a T. So, too, did the reproach levelled at Ronald Reagan for having stated when accepting his nomination for a second presidential term (in August 1984): "Since January 20, 1981, not one inch of soil has fallen to the communists."

In 1988 PW Botha, who knew about my contact with Crocker, asked me to see him about a number of issues. He was affable during my visit, and came to the point as we concluded our conversation: "You and Crocker know each other. I can't stand the man, and I don't trust him. Tell him we have to talk some more about the conflict in Namibia and Angola; there are a few conditions we need to agree on first. South Africa and the SADF must be able to withdraw with dignity. There are also costs that need to be looked at." And then, as an afterthought: "I don't like the idea of my young men being killed and maimed. The war is becoming too costly." The preparatory processes for a settlement were well on track at that stage, and Botha was aware of what lay ahead. This conversation was one of the times where he revealed his human side. Crocker did not like Botha either. According to him Botha exhibited "xenophobic rage" on more than one occasion, especially in critical situations, when he would sweep reasonableness and ordinary practical realities off the table. For my part, I always thought that Botha had an ambivalent personality: he was addicted to power, yet still wanted to accommodate morality. His political and moral sensibilities were constantly in conflict and, like his predecessor BJ Vorster, he could not deal with that. His successor, FW de Klerk, managed to cope better with this conflict. Presumably that was the reason why Botha resorted to a fundamentalist interpretation of the Bible after his retirement.

From the start of 1988 I heard much about the conflict in Angola-Namibia from an ANC perspective. It made me realise very quickly that the settlement of this conflict would be a prelude to the resolution of the civil war in South Africa. And also, that while the former conflict could not be resolved by means of a military solution, this was even more true of the latter. Thabo Mbeki and I agreed about this from the outset. To my mind, few dates in our history are as important as 22 December 1988, a few days before Christmas. On that day the trilateral agreement between South Africa, Cuba and Angola was signed. A gruelling and expensive war was over. General Jannie Geldenhuys, Niel Barnard and Neil van Heerden (foreign affairs) had been decisive peace brokers. In 1989 the Namibian negotiation process led to an inclusive election, and in March 1990 Swapo was in power in Windhoek.

After the Rubicon speech Botha's government became more and more mired in difficulties. Key opinion leaders withdrew their support for the notion of reform from within. Others lost their enthusiasm for this strategy and rather kept quiet. As someone from the ranks of the NP put it in 1988: "Intellectual bankcruptcy set in in the NP. The only thing that remained was the use of instruments of power."

Later it would emerge that moral bankcruptcy had set in as well. Elements of the state had been turned into killing machines. The Botha regime and its security forces had their hands full with severe civil resistance among the majority of the population. An internal erosion process set in after PW Botha's Rubicon speech. This process accelerated as external pressure and internal extraparliamentary resistance intensified. The security forces were never really in control, despite bombastic assurances. The extended states of emergency attested to that. As Franklin Sonn told me in 1988: "A government that rules through states of emergency is a government in dire straits. It's only a matter of time. Apartheid is teetering on the edge of its grave." I was able to witness this erosion from close up through my involvement with the Urban Foundation from 1985.

# 3
## Hospital visits and secret meetings: Mandela, Coetsee and Barnard

It is one of the great historical ironies of South Africa's process of transition to an inclusive democracy: the fiery and charismatic Winnie Mandela, then still the wife of the political prisoner Nelson Mandela, threw out a line to NP minister Kobie Coetsee, which was the start of something that would lead to Mandela's meeting with Botha in his Cape Town residence, Tuynhuys, on 5 July 1989. It is unlikely that she herself would have hoped for such an outcome. It was rather a case of an ever self-assured Winnie Mandela who refused to let herself be intimidated by anybody or anything. Kobie Coetsee *had* to give her a hearing. She was, after all, Nelson Mandela's wife, she had been banished to the Free State, and on top of that she was friends with (white) acquaintances of Coetsee's. A few days after her husband's second hospitalisation with tuberculosis (on 12 August 1988) I ran into her at the then DF Malan Airport, now the Cape Town International Airport. Her lawyer, Ismail Ayob, was among her entourage. I happened to be on my way to England for discussions with Thabo Mbeki and his group. Unthinkingly, I walked up to her to say hello. We greeted each other. At that moment, hordes of photographers and journalists descended on Winnie and her entourage to take pictures and ask questions. I fled hastily. This was not a photograph in which I could appear.

In November 1985 the 67-year-old Nelson Mandela was admitted to the Volks Hospital in Cape Town for a prostate operation. The "Volks", as it was commonly known, a Dutch Reformed Church-inspired initiative, had opened its doors in 1930. The inaugural address was delivered by former clergyman and later prime minister of South Africa, Dr DF Malan, one of the fathers of apartheid, who said: "This is no local institution. It belongs to the entire volk [Afrikaner nation]. This is not just a hospital. It is a hospital for the volk." In 1981 the hospital had to be taken over by the Cape

Provincial Administration, and in 1998 it was acquired by Medi-Clinic. An ancedote that is told about a visit to Mandela in the Volks Hospital by George Bizos, his senior legal representative, says much about Mandela's personality. The Afrikaans-speaking nurses had to change his dressings at regular intervals. At some point, Mandela cut short his conversation with Bizos: the nurses needed to do their work so that they could go home to their families.

Winnie Mandela, who was on her way to visit her husband in hospital, happened to be on the same flight as Kobie Coetsee, who had taken over from Jimmy Kruger as minister of justice, police and prisons (in October 1980). It was Jimmy Kruger who had remarked infamously in 1977 that the death by torture of the dynamic Black Consciousness leader Steve Biko "left him cold". This statement was like a cannon shot to the hearts of many NP-supporting Afrikaners whose consciences were increasingly troubled by the megalomania of their leaders. Kruger had banished Winnie Mandela to the small Free State town of Brandfort, about 60 kilometres from Bloemfontein (1977). He wanted her away from Soweto, which had exploded in 1976, but not too far from the watchful eyes of the security police. It was in any case easier to spy on her in Brandfort than in Soweto. In those days the police station in Brandfort had an address of symbolic significance to Afrikaners: Voortrekker Street. Another symbolic name, but with a good dose of gallows humour, was that of the black township where her new home – without running water – was situated: Phathakahle. The word can be translated as "handle with care". With Winnie Mandela's presence, this name acquired new political significance. It was from this small town that she set out on her officially sanctioned trip to the Volks Hospital.

Coetsee, who had been born on 19 April 1931 in Ladybrand, a small town in the then Orange Free State (OFS), studied law at the University of the Orange Free State in Bloemfontein. In 1968 he became the NP member of parliament for Bloemfontein West, which had become vacant when Jim Fouché was named as state president. PW Botha appointed Coetsee as deputy minister of defence and national intelligence in 1978. He eventually became minister of justice, with prisons added to his portfolio at a later stage. In 1985 he was elected leader of the NP in the OFS. It is significant to note that after the first democratic election in 1994, Coetsee was elected president of what was then called the senate, with the support of the ANC. He died of a heart attack in 2000. Mandela had held him in very high esteem.

During the flight to Cape Town, Winnie Mandela went up to Coetsee and sat down next to him. And spoke to him in her inimitable fashion. Jimmy Kruger had not succeeded in demoralising her. The conversation was facilitated by an important factor, one that would also play a huge role in the long mediation and negotiation road to the election in 1994: the effect of personal relationships and the experiences of a shared South African identity. Aziz Pahad put it very aptly when he spoke of our "common destiny and common country" during our first meeting in October 1987. Coetsee was also no Jimmy Kruger, but a sensitive person despite his strong will and ego that were too obtrusive at times. Kruger's banishment of Winnie Mandela to Brandfort had "fortunate unintended consequences" (*felix culpa*). The only lawyer in the town, Pieter de Waal, and his wife Adéle (née Retief) got to know Winnie Mandela well and their relationship grew into a special friendship. De Waal also knew Coetsee. Sadly, his wife Adéle could not share in the joy of the first truly democratic election (in 1994) as a sign of her and her husband's contribution to the healing of relationships. She died in a car accident in 1990.

This is a little piece of history that illustrates what the positive and boundary-transcending role of personal relationships, a culture of trust and confidence, mutual respect, and unofficial or private interaction can be within a bigger political picture. In the Brandfort episode it happened within two dimensions: the relationship between Kobie Coetsee and Pieter de Waal, the lawyer in the town, and the relationship between Adéle de Waal and Winnie Mandela. Pieter de Waal and Kobie Coetsee had known each other personally since their university days in Bloemfontein. They played tennis together. Hence De Waal had access to Coetsee. If there is one thing I learnt in this period of our history, sometimes harshly, it is that without access, you are "out". In all societies, access is "informal" *and* "formal". The business world is a textbook example of this, as the word "contacts" implies. The formal and institutionalised forms of access, as laid down procedurally in communication channels, spheres of authority (authorised persons) and diaries, generally take longer. Such access can become bogged down in red tape, which is frequently used as a delaying and exclusionary technique. Informal access is often more effective and mainly timesaving. It is determined by the nature of role players' networks.

De Waal used to leapfrog over all the formal gatekeepers and talk directly to Coetsee – before he succeeded Kruger and also after he became the minister. De Waal also wrote Kruger a letter to say that Winnie Mandela was causing more problems in Brandfort than those Kruger had wanted to solve. The De Waal family were unhappy about the conditions in which Winnie Mandela had to live. They tried to make things easier for her by, for instance, making their house available to her and her guests from abroad that the authorities permitted her to see. She also used their house telephone at times. Adéle de Waal once caused great consternation when she had to rush to drop Winnie at her home in the township in order to meet the time limit stipulated in her friend's banning order. Adéle, like her friend, came up against an overzealous policeman, Gert Prinsloo, who had been indoctrinated with the word "arrest". Her husband's reaction to this threat, and his intention to phone the minister, resolved this explosive situation. In a hierarchical system of authority, the person who knew the minister had more influence than a policeman did.

It was after the conversation on the plane that Coetsee decided to visit Nelson Mandela in hospital. There was an important context to this visit, as well as the conversation, that needs to be repeated briefly despite it being familiar history. For about half a century the ANC had been an organisation that did not endorse violence as a means of furthering political objectives. The watchwords were rather dialogue and negotiations. Even when Nelson Mandela and a number of other new-generation liberation leaders formed the ANC Youth League and got rid of dead wood, their more militant approach did not translate immediately into a call to arms. A radical change occurred in 1961. Before South Africa became a republic outside the Commonwealth, and with the memory of the Sharpeville massacre still fresh, Mandela wrote a letter to then prime minister, Hendrik Verwoerd. He proposed a National Convention with a view to the drafting of a new, nonracial and democratic constitution. He received no response. Thereafter the ANC's decades-long policy of nonviolent action came to an end, and UmKhonto weSizwe (MK) was founded. Mandela later admitted he had never believed that the ANC's armed struggle would topple the apartheid state. But it did, of course, put great pressure on the apartheid state.

Mandela himself, like Tambo and Mbeki too, had always been in favour of dialogue in a qualified manner. During the 1980s those who did not exclude dialogue in principle were increasingly concerned about the growing militancy among the youth in the ANC after 1976 and the influence of communist regimes that had started exporting revolution to other countries. This applied mainly to those who were strong adherents of the tradition of the Freedom Charter that had been adopted at Kliptown in 1955. In the Afrikaner-ANC talks the ANC participants, and Thabo Mbeki in particular, regularly made mention of the fact that the Charter was steeped in a pro-negotiation philosophy and spelled out the contours for a dialogue about black people's expectations and rights. The Freedom Charter was undoubtedly Mbeki's political and intellectual point of reference, his primary text and fundamental vision of the future. That was also the reason why he could hold his own within the ANC with its mounting revolutionary militancy and revolutionary dreams of power. No one dared to question or disregard the Freedom Charter. In the interpretation of the Charter, Mbeki was the militants' superior.[1]

An important shift had taken place in the 1960s when the idea of an armed struggle and a military takeover of the South African state became prominent. This prominence, along with the expectations of the ANC's military wing, was boosted sky-high by the then Soviet Union in particular. Financially, militarily and politically, the external wing of the ANC became highly dependent on Moscow and its camp followers. It was sucked into the East-West conflict as well as Moscow's ideological dreams. Naturally, the Freedom Charter's emphasis on the idea of nationalisation was a source of inspiration in these circles. Mandela, who had been arrested in 1963 and sentenced to life imprisonment during the Rivonia trial in 1964, was incarcerated on Robben Island for many years. He was not a communist or a supporter of Moscow's ideological dreams. It was rather a case of "my enemy's enemy is my ally". In his cell and in the quarries of Robben Island, he thought and dreamed about the future instead of passively bemoaning his fate. In March 1982, his circumstances improved substantially. Mandela, Walter Sisulu, Ahmed Kathrada, Raymond Mhlaba and Andrew Mlangeni were transferred to the third floor of Pollsmoor Prison, where they were housed in more civilised conditions than on Robben Island. They even had beds with sheets, not to mention towels. Occasionally they were allowed to receive foreign visitors. At that stage Kobie Coetsee was the political head (minister) of the department and also responsible for prisons. He had been a Botha appointment. It was also Botha who had excluded Kruger from his cabinet.

Mandela's memory of the move to Pollsmoor is particularly touching. "A man can get used to anything, and I had grown used to Robben Island. I had lived there for almost two decades and while it was never a home – my home was in Johannesburg – it had become a place where I felt comfortable. I have always found change difficult . . . I had no idea what to look forward to." As would emerge later, however, this transfer to Pollsmoor was ultimately of great political significance – albeit that the government had other objectives in mind with the move, such as disrupting the global identification of the name Mandela with Robben Island. In the ranks of the resistance movements and the anti-apartheid campaigners, the political symbolism of this island was as powerful as the political symbolism of the Voortrekker Monument among Afrikaners, if not more so.

It was from Pollsmoor that Mandela was taken to the Volks Hospital where he was operated on and received post-operative care. Paul Cluver, then a well-known Cape neurosurgeon and today a respected wine farmer, used to perform brain operations there. He relates that when he arrived at the theatre section of the hospital one day, everything had been closed off. He was given a vague explanation about essential repairs and was only informed of the real reason later. Secrecy was at that stage considered to be in the interest of national security. There was an important side effect once it became known that Mandela had had an operation. The question was suddenly asked with great urgency: what would happen if Mandela died in imprisonment? This question could not be answered in a Jimmy Kruger-like manner. Coetsee was well aware of that.

When Kobie Coetsee paid Mandela a visit in the Volks Hospital, it was the first time that a minister of the ruling party visited South Africa's world-famous prisoner. Personally, I doubt whether Coetsee had any long-term strategic or even tactical objectives; it was rather a goodwill visit with a strong dose of curiosity. And it held risks for both Coetsee and Mandela. Yet Coetsee, and particularly Mandela, were quick to grasp its significance, even though it would take a long time before subsequent visits led to an exploration of negotiation possibilities. It was, however, the start of a process where "enemies" began talking informally to each other, a track-two interaction within the system and, above all, confidential. What followed directly afterwards was a decisive key in the lock of South Africa's politically bolted-down doors: the forging of personal relationships on the basis of trust and (self-)confidence. A process on a personal level, based on mutual respect and confidentiality, was set in motion. As Thabo Mbeki put it to me early in 1988, the ANC had a principled position, which was that the regime had to take the initiative to start a dialogue with the ANC. It was not the ANC that should make the first move. That was why Mandela took a great risk and later also had to face severe criticism from his fellow prisoners about his initiatives from prison.

It was another lesson that I learned very swiftly: trust between historical political enemies is also built as a result of shared risks. Building and sustaining trust and (self-)confidence is not simply a moral choice or a kind of conversion. It includes important strategic and tactical facets. The business sector is a good example of this. Sound and well-functioning partnerships are built not only on reward-sharing, but also on risk-sharing. In short: trust is fostered when the parties share both rewards and risks. That was what Kobie Coetsee did, who kept his fellow cabinet members in the dark about his conversations with Mandela. That was also what Mandela did. He and Kobie Coetsee eventually had much more than just a goodwill or moral interest in their conversations. Over time it became a strategic and tactical interest.

Mandela, notwithstanding his imprisonment of many years, knew exactly what he wanted to do and how he wanted to do it. He knew that if the Botha regime isolated him from Lusaka, other ANC leaders and also the

UDF, it would undermine his own political credibility. He neither wished to, nor could he afford to, fall for a "divide-and-rule" strategy. Yet he did not want to broadcast his conversation with Coetsee and their subsequent discussions. Politically and morally, that was his most difficult decision. His "constituency" were people who liked to take collective decisions. He had to choose between either talking privately or protesting publicly and endorsing all kinds of protest actions and public conferences. He chose the former. And he did not even inform his own political comrades in Pollsmoor. It was a choice that held enormous risks. He did take one person into his confidence: George Bizos, his senior legal representative, who had access to him. Bizos, whom I have read about, talked about with others and once or twice had personal conversations with, is a remarkable man. He and his father fled from Greece during the Second World War and ended up in South Africa by way of Egypt. His father opened a café directly across the street from the offices of the now defunct *Vaderland* newspaper. When I read that, I could not help laughing aloud about South Africa's ironies.

From his hospital bed on the third floor of the Volks Hospital Mandela informed Bizos about his meeting with Coetsee. He wanted Bizos to convey a personal message, confidentially, to Oliver Tambo in Lusaka. Bizos, not someone who talked indiscriminately to others about his contacts in order to impress, consented. He decided to talk to Kobie Coetsee about it beforehand to avoid any unpleasantness. The conversation eventually took place on an aeroplane, of all places. Bizos's meeting with Tambo, who had gone into exile in 1961, was held in a hotel in Lusaka. It turned into a lengthy discussion and Tambo was briefed in full. He, too, accepted that exploratory talks, later referred to as "talks about talks" by the ANC-Afrikaner contact group, had to be kept confidential and confined to a small group. A communication channel now existed between Mandela-Coetsee and Tambo. In Lusaka, Thabo Mbeki was among the few people who had been informed.

Bizos paid a second visit to Lusaka in February 1986. This time President Kenneth Kaunda was also briefed in broad terms. Bizos stayed in Kaunda's guest house, where I also stayed on occasion. Apparently, Oliver Tambo stayed there as well during the Bizos visit. President Kaunda knew, of course, which way the wind was blowing, albeit that it was still only a slight breeze. Back in South Africa, Bizos decided to brief Coetsee on the positive reaction to his contact with Mandela. Accompanied by Judge Johan Kriegler who had arranged the meeting, Bizos visited Coetsee at his home in Pretoria. Any expectation Coetsee might still have harboured that a wedge could be driven between Mandela and Tambo, the "inziles" and the exiles, and that "divide and rule" would prevail, was quashed by Bizos. Coetsee also got this message: There was a serious and honest desire to have discussions with the government. The idea of a negotiated settlement was now on the political agenda, though it would take a long while still to put flesh on the bones. But a *process* had started.

On Mandela's discharge from the Volks Hospital on 23 December 1985, two days before Christmas, he was given a groundfloor cell in the hospital section of Pollsmoor. Some believe that this was an attempt to isolate Mandela from his fellow political prisoners and make him more amenable to compromises. That might have been what PW Botha, who had been briefed by Coetsee on his visit to Mandela, had in mind. He knew full well that when the day should come for serious deliberations about the political future of the country, Nelson Mandela had to be present at the table. Hence Botha had to find a way to release Mandela and other political prisoners without relinquishing control. Even his good friend, the conservative German politician Franz Josef Strauss, was putting pressure on him. I have also been told that Botha became more aware of the issue of the release of political prisoners as a result of the prison sentence imposed on the Afrikaans writer Breyten Breytenbach, then an ANC courier. Breytenbach's brother was one of Botha's valued military leaders. In Coetsee's case, though, there was in my view a more basic reason: he wanted to make it easier for Mandela and himself to talk privately and confidentially, and he wished to acknowledge Mandela's dignity as a leader. Mandela went to a lot of trouble to keep in touch with his fellow political prisoners, despite having his own private bathroom and even an exercise room.

Several meetings took place between Coetsee and Mandela. Coetsee did not treat Mandela like a prisoner, but went out of his way to show him respect. The meetings were held in elegant surroundings and Mandela was treated like a leader. At one point Coetsee even hosted Winnie Mandela at his official Cape residence, Savernake. He told her that he had decided she could return to her home in Soweto. To Winnie Mandela, this was manna from heaven. After her return to Soweto, though, her public activisim reached new lows. She flouted Coetsee's friendly but paternalistic request that she should exercise restraint and not let him down.

Eventually Mandela grew impatient. He wanted to meet the president, PW Botha, the "Great Crocodile", face to face. A long time had passed since the EPG's departure from the country. Some of the members had met Mandela. It was at the same time, in fact, that Bizos left for his mission to Lusaka. Botha was at that stage still adamant that ANC-orchestrated violence ruled out the possibility of official talks. ANC leaders and Mandela first had to renounce violence publicly. It is unlikely that Coetsee took particular trouble to persuade Botha to moderate his stance. Botha not only ruled the country with an iron fist, but his cabinet as well. The cabinet were in any case unaware of Coetsee's initiatives, as Botha had kept them in the dark. He encouraged Coetsee to continue with his personal contacts. Undoubtedly his intention was to learn more about Mandela and his views. PW Botha was someone who put much effort into finding out more about the personalities and positions of leaders he interacted with.

At this point, I need to say something about my contact and interaction with Botha. I was never an adviser of his, as was sometimes claimed. Our relationship was personal rather than political. His daughter Rozanne was in my philosophy class (for three years), as was Jimmy Kruger's son Eitel, who would later play a prominent role in Pretoria. I had great appreciation for both of them as students and as individuals. Chris Heunis, a political colleague and friend of Botha's, also regularly invited the Stellenbosch *verligtes*, including Sampie Terreblanche, Julius Jeppe, Christoph Hanekom and myself, to NP conferences, particularly youth conferences.

When the former rector of SU, Professor HB Thom, who was chancellor of the university at the time, died on Friday, 4 November 1983, Heunis was the first to put his candicacy on the table the day after Thom's death (Saturday). He was strongly supported by a leading academic, Professor Christo Viljoen, and a few others. Heunis had something of an obsession about becoming SU's chancellor. On John Vorster's resignation he had also made himself available for the position, but Thom stymied his candidacy at an early stage. Heunis's second attempt had failed as well. The chairman of the SU council, the dignified Jan van der Horst, and the SU rector, Professor Mike de Vries, contacted me. They were also of the view that Heunis, who couldn't help "interfering in everything", had to be "kept out". The only way in which this could be achieved, was to persuade PW Botha to make himself available for the chancellorship. And they wanted me to put the idea to Botha. I consulted Piet Cillié, the former editor of *Die Burger* and later professor in journalism at SU. Cillié's advice was: "Keep Heunis out. It wouldn't be good for the university and for him if he became chancellor."

Minister Dawie de Villiers and I talked to Botha in his office in the Union Buildings about the possibility of his candidacy. He would only consider it, he said, if I could give him satisfactory answers to the following questions:

- He doesn't have a university degree. How can he become chancellor?
- He knows that his "colleague Heunis" aspires to the position. How will I handle that?
- He can only fill the position for one term at the most. Can he make a contribution? He has more than enough work.

The second question was the trickiest. I told Botha I would inform Heunis personally if he, Botha, made himself available as candidate. Botha wouldn't have to tell Heunis. After a few days, Botha accepted his candidature. I visited Heunis in his office at the parliament buildings and gave him an honest explanation of the situation. It turned into one of the most unpleasant experiences of my life. Heunis exploded, with good reason. The rift between us never healed completely. Botha contacted me and said: "Thank you. If you feel strongly about something, you shouldn't act like a coward." From that day on there was a relationship of mutual respect between us.

Towards the end of 1988 Botha and I met by chance and exchanged a few words. As we concluded our brief chat, he remarked: "I know about your contacts with the ANC. If the news leaks out, I'll have to haul you over the coals in parliament." He laughed when I replied: "Sir, that will boost my credibility." It would take many months before he himself talked to a formidable ANC leader. He knew that this conversation was unavoidable, but wanted to determine the time and terms of the conversation himself.

I had left it up to Niel Barnard to brief Botha about the dialogue project or not. In fact, I realised very soon that in the undertaking in which I had become involved, one could not bypass Barnard. It required discipline to act professionally since I prefer informal, unofficial and unconventional interaction. I also have an aversion to protocol. Barnard did not inform Mandela himself about the dialogue project with the ANC exiles. Mandela, I was told by a senior member of the NIS, did not want to share the informal, non-public talks with anybody else from the ranks of the ANC. Especially not with Thabo Mbeki. One evening in Pretoria in the late 1980s, a few NIS members and I even speculated wildly whether we shouldn't smuggle Mbeki into South Africa to hold discussions with Mandela. This idea was shot down because it was believed that Mandela would not go along with it. At some stage Mandela was informed about the talks in England from within the Tambo-Mbeki inner circle.

Mandela, frustrated with the slow progress of the dialogue and concerned about the waves of resistance and repression sweeping the country, requested to speak to the commissioner of prisons, Commissioner Willemse. Within days Willemse arrived in Cape Town from Pretoria. At Pollsmoor, Mandela told him: "I want to talk to PW Botha." The general, slightly surprised, but someone who was well versed in protocol and also had respect for Mandela, said immediately that Kobie Coetsee was in Cape Town and that he would speak to him. Once again Coetsee and Mandela met at Coetsee's official residence. The conversations between them became more frequent. It is not widely known, but in 1987 Coetsee, Mandela and George Matanzima, the brother of Paramount Chief Kaiser Matanzima, the political leader of the "independent" Transkei, had a meeting at Kobie Coetsee's home. PW Botha was keen to get rid of the "Mandela problem" by giving Mandela his freedom in the Transkei subject to certain conditions. This meeting produced nothing of political significance except friendly words. Mandela had a greater political dream than merely his own personal freedom. He wanted to help achieve the liberation of all oppressed people in South Africa. And he wanted to do this by means of dialogue with "the enemy". Looking back on his conversations with Coetsee, he wrote in his autobiography *Long Walk to Freedom*: "It was clear to me that a military victory was a distant if not impossible dream ... It was time to talk." This memory of Mandela's is of great significance when it comes to answering the complex question: why did the leaders of the South African government and the leaders of the ANC finally opt for a negotiated settlement?

On the side of both the NP government and the ANC there is no single answer to this question, except that one can say with certainty: it was visionary strategic leadership that helped to make it possible, not a sudden moral conversion or miracle. Mandela assists us with his remark by focusing on one very important issue: a military solution was not possible. The ANC's revolutionary agenda was wishful thinking. The political, financial and military sponsorship for this fantasy, Moscow, was no longer guaranteed. Independent of Mandela, Thabo Mbeki also expressed this view during our discussions in England. The military option of PW Botha and his defence minister Magnus Malan suffered the same fate. The idea of a Total Onslaught and Total Strategy was being scuttled in Angola-Namibia, in the streets of black and coloured townships such as Soweto and Bonteheuwel, in the parental homes of young white conscripts, and in London, Washington, Paris and Amsterdam.

Early in 1988 there was a significant indication that progress was now being pursued purposefully by government representatives. A formal and special committee was established that included Niel Barnard and Mike Louw of the NIS, Commissioner Willemse from prisons, the director-general of the department of prisons Fanie van der Merwe, and of course Kobie Coetsee himself. The NIS became a key player in this initiative. The first meeting took place on 28 March 1988, and 48 meetings were held in all. Some of these were one-on-one discussions between Barnard and Mandela. (One such conversation was extremely delicate and personal as it related to the activities of Winnie Mandela, then still Nelson Mandela's wife.) With this initiative, preparations for the release of Mandela and other political prisoners and dialogue about a good understanding of the kind of conditions formal negotiations would be subject to, were started in earnest by informed insiders on a confidential basis.

The establishment of this highly confidential committee as a track-two project within the state was in every sense a watershed. Kobie Coetsee cleared its composition with President PW Botha; to the surprise of some members, Botha gave the project his blessing. Fanie van der Merwe, who would become a central figure at Codesa and the constitutional negotiations, played a key role in this commitee. Being involved in prisons and accountable to Minister Kobie Coetsee, he provided "justification cover" for the structured discussions with Nelson Mandela. If they should leak out, he could say that it was his "job" to hold discussions with political prisoners about their well-being from time to time.

Commissioner "Willie" Willemse should also be mentioned in this regard. He and Mandela respected each other and their relationship was characterised by goodwill. Willemse acknowledged the dignity and rights of political prisoners. Through his conduct, he, like Van der Merwe, repudiated the political image of brutal, megalomanic Afrikaners.

I first heard about these talks in August 1988. They were incisive discussions that sometimes lasted up to eight hours. At that stage the Afrikaner-ANC contact group had already met three times, with the third meeting held in August 1988. What Barnard of the NIS did was to bring about a transfer of the prison talks with Mandela to a broader group of stakeholders. After Mandela had been moved to Victor Verster Prison in Paarl, Koos Kruger said, admittedly in light vein, that I should please not ask to visit Mandela as well. After his release, Mandela asked me: "Why didn't you come to visit me?" I replied that there were many other people he had to see. One of the moving stories Barnard told me later was about the committee's second meeting with Mandela, which took place at Willemse's home. Willemse's wife cooked a meal for the participants and treated Mandela as simply another guest, an equal of the others.

It needs to be pointed out that Kobie Coetsee, Niel Barnard and Pieter de Waal were all "Free Staters". Barnard had lectured in political science at the University of the Orange Free State (now the University of the Free

State) in Bloemfontein. He was not a publicity seeker; a widely read academic who was also a strategic thinker, Barnard had solid credentials in the Afrikaner community. As a former student of his put it to me, he was "someone of strong convictions and will. Stood no nonsense from anyone. And although he never put all his cards on the table, he commanded respect and trust. He despised anyone he considered a 'weakling' and a 'bungler'." PW Botha, then still prime minister, had appointed Barnard as head of the NIS in 1979. Within months, the NIS was transformed into a professional and highly effective service. The notorious General Hendrik van den Bergh's Bureau for State Security was no more.

Kobie Coetsee played an important role in the opening moves for a non-public dialogue. He was the one who paved the way for a dialogue process with Nelson Mandela within a limited and carefully selected circle between 1985 and 1986. Mandela referred to Coetsee as a "new kind of Afrikaner", particularly after Coetsee had authorised visits by Lord Nicholas Bethal, a member of the British House of Lords and the European Parliament, and Samuel Dash, an American professor and former adviser to the US Senate's Watergate Committee. Barnard and Louw of the NIS had respect for Coetsee, even though Louw thought that Coetsee had an "obsession" about personal secrecy and was "paranoid" about not being proved wrong. It was actually a most remarkable mental shift that took place from 1988. In January 1985 PW Botha, supported triumphantly by his securocrats, still thought he had a trump card: Mandela was offered his freedom on condition that he unconditionally renounced violence as a political weapon. They knew, of course, that Mandela would never accept such an offer. How could a founding father of MK do that? According to what I was told later by a member of the NIS, it was purely and simply an ill-considered trap set by Botha and his securocrats in the hope that if Mandela rejected the offer, the Western world would accept that the South African government could not take the risk of releasing him.

At a gathering in Soweto where Bishop Tutu was honoured for his Nobel Peace Prize, Zindzi Mandela read her father's statement about the offer to the audience. It was perfect timing that made Botha and his securocrats look like political dunces. Mandela declared: "I am a member of the African

National Congress. I have always been a member of the African National Congress and I will remain a member of the African National Congress until the day I die."Then he said something that I still find deeply moving: "Oliver Tambo is much more than a brother to me. He is my greatest friend and comrade for nearly fifty years." Mandela knew what friendship and loyal personal relationships meant. He also said: "I am not a violent man. . . It was only then when all other forms of resistance were no longer open to us that we turned to armed struggle."Then came a political *coup de grâce*: a challenge to Botha to show that he was different from Malan, Strijdom and Verwoerd. "Let *him* renounce violence."

Coetsee was always solicitous of Mandela's dignity and comfort. Their meetings were never held in prison. He also did something that was not only extremely risky, but unique in preparatory phases of complex political-settlement processes. On the one hand it was a daring exercise in trust- and confidence-building, and on the other a way of introducing Mandela to a world from which he had been excluded for decades. Shortly after his discharge from the Volks Hospital on 23 December 1985, Mandela was taken on excursions. Without being conspicuously accompanied, guarded or protected by security guards. He became a prisoner – the world's most famous one – with freedom! And it was not only a question of Mandela being trusted by Coetsee and from 1988 also by other members of the committee. Mandela trusted them in turn. As someone from the NIS remarked to me: "There wasn't a snowball's chance that anyone would recognise him, because there weren't photos of him floating around. And he didn't want to be recognised either. He clearly had more important things on his mind."

At first the outings were confined to Cape Town and the surrounding area. Later the trips became longer and longer: towns such as Paternoster, Saldanha Bay and Worcester were visited. Mandela could also put in requests. A visit that left me very excited when I heard about it later was the one to the Karoo town of Laingsburg, my home town. Apparently, Mandela asked to visit Laingsburg after reading about the flood disaster that had ravaged the town. His long stay in prison and his labour on Robben Island had toughened his hands and his body, but not his heart. He is someone with steel in his will and in his teeth, but not, in a manner of speaking, in his heart. One should be wary of overemphasising personal relationships in exploratory, mediation and negotiation processes. Other factors also play a role: power relations, vested interests, aspirations, violence, economic realities, and so on. But building and sustaining trust and confidence can only be achieved through personal relationships. In the case of Mandela, it is a remarkable story that has been referred to many times. Its impact was so great, however, that it needs to be repeated here in outline: the relationship between Nelson Mandela and James Gregory, whose son Brent – a trainee prison warder – was also involved when Mandela was transferred to a house in the grounds of Victor Verster Prison.

Born on a farm in Zululand, Gregory was 23 years old when he started working on Robben Island as a warder. And he could read and speak Zulu. He grew older with Mandela and the other black leaders on Robben Island. He was also the one who mostly took Mandela on his outings after the transfer to Pollsmoor. And when Mandela was moved to a house at Victor Verster Prison near Paarl, Gregory went along. It was inevitable that a meaningful personal relationship would develop between this warder and South Africa's internationally renowned prisoner. They talked about the country and its people. And Mandela, especially during his excursions, could experience the environment and the inhabitants through the eyes and observations of his warder. In my opinion, Mandela had a better understanding of white people, and notably Afrikaners, than they had of black people.

The talks with Coetsee's committee, along with his excursions, undoubtedly gave Mandela much hope. He even wrote a letter to PW Botha in 1988, and by August he got a good indication that a meeting was imminent. Then fate intervened: on 12 August 1988 Mandela was hospitalised again and diagnosed with tuberculosis. He stayed in hospital until September 1988, and then recuperated in a private clinic. It is interesting to note that the third meeting of the unofficial Afrikaner-ANC contact group took place from 21 to 24 August 1988. In December of that year Mandela was moved to a very comfortable house in the grounds of Victor Verster. The NIS had furnished the house in two days. Here Mandela was able to receive a wide variety of liberation activists and community leaders. The settlement process was gathering momentum, even though the country was still burning.

In my view, PW Botha had already realised by 1985 that the release of Nelson Mandela and other political prisoners was inevitable. International and domestic pressure, and Margaret Thatcher's stance in particular, were the push factors in this regard. He just didn't know how and when. And of course he wanted to do it on his own terms. Two issues carried much weight with him: the renouncement of violence, and the position and role of the communists (the SACP). By 1988 he realised that a hope-giving compromise was needed. The proposal from the Coetsee committee that Mandela be moved to a house in the grounds of Victor Verster was a godsend to him, and the first public signal on the part of the Botha regime that Mandela's release was only a question of timing. Botha had realised by then that if black leadership had to play an essential role in dealing with the political conflict in South Africa, Nelson Mandela had to be a central figure within such leadership. But Botha had an intense aversion to all leaders who were communists or who, according to him, had even just a "whiff" of communism about them. Along with the issue of violence, Botha's fanatical anti-communism was a psychological and political obstacle to Mandela's release. Barnard, however, immediately recognised Mandela's leadership qualities. Mandela's international political and moral status in any case made his leadership role inevitable. This was initially a problem for the Lusaka ANC. Oliver Tambo was, after all, the official leader.

Convincing PW Botha that a personal meeting with Mandela was politically necessary was a tricky job. The preparatory phase for an official settlement process also required the preparation of PW Botha. In a 2004 interview, Niel Barnard summed up the delicacy of the problem: "To put the matter of discussions with Mandela into perspective, let me suggest a comparison . . . The state of national security at that time in South Africa made it as likely for PW Botha to talk to Mandela as it would be now for President George Bush to invite Osama bin Laden to the White House" (Heald, p. 102). The preparatory phase, which had begun as early as Mandela's first spell in hospital, was much more complex than many present-day commentators imagine. And then fate intervened once again: in January 1989 PW Botha suffered a stroke, something that befell Oliver Tambo as well in August 1989. In the meantime the protests in South Africa and the talks between the committee and Mandela continued. Botha recovered to such an extent that he was able to resume his duties as state president. By then he was no longer the leader of the National Party. FW de Klerk, who had become the Transvaal NP leader at the age of 47, took over the national leadership as well on 2 February 1989.

At this stage I need to touch on an aspect that was a sensitive matter to all parties to the dialogue: the reaction of supporters if the talks were to leak out. The control that Botha, Coetsee and especially Barnard could exercise in this regard was watertight in many respects. They operated within a "system" with bureaucrats who did not indulge in indiscreet talk. Mandela did not have such a "system" at his disposal. He had to put his trust in a small number of people and also accept that the bureaucrats would not embarrass him politically through leaks to the media. Trusting them was one of the greatest risks he took. Granted, his government interlocutors were dependent on his goodwill and cooperation. Trust also has a lot to do with accepting a relationship of interdependence, along with the nature of the aspirations of the parties concerned. In the case of Mandela and his interlocutors, the expectations were both strong and high: an end to political violence and a process that would bring peace.

Besides the contact avenue to Lusaka opened by Mandela and Bizos, of which Kobie Coetsee was aware, another avenue was developed as well: Operation Vulindlela (Vula). This was the brainchild of the revolutionary militants who dreamed of a military takeover of political power in South Africa. Among the exiled revolutionaries, the successful mass mobilisation by the UDF and other organisations had inspired visions of a Leipzig option where mass mobilisation would lead to regime change. They also feared being marginalised by the leaders of the mass action. Hence it was decided to infiltrate South Africa, establish underground military structures, set up arms caches, and cooperate with the mass movement. Strangely enough, Oliver Tambo had given the operation the green light, apparently without informing his pro-negotiation inner circle. In the late 1980s, after numerous intrigues and plans that had gone awry, Mac Maharaj and Siphiwe Nyanda established their base in Durban in order to orchestrate the ANC's revolutionary project from there. They were later joined by Ronnie Kasrils. Meanwhile Mandela held talks with the Coetsee committee, blissfully unaware of the military plans of Maharaj and his revolutionary comrades.

In this preliminary phase of the negotiation process, Mandela was undoubtedly the one who ran the greatest risk of losing his credibility. This realisation struck me on my birthday on 19 August 1988. An NIS official had spoken to me about the issue of confidentiality and credibility. And that credibility was also connected with disciplining oneself not to violate confidentiality. As he told me: "It's actually very easy to destroy someone's credibility in public if you and that person have shared confidential and private matters." After that conversation I understood that Coetsee, his NIS team and the other officials really meant business with the private and inner-circle discussions. The confidential nature of the talks was proof of the seriousness with which they approached the project. What happens in a case like this is that the participating parties ("enemies") deliberately and in a highly disciplined manner detach themselves from the prevailing views and positions of their respective constituencies and the latter's elites. In sharply divided and polarised societies where a culture of violence has become the norm, confidentiality and integrity are essential from the outset. That is why middle-ground growth points seldom, if ever, have a public start. In fact, the official preparation for the negotiation process after FW de Klerk's epoch-making and brave speech of 2 February 1990 was initially not a public process, as illustrated by, for example, the secret visits to Pretoria by ANC leaders from Lusaka.

Mandela ran into difficulties at one stage. As in the NP, there were power and personality struggles within the ANC, not only in Lusaka but in South Africa too, where the UDF's actions were highly successful. There were also different agendas among the Robben Island prisoners. Thabo Mbeki's father Govan Mbeki, for instance, was a die-hard Marxist. Ideologically, he and Nelson Mandela were poles apart; what united them was the common enemy, apartheid. There was continuing tension between Mandela and Govan Mbeki, as would be the case later, ironically enough, between Thabo Mbeki and the "leftists". The disagreements between Mandela and Govan Mbeki had a long history. In the 1960s there had been an intensive debate within the ANC about the ANC's approach to the so-called Bantustans. People like Mandela,

Walter Sisulu and Tambo, who had become acting president after Albert Luthuli's death in 1967 before being elected president, adopted a qualified pragmatic position: the Bantustans could be used as bases for mass mobilisation. They did not even want to use the term "sellouts". Mandela adhered to this position even in 1976. Rural areas were, of course, crucial to successful guerilla warfare. Govan Mbeki was vehemently opposed to this view. As a hardline Marxist, he found it impossible to support Mandela's pragmatism regarding the Bantustans. Within the external wing of the ANC, especially after a 1978 visit to Vietnam by members of the leadership, the accent eventually fell very strongly on mass mobilisation. And that was what the UDF managed to achieve.

An issue Mandela felt strongly about for humanitarian reasons, among others, was the release of the 78-year-old Govan Mbeki. Coetsee and his team saw this as a unique opportunity: an experiment in controlling public reaction to the release of political prisoners. Walter Sisulu, who would be released later, was 76 years old at the time. The process that led to Govan Mbeki's release is a story in its own right. Mbeki had remained on Robben Island when Mandela and the four other political prisoners were transferred to Pollsmoor. He was then brought from Robben Island to Mandela via a circuitous route. In talking to him, Mandela was quite vague about everything that was happening. In November 1987, Govan Mbeki was released. He had not been informed at first hand about the Coetsee-Mandela talks. Even when the two of them met again later in Victor Verster, Mandela still remained vague. It may well be that he didn't trust Mbeki, the Marxist. In 1989, when he lived in Port Elizabeth, Govan Mbeki was responsible for a rumour taking root among the UDF that Mandela was too conciliatory in his talks with government representatives. It created great consternation in UDF circles. Allan Boesak, a gifted and charismatic UDF leader, was particularly indignant. The NP government, it must be remembered, had no credibility whatsoever in UDF circles and was viewed with mistrust and suspicion. Mandela did not have a "mandate from the people" (in other words, the UDF). The crisis was eventually defused. It was a shortened version of Mandela's memorandum to Botha that had sparked the UDF crisis about "consultation with the people".

There were also other attempts from within official government circles to make contact with the ANC and hold discussions. These initiatives tell a story of desperation with the official public position, on the one hand, and the tight control that the NIS exercised over the process on the other. The NIS was adamant that it was the appropriate and best-equipped state institution to manage and control the process, as proved by the confidential talks with Nelson Mandela. The involvement of too many players, for example foreign affairs and even Minister Chris Heunis's department of constitutional development, could cause political short-circuits. Naturally, these departments were not fully informed about the informal and confidential talks that had already taken place. When Fanie Cloete, a political scientist and later a professor, and Kobus Jordaan, an intelligent and committed individual, put out feelers regarding an informal discussion with the ANC in their capacity as constitutional development officials, their security clearances were summarily withdrawn. The NIS was opposed to foreign affairs as well, and especially the attempts of that department's overenthusiastic minister, Pik Botha. These were stymied in subtle ways. Pik Botha was also not a key player in De Klerk's negotiating team.

★ ★ ★

A more senstive and problematic initiative was that of Richard Rosenthal, whom I got to know at the Urban Foundation. He was a highly intelligent lawyer, but very emotional when it came to political issues. At one stage he was so pessimistic about the Botha regime's handling of the political conflict in South Africa that, like many other people, he considered emigration. In 1987 he did something that many others wanted to do except that their courage failed them. He wrote a letter to PW Botha, saying that he was prepared to facilitate a process that could lead to formal negotiations with the ANC. It is uncertain whether Botha himself read the letter. Deputy minister of constitutional development Stoffel van der Merwe, a supporter of his minister Chris Heunis, replied to Rosenthal's letter. Van der Merwe conveyed the impression that Botha concurred with Rosenthal's ideas, and over the next 18 months Rosenthal played a mediatory role in contacts with mainly Thabo Mbeki. Rosenthal was supported by the Swiss government.

During 1988 Thabo Mbeki informed me about the contacts with Rosenthal and asked what I thought of this initiative. It became a very awkward matter. Rosenthal and I met a few times. The NIS had requested me to persuade him to call off his initiative before it turned into a public dilemma. I was at that stage already involved in the NIS's initiative and later also aware of the talks with Mandela, which put me in an impossible situation. I was unable to inform Rosenthal fully about everything that was already under way.

Stoffel van der Merwe, I was told, had no mandate for the initiative he took. This was not an undertaking that belonged with him and his department. It would "blow up in his face". I was told that the blow-up came during Botha's private visit to Switzerland in 1988. At the reception for Botha, a member of the Swiss government declared their support and thankfulness for the Rosenthal-Van der Merwe initiative. Later that evening, Botha grumbled to some members of his delegation. He was hopping mad at Van der Merwe. Even felt like firing him, he told one of his few confidants. In my opinion, Botha had not been briefed fully about this initiative, or maybe not at all. Van der Merwe was only a deputy minister at the time; there was no way he could play the key part he had hoped to play. The NIS was in any case dead set against someone from constitutional development undertaking a "very delicate operation" with the assistance of a person they didn't know. There was a lack of good control and accountability, it was stated. Rosenthal eventually became very despondent, as his book *Mission Improbable: A Piece of the South African Story* testifies.

At the time of the Swiss meeting, President PW Botha was visiting Europe to attend the funeral of the conservative Bavarian politician Franz Josef Strauss. On this occasion he also had talks with the German chancellor Helmut Kohl. Margaret Thatcher and Kohl had regular discussions about South Africa, particularly about the Namibian issue where German interests were also involved. Both of them gradually became frustrated with the slow pace of reform and the "militarisation of South Africa under PW Botha". In conversations with people from Thatcher's and Kohl's circles during the 1980s, I increasingly heard the word "militarisation". In light of their own history this word was like a blood-red flag in West Germany, read together with the prevailing state of emergency in South Africa. PW Botha desperately needed credible international meetings. There were few of these. His reform initiatives were too meagre and too late. They failed to open diplomatic doors. The international consensus on what had to happen was ahead of the reform initiatives.

★ ★ ★

The Coetsee-Mandela-Barnard talks progressed extremely well during 1989 and culminated in the meeting between PW Botha and Nelson Mandela on 5 July of that year, three weeks after the annual commemoration of the 1976 youth uprising in Soweto and elsewhere. Thereafter it was only a matter of time before the negotiating process would start more officially in earnest. What most of those who at that stage saw the photo that was taken of Botha and Mandela at their meeting didn't know, however, was that another process was also under way: talks between Afrikaners and the ANC in exile, with the knowledge of Niel Barnard. Even Mandela was unaware of this dialogue channel for quite some time. Tambo and Mbeki had been informed about both channels. This gave them a competitive advantage over the "gunmen" in their own ranks. The same applied of course to the pro-negotiators within the regime. While the securocrats supported a state of emergency, the pro-negotiators worked behind the scenes at developing and exploiting the political possibilities that were inherent in a possible negotiating process. Intensive dialogue was the vehicle for this.

During the first part of the 1980s, the ANC regarded dialogue and contact with (white) South Africans as a component of a strategy to subvert and put pressure on the prevailing political system. On the part of the ruling elite, who had infiltrated the ANC very successfully, the aim was to instigate division, confusion and even conflict within the liberation movement. The model was: revolutionary versus counterrevolutionary. This strategic paradigm, which was set in ideological concrete, first had to be broken down. The now famous prison talks were an important chisel in this regard, as were the Afrikaner-ANC talks. And the NIS-ANC talks in Switzerland and later in Pretoria were yet another chisel that helped to cut open a new path. So, too, were Idasa and other organisations, countries and leaders.

# 4
# Talks in the basement

To prepare myself for my first face-to-face talks with exiled ANC leaders, I took trouble to learn more about the views and especially the
personality profiles of the people I expected to meet. I was able to read a
good deal of "banned literature" in the process, which was later supple-
mented by material provided to me by ANC participants such as Aziz Pahad
and Tony Trew. It was also necessary to get an idea of the propaganda the
two archenemies used against each other and to try to separate the political
wheat from the political chaff. In conflict situations of the kind in which
South Africa found itself, propaganda and politics are like conjoined twins:
one cannot exist without the other.[1]

It was important to have an understanding of the context within which
the ANC operated during the 1980s in order to prevent the envisaged talks
from becoming bogged down in too many analyses, self-justifications and
accusations. We had to be able to talk about the way forward. Of course, all
exploratory talks between political enemies that are also involved in armed
conflict eventually need to focus incisively on the past when the settlement
process is more specifically about peace and reconciliation. In a preparatory
phase, however, a broad consensus on the possibilities and necessity of a negotiated settlement precedes in-depth discussions about the past and how
it should be dealt with. Since 1961, the broad contours of the political context that typified the ANC had been very closely connected with the ANC's
revolutionary agenda. Initially it proved difficult to get this agenda off the
ground. A prominent leader, Nelson Mandela, and many others were in
prison. The ANC was infiltrated by informants (*impimpis*). As someone put it:
from Soweto, Lusaka, London, Paris, Amsterdam and Geneva to Moscow
itself.

The revolutionary agenda was eventually boosted by three political drivers. The first was the role of the SACP, and leaders such as Joe Slovo, in this

agenda. They referred to themselves as professional revolutionaries and were networked with the Soviet Union's notorious but competent KGB and the East German Stasi. It was mainly they who kept the dream of a revolutionary takeover of political power alive and also dominated the ANC intellectually and ideologically.

The second driver was a radical one that came as a shock to the NP government, the business sector and many other whites: the revolt of the black youth in 1976. Few events validated the revolutionary agenda as strongly as did this eruption of mass popular protest and rage against the system and its white and black supporters. The seeds of mass mobilisation were sowed far and wide, and the security forces had to be deployed to attempt to suppress the uprisings forcibly. Many young blacks fled the country and joined MK. Their anger against the apartheid system and its white beneficiaries astounded even the older generation who had grown up with the Freedom Charter. It was during this time that the construct of the system and its supporters as "the enemy" was strongly incarnated in the psyche of a new generation of blacks. Necklace killings eventually became a grim illustration of this incarnation. The Urban Foundation, an initiative of the business sector, was born during this period.

From a political and strategic perspective, the third factor was probably the most decisive. The information given to me about this by Mbeki and Pahad in 1988 deepened my understanding of the historical context. Following the 1976 youth uprisings, Oliver Tambo, Thabo Mbeki, Joe Slovo and a few other ANC leaders visited Vietnam in October 1978. It was not a goodwill visit, but related specifically to the ANC's communist-driven revolutionary agenda and the role played in it by MK. The revolt of the youth had put new heart into MK. Tambo, Mbeki and Slovo were given a hearing by none other than the guerilla leader who had bloodied the noses of the French and the Americans both politically and militarily: General Võ Nguyên Giáp, famous in some circles and infamous in others.[2] When I heard this story, it struck me once again how one can be a prisoner of one's constructs of political enemies and how relative the "truth" is when it comes to political processes and events. Giáp's story increased my admiration for my Anglo-Boer War hero General Christian de Wet, although De Wet's strength with regard to guerilla warfare lay in military mobility rather than mass mobilisation. (South Africa was also a far cry from a Vietnam where underground networks, including tunnels, could be established.)

General Giáp, more than anyone else, directed the ANC onto a track that was crucial in the systematic shift towards a choice in favour of a negotiated settlement. According to my interpretation, Thabo Mbeki played a decisive role in this. Thus the 1978 visit to Giáp was an important station on the way to what happened in South Africa after 1985. Giáp had not been enthusiastic about the idea of an exclusively military offensive, led by MK and its communist professional revolutionaries, to achieve a takeover of political power. The political struggle was fundamental. Hence the military struggle had to be integrated into the political struggle. If "the enemy" could not be defeated militarily, only one option remained: a political option, with military support. The ANC's three-year plan was born out of this: to generate mass action in South Africa around political and social objectives and to build up underground networks, with the armed struggle as only one element of the political struggle and not its principal vehicle. After learning about this, I understood for the first time that "people's war" was not just a propagandistic slogan. It was a well-calculated and strategically considered term.

From 1980, South Africa entered a "people's war". This was not a war that could be fought by the South African security forces only. Of course the South African government, in a move that was not as stupid as is sometimes claimed, itself used the so-called WHAM strategy: Winning Hearts and Minds. But its credibility was sabotaged in townships and on the streets of South Africa by tear gas and bullets. According to my profile analysis of him, Thabo Mbeki was the chief architect, the General Giáp of the ANC's rethought strategy. By 1985, the year of PW Botha's Rubicon debacle, "people's war" had become a hackneyed term. It signified mass mobilisation. By then Mbeki had believed for quite some time that the armed struggle had to move past the point of "armed propaganda" to "people's war". What he meant by this seemingly paradoxical formulation, was blatantly obvious to the ANC militants and professional revolutionaries: a military seizure of political power was a pipe dream. The struggle against the apartheid state was primarily a political struggle. MK was just an auxiliary resource. The professional revolutionaries and militants never forgave him for this. Within the exiled ANC it was Mbeki, more than Tambo, who promoted the pro-negotiation option very actively and deliberately. Tambo was somewhat ambivalent. He also had to keep Joe Slovo, Mac Maharaj and Chris Hani happy. That was why he supported Operation Vula.

The global political tide favoured Mbeki, however, not Slovo and Hani. It had not only turned more strongly against the apartheid state, but also against the MK militants, so much so that by 1988 the ANC was rapidly losing its position of moral advantage in the international arena. Chris Hani and Co's military actions against white "soft targets" did not go down well. Neither did the political intolerance among blacks. This intolerance was a major impetus behind the swing to an inclusive settlement process. One of the occasions Thabo Mbeki became visibly annoyed with me was when I referred to the intolerance in black ranks and the brutality of black-on-black violence. He put the blame for that on the apartheid state. For politically correct reasons, the destructive role of black-on-black violence does not receive enough attention. It is a fact that mass mobilisation had ghastly side effects in black society: not only a political deadlock between some black leaders, but also escalating black-on-black violence and black corpses in the streets. I remember how, in an emotional moment, Enos Mabuza and I tried to comfort each other about this situation while tears ran down our cheeks. As Mabuza put it to me: "We blacks have become each other's enemies." Because I am strongly opposed to violence, I told him with despair in my voice: "The struggle against apartheid cannot be won if black people wage war against themselves." The impact of black-on-black violence on the shift to a negotiated settlement was just as important as all the other reasons one may cite.

It was therefore not a coincidence that negotiation was already discussed at the ANC's Kabwe conference in Zambia in 1985. This was not a sudden conversion or moral choice, but a calculated strategic choice. Within the ANC, which was at the time still strongly committed to "people's war" and mass mobilisation, some were experiencing a growing unease about the question as to whether they would be able to exercise control over mass actions and the accompanying violence. Referring to this period, Thabo

Mbeki told me in 1988: "War and violence can never be permanent strategic options. It must always be assumed that negotiations are an option, even with a defeated enemy. In the case of South Africa, black leaders will also have to start talking to each other eventually." In his opening address at the conference, Oliver Tambo, in a tentative and qualified manner, sent out a signal to the delegates and also to MK: "... no revolutionary movement can be against negotiations in principle." But Tambo's ambivalence, which has been mentioned before, was also apparent in 1985 when he declared in typical propaganda style on Radio Freedom that "the struggle" had to be taken to white suburbs. Whites could not be allowed to live peacefully while black townships were burning. Thabo Mbeki nevertheless emphasised in 1988 that MK had been ordered to avoid civilian deaths. This order was not observed in practice.

Two years after the Kabwe conference, the Afrikaner-ANC contact group met for the first time. The Dakar conference, with all the publicity – both positive and negative – it had attracted, had been held three months previously. The unofficial exploratory talks between the Afrikaner contact group and ANC leaders took place from 14:00 on 1 November until 12:00 on 3 November 1987 in the south of England in a basement of the Compleat Angler Hotel in Marlow in Buckinghamshire, next to the Thames River. We arrived on a typical English October morning with autumn colours all around. Outside, a few white swans were floating tranquilly on the water. Sampie Terreblanche, a member of the group who was always quick to spot an irony, remarked immediately: "Trust us to meet the ANC in a basement!"

For the purposes of the dialogue project it was important to avoid any publicity whatsoever. A communication channel had to be opened that would neither cause public embarrassment for participants nor broadcast tentative proposals by leading figures regarding the way forward that might inflame public emotion. As Niel Barnard once explained to me: "You don't start a dialogue with political enemies by means of conferences and newspapers if you're seriously interested in negotiation. You start with a private clarification of positions and possible ways to resolve deadlocks and strategic impasses. It's a slow process. Patience is more important than publicity."

Our meeting in November had been preceded by something significant:

the ANC's public statement in favour of negotiations on 9 October 1987, which said: "Once more, we would like to reaffirm that the ANC and the masses of our people as a whole are ready and willing to enter genuine negotiations provided they are aimed at the transformation of our country into a united and nonracial democracy." Aziz Pahad told me later that the intention with this statement had been to take a strong moral stand against the Botha regime on the necessity for negotiations, as well as to convey a clear message to the militants in the ANC and the broad mass movement.

This historic first meeting, admittedly an experiment and not at a high level, took place against the background of an event that had dampened our spirits somewhat: the failure of the White Plains conference in New York in September 1987. The ANC itself had not accepted invitations to this conference. Kobus Meiring, the deputy minister of foreign affairs and a very progressive thinker, was among those who attended. The South African government, however, refused to grant passports to the prominent trade union leaders Cyril Ramaphosa and Jay Naidoo as well as Fatima Meer, a well-known academic from the University of Natal. The conference, which had raised high public expectations, collapsed on 30 September when eight black South Africans walked out in protest at the government's action. They included the respected Dr A Motlana, Cassim Saloojee of the UDF, Phiroshaw Camay of Nactu and the venerable Sam Motsuenyane, whom I had come to know well at the Urban Foundation. The eight issued a scathing statement which read in part: "The very fact that certain key organisations and their views will not be heard at this meeting is the direct responsibility of the minority racist regime. No prospect of dialogue therefore exists."

Sampie Terreblanche, myself and others were incensed at the government's short-sightedness. I, for one, knew about the tentative attempt to start making contact. We mobilised support for a public statement. Together with Inkatha's representative Oscar Dhlomo, Denis Worrall, Willem de Klerk, Van Zyl Slabbert and others, we drafted a statement in which we didn't mince our words: "We strongly condemn the refusal of the government to grant passports to a number of fellow South Africans who were invited to attend. The aim of this conference was to create a climate in which South

Africans of all political persuasions could talk calmly and creatively about their country's future. Under these circumstances, to deny people with differing views the opportunity to put those views not only undermines the aims of the conference but grievously damages the credibility of the Republic's official delegation."

I felt particularly strongly about a sentence condemning the government's action for being "short-sighted and morally unacceptable". This was also one of only a few occasions where I had doubts about the wisdom of my involvement with the NIS. Kruger of the NIS subsequently asked me in a fatherly tone: "Do you think that was prudent? The *Cape Times* says you were the chief organiser? The president won't be impressed with your activism." Later, after a discussion about the matter, he said: "Things are becoming increasingly difficult. I'm not always sure of what we should do. The security of our country and the stability of our state are making heavier and heavier demands."

It should also be mentioned that a new British ambassador arrived in South Africa in April 1987: Robin Renwick. Kruger told me very soon: "You must get to know the man." Renwick himself took the initiative in making contact with me, and over time we developed a good relationship of trust and often held private discussions. Since the meetings of the dialogue group took place in Britain, it was necessary to have an informal connection in this regard. Renwick was a confidant of Margaret Thatcher's and made it his aim to stimulate change processes in South Africa. Funds were even made available to black organisations and leading figures. These contributions were intended to keep hope alive and to avert a total organisational and institutional collapse in black communities.

It was important that the process which was started in the Compleat Angler Hotel had to be kept out of the media. One way to achieve that was to impress on the participants that the talks were unofficial and private, which they were in any case, and that the Chatham House Rule, which promoted confidentiality, applied. Besides, the talks had been initiated and were organised by Consgold. The project was not a state-driven initiative. It stands to reason that my involvement required personal discipline and even calculated compromises. Most of the Afrikaner participants – if not all – were aware of the existence of some or other "Pretoria" connection, but not of its exact nature.

Deciding which Afrikaner opinion leaders should be asked to participate was a thorny issue. This question answered itself: among those who were invited, only the Stellenbosch contingent were prepared to dip their toes in a raging, ice-cold river. It turned out to be a blessing in disguise. The participants knew each other well, did not have public political aspirations and did not occupy important institutional positions in the Afrikaner establishment. They were *verligtes*, they were well informed about what was happening in the country, and they were not alienated from the broader Afrikaner community. They might have jumped out of the NP laager by backing the Independent Movement, but the regime could not disregard or isolate them. Even though they were Afrikaner rebels, they could not be vilified politically as traitors to Afrikaner-nationalist ideals. By 1987 the NP was in any case no longer supported by a powerful Afrikaner-national movement; it was a reeling party that lacked the capacity to cast *verligtes* into the wilderness. *Verligtheid* even gave the NP a measure of credibility. Foreign diplomats and journalists beat a path to the office doors of some *verligtes*. The ANC took note of this phenomenon.

Before the meeting at the Compleat Angler I had a long talk with Fleur de Villiers in London. She told me that during a study visit to Harvard University she had been highly impressed by the lectures and books of Roger Fisher from the law faculty, who was a director of the Harvard Negotiation Project. He specialised in negotiation processes and conflict management. Fleur said: "Take cognisance of Roger Fisher." I followed her advice and was particularly impressed by his well-known book *Getting to Yes*, which he coauthored with Bill Ury. It focuses strongly on an interest-based approach to negotiation, which means that one has to understand the interests of the contending parties and look for common ground. He is also of the view that negotiators have to be insiders with influence and persuasive powers. After all, they have to sell negotiated settlements to their constituencies. I became very conscious of this facet of negotiation processes. It must be possible for that which is achieved on paper inside the negotiation chamber to be put into practice outside the chamber. Conferences and seminars are valuable, but they are of only limited consequence if the question of practical implementation is omitted. It is interesting to note that in the formal negotiation process, Fisher's ideas also played a role in the thinking of people like Maharaj, Theuns Eloff and Roelf Meyer.

Fisher and Ury make a distinction that I found very useful in the Afrikaner-ANC talks as well as in my private conversations with Thabo Mbeki, namely that between interests and formal positions. A central question in this regard is: What are the interests that underlie the formal positions? Is there perhaps a relative degree of consensus with regard to the interests that is not reflected in the formal positions adopted by the parties? Once you have uncovered this, according Fisher and Ury, it is easier to come to an understanding about the rules of engagement.[3]

Fisher, in turn, put me on the philosophical tracks of Karl Marx and Herbert Marcuse: How can theory and practice be synthesised? Can proposals on paper become meaningful practice? Can intellectuals also be project managers? During this time I was also referred to George Kelly's book *A Theory of Personality: The Psychology of Personal Constructs*. Kelly holds that a construct is a frame of reference and interpretation that we use in looking at people and phenomena. This frame or mental mould determines individuals' opinions on issues, their interpretation of people and experiences, and what they accept or reject. The construct, in turn, is created by emotions, perceptions and ways of thinking with which a person is confronted in the socialisation process and in interpersonal interactions. In other words, personal identity is constructed through our (contextual) interactions.[4]

The informal talks were an attempt to dismantle the *enemy construct* and to create a construct around the idea of *negotiation partners*. This objective was the main reason why the discussion forum was not a public one, and also why the dialogue was limited to politically influential Afrikaners and pro-negotiation ANC figures. Hence the decision to opt for a *process* rather than a sensational *event*.[5]

In her forthright manner, Fleur de Villiers gave me several tips that I took to heart. Looking back on the whole process today, I can see what an important mentor she was when it came to understanding exploratory and mediatory processes. Unfortunately, she and Thabo Mbeki failed to hit it off at one stage. Many men don't like intelligent women with strong views! One of her tips was: "Don't compete with others who are keen to be involved in advancing the cause of negotiations. Remember, everyone's going to descend on people like Tambo, Mandela and Mbeki to get their ears. Just let them do their thing. That's also necessary." She was nevertheless blunt about the limited influence of public dialogue in advancing the possibility of a negotiated settlement. In her view, it was mostly a case of "liberals talking to other liberals". Moreover, she said, with Afrikaner nationalists and ANC representatives in the same public forum, what you get instead of dialogue is "public positioning and grandstanding". She was also frank about another matter: "Don't talk to just anybody. Choose your confidants carefully. You academics talk and write too soon and too easily, because you think that's how you have to market yourselves. And when you attend seminars and conferences, don't try to impress people by insinuating that you have more information than they do." It was this point that made Thabo Mbeki and me decide not to appear together at the same international conferences and seminars. When we did appear together, it was as a result of carefully judged timing.

De Villiers's tip about competition was spot-on. In my view, few things bedevilled the transitional process to a new, inclusive democracy as much as the obsession of those from the advantaged race group to be hailed as Voortrekkers to a new South Africa. The rivalry was fierce at times. It is partly understandable: whites in general, and Afrikaners in particular, sought recognition. So did leaders from their ranks who had helped to give shape to the new South Africa. Nor was it a misguided expectation. There was a host of whites, English- as well as Afrikaans-speaking, who helped in various ways to make the first inclusive and democratic elections of 1994 possible.

The rivalry also needs to be contextualised. There were individuals and groups in South Africa that, for good moral and strategic reasons, did not want to be seen sharing forums with government representatives. They firmly believed that they would be more effective from outside the government system. A good illustration of this is a conference that took place in October 1988. Idasa had arranged a meeting between Afrikaners, Africa experts from the Soviet Union and ANC officials in Leverkusen, West Germany. The Angola-Namibia peace settlement was in the planning phase at the time. When an official from the South African government's department of foreign affairs requested to attend the Leverkusen conference incognito, the request was declined. Alex Boraine of Idasa thought it fit not only to make this request public at a seminar at the Centre of Strategic and International Studies in Washington in November 1988, but also to comment on it. In his view, it would have been a "breach of faith" if Idasa had granted the request. He opined that "Pretoria" was attempting to make use of some of the communication channels that Idasa had opened.

Not beating about the bush, Boraine declared that Idasa would make it a test case if the government labelled contacts with the ANC as treason. In an attempt to hoist Idasa's banner as a mediator higher, he noted with scarcely disguised smugness that while PW Botha was "ranting" about Idasa's Dakar conference, some politicians and officials of his government regularly asked Idasa to convey messages to ANC officials. Boraine's view that many South Africans envied the Soviet Union for having a leader like Gorbachev was understandable. Botha was certainly no Gorbachev. But what Boraine did not know, unlike Tambo, Mbeki and a few others who did, was that by that time much spadework had already been done behind the scenes with regard to opening reliable and confidential communication channels with the ANC. Similar channels, also with Russian representatives, were functioning in respect of the Angola-Nambia issue by then. And in November 1987 yet another initiative was launched, this time with the exile wing of the ANC.

★ ★ ★

Willie Breytenbach, Sampie Terreblanche and I were pleasantly surprised by the Compleat Angler. Having arrived first, we had an opportunity to explore and appreciate the surroundings. It was a convivial country hotel, isolated, typically English and not quite an address for a momentous meeting. If any of us might have considered ourselves "important", this address swiftly relativised our status to that of ordinary visitors. As a result of my contact with the NIS of which the other discussion partners were still unaware at the time, and also apropos of Michael Young's own contacts, I thought that this idyllic and tranquil setting was just too perfect to have totally escaped the attention of the British intelligence service. Thanks to Young's excellent logistical arrangements, the ANC participants arrived in a comfortable black car with a chauffeur. We three Stellenboschers stood waiting nervously in the parking area, not exactly well prepared for what might happen with this meeting. We knew intuitively that it was a test run. Breytenbach, who had civil-service experience, even within the State Security Council, was probably the best prepared. Sampie Terreblanche, someone with his own objectives and a passion about apartheid injustices, was pacing up and down. I had heard in the meantime that Harold Wolpe, a staunch Marxist who had pulled off a spectacular escape from prison after the Rivonia trial, would be one of the participants, and told myself: "I'm going to meet the devil incarnate. And I have to try to be friendly."

Aziz Pahad, from the ANC office in London, headed the ANC group. He put out his hand to me jovially, greeted me and said in Afrikaans: "What's the weather like in our country? Is the sun shining? Of course, we don't see much sun here." I greeted him in Afrikaans as well. Thought to myself, at least we have something in common: South Africa's sun and warm weather. It was to be the start of a lifelong friendship. Thabo couldn't make it, he explained. He had another appointment. I knew he was really saying: Thabo first wants to see if the dialogue group is worth the trouble. Pahad's Afrikaans, I realised, was a good tactical start. Nothing worked better to make Afrikaners well-disposed towards someone than addressing them in their own language. It was a form of recognition, even though Afrikaans was branded as the language of the oppressor. Nelson Mandela did the same. On Robben Island he took trouble to understand Afrikaners and their culture. Mandela encouraged some of his fellow prisoners, such as Mac Maharaj, to do likewise. He knew that when the ANC were to sit down at the negotiation table one day, Afrikaners would be the main adversary. Psychologically, of course, he was a masterly seducer. That was why he liked to use Afrikaans in conversations with Afrikaners. And why he bestowed political fame on the Afrikaans poet Ingrid Jonker in his first presidential address.

Marinus Wiechers, who had initially indicated that he would attend the meeting, was unfortunately unable to come. On the ANC side, besides Aziz

Pahad there was the poet/writer Wally Serote, who was also associated with MK. It was clear that he didn't exactly consider the discussion opportunity important. (Many years later the two of us would work together cordially on the board of Freedom Park.[(6)]) Another participant was Tony Trew, who attended all meetings. He was the ANC's "scribe" for many years. Trew had been a first-year student in the male residence Dagbreek of Stellenbosch University at the time when I was a senior student there. Harold Wolpe, a university lecturer and a relative of my good American friend Howard Wolpe, who was then a Democrat member of the US House of Representatives and a fiery anti-apartheid campaigner, was also present. Initially I had strong prejudices against Wolpe and Serote, and I often wondered whether I would have attended the first meeting if I had known about their participation beforehand. In the 1960s, Wolpe and his comrades had been arrested at Rivonia in Johannesburg for revolutionary conspiracy against the state. As is the case with prejudices, to me his name and surname had come to symbolise all that was politically evil. He had been helped to escape, and Mandela and others were left to carry the can. I also did not think of Serote as a poet/writer who could conjure with words and cared about his traditional culture. According to my information, he was an MK soldier and an evil enemy. Years later I admitted to him: "I always thought of you as someone walking around with a Russian pistol who would rather shoot 'Boere' than write poetry." At our next meeting, in February 1988, he gave me one of his books and told me about his mother.

Before we come to the substance of the first discussion, something of a more personal nature: the advantage of the convivial atmosphere in the Compleat Angler Hotel was that we could talk comfortably between discussion sessions. The contact group was small and there was enough time for informal socialising. This facet of our interactions was undoubtedly of crucial importance.

The first evening Aziz Pahad and I talked alone. I told him that I came from Laingsburg and had grown up on a farm. Also that my mother had been my father's teacher, that Annemarie and I had six children, and that she had obtained her doctorate in mathematics in 1978. Like me, she was a lecturer. Pahad remarked: "Oh, you're building a tribe to counter us blacks' numerical superiority!" He told me that he knew Johannesburg very well, liked the place and had good friends in Roodepoort's Indian community. I asked him: "Do you know the Desai family?" He was flabbergasted. "They're good friends of mine. How do you know them? Do you know Bahia? And her sister?" I told him the story in detail. Realised for the first time in my life how the telling of shared stories builds bridges, treads footpaths out of cul-de-sacs, and plaits sturdy ropes for suspension bridges across abysses. My story became a plaited rope between me and Aziz. Later Tony Trew joined us and stood listening intently. It is a long story that I can only tell in broad outline here.

From 1965 to 1967 I lectured in political science and philosophy at the then University College for Indians on Salisbury Island in Durban's harbour area: an Afrikaner from the Karoo amid students of whom the majority was imbued with political activism. Bahia Desai was one of them, openly hostile. And brilliant. She and my only student in the second-year philosophy class of 1965, Munirah Lahki, were good friends. I took particular trouble to communicate with Bahia. At a later stage she told me her story in my office, and about her loathing for the security police that harassed her family.

Towards the end of 1967 I decided to join the staff of the new Rand Afrikaans University (RAU) in the coming year. Bahia Desai came to see me in my civil-service-like office, extremely upset about my intended departure. You're leaving your students in the lurch, she said at one point, and burst into tears. Her reproach made me feel rotten, and I offered her my handkerchief. She took it and wiped away her tears. The next day she returned the handkerchief, washed and ironed, and told me: "Thank you. That you offered me your handkerchief and that I accepted it, was a liberating experience. We *can* shake off prejudices."

One day in Johannesburg I was standing in a parking area of the then temporary RAU campus in Braamfontein. In the street in front of RAU, I spotted an agitated Bahia running from the campus of the University of the Witwatersrand in the direction of Hillbrow. When I intercepted her, she screamed at me: "Bring your car, bring your car. Take me to the hospital. My sister tried to commit suicide." I went to fetch my Volkswagen that was parked nearby. But when she saw me behind the wheel in my car, she shouted angrily: "Racist Afrikaner pig. Get out of my way." I tried to calm her down, with no success. She ran off in the direction of the Johannesburg General Hospital.

Bahia contacted me after a few days. She did not apologise, but explained her behaviour. When she saw me in the car, she also saw the security police in her mind's eye. I became a symbol of the system. The security police had "caught out" her sister, a medical doctor, and Professor Blacking of Wits in terms of the provisions of the Immorality Act, and were harassing the family. Her sister, a beautiful woman, had cracked up under the strain of the harassment. So had her father. Bahia's story was one of the most politically and morally tragic tales I had ever heard, and I apologised to *her*.

Aziz Pahad put his hand on my shoulder: "Weellie, thank you for telling me your story. We are brothers." A kind of declaration of common ground that affirmed Roger Fisher's accentuation of the importance of a good understanding and recognition of shared interests, also on the personal level. Munirah Lahki and Bahia Desai, together with another of my students on Salisbury Island, Gunvantrai Govindjee who also hailed from the Karoo and spoke fluent Afrikaans, had prepared me well.

★ ★ ★

The talks in the basement room of the Compleat Angler Hotel did not have a predetermined agenda. As an employee of Consgold, Michael Young, the coordinator, naturally had his own ideas. But he made no attempt to impose an agenda on us. Along with explanatory statements about the situation among exiles and also in South Africa, we inadvertently chalked out the main agenda items of subsequent talks in the course of the discussions.

The basement talks were particularly probing and by no means as stressful and even aggressive as claimed by some who have written about them as outsiders, for example Robert Harvey in his book *The Fall of Apartheid*. To be sure, we started off tentatively and somewhat hesitant to speak to each other, as if each side was waiting for the other to say something specific and dramatic. It became a cautious verbal chess game. We knew intuitively what the central theme of our discussion should be. Someone – I can't remember who – articulated the intuition: "Methods facilitating transition". It was as if there was a collective sigh of relief: the keyword was on the table – *transition*. Three elements were identified directly hereafter: the political process; the role of the economy; security issues. The question that tied the discussion together was what we, the participants, understood by these elements and what the obstacles were.

We talked at length about the political process. Harold Wolpe drew me aside during a tea break and asked what the chances were that Afrikaner-dom could split more deeply than had been the case with the Independent Movement. He repeated the question during a session. It was very clear that this issue was crucially important to the ANC members. Throughout, they wanted to know what was really happening within the Afrikaner commu-nity and the NP political elite. The liberal English press and Dakar had not been of much help in their attempts to understand the dynamics within the so-called Afrikaner establishment. I couldn't help thinking of an inference I had drawn from Roger Fisher's views: the difference between the percep-tions of outsiders and the experiences of insiders.

Sampie Terreblanche made the ANC participants sit up: "At least twenty per cent of Afrikaners are disillusioned with the NP and want credible re-forms." This observation was not based on a haphazard guess. Terreblanche had been, like Breytenbach and me, a signatory of the press statement of 8 March 1987, which was based on the memorandum that Discussion Group '85 had handed to Minister Chris Heunis on 1 July 1986 and then discussed with President PW Botha on 20 February 1987. The ANC participants, pris-oners of perceptions about Afrikaners that the English press had helped to construct, were dumbfounded. Even the Marxist Harold Wolpe was sud-denly less dogmatic and genuinely curious.

Later on in the dicussions I discovered why his interest had been aroused. "Is the hegemonic power that has been consolidated around the NP and its leader really crumbling? Won't Magnus Malan and his military inter-vene? Surely they would have to?" – he asked at tea time. Though I didn't understand his question at first, I soon realised that he was alluding to the possibility of a military coup. It was a possibility that had not occurred to me before, and I felt a chill run down my spine: what prevented the apart-heid ideologues and securocrats from coming up with this as a "last resort" in the interest of "security and stability"? What would the NIS's stance be? How would I personally respond to such an action?

The first question the ANC participants threw at us was: What do the twenty per cent of Afrikaners want? What should the agenda be? What is meant by "genuine" negotiations? What are the real issues? And what do the securocrats want? Willie Breytenbach then made a point that I considered to be of fundamental importance. In his calm and reasoned manner, he said: "The parties to the conflict must accept that a serious deadlock exists. Only then can one start talking about core questions and a settlement process." He asked: "Maybe there first have to be even more crises to force us to negotiate a settlement? Or do we have to realise that the process should begin *before* more serious and perhaps catastrophic crises occur? Has the time not come for us to develop a platform of networks to prevent the inevitable catastrophe?" His questions made me realise that the NP government and the ANC were each other's veto powers. Both were already in strategic and tactical positions that enabled them to deny the other party a victory.

Breytenbach's questions were an important agenda item. For practical reasons he was unable to attend the subsequent meetings of the contact group, but his questions were always present in the discussions. The ANC had realised that the settlement had to be reached with Afrikaners and their elite, and with no one else. How, on what conditions, and when, had become the real issues.

Aziz Pahad, who was already aware of the Coetsee-Mandela initiative, then also said something that stunned me, and Serote and Wolpe even more. "The ANC not only has a military option. There is also a political option," he said vaguely, waving his hands around and looking at Wolpe. Wolpe, first rendered speechless and then irate, heard from Pahad: "Genuine negotiations have never been rejected by the ANC. The issue is the how and the what of the negotiations." Serote was visibly annoyed. Trew, as was mostly the case, was deadpan as he sat writing his notes. I wrote in my notebook: "If words mean something, we will have to clarify what 'genuine' implies. We will also have to gain a good understanding of what the contending parties mean by conditions for negotiations." By then the ANC, through the inspiration of Thabo Mbeki, had already won an important round. In October

1987, a few weeks before our meeting, they had issued a statement on negotiations and the conditions that first had to be met.

In the course of the discussions Wolpe put a genuinely meant question on the table: "What would make the Afrikaners and the oppressed who are in revolt excited for a more dynamic negotiation process?" It was an important question, one which caused me to start changing my attitude towards him. During the sessions in the basement, a great deal of time was subsequently devoted to the preconditions for a settlement process. Trew, who didn't say much but as an informed member of the Mbeki inner circle always asked good questions, inquired: "What about the constitutional issues? Surely you can't orchestrate that without the ANC? Do you accept that the most important agent of change is already situated outside of the regime? And why does the regime now suddenly want to release political prisoners? What is the short- and longer-term agenda? You have to accept that the demand for the release of political prisoners as a precondition for the start of a negotiation process is by now a universal international demand." Pahad emphasised: "The political regime in South Africa won't be able to use that as a political game. Divide-and-rule won't work. Nor will deals with so-called nonviolent black groupings and leaders."

Pahad's remark gave me sleepless nights. On the one hand, there was the essential and morally compelling argument of an eventual inclusive negotiation process in which all political groupings had to participate. This was what the dream of a nonracial, inclusive democracy implied. This dream had to start with an agreement on who all had to participate in the negotiation process. On the other hand, it was as clear as day to me at this meeting: the primary participants in the preparatory process were the ANC and people close to the government elite. In fact, this was what the basement talks symbolised: a dialogue between people of the ANC and Afrikaners "only". At that stage I already told myself that this would also be the case in the formal negotiation process. Afrikaners (the NP) and the ANC would be the primary negotiators. If these two groupings were unable to reach agreement, there would be no settlement.

We talked incisively and at length about the economic dimension of a possible transitional process, with Sampie Terreblanche and Harold Wolpe the dominant participants. Michael Young also aired his views. After all, he was from Consgold that had business interests in South Africa. Terreblanche was in his element, using terms such as "declining economy", "siege mentality" and "wrong allocation of public funds". And then came his point: "The main reason for the economic crisis is apartheid. We need a booming economy. Political reform is a precondition for economic growth."

Unintentionally, he had touched on a hot potato: whether or not sanctions were desirable. The result was some lively verbal sparring. Terreblanche, no capitalist, trod on many sensitive toes. Sanctions were a sacred cow to the ANC, and Terreblanche, a social democrat, had started slaughtering it. Wolpe exclaimed in desperation: "Why would apartheid be dismantled in a booming economy? It would result in resistance to political change. More and more economic pressure has to be put on the political system." Terreblanche, who was not wholly opposed to pressure and economic sanctions, asked: "Are you following a scorched earth economic strategy? Do you think the multinational companies are going to return to such a landscape? You can't build with economic ashes."

Wolpe reached back to the Freedom Charter: redistribution of wealth; socialism; mixed economy. He assured us, somewhat half-heartedly, that the ANC was neither socialist nor capitalist. Terreblanche looked at him sceptically. Wolpe tried again: "We don't want to destroy the economy. We *need* economic development. But there is a precondition: the economy may not dictate the politics. We do accept that there has to be 'money in the treasury'." Trew came to Wolpe's aid: "It's the inequalities that have to be changed. For the purpose of redistribution, some must be prepared to relinquish wealth. Growth alone won't help. And there has to be a transitional period."

Terreblanche, Breytenbach and I expressed our enthusiasm for the idea of a transitional period. Trew emphasised: "We want whites to come over and share the [ANC's] aspirations." My enthusiasm faded: do we then all have to join the ANC ? Wolpe went further: "You should link up with the mass democratic movement and learn what it is all about." Terreblanche looked even more sceptical. Michael Young, a very disciplined and calm person, couldn't help saying: "You terrify the outgoing order. You instil expectations on which you cannot deliver." At least the term "transitional period" had been uttered. It became a kind of window onto the future throughout our meetings. During later meetings we started focusing on the "how" regarding such a period.

In the course of the discussion that was threatening to get bogged down, Pahad asked a vital question: "What can we do to avert an economic catastrophe? What should the post-apartheid economy look like? And if sanctions had to be lifted, what then would be the pressure mechanisms to advance political change?" It became a fruitful discussion. We did not arrive at answers, but we gained a better understanding of each other's views and especially of the magnitude of the economic problems that were already facing South Africa and that would also be carried into the future after democratisation. Breytenbach and I, and especially Terreblanche, were well informed about the poverty of the oppressed masses. Owing to my involvement with the Urban Foundation, I could "see" it instead of just knowing about it from reports. The discussion became a significant turning point in one respect: the ANC participants accepted our concerns and our seriousness about the severe poverty among the majority of South Africa's people, a majority that was black. Serote, a good listener but not someone who talked a lot, asked at one stage: "How do the reforms that the twenty per cent of Terreblanche's Afrikaners want compare with the needs of black people?" He hit me between the eyes. Serote was also the one who pointed out the armed struggle. It was a "strong movement" towards a broad, extra-parliamentary stance. It promoted "mass mobilisation".

He also put the issue of Afrikaner fears on the table: "They are an ethnic minority, accustomed to power and without an escape country. They have their own language and their own institutions. And they have been raised with racism – in school, church and state. They know they may lose a lot. How should one deal with them so that their physical and political survival wouldn't be threatened?" We all realised that this was a cardinal and sensitive issue. The discussion around this topic was hesitant and cautious and we did not make much headway, except for agreeing that in this regard it would probably be necessary to talk about guarantees and the rights of minorities. Thereafter the tone of the discussion became noticeably more sober, particularly after one of the Afrikaners remarked that the full might of the state had not yet been unleashed against the ANC's military and civil resistance. The NP was also far from unravelling, even though the Conservative Party had become a political factor. All three Afrikaners were agreed that the Independents did not offer an alternative government and that the Progressive Federal Party stood no chance of signifcantly increasing its voting strength. That was one of the reasons why Van Zyl Slabbert had abandoned this particular political ship. There should therefore not be any expectations that divisions in white ranks would promote a military takeover of power by MK or a political watershed that would benefit the so-called mass democratic movement.

The ANC participants, especially Wolpe and Serote, were visibly disappointed. Pahad remarked that it was proving to be a big problem to bring about unity between the different liberation movements and particularly between Lusaka and the UDF. He was somewhat philosophical, as if he wanted to convince himself: "The eighties is different from the sixties. The political argument is predominant. Hence ungovernability should not be regarded as a type of anarchism. It is an experiment in and motivation for alternative forms of government."

Without taking a formal decision or even talking it over as a way of summarising the discussion, we knew what the real issues were:

- Preconditions for a settlement process and the necessity of "talks about talks";
- The issue of violence as an instrument of political power and how it should be dealt with;
- The issue of sanctions and what a post-apartheid economic dispensation should look like;
- Consensus about a transitional process;
- The release of political prisoners and especially the position of Nelson Mandela in this process; and
- How to deal with, on the one hand, the expectations of people who had been disadvantaged and oppressed because of their skin colour, and, on the other hand, the political reality of the fears of whites and the position of Afrikaners in particular.

Harold Wolpe made an incidental remark that provided some relief: There is no Big Bang solution. It's a laborious process. He was spot-on. What he was unaware of, however, was that this laborious process had already begun in a Cape Town hospital. Wolpe's attendance at the dialogue session in the basement of the Compleat Angler Hotel in Marlow was the start of a dimension of this process where the participants had no idea of what the outcome might be: at this stage I did not have high hopes of the subsequent course of the dialogue process. If one comes from the arid Karoo, hope is a way of life, but one also has to be realistic: if the sky is blue, it can't rain. Our meeting was only a first exploratory and clarification move. For their part, the ANC experienced a "crucial lack of clarity" about the Afrikaner participants' status within the ruling power elite and their likely influence, as spelled out in *Report of a Meeting Held in England on 1st and 2nd November 1987*. The view was expressed, though, that they had more "political influence" within the ruling elite than the participants at the Dakar conference. Other instructive points were also made in the report: first, the pro-negotiation elements within the state were of the view that the extraparliamentary protests, the armed struggle and the impact of the ANC had been sufficiently controlled and that a considerable degree of stability had been re-established. Second, the state could now act to take steps which, "if properly responded to" by the ANC, could lead to full-scale negotiations. This was a key point, with the critical question being: Would the state comply with certain fundamental preconditions for negotiation? Such as the release of Nelson Mandela and other political prisoners?

That process kicked off a few days after our first contact meeting with the release of Thabo Mbeki's father, Govan Mbeki. But I remained sceptical about the sustainability of the dialogue progress, mindful of the ambivalence of the Kabwe conference in 1985. On that occasion it had been said very specifically that there would be no meaningful negotiations with "the enemy" "whilst he feels strong". The enemy was in any case not interested in negotiations, and military and other forms of pressure had to be applied to force the NP government to the negotiating table. "Dialogue" was still mainly viewed as a means of demoralising the regime and sowing division in white ranks. In Dakar Thabo Mbeki not only declared that he was an

Afrikaner, but also made a strong appeal: "We need white support." The South African Communist Party was the leading light in a divide-and-rule strategy. In 1987, a few weeks after the Dakar meeting, the *African Communist* hailed "the splitting of Afrikanerdom" as one of the liberation movement's most important achievements. This made PW Botha even more infuriated with the Dakar participants and people such as Theuns Eloff.

My scepticism was confirmed shortly after the first meeting: General Bantu Holomisa staged a military coup in the "independent" Transkei and seized power. Militants in the ANC were over the moon because they considered Holomisa a possible ally. It was also Holomisa who would later frequently leak secret documents about the South African security forces' elimination and murder campaigns against political enemies. This landed the South African state and its ruling elite in deep trouble.

# 5
# Thabo Mbeki joins the dialogue

The year 1988 was one of monumental historical significance for South Africa. It saw important inner-circle talks about the conflict in Angola–Namibia and eventually also the start of far-reaching settlement processes in that region. As a result, the settlement idea was irrevocably placed on the agenda of South Africa's internal politics as a way of resolving the prevailing low-intensity civil war between the historically advantaged and the historically disadvantaged. Although there were whites fighting side by side with the resistance fighters and nonracialism was propagated, according to the general political perception this was a racially oriented black–white war, whatever the more theoretical explanations about, say, Afrikaner nationalism and black nationalism suggested. As far as South Africa's internal politics was concerned, 1988 was a year of political catastrophes and heightened political temperatures. Two interrelated examples can be to used to illustrate this.

One had its origins in September 1984. Black rage had erupted like a dormant volcano in Sharpeville and the adjacent Sebokeng in what was at bottom a revolt against the government's local authority system – another supporting pillar of the apartheid state. The revolt manifested itself through fires, blood and fierce clashes with the police. Besides the deaths caused by police bullets, murder dockets were opened in the case of deaths caused by people from among the enraged crowd.

The deputy mayor of Sharpeville was one of the victims. He had opened fire on the enraged crowd with his gun and had paid with his life. In Sharpeville, which had been a powerful political symbol in the resistance movements and internationally since the 1960s, the unacceptability of the local authority system through which the government aimed to unilaterally implement its obsession with ethnicity and group rights was challenged with fury. A new political symbol was created: the "Sharpeville Six", who included the local Vaal Professionals soccer player Francis Mohkesi. Six people who had been among the crowd were arrested and charged with murder under the controversial "common cause" clause. There were even black state witnesses, such as Joseph Manete. The Sharpeville Six became "martyrs" for liberation. The state, through its judicial system, demanded the death penalty and said that they should be hanged. The court case provoked severe protests and rioting in black ranks and caused a stir internationally. The six were sentenced to death at the end of 1985. I was involved with the Urban Foundation by then and experienced black people's anger about this at first hand. Political unrest continued unabated, and in June 1986 a state of emergency was declared.[1]

The hangings were stayed by an appeal. The renowned Sydney Kentridge and Denis Kuny were among the legal personalities who battled for the lives of the Sharpeville Six in a protracted case that increased the political temperatures at home and abroad. When the appeal was finally rejected in December 1987, it had international repercussions. For months thereafter the six symbolic political martyrs lived, so to speak, in the shadow of the gallows. President PW Botha eventually yielded to mounting national and international pressure, and the death sentences were commuted to imprisonment. The regime's attempt to portray this as an act of clemency failed dismally. Blacks increasingly expressed their lack of faith in the courts. Official justice was for "whites only", it was said. Few issues inspired black protest politics and eruptions of anger against the prevailing system and its judicial order during the 1980s to the extent that the state's handling of the Sharpeville Six did. The year 1988 saw the collapse of all remaining positive reactions to the South African government's reform initiatives among blacks and in the ranks of Western governments, including the hope of meaningful renewal under PW Botha. In addition, a significant number of Afrikaners were no longer convinced of the credibility of the Total Onslaught and Total Strategy as understood by the South African government and President PW Botha. A strategic vacuum developed.

The second example that illustrates the raised political temperature was the government's response to the ongoing unrest, the rage-inspired actions of the oppressed, and the relative success of what was later called the Mass

Democratic Movement (MDM), in other words, the UDF with its supporting organisations and charismatic leaders such as Archbishop Desmond Tutu,
Dr Allan Boesak and Mawlana Esack. The regime hit back with bannings.
This occurred in the same month as the second meeting of the Afrikaner-
ANC contact group, also referred to by the more neutral name of the Consgold contact group with an eye to possible leaks. The UDF was banned along
with 16 other organisations, and Cosatu was restricted from engaging in
activities that were not specifically trade union related. Yet the dialogue with
Nelson Mandela continued, though the risks for him had increased. The
unofficial contact between Afrikaners and ANC leaders continued likewise.

In the meantime the spheres of influence within the government and the
people who called the shots had changed. Like many other power-besotted
politicians and heads of state, President PW Botha was politically arrogant.
Power and position tend to have that effect on people. He knew that his
political shelf life was close to its expiry date. His former confidants and
friends in his party were deserting him. A cabinet minister, who was not
among those who had high leadership ambitions, told me in an unguarded
cynical moment: "The vultures have gathered on the branches of the NP
tree and are on the lookout for what they can prey on when Botha passes
away politically." But it would still take a while before that moment came.

The exile ANC had its own share of internal problems, notwithstanding
wild and propagandistic pronouncements by militants in particular. Moscow had stopped exporting revolutionary dreams to other countries and
was unenthusiastic about a military takeover of power in South Africa. A
negotiated settlement in Angola-Namibia was on the cards. As a Russian
envoy put it to me during a reception hosted by Pik Botha in Cape Town:
"Angola doesn't need Cubans." Any expectation the ANC's militants might
have had that Moscow and Havana would boost them with manpower,
perished in 1988. But that neither dampened the exile militants' militancy
nor inclined them to concur with Thabo Mbeki's diplomatic and pro-
negotiation initiatives. To them, he was competition. At that stage already
this rivalry caused a rent in the seemingly firmly woven ideological fabric
of the ANC that would never be repaired but instead kept growing bigger
as time went on. It was also in the turbulent 1988 that Niel Barnard and his

NIS team started featuring prominently in the behind-the-scenes talks. The discussions with Mandela became more focused, and Barnard became the key person.

PW Botha, increasingly isolated, often sat alone in his well-equipped situation room and watched what appeared on the screens. He also read reports. "Not longer than two pages and no spelling errors" was his guideline – so I was told. He took a special interest in Pik Botha's activities. According to PW Botha, Pik was energetic and intelligent, but a "political sieve" who leaked too many things and talked too indiscreetly. One day, I was told, Barnard walked into the Pretoria office of a young and dynamic NIS official, Theo de Jager, and announced: "Pack your bags. You're going to take over from the 'policeman' in the president's situation room." The official was someone that I had for some or other reason convinced to study philosophy in his student years. With that, Barnard took over the inside track to Botha. The military shifted politically and strategically to an outside track. By 1988, Botha was not only isolated; he was also a lonely politician, a victim of a policy – apartheid – that was systemically immoral and politically destructive. Of course, his personality had also played a part. Both Barnard and Louw considered him a "hard person".

★　★　★

The relationship between Mandela and Barnard was not very spontaneous at first. South Africa's most famous prisoner, and by then occasionally "host" in prison to people who wanted an audience with him, was used to Kobie Coetsee. He trusted Coetsee, who went to great lengths to show him respect and to recognise the human dignity of the political prisoners, unlike Jimmy Kruger. Botha was informed of all of this and did not interfere with Coetsee. The dialogue with Mandela was a *private* matter, not a *public* rapprochement initiative, it was argued, and of course confidential; nothing more than a second-track interaction without a link to a first track. It took Mandela a while to accept Barnard's key role. I realised subsequently that his hesitation had not been directed at Barnard personally, but was meant to protect his own position. Coetsee and his officials were from the department that dealt directly with the political prisoners. There were enough plausible

reasons for them to talk to each other if word had to leak out and explanations had to be given. But Barnard? He was director-general of the National
Intelligence Service and had a seat on the State Security Council, besides
being chairman of the Coordinating Intelligence Committee. His participation would lend another dimension to the prison talks, a dimension that
other political prisoners, the UDF and Lusaka might misunderstand. Mandela put up with Barnard's involvement nonetheless. Barnard was, after all,
a key figure in the inner circle. In the end Mandela lauded Barnard and
regarded him as an intelligent person, someone with discipline. It was a
quality that Mandela rated highly.

The "Great Crocodile", isolated in his situation room, relied increasingly
on Barnard. He knew that his time was running out. Some of the younger
crocodiles in the NP pool were lying in wait. He agreed to a settlement of the
conflict in Angola, with the US a prominent mediator. By mid-1988, with
Russian representatives as "observers" mainly to keep the Cubans in check,
South African, Angolan and Cuban representatives reached an agreement.
Fourteen principles were adopted, and South Africa made a significant concession: the Cubans were not required to withdraw before peace negotiations could start. They could withdraw from Angola over time in light of
South Africa's implementation of Resolution 435. This concession would
later also have an effect on Botha's unwavering demand that Mandela and
the ANC had to renounce violence as a means of furthering political objectives before the negotiating process could begin. The resolution and the
question as to whether South Africa would respect it became a salient
talking point in the informal, track-two talks with members of the ANC and
with foreign leaders, and even among progressive Afrikaners.

These developments, while purely coincidental, had a material influence
on the unofficial dialogue group in England: the talks were given a new
impetus and direction. On 1 September 1988 South Africa, Angola and Cuba
signed the Geneva Protocol that ushered in a ceasefire in Namibia.

The background to the signing of this tripartite agreement is a remarkable
tale that is also analogous to the story told in this book. General Magnus
Malan and his hawks, the South African Police and the securocrats within
the higher echelons of the South African state, were convinced that the

Total Strategy had everything under control. This militarised discourse had helped to create a false perception of the conflict in South Africa and how it should be dealt with. Along with this discourse that promoted repression, limited reforms were introduced: a start was made with scrapping certain apartheid measures, especially from 1985 when the Mixed Marriages Act and the Immorality Act were repealed on 19 June. The abolition of other measures followed, and on 1 July 1986 a linchpin of the apartheid system was removed: the influx-control measures that regulated blacks' freedom of movement in a dictatorial manner. On 15 September 1986 black people were even granted the right to own property in black townships. In June 1988 tertiary education received a bonus: the state would no longer insist on segregated student residences. This reformism went hand in hand with harsh security measures, in other words, counterinsurgency actions.

All of this fostered a new discourse among important players in the state bureaucracy, notably in the NIS and the department of foreign affairs, and even among elements of the SADF. The names that crop up in this regard are those of Jannie Geldenhuys, Niel Barnard and Neil van Heerden, the troika who were intimately involved in the settlement process in Angola-Namibia. Geldenhuys and Barnard were close friends. The trio exemplified a discourse that had also hit the SADF's militants like a bolt from the blue: the regional conflict in which South Africa had become embroiled, as well as the country's internal conflict, could not be resolved by military means. A political solution had to be found. Geldenhuys was a key figure in this discursive shift. He had at one stage been directly involved in the conflict in Angola-Namibia.

There are a few other aspects that should be touched on as far as 1988 is concerned. The Botha regime might have had a power struggle between the hawks and the doves within its ranks, but so did the external wing of the ANC. Oliver Tambo was getting on in years. Umkhonto weSizwe (MK) had become bolder and even believed that MK was winning the armed struggle. By this time Thabo Mbeki had long been part of Tambo's inner circle. Chris Hani, MK's new chief of staff, brimmed over with confidence: the perception that was created by the NP regime and its progagandists that the ANC's military setbacks between 1985 and 1986 signalled the failure of the armed struggle, had to be turned around. And *he* would make sure that it happened. They should attack soft targets. Thabo Mbeki, together with Oliver Tambo the strong voice in the political wing, did not agree. They knew about the tentative talks in Pollsmoor and in England, of which Hani and other ANC leaders had not been informed at first. Tambo's attempts to moderate Hani's stance were unsuccessful. It was not only a case of Chris Hani believing that he could defeat the apartheid state militarily; he actually wanted to get Thabo Mbeki out of the way as a possible successor to Tambo. It became a bitter power struggle that would later be continued in South Africa as well.

Mbeki never thought much of MK's military capabilities, and made no secret of his opinion. He was a negotiator. The tension between him and people such as Mac Maharaj and Siphiwe Nyanda, who would later become a general and also a cabinet minister, had come a long way. In an attempt to defuse the power struggle in Lusaka, the National Executive Committee (NEC) of the ANC was expanded to more than 30 members in 1988 and the top leadership of MK was included. Mbeki travelled incessantly, participating in conferences, seminars and discussions. He held talks with Idasa and Van Zyl Slabbert, with Richard Rosenthal from South Africa, with numerous South Africans and various international leaders. He knew what was happening in the world and in South Africa. He listened to others and did not come across as opiniated. When he expressed his views, it was in a reasoned manner and without slogans. In Western capitals he was regarded as a reasonable person, not doctrinaire, and a sophisticated politician who commanded respect universally as an African politician. He also enjoyed the support of President Kenneth Kaunda of Zambia.

The power struggle within the ANC's external wing, an aspect Mbeki sometimes alluded to during our talks, flared up every now and again from 1988 onwards. There is little doubt that the Angolan settlement process was a contributory factor. The ANC had military camps in Angola. Hani was of course also an enthusiastic supporter of the SACP and an esteemed party member. I met him in Lusaka in 1990. Whites were especially impressed by his knowledge of the English literary classics, including Shakespeare. I must admit that I always had a prejudice against him, and saw him as someone with a Russian pistol in his inside pocket. He was extremely intelligent and charismatic, passionate about the armed struggle and the ideal of a military takeover. I caught on swiftly that the power struggle between him and Mbeki was not just about succession. It was also about negotiations versus a military takeover. And this power struggle was not even between communists and non-communists. Hani's "boss" was Joe Modise. Modise's wife, Jacqueline Sedibe, was also involved in MK as head of communications. Hani's good friend, Ronnie Kasrils, was a member of MK's military intelligence. And Steve Tshwete was MK's political commissar. I heard later that Joe Modise shielded Mbeki, and eventually got to know him reasonably well.

In light of this context, it is important to take a brief look at the position adopted by the ANC with regard to negotiations with the South African government. Up to 1985 an ideological hard line held sway, as expressed in the ANC's *Strategy and Tactics of the South African Revolution* (1969). Marxist ideology and communist political dreams about an assumption of power figured prominently, as did the ideal of a two-phase revolution. This stance was reaffirmed during the ANC's Kabwe conference, qualified by a lukewarm mention of the possibility of negotiation. At that stage the primary objective of the ANC was still "takeover of power". Liberation was seen as "just around the corner ". The torch of revolution burned high, as did the flames in black neighbourhoods where township wars raged. In October 1987, the banned ANC issued a statement on negotiations. This occurred about eight months after Discussion Group '85's disastrous meeting with PW Botha in Tuynhuys, a few months after the formation of the Independent Movement, and not long after Idasa's Dakar conference. It was once again good timing on the part of the ANC. Making a mental and strategic shift was a difficult and sometimes dangerous juggling act, Thabo Mbeki told me during our first meeting. To the militants, wedded to the notion of an imminent revolutionary takeover, the word "negotiations" was synonymous with "betrayal". It was primarily the SACP that advocated a revolutionary takeover of power. The view held by Tambo and particularly Mbeki was: Given the international situation as well as the mental shifts in South Africa, negotiations were not excluded in principle. Was the ANC prepared for that? And did they have a strategy and proposals ready?

To capture the initiative from the South African government in the battle for the moral high ground, the ANC announced a set of preconditions for a negotiated settlement in October 1987. There was no reference to the two-phase revolution or a takeover of power. The goal was the transformation of South Africa into a unified, nonracial democracy and the transfer of political power to "the people". The South African government was on the back foot. There was no undertaking to renounce violence. A committee of the former Organisation of African Unity (OAU), now the African Union (AU), talked instead of "agreeing to a mutually binding cease-fire". Such a move would, of course, imply recognition for the ANC's armed struggle on the part of the South African government. The military cabal, with Modise powerless, nevertheless started focusing on soft targets in mainly white areas. Hani and Tshwete even issued press statements. Tambo and a few others tried to do damage control by declaring that attacks on civilian targets were not ANC policy. It became a battle between the "old" and the "new" generation, the "negotiators" and the "militants". In June 1988 the ANC's National Executive Committee (NEC) in Lusaka attempted to defuse the crisis. Tshwete was "redeployed" to a position on the NEC, while Kasrils became the second white NEC member. Jackie Selebi, too, became a member of the committee. These developments did not give me any hope. In the concept of soft targets I recognised a hideous face of the ANC: terror in its most extreme form. I have always taken a strong moral stand against violence, especially violence aimed at gaining political and other forms of power over people. Hence I was thankful that MK's attacks on soft targets undermined the ANC's moral position in the international community.

During this period some black African leaders, including President Kenneth Kaunda, started pressurising the ANC more strongly to advance the negotiation option. The ANC's recognition in Africa as the most important South African liberation movement had been a long and laborious process, particularly among the Francophone countries. The concept of "frontline states" was a political bonus for the ANC. Economic and trade relations meant that this bonus was of little value, however, except that it gave the ANC "addresses" in these countries. Lusaka was an important address. But President Kenneth Kaunda of Zambia was not very enthusiastic about the armed struggle. He had been an advocate of dialogue for years, and exerted pressure in this regard on the ANC leadership at every opportunity. He was outspoken in his appreciation for Mbeki, as was apparent at a Lusaka prayer meeting I attended with Mbeki and others at the invitation of Kaunda and the Fellowship Movement following De Klerk's historic speech in February 1990.

Within the ANC's leadership there was nonetheless opposition to Hani's militancy. Among the majority of the world's opinion leaders too, including Mikhail Gorbachev. In the end Hani and the other militants were given a political thrashing by Thabo Mbeki that they would neither forgive nor forget. Of course, Mbeki had had a strategic and tactical advantage. Like many young blacks who had left South Africa for political reasons, he wanted to participate in the struggle by preparing himself militarily in the Soviet Union. He, too, had set his mind on joining MK. It was Tambo who had influenced him to play a political leadership role instead. Mbeki eventually became the ANC leader who shuttled between capitals, conferences and discussions, who observed and understood the international political trends from Moscow to Washington, and who built up an exceptional network of contacts. It soon became clear to me that Mbeki had jumped at the Consgold project as an opportunity for signalling the commitment to negotiations. That was also the reason for his enthusiasm to talk as often as he could to the visitors from South Africa that flocked to Lusaka. In fact, he encouraged the visits. In the course of the meetings of the Afrikaner-ANC dialogue group he was able to convince prominent members of the Afrikaner community of the ANC's reasonableness. Whereas Hani and his MK comrades wanted to blast open their road to Pretoria with bombs in the streets, Thabo Mbeki and his negotiation comrades helped open the road to Pretoria, in the heads of Afrikaners in particular, by engaging in dialogue. His primary objective, however, was not to talk to Afrikaner opinion leaders only. He wanted to talk to representatives of "Pretoria".

The ANC's preparations for inevitable negotiations with the South African government started with greater seriousness in 1988. Tambo appointed a small task team to draft a working document that would set out clearly and unequivocally the ANC's conditions for negotiations. This eventually became the Harare Declaration, which was ratified and made public by the Organisation of African Unity (OAU) on 21 August 1989. It caused turmoil in the ranks of the ANC hawks in particular. Tambo, Mbeki and other proponents of negotiations had their hands full to get the document accepted. With the OAU on the side of Tambo and Mbeki, the militants lost. It was a very significant political move, and, as far as the rest of the world was concerned, another public diplomatic victory for Thabo Mbeki. The South African government was at that stage neither willing nor ready to discuss a solid document on negotiations within a party context, or to table such a document in the public sphere.

★ ★ ★

Something else that needs to be mentioned here is my participation in another unoffical track-two dialogue process, also in Britain: the Jubilee Initiative or Newick Park dialogue group that was organised by the Jubilee Centre in Cambridge, a Christian organisation. It ran parallel to the Consgold dialogue group, but without the two groups knowing about each other or exchanging views. The Newick Park Initiative, too, was confidential. The executive director was Dr Michael Schluter, who had close ties with Kenya. One of his strong supporters, and the chairman of the dialogue group, was the owner of the Newick Park estate Lord Brentford, who had good access to the Thatcher regime. Donald Anderson, an influential member of the Labour Party with strong ANC connections, was among the participants. The first meeting had taken place as far back as March 1987 and the second was held in March 1988, where the conflict between the UDF and Inkatha and the effect of Govan Mbeki's release were discussed. At a subsequent meeting from 3 to 5 November 1988, the discussions focused on topics such as trust-building and guidelines for a constitutional settlement. An exceptionally informative talking point was: "The transfer of business ownership and control to Africans in independent African States: a study of Kenya, Tanzania and Zimbabwe". In 1989 this issue would be an item on the agenda of the Consgold dialogue group, and in this way Newick Park was nevertheless of consequence to the Consgold talks.

In preparation for the Newick Park session, a meeting that dealt specifically with "Alternative constitutional settlements in South Africa" was held in Pietermaritzburg from 9 to 11 June 1988. An advantage of this track-two dialogue group was that the participants included black and coloured leaders from South Africa and Africa. It also had a strong research component, and working papers on topics such as land reform, negotiation and white fears were discussed. Washington Okumu, a Kenyan, was a member of the group. It was he who persuaded Inkatha to take part in the processes that would lead to the first inclusive election (1994). Another advantage was the participation of black religious leaders. Two of them made a deep impression on me: Caesar Molebatsi and Dr Elias Tema. Other leading participants were Enos Mabuza and Marinus Wiechers.

Mabuza, whom I came to know very well over many years, was the chief minister of the so-called self-governing state of KaNgwane. He made no secret of his support for the ANC, and had a good relationship with Thabo Mbeki. Early in the eighties he had led a delegation of his political party, the Inyandza National Movement, to Lusaka, where Oliver Tambo and senior ANC officials gave him a hearing. Mabuza was a very calm and reasoned person, but vehemently opposed to apartheid. Tambo, Mbeki and other exiled leaders considered him "a comrade within the system". It was Mabuza who convinced me that acceptance of an inclusive and meaningful negotiation process implied a fundamental, non-negotiable assumption: the release of imprisoned political leaders.

Thus I was able to participate in two dialogue processes in Britain that provided for political cross-fertilisation. The Newick Park Initiative, too, did not issue public statements or seek publicity. It was rather a search for consensus within the group and its networks on a way to resolve South Africa's impasse, prevent large-scale and prolonged bloodshed, promote an inclusive climate for negotiations, and understand white fears. The group also debated proposals on how the political crisis in South Africa should be responded to from a Christian perspective. It was necessary to achieve this consensus, it was argued, before there could be public opinion-forming action. Both the Consgold dialogue group and the Newick Park dialogue group strongly emphasised the economic dimension of the envisaged consensus. For example, on 18 June 1988, two days after the commemoration of the June 16 Soweto uprising, an economic consultative meeting of the Newick Park dialogue group was held in Dube, Soweto. Among those who participated were Dr Simon Brand, Professor Sampie Terreblanche, Dr Sam Motsuenyane and Dr Elias Tema, who acted as chairman. The group agreed that "ethnicity should play less of a role – as a prescriptive criterion, for social policy, and that 'melting pot processes' were needed to achieve this".

This notion was later also heavily accentuated by the ANC members of the Consgold dialogue group. During the second meeting, Thabo Mbeki stated that group thinking was a "political anachronism" – the "principal driver" of apartheid and the violence in the country. It fed on centrifugal forces whereas the economy was a centripetal force, he added. The latter force would crush forms of group thinking.

Between 15 and 19 February 1988, a few days before the second meeting of the Consgold dialogue group, a significant conference took place at Wilton Park, Steyning, West Sussex. As someone with a passion for ancient things, I was overawed by the history of the conference centre that dates back to the time of William the Conqueror (1066+). In those days loyal followers of the king were granted land and other benefits – a practice that has continued through the ages and has merely taken on other forms today. William de Braose had been the beneficiary in this case. There was even an old church where I could sit and reflect. Ecclesiastically sanctioned political power was an important element of a ruler's success.

The theme of the conference was very pertinent: "South and Southern Africa – Prospects for ending apartheid and restoring regional stability". When I received the programme and saw the theme, I knew: Margaret Thatcher had had enough of the NP's bungling. The Wilton Park conference centre, as a project of the Foreign and Commonwealth Office, was an important think tank and influencing platform of the British government. A very conservative member of the ruling NP, André Fourie, would speak on the government's approach to reform. Sampie Terreblanche and I had to present brief introductions. So would prominent South Africans such as Hermann Giliomee, John Kane-Berman, André Odendaal, Patrick Pasha, Aggrey Klaaste, Sebolelo Mohajane, Frederik van Zyl Slabbert and Vusi Khumalo, who had to speak on problems regarding South Africa and the region. There were other participants from countries such as Canada, Mozambique, France, Nigeria, Britain, Zimbabwe, the US, the Netherlands, Portugal and Germany. Patrick Fairweather, undersecretary at the British foreign office, and Fleur de Villiers were also in attendance. It was stipulated that the discussions were "off the record". The conference, which was partly sponsored by Anglo American, was characterised by robust debate – both inside and outside the seminar room. All the participants were housed on the premises of the conference centre, and there was ample time for private conversations.

Aggrey Klaaste, whom I had come to know through the Urban Foundation, told me at some point: "It's never too late to talk." It became a refrain in my mind. I considered informing Klaaste about my participation in the Consgold talks, but decided against it so as not to compromise him. Towards the end of 1988 he gave me a copy of the September publication of the Transvaal United African Teachers' Association (TUATA) apropos of this organisation's congress. An article entitled "From paralysis to nation-building" referred to the views of Klaaste (editor of the *Sowetan*), Sam Mabe (assistant editor) and Nomavenda Mathiane (an article in the magazine *Frontline*). The editor of the journal, P Rikhotso, wrote about "The child in tomorrow's world", little knowing how dramatic the political changes in South Africa would be after 1990. Klaaste, Mathiane and Mabe appealed for "nation-building" – for the sake of the new generation. They were critical of blacks, especially opinion leaders and teachers, who failed to take a stand against practices such as necklace killings. It was a plea for self-examination.

Signs of this were also evident at the Wilton Park conference. But they were not picked up by many of the white South Africans, particularly not those who still believed that the Botha regime's path of gradual reform deserved more support. Unlike before, the black South African delegates did not walk out of the conference when they had to listen to a government representative. A protest was registered all the same. Fleur de Villiers told me: "There is a new realism among black people about dialogue sessions like these." This was later confirmed to me by Thabo Mbeki. The ANC had told some black participants and also those from other African countries that participation in the conference would not be illegitimate for "pragmatic reasons" (among others, the prospective settlement in Namibia–Angola). Black participants were given a hard time when it came to sanctions and the possibility of a wasteland. The moral argument from anti-apartheid ranks, namely that sanctions were the only nonviolent means of resisting apartheid, was weakened by the wasteland argument, particularly also in light of the unbridled black-on-black violence in various parts of the country. Regarding "white fears" about which the Zimbabwean delegate had grumbled, Patrick Fairweather had the last word: "The best way to address white fears in South Africa is to make an economic success of Zimbabwe."

The second meeting of the unofficial contact group in England was scheduled for 21 to 24 February 1988. This time Thabo Mbeki would act as leader of the ANC participants. Our meeting was held in impressive surroundings: the Eastwell Manor Hotel in Kent. The ANC was also 75 years old that year, and the occasion was celebrated with a conference in Tanzania attended by delegates from numerous countries. Coetsee, Barnard and Mandela's more intensive talks were in the offing. Mbeki knew about the talks via Tambo. His presence would enhance the status and legitimacy of our contact group. The news of his participation had me both excited and worried. He was part of the committee of the ANC's NEC that was tasked with reflecting on negotiations and constitutional guidelines. Pallo Jordan also served on the committee. Furthermore, Mbeki was the ANC's most famous diplomat, intelligent, well read and well travelled. He was not someone to be underestimated. True, he was known for his charm and composure, but he was also resolute and unwavering in his purpose of destroying the apartheid system. I had wondered beforehand whether we as Afrikaner participants would be a match for him. Some of my NIS contacts warned me against speaking too much; I should rather listen carefully to what he said. Koos Kruger asked me to keep detailed notes because Mbeki was an important ANC leader. It was also Kruger who arranged for me to meet Barnard in Pretoria after my first meetings with Mbeki.

Michael Young, together with Aziz Pahad who had joined us, introduced me to Thabo Mbeki. He was cordial, put out his hand to me spontaneously, and said something like: "Oh, the professor of philosophy from Stellenbosch." My first sensation was that he was shorter than I had imagined.

I made a mental note: "He's short, but he seems composed and bold." I was extremely tense, and felt relieved that I was taller and more strongly built than him. Koos Kruger had warned me that Mbeki would be very well informed about his Afrikaner interlocutors. And an expert in the art of communication. Hence I had decided beforehand to be friendly, but to say little and rather sum him up first. If this was a chess game – which it was in a certain sense, albeit with words and body language – I lost the first round.

Mbeki said: "I've read your book *Apartheid Must Die*. It was a risky book for you to have written. Apartheid was supposedly intended to protect Afrikaners, but your book actually says that apartheid would lead to their self-destruction." He caught me unawares, and forced me to talk about something that indeed gripped me intensely: apartheid as both a political and moral systemic evil. The book, which was then ten years old, had already been overtaken by events in many respects. I assumed that he wanted to say: "You and I have a common goal: the end of apartheid" – and I asked myself: "Would the two of us also learn to find common ground about the route to this goal, given the ANC's violence option?" This question, more than anything else, was the start of a relationship of trust and friendship that has been very enriching.

Meanwhile the political climate in South Africa had become hotter. Niel Barnard admitted in 2004 that South Africa found itself in a very tight corner by March 1988. He noted that the minister of police, Louis le Grange, had assured the cabinet that they had everything under control. In reality, however, in many parts of the country and in certain townships things were totally out of control. The political risks kept mounting. It was at this time that a committee was formed with a view to more structured discussions with Nelson Mandela. This pre-negotiation move was in my opinion the decisive factor in the preparatory phase. The first conversation with Mandela took place on 28 March 1988 in the office of the head of Pollsmoor Prison. Mike Louw even opined that PW Botha had dug a hole for himself and that it was the committee's responsibility to extricate him from that!

Thabo Mbeki's participation put me in a dilemma: should I wait for the green light from Barnard before informing Mbeki about my contact with the NIS, or should I tell him from the outset? The talks might have been unofficial, but they were confidential. In any case, I had no mandate from the NIS. The role of a go-between and talks in which positions are clarified and options explored, are more complicated than is sometimes thought. Trust and integrity are at stake. I decided to seek Fleur de Villiers's advice before the meeting. She stared at me in amazement when she heard about my connection with NIS, uttered a swear word, and wondered whether I knew what I had let myself in for. In liberal circles, misgivings about the NIS were primarily informed by notions of bugging. After recovering from her shock, she said firmly: "You can't keep Mbeki in the dark." I decided to inform him.

When we were alone, underneath a tree in the icy grounds of the East-well Manor, I told Mbeki that our dialogue group actually also amounted to "talks within talks": one form of dialogue involved the whole group; the second was private and personal between him and me. I informed him that I would report everything as correctly as possible to Barnard and his team. Any questions "Pretoria" might have, I would also relay to him for his re-sponse. I emphasised: "I haven't spoken about this to anyone in the contact group, also not to Michael Young. And I don't intend to tell them, even though they might start suspecting it." I emphasised: "We are busy with ex-perimental explorations. Our dialogue should be a form of talks about talks. And should remain unofficial and confidential."

I stressed the fact that I had no mandate, that I had no knowledge of the NIS's game plan, and that I could only be a bearer of messages and infor-mation. I remember adding that, as someone who concerned himself with philosophy, I did not accept that there was something like "bare facts"; facts were invariably interwoven with interpretations.

Mbeki looked at me with dark eyes, not at all surprised or even excited. He lit his pipe: "You are aware that you're taking a risk by informing me? Why are you doing it?"

I replied: "Not informing you is a greater risk. What do I do if the talks leak out, and also if it should take longer than was anticipated and we make progress?"

He said: "Good. I hear you."

There was little doubt in my mind that he had suspected there might be a Pretoria connection in the group. After all, he knew about the Coetsee-Mandela communication channel and, as he later confirmed to me, he had anticipated that informal contact would be made with the exiled leadership at some or other point.

There was also little doubt in my mind that Mbeki considered me an unlikely candidate for contact with "Pretoria". He was already in contact with a number of leading and opinion-forming whites from different spheres of South African society, some of whom had presented themselves as intermediaries. Many of them would have been able to play that role well. My announcement that I had contact with the NIS, and to which he had listened dispassionately — his self-discipline in this regard always amazed me — did come as a great surprise to him. Years later he specially emphasised in public that I had taken him into my confidence. Both morally and strategically it had been a wise move, albeit a rather impulsive one. Mbeki, I soon established, sought a contact channel with "Pretoria". At that stage the confidential Coetsee-Mandela channel was not for him and Tambo the only dialogue access they could or wanted to count on. The exiled ANC in Lusaka could not afford not to be part of a track-two exploratory dialogue.

The meeting at the Eastwell Manor Hotel, Ashford, Kent was attended by Mbeki, Pahad, Serote and Trew. Terreblanche and I had been joined by the constitutional law expert Marinus Wiechers of the University of South Africa (Unisa). The blazing fires, good food and fine wine made for an atmosphere that facilitated incisive, honest and straight-from-the-shoulder discussions. We did not mince our words when it came to sensitive topics. The touchiest, though, was the question of violence as a means to achieve political objectives. As had already been apparent at the first meeting, this issue was to people like Wolpe and Serote a "moral stand" and a justification for both the existence and modus operandi of MK. The Afrikaners had to tread lightly around this topic. We knew that to the Botha regime with its securocrats, the renouncement of violence was a non-negotiable precondition for a settlement process. The violence that raged among black people in Natal at that stage made it easier for us to talk less emotionally about the ANC's violence option and more in rational and strategic terms. The ANC participants were in a quandary about this violence, even though it was implied that Inkatha was "government-sponsored" and therefore part of the apartheid system. Thabo Mbeki, in his calm and reasoned manner, was quite outspoken. He objected strongly to necklace killings and said that the ANC leadership had neither recommended nor sanctioned necklacing. But the leadership would not condemn necklacing in public.

He told us that during a closed meeting in Harare in September 1987 it was insisted that this practice had to be stopped. Necklace killings, where car tyres that had been soaked in petrol were hung around a victim's neck and set alight, claimed the lives of many blacks between September 1984 and December 1989. Victims were branded as *impimpis*, namely people who had given information to the police and the state's security forces, and killed in mass action. As a result of my involvement with the Urban Foundation, I had stood at a number of places where the scars left by this barbaric execution method on our fatherland made me weep for our country and its people. Winnie Mandela, acting impetuously and irrationally as she did at times, caused an uproar both nationally and internationally when she declared in April 1986 that the freedom fighters in South Africa did not have guns. They only had stones, matches and petrol; with their boxes of matches and necklaces they would liberate the country. Her statements were a huge embarrassment to the external wing of the ANC and the UDF because they sabotaged the liberation movement's claim to the moral high ground. But the ANC leadership and people like Bishop Tutu were unable to put a summary stop to this barbaric form of populism.

The Total Strategy had of course been instrumental in creating a dark night of mistrust and suspicion in South Africa. In our discussion on violence at the Eastwell Manor, Mbeki admitted that violence had spiralled out of control in Natal, as well as in a few other places in the country. He reckoned that the warlords in Natal were being encouraged by the government to commit violence. By means of Inkatha, the government wanted to create the perception that rifts existed among blacks. He made Terreblanche, Wiechers and me sit up when he contended: "Brigadier Buchner was sent to Pietermaritzburg to orchestrate the violence. The South African government had believed that Inkatha would win the power struggle. That's why they also acted against the UDF and Cosatu when they realised they had miscalculated. Inkatha can't win. It's a people's war, after all. What the regime has done, is to let the violence get out of control."

Before my first personal meeting with Mbeki at the Eastwell Manor, I had taken careful note of what I could read about him, such as his Transkei background and his study years at the University of Sussex. I also spoke to someone who had met him at Idasa's Dakar conference in Senegal, who was filled with admiration: "Mbeki is an intellectual as well as a political strategist. When discussions bore him, he becomes distracted." My informant added: "At Dakar, Mbeki had been especially impressed by the clergyman Theuns Eloff, from the Dopper church." On his return to South Africa after the conference, Eloff had found himself in hot water in both the political and ecclesiastical spheres. The irate PW Botha picked on him in particular. He eventually had to find a means of livelihood outside the church. In hindsight, this was providential. Eloff later played a key role in the official processes that led to the negotiated settlement.

As I sat listening to Mbeki's exposition of the violence in KwaZulu and Natal and the state's involvement, I witnessed his sharp analytical ability, stripped of emotion but imbued with intense seriousness. By that time rumours about state-orchestrated violence and killings were rife. Mbeki stated unequivocally: "This is not leftist progaganda, but hard facts, part of PW Botha's so-called counterrevolutionary Total Strategy, with Inkatha a political sweetheart of the government." I told myself that I had to talk to Oom Koos about this, and also asked myself: "Do Leon Wessels, Dawie de Villiers and other cabinet ministers know that there may be a hidden land mine here that could be detonated at any moment?" That day I accepted that something diabolic lay behind the rumours and accusations of state-orchestrated violence and killings. Mbeki had convinced me. I wrote in my notebook: "How is it possible that the notion of 'the enemy' can inspire state-sponsored violence and murder?"

This was not the first time I had to hear that the primary cause of the violence was in fact the apartheid state. The jovial Pahad became annoyed with me on one occasion when I declared angrily that both the state and the ANC were implicated in the culture of violence in the country, and that it was time for the ANC to publicly accept responsibility for their complicity and stop putting all the blame on apartheid. I added: "Maybe the government and the ANC should start with confidential talks specifically about violence and acknowledge that structurally and in practice, we are all prisoners of a culture of violence." Pahad and I later confessed to each other that we despaired of a violence-free future. Wiechers put it blatantly in one of our dialogue sessions: "The ANC is unable to stop the violence in Natal on their own. There has to be joint discussions about a ceasefire with a view to dialogue." When the Afrikaners agreed with this view, some of the ANC interlocutors were visibly surprised. I got the impression that they had actually wanted us to defend the idea of a "renouncement" of the violence option. They had come well prepared to argue against this precondition. Mbeki, aware of what was already being discussed regarding regional conflicts and of the conversations with Mandela, was more sympathetic. He could understand the Afrikaners' point that there was not only growing right-wing resistance among whites in South Africa, but also a view among securocrats that the government was fully in control militarily and could clamp down even more forcefully if need be.

During the dialogue session Mbeki gave a lengthy explanation of the most important conditions for a settlement that represented the stance of the ANC and other liberation movements. What he said, would later become the basis of the Harare Declaration. Two conditions were stressed in particular: the release of *all* political prisoners; the unbanning of *all* banned organisations. He spoke about this with great authority and confidence. I later asked him about it in private. It was a "message" I wanted to convey in Pretoria. He said: "All Western countries support us on this. There's an international consensus." It became clear to me that Thabo Mbeki and those who were close to him had read the settlement drivers in the rest of the world better than the South African government. Of course, they were also better placed than the government to understand these. I was fairly disheartened when I realised that while these two conditions had already acquired a non-negotiable status, the Botha regime was still very far from this position. I shared my pessimism with Wiechers. He was not optimistic either, but remarked: "In situations where negotiation has become the only option for the main parties, things can change very quickly. Just remember how long we were pessimistic about South West Africa (Namibia) and the likelihood of a settlement there. And how complacently Botha and his generals had assured us that they had everything under control in that region."

Thabo Mbeki confirmed the non-negotiability of the conditions in question when I spoke to him about my pessimism. When I just looked at him silently, he said: "Of course, the 'how' of the conditions have to be discussed. The ANC would like to talk about their implementation. But we seek in-principle acceptance, even if it's not via a public announcement."

While the sanctions sword cut deeper and deeper in South Africa, Tambo and Mbeki travelled from platform to platform to convey the ANC's stance on a settlement and the conditions that had to be met. The South African government was not in a position to do the same. The US became an important target, and later also Britain and other Western countries. Africa was in any case inside the ANC's fold. And because they had been informed of the talks that were by that time already happening on a confidential basis, they acquired a competitive advantage. Thabo Mbeki did not exploit this. It helped him to plant the pro-negotiation flag in the ranks of the external ANC: negotiations became accepted in wide circles as "a pillar of the struggle".

During our meeting I realised just how strongly Mbeki had committed himself personally to the negotiation option as the only way to escape from the broadening spiral of violence and to meet the requirements of justice and peace. He had mustered all his intellectual and strategic ingenuity to advance this option. I wrote in my notebook: "He reminds me of Martin Luther's position of 'here I stand, I can do no other'. A position that is both strategic and moral." It also became clear to me why he had valued the Dakar conference, but was not optimistic about its influence on the advancement of a negotiation process. To the ANC, Alex Boraine was a typical liberal. And Mbeki was really seeking contact with the inner circle of the NP and the Afrikaners. He did not find these contact points at Dakar.

It was in the Eastwell Manor that Mbeki put forward a proposal that was not only of decisive importance but also illustrated his strategic ability. No doubt it had been cleared with Tambo and his inner circle. Aziz Pahad kept nodding his head approvingly. Serote's face was expressionless as he listened. Mbeki accepted the argument that right-wing Afrikaners could create a political problem along with the miltary hawks of the SADF.[2] That would be the case, he said, if the release of political prisoners had to be greeted with chaotic street celebrations, defiant political demonstrations and damage to property. Hence the question was: How could such a situation be avoided, and could the ANC leadership play a role in this regard? And how could they play a role if they were banned or still in exile? He had trumped us. And immediately relativised his trump card: the release of his father, Govan Mbeki, had proved that the internal leaders were able to keep "the people" in check. It had been very positive. Govan Mbeki, a hardline Marxist, was an important leadership icon among radicals in particular and in the Eastern Cape. He was the first prominent political prisoner to be released from the prison on Robben Island. Nelson Mandela had played a key role in his release. It became a successful move on the political chess board. Also a signal to the securocrats and the military fundamentalists: the game was changing. In time a political settlement had to be sought, and the release of political prisoners and the unbanning of all resistance movements would be crucial in this.

The issue of prisoner releases was a topic to which Mbeki and Pahad returned repeatedly during the discussion. Their focus was not only on who had to be released, but especially on the role that freed political prisoners could play. In fact, the ANC had instructed Govan Mbeki not to position himself as a leader of the ANC, one of the liberation movements, but as a national leader. He also had to honour the restrictions that had been placed on him and contribute towards the release of other prisoners. Thabo Mbeki related that his father had only been told shortly before his plane landed in Port Elizabeth that a "welcoming function" awaited him. He was totally unprepared for this, and it caused a serious problem with his first press conference. Thabo Mbeki believed it had been a planned trick on the part of the government. They had intended that, as a self-proclaimed Marxist, he should walk into a political trap. The ANC was in favour of a "controlled reintroduction" of freed political prisoners into the community. This phrase would crop up repeatedly in all our dialogue sessions. According to Mbeki, Kobie Coetsee had informed Lusaka via a go-between about Govan Mbeki's planned release. He provided no details, however, and did not send a follow-up message. But he did create an impression with the first message that Govan's release would be a prelude to Mandela's release.

With regard to the role of freed political prisoners, I could convey the following "message" to the NIS:

- They should initially, after the anticipated welcoming celebrations, keep a low profile. This would give them the opportunity to gain a better understanding of what is happening in the country so as to enable them to position themselves well.
- They should play a role in ending black-on-black violence and eliminating divisions among blacks. This should be regarded as a main priority in light of the government's divide-and-rule tactics.
- They should help to strongly consolidate the political image and function of the ANC. The ANC is in the first instance not a terrorist organisation, but a political movement. The accent has to fall on what Thabo Mbeki calls the "institutionalisation of the political process".
- They should contribute towards acceptance of the "legitimacy and legality" of the ANC. Prisoner releases must be part of a process of which the objective must be the unbanning of all black organisations.
- They should help to provide internal leadership since a vacuum and other deficiencies exist on certain levels. One such deficiency was discipline.

In light of the above, we talked at length and incisively at our meeting about the question of quid pro quo, in other words, the necessity of an attitude of give-and-take in order to bring about a climate that was conducive to sustainable negotiations and would create "a measure of trust", as Serote put it. This needed to be discussed in depth in view of the government's handling of the Nkomati Accord, the visit of the EPG, and the banning of legitimate black organisations. What exactly this give-and-take would entail in practice was not discussed in full on this occasion, particularly not in respect of the violence option as exercised by the ANC.

An important accent in the conversation was the ANC participants' strong view that the ANC did *not* regard negotiations as merely another form of

ANC-driven transfer of power. Negotiations had to be about the establishment of an inclusive, nonracial democracy. This pointed to the need for a
credible election. Indeed, the election process and system would have to be
one of the major items on the negotiation agenda. It was emphasised once
again that a transitional period would be essential, especially also in light
of white fears and the possibility of right-wing resistance. "Guarantees for
minorities" were even mentioned approvingly. The ANC interlocutors' repeated references to right-wing resistance were striking. This was also the
case during the official negotiation process. I think it was Tony Trew who,
during a tea break, cautioned me against underestimating right-wing resistance; I should remember what happened to Abraham Lincoln.

The concept of a transitional period was debated from another angle as
well: the necessity of building a political culture of mutual trust in democratic processes and institutions. Thabo Mbeki, who at one point reacted
caustically to the view that the ANC was not ready to govern, was of the
opinion that, given the past, democratisation would be a learning process
for all of us. A transitional process could help us with this learning process,
he said pensively. With reference to this discussion, I found it necessary to
report to the NIS that there was deep-seated distrust and even fear on the
ANC's part about the motives of "Pretoria". As Mbeki put it: "Our perception is – we are dealing with a group of people interested only in maintaining the status quo."

This distrust ran widely and deeply on both sides. But in the public sphere
it was mainly the South African government whose bona fides were in
doubt. The Nkomati Accord (March 1984) – a non-aggression pact between
South Africa and its neighbour Mozambique – and the activities of the
Renamo rebel group were the sharp thorn in the flesh. On Wednesday,
24 February 1988, which was the last day of our dialogue group's talks at
the Eastwell Manor, a full-page report was published in the British newspaper *The Independent* under the headline "Tearing Mozambique apart".
It dealt with Renamo's efforts to destabilise Mozambique and overthrow
President Chissano's Frelimo government. As if it had been planned, the
report appeared on the same day that the South African government banned
17 organisations.

Renamo, which had been founded by the former Rhodesian intelligence service and was reportedly also supported by South Africa's Military Intelligence (MI), did not disappear from the scene after the signing of the Nkomati Accord. The report in *The Independent* had a subheading: "Renamo supply trail begins in South Africa". An interesting bit of information was the reference to two ANC spies who had infiltrated MI's Renamo programme *Voice of Free Africa*, which was broadcast from Hillbrow. The message of the report was clear: South Africa was violating the Nkomati Accord. The South African military was still supplying Renamo with weapons. The two ANC spies in question were Derek Hanekom and his wife. After reading this report, I understood Van Zyl Slabbert's emotion at Wilton Park when he commented on the atrocities committed by Renamo and the alleged role of the South African military. I reported back to the NIS about the "growing suspicion" on the part of key persons that South Africa was not honouring the Nkomati Accord and not opting "for peace and stability", and noted that it was openly claimed that PW Botha and Pik Botha were either unaware of what the South African Defence Force was doing or perhaps turning a blind eye to its activities.

It was a question that surfaced repeatedly during the first half of 1988 in particular: Can the South African government be trusted? Does it have the political will to abide by and implement agreements? Can the South African government put demands to the governments of neighbouring countries about the ANC's presence and activities if there is cooperation with Renamo? It became glaringly obvious that the resolution of regional conflicts was closely connected with the resolution of the civil war in South Africa. Along with this, the bona fides of the Botha government were increasingly called into question.

One facet of the Eastwell meeting was a big eye-opener to the ANC members, even Mbeki, and helped to foster greater understanding of the position of the white pro-negotiation elements in South Africa: the three Afrikaners were very frank in their views about the way in which the military had taken over civil society and the political processes. Yet there were signs of a shift, we argued. Contacts from the military sphere were of the opinion that the political leaders needed to take a much stronger lead in finding a way to resolve impasses. There were also generals who maintained that 80% of the solution lay with the politicians and 20% with the military. Pahad remarked: "We also say that the solution to the struggle is mainly of a political nature."

Terreblanche brought us all back to earth; he reckoned that the South African Police (SAP) was a serious problem, and that they opposed radical political reform. Thabo Mbeki was also dumbfounded when I said that PW Botha would retire within two years. With Wiechers among the participants, much time was devoted to constitutional issues, including the ANC's insistence on "one person, one vote in a unitary state ". Mbeki went out of his way to explain the ANC's position. It quickly became clear that the idea of a multiparty democracy in a unitary state was non-negotiable to the ANC. There was a strong consensus on a *transitional process*. So something had happened at this meeting in Kent that was very significant for the nature of the process itself: we had moved away from analyses and explanations of the past towards more candid reflections on what Pahad at some point referred to as "the way forward". At the conclusion of the three-day meeting, we decided that future talks had to focus on the theme "Creating a climate for negotiations". Five facets had to receive attention: negotiation strategies; obstacles; black aspirations; white fears; mechanics of change.

On the last day of our meeting, 24 February 1988, there was a dramatic event in South Africa: the government banned 17 organisations, including the UDF. Mbeki told me in a private conversation that the bannings, totalitarian as they were, would unite black resistance against the apartheid regime and promote solidarity. He added: "The Botha regime's action will turn many Afrikaners against the NP. It's politically inevitable. Especially among young Afrikaners. They're tired of fighting for an immoral cause. The UDF, with more than two million members, won't collapse. It's a movement that arose out of, and for, civil society. A truly democratic protest movement." He also remarked with a measure of uncertainty: "How the ANC (in exile) can collaborate in a coordinated and integrated manner with the UDF (inside South Africa), is the big strategic question." Tambo, he stated, had lauded the UDF at the ANC's Kabwe conference in June 1985. At this conference a *Decade of Liberation* was announced. According to Tambo, the UDF was an outstanding example of the "political maturity of our people".

Mbeki later added a short footnote to the conversation: the position of Inkatha and its future role. He asked somewhat cynically why Inkatha had not been banned. Was it because Inkatha was part of Botha's co-optation system? Or because Botha deliberately wanted to undermine the credibility of Buthelezi and Inkatha, and increase the tension between them and the UDF? He regarded me sceptically when I said it was the latter, and asked me to explain what I meant.

A supporter of Dr Buthelezi at the time, I said that the Botha regime was doing all in its power to drive a wedge between Dr Buthelezi and his Inkatha party, and other black leaders and their organisations. The regime followed a policy of co-optation and divide-and-rule. Dr Buthelezi was an embarrassment to the regime. Owing to Dr Buthelezi's status and influence, it was impossible for the regime to ban him and Inkatha. The conditions that he and his party set for negotiations were also similar to those set by Western leaders and the ANC. Inkatha and its leadership were part of the general international consensus against apartheid and for an inclusive negotiation process. Mbeki said: "It's possible that you may be right."

In the course of 1988 Inkatha and its leaders, including Dr Buthelezi and the respected Dr Oscar Dhlomo, were scathing in their criticism of the bannings and restrictions. Dhlomo was the secretary-general of Inkatha and the minister of education and culture in Dr Buthelezi's KwaZulu government at the time. He made a good point at the joint meeting of the Inkatha Youth Brigade and the white *Jeug vir Suid-Afrika* (Youth for South Africa) in April 1988: By banning and restricting democratic organisations while black leaders and foreign governments demanded unbanning as a condition for negotiations, the Botha government was creating a climate for more violence. The role of Inkatha in the resistance process and particularly its future position in a negotiation process came up repeatedly in subsequent discussions of the dialogue group. The ANC interlocutors regarded Inkatha as an important political player, but not as an influential resistance movement. The conflict with the UDF precluded the latter. The UDF had been started as a resistance against the NP regime's constitutional plans. Inkatha was never seen or accepted as a political player in this resistance. Thabo Mbeki was vague when I asked him whether the external ANC had been informed about the formation of the UDF and the Reverend Allan Boesak's leading role in that regard.

During the Eastwell Manor meeting I abandoned most of my reservations about the significance of the Consgold project. For a considerable time the ANC had interpreted track-two talks as a way of creating divisions in the camp of the "enemy".Whites, and notably Afrikaners, had to be "won over" to the cause of the ANC. Hence, identification with the extraparliamentary opposition was a high priority. Even Thabo Mbeki was still "officially" convinced of a similar position during September 1987. But his participation at the Eastwell Manor talks convinced me that he, Pahad and Trew were taking a broader approach: divisions among "the enemy" would not bring the enemy down. There were other, more relevant "interests". Dialogue with "the enemy", which had by then started tentatively in Pollsmoor Prison and became more structured in 1988, was necessary to ensure a sustainable negotiation process.

Mbeki got into political hot water in Lusaka because of the Eastwell Manor meeting. Hani had heard about it. He registered a strong protest during a meeting of the National Working Committee in February 1988. Mbeki was not present. It was the last day of the Eastwell Manor meeting. Hani declared that Mbeki was holding discussions with "Afrikaner intellectuals" without a mandate and without prior consultation. Joe Nhlanhla, too, objected strongly: there had been neither consultation nor coordination, which suggested a loss of control. Track-two discussions always run the risk of coming up against the demand of an institutional mandate. Hani was adamant: anyone who wanted to attend such a meeting should be delegated by "the movement" to do so.

But with Oliver Tambo as Thabo Mbeki's political patron, Mbeki survived the Hani salvo.

# 6

## Mells Park: "Consensus
## is not just a dream"

The third meeting of the Afrikaner-ANC dialogue group took place at
Mells Park from 21 to 24 August 1988. It was summer in England. In
South Africa it was winter, also in a political sense – 1988 was one of the
country's most violent and bloody years.

Already in March that year, when the Newick Park dialogue group met
on 2 and 3 March in Britain, the general spirit was one of dejection. The
conflict between Inkatha and the UDF in the Pietermaritzburg area was
discussed. Some of the participants had pro-Inkatha sympathies. Dr Mangosuthu Buthelezi had good connections with national and international
Christian networks. Also with the US-oriented Fellowship Movement, which
in turn had good contacts with important US politicians. Even as far as the
White House.[1] Buthelezi knew the value of networks and was popular
among conservative Americans.

At Newick Park we discussed the effects of Govan Mbeki's release on
the black community. Much time was devoted to the "dilemmas" of the NP's
reform process. We also focused at length on constitutional settlement processes and the question as to whether the government might be landing
itself in an even worse cul-de-sac constitutionally as a result of some of
its reform initiatives. All the participants believed this to be the case. They
reckoned that it was a futile attempt on the regime's part to install (ethnic)
local authorities and even provide for a "Great Indaba", or overarching
institution. After all, the whole notion was based on the race-based Population Registration Act. This central pillar in the apartheid temple had to
be toppled.

I was invited by the department of foreign affairs to address the South
African missions in Bonn, Munich and Amsterdam the week after the
Newick Park meeting. The topics on which I had to speak included "The

democratisation of South Africa". Foreign affairs minister Pik Botha and his officials went out of their way to promote negotiations, but they were hamstrung. The Botha government had not come up with a cogent policy proposal, and the release of Nelson Mandela and the unbanning of all liberation movements were not in prospect. By then there was already an international consensus on these two elements of a settlement process. All foreign affairs could achieve through their initiatives was to keep the hope of a settlement process alive.

There was a second ambush: PW Botha and his securocrats had no confidence in Pik Botha and the senior foreign affairs officials when it came to what they identified as strategic security issues. PW Botha, given his personality, also had his own, subjective view of Pik. PW Botha was of course in a certain respect dependent on his minister of foreign affairs. Pik Botha had excellent international contacts, better than those of any other cabinet minister. And Pik Botha was, in turn, dependent on PW Botha for his ministerial office. The NIS, too, sometimes had reservations about Pik Botha, mainly because they maintained, and to my mind rightly so, that the planning, preparation and initiation of a settlement process with, say, the ANC was a strategic security issue. It was argued that this was not something to which Pik Botha and his department could contribute under their own steam.

The visits to Bonn, Munich and Amsterdam were highly informative, even though the Dutch government caused considerable drama by cancelling my visa in light of an intensified sanctions campaign. After the visits it was clear that businesspeople who were still attempting to promote and maintain trade relations with South Africa were also losing heart. The "hassle factor", as someone in Munich put it, had simply become too big and even too expensive. There was a very strong consensus: "While we do not approve of the violence that the ANC and the UDF are inflicting on the country, a negotiated-settlement process is the only way out of the political impasse. This process can start with the release of Nelson Mandela and other political prisoners." Someone in Munich observed cynically: "You can jail people, but not the dream of freedom. If PW Botha carries on like this, he'll run out of prisons."

Meanwhile the possibility of more stringent sanctions against South

Africa featured more and more strongly on the international agenda, driven mainly by the US. This intensified the pressure on Britain and particularly Prime Minister Margaret Thatcher. I discussed this issue in detail with my NIS contacts in a safe house in the north of Pretoria. It became a good discussion during which we also talked about the strategic consequences of intensified economic sanctions. By August 1988, after the third meeting, I found myself in an impossible situation, and wondered whether I was the right person for this project. My wife Annemarie said what she always says in situations like this: "You don't stop halfway with what you've started." I tried to explain my dilemma to her as concisely as possible: "Thabo is restless. He expects progress, because he and Tambo are being pressurised by the ANC hawks. And Thatcher has also given up hope." Annemarie likes detail. She asked for more information. Especially about Thabo Mbeki's expectations. Eventually I had another meeting with my NIS contacts. The unofficial nature of the talks in England had once again brought home to me the delicacy of this kind of "talks about talks". In our conversations about the meetings in England, Barnard usually qualified everything, very professionally and correctly, with phrases such as "maybe if we ...". I was motivated anew when I left the meeting with the NIS.

In April 1988 I wrote an article for the Afrikaans Sunday paper *Rapport* under the headline "The sanctions sword is being sharpened once more", with reference to the discussion of the Dellums Bill in the US. Oil companies such as Mobil and Japan's trade relations with South Africa were being targeted by sanctions campaigners, as well as academic and cultural ties. I posed the questions: "Do we accept that Africa needs us whites? Do we know what to do about that?" In May 1988 I also gave a lecture at the Stellenbosch University's Business School that was reported in the *Financial Mail* (6 May), among others. I emphasised in the lecture that South Africa needed to give Thatcher something in return to enable her to maintain her well-disposed stance. And South Africa was not doing that at that stage. What I wrote and said, expressed something of my growing frustration with the slow pace of progress towards a negotiated settlement and with the violence in the country. Several church and faith leaders, such as Archbishop Tutu, Allan Boesak, Imam Solomons and Nazeem Mohamed, had by then assumed the role of spokespersons on socioeconomic rights for blacks, with the Afrikaans "white churches" light years behind these developments. By that time I was already convinced that within the Afrikaner community, all hope for a negotiated settlement had to be pinned on business leaders. My NIS contacts never exerted any pressure on me as far as my public views and participation in conferences and seminars were concerned.

Later that year, a birthday was celebrated: Mandela turned 70. The celebration, with a concert at the Wembley Stadium on 11 June, was a massive event. Among the renowned artists who appeared were Miriam Makeba, Whitney Houston and Harry Belafonte, one of my favourite singers. I met him later at a Christmas dinner hosted by Thabo Mbeki. I told my NIS interlocutors: "The government can't win. The concert is organised by 'Artists against Apartheid'. Does South Africa have 'Artists for Apartheid' that can organise a spectacular event?" The concert projected the image of the ANC as a "civilised and cultured group of people". The propaganda war against the South African regime was won decisively in 1988. Nelson Mandela celebrated his 70th birthday in prison in a blaze of international glory. Coetsee and Barnard needed to pull a big rabbit out of the hat. At least the committee was already fully engaged in incisive discussions with the world's best-known prisoner and the South African government's biggest "enemy".

In 1988 we also experienced something that has not received much attention to date: political Trojan horses within the system itself. They were the then reviled chief ministers of the so-called self-governing black states. This project was the most grotesque expression of Afrikaner nationalists' ideological addiction to the notion of ethnic politics. Two of the chief ministers in particular repeatedly left the system and its ruling elite incensed. But they were powerless to give vent to their anger. These two were Mangosuthu Buthelezi of KwaZulu and Enos Mabuza of KaNgwane. I would like to refer to the latter, because he was a special friend who also participated in the Newick Park Initiative. His solid ties with the ANC put him in a different position from that of Buthelezi. The South African government were dependent on Buthelezi and hoped that he would assist them in the government's battle against the ANC.

On 28 July 1988 Mabuza, with the knowledge of other chief ministers
of the "homelands", signed a memorandum he had drafted for a meeting
on 1 August 1988 with Chris Heunis, the minister of constitutional development and planning. Mabuza gave me a copy of the document and said in
his quiet and non-aggressive way: "The minister is the political head of a
department with a particular name. Yet he and his department believe they
can plan everything unilaterally on behalf of and for others. He also doesn't
know the difference between dictating to others, consultation and negotiation. Is he perhaps going to be the ruling party's chief negotiator with
the ANC and the PAC one day? What a bleak prospect!" The memorandum
pulled no punches. The NP government's proposed National Council that
was intended to involve black leaders in government processes, was still based
on the disastrous policy of separate states, race and ethnicity. Moreover, the
minister and his officials had determined the agenda unilaterally. There had
been no prior consultation with the chief ministers to ascertain what they
regarded as priorities. Mabuza reminded the NP minister that since 24 November 1986 he, Mabuza, both on his own and with others, had been high-
lighting the crucial issues ad nauseam, for instance the Population Registration Act, the state of emergency and the release of Nelson Mandela. All in
vain. The minister had not heard them.

Buthelezi didn't even attend the meeting. His argument was: How can he
attend a meeting like this with a unilaterally determined agenda while a
state of emergency and bannings are in force? Surely it can't be "business
as usual"?

Mabuza, who consistently took a strong and well-articulated stand against
apartheid, did not mince his words. He wrote: ". . . we maintain that for
any initiative to be acceptable and to hold the promise of eventual success,
neither its agenda and participants nor its outcome can be unilaterally determined." Heunis was at his wits' end. Black leaders who were prepared
to fall in with his plans had become an extremely scarce commodity. He
was in a political impasse. At the Newick Park discussions, Mabuza frequently made the point that the style of the NP government also symbolised the nature of the political system: authoritarian. Without the cooperation of black leaders, the government would have two options: either to

proceed with its plans unilaterally, or to abandon them. Both these possibilities were serious political and strategic disadvantages for Heunis and his government.

The next meeting of the Consgold dialogue group was scheduled for 21 to 24 August 1988, about three weeks after Mabuza's confrontation with Heunis. Prior to this meeting, from 9 to 11 June, the Newick Park Initiative gathered in Pietermaritzburg. The theme was "Alternative constitutional settlement in South Africa consultation". Participants from the ranks of black churches were Elias Tema, Caesar Molebatsi, Stanley Magoba and Richard Stevens. Magoba later played a big role in the Pan-Africanist Congress (PAC). Mabuza also attended the meeting. Theuns Eloff became a driving force. We analysed not only the existing climate for negotiations, but also issues such as land reform, ownership and management hierarchies in the South African economy. This was identified as one of the major issues in a democratised South Africa.

In August the Consgold dialogue group met at Mells Park – an extensive estate near the picturesque village of Mells, not far from the city of Bath with its Roman ruins. We would meet at Mells Park on several occasions, including the weekend of Nelson Mandela's release (11 February 1990). There were open parklands, walkways and wooded areas where we could walk and share our personal experiences. Serote and Wolpe had been left out of the ANC group, and only Thabo Mbeki, Aziz Pahad and Tony Trew were present. It was a sign that Mbeki considered the dialogue group important. As we stood outside the manor house and admired the surroundings, he remarked to me half casually: "If we make progress this weekend, other participants would have to be added." I didn't ask him what he meant by "progress". Apart from myself, the Afrikaner participants were Sampie Terreblanche and Willem (Wimpie) de Klerk.

De Klerk was an important addition. A former professor at the then University of Potchefstroom, he was a member of the smaller Reformed Church (known as the "Doppers"), a prominent opinion leader, a brother of FW de Klerk and a senior figure in the Afrikaner Broederbond (AB), from which I had resigned by then. Like me and Terreblanche, he had joined the ranks of the Independent Movement in 1987. The Sunday evening at the dinner table, Pahad inquired jokingly: "Where are the Nationalists? Have you squeezed them out, or are they irrelevant? And what about the Progs?"

The meeting at Mells Park turned out to be one of the most decisive gatherings of the unofficial dialogue group. It started two days after my 53rd birthday on 19 August, and lasted until our departure just after breakfast on 24 August 1988. Fleur de Villiers met me at Heathrow Airport before the meeting. I stayed with her and her mother until Sunday, 21 August. Willem de Klerk and Sampie Terreblanche had arrived on Saturday, 20 August, and were taken from Heathrow to the Connaught Hotel, Carlos Place, London. On the Sunday, the three of us travelled to Mells Park House by car and arrived late in the afternoon. The ANC members, Thabo Mbeki, Aziz Pahad and Tony Trew, arrived in another car. We spent a pleasant evening in each other's company.

Dinner was always very formal: jackets and ties, silver Victorian cutlery. Mbeki sent Pahad to his room to put on a tie. We dined in classic style. Besides an official dining room, Mells Park had a library and a recreation room. Michael Young and I had arranged with each other that there would be two "processes": formal meetings inside the seminar room in terms of an agreed agenda; informal gatherings outside the room without his presence. Mbeki and I stayed in the main house in adjoining rooms. We had agreed beforehand on a programme for the dialogue sessions. We called it "bilateral programme", and the participants received it beforehand. As at the previous meeting, Mbeki and I "clicked" from the start even though we are different personality types. We shared similar philosophical and literary interests, as we would later discover in more depth. I had no aspirations or capabilities to play any leadership role in a new dispensation that would make me vie with him or anyone else. And he had no desire to become a philosophy professor in Stellenbosch. We were not in competition with each other. I realised at this meeting: If the South African government and the ANC and other organisations were to achieve a settlement, there would be difficulties on other levels. There would be increased competition for power and influence. As Aziz Pahad put it to me in his explanation of the strategic importance of Dakar: "There's a big problem. Everyone who attended is excited about playing an influential role in future. And there are many who weren't at Dakar who want to do so as well. We have to discuss this serious problem." Unfortunately, we never did. I think he had been spot-on.

The idyllic yet stately surroundings contributed greatly to the success of our interaction. Nature and architecture created an atmosphere of civility where harsh words, arrogance and rudeness were out of place. We were only six participants, a small enough group to let the process flow and deepen. We could look each other in the eyes and we not only discussed compli- cated issues, but talked nineteen to the dozen to each other, told jokes and exchanged anecdotes. I asked Mbeki about his mother (Epainette) and her shop, and whether he had at least given her a hand at times and not only read books. His face and eyes brightened when he talked about this period of his life. I told him how my mother had instilled a love of books and reading in me and how she had prevented my father from giving me too many chores on the farm, because I was busy with my books. We discov- ered that we were both crazy about Yeats. He drew my attention to black writers whose books I should read. We found ourselves in agreement not merely about the importance of a negotiation process, but personally as well – the kind of person, as I told the NIS, to whom I would entrust my life. My remark was meant sincerely. But I also intended it to undermine the "terrorist" construct.

The Mells Park meeting brought clarity about six cardinal issues:

- Evaluation of the previous meetings, whether there has been progress and on what;
- An understanding of the internal political processes and where our country is more or less;
- Constitutional issues, particularly as seen by the ANC;
- The violence issue;
- Angola and what effect it will have on Namibia and South Africa; and
- The way forward.

The meeting took place shortly after attacks on soft targets in South Africa, at the Ellis Park sport stadium and in Hyde Park, Johannesburg, among others. It became a fairly emotional discussion. In South Africa and among certain church groups there were serious questions about the advisedness and morality of this strategy. The moral advantage that the ANC used to enjoy was suddenly in question. The ANC interlocutors, clearly not in favour of attacks on soft targets and civilians, were on the back foot. Mbeki, who knew about the Coetsee-Barnard-Mandela connection and was strongly pro-negotiation, then did something that was a huge contribution to trust-building in the exploratory process. It was also interpreted as such in "Pretoria" after my report-back. He gave a detailed explanation of the official policy of the ANC: attacks on soft targets was not policy.

The violence option had of course been a very emotional issue from the outset. It was brought to a head in South Africa and in countries such as Britain when a car bomb exploded in front of the Nedbank building in Church Street in Pretoria on 20 May 1983. Nineteen people (12 civilians and seven members of the SADF) died, while 219 were seriously injured or maimed. Only two of the latter were SADF members and the rest, 217, civilians. In 1961, with the founding of MK, the ANC had decided to proceed to violent actions; if there had been a position since 1961 that soft targets would not be attacked, that standpoint died in Church Street. Oliver Tambo, who had left South Africa in 1961, and people like Thabo Mbeki had great difficulty in trying to explain this shift. They were not successful.[2]

The two of them held a stereotyped view: the apartheid state had started the violence. For nearly 50 years the ANC had been a peaceful liberation movement. With the intensification of the "people's war", it was inevitable that civilians could die too. As Tambo put it to the British Foreign Affairs Committee with reference to a question about black-on-black violence: "We think it is unavoidable in a way. It is a product of the violent system in which we live." He did admit on this occasion: "I regret all these things. I regret them, but I would refuse to be asked to condemn . . ." In his book *Long Walk to Freedom* Nelson Mandela also expressed his "regret" about the Church Street bomb, but explained the incident in the same way as Tambo did. The issue of violence and its aftereffects would remain a vexed question for a long time, even after the Truth and Reconciliation Commission – like a sore that continued to fester. Since 1988 I personally came to the conclusion that Hani and his hawks were firmly convinced that they would be able to take over South Africa by means of violent resistance. It was not just propaganda talk. Their dream of a military revolution was stronger than most people thought. Concepts such as "settlement" and "negotiation" did not feature in their vocabulary. "Takeover of power" by force of arms was the dominant motive. And even after the start of the official settlement process this motive was also a political issue on the part of certain elements in the ANC. Operation Vula was an illustration of this.

De Klerk, Terreblanche and I were unanimous and at times even emotional: "ANC-inspired violence is counterproductive. It fuels right-wing solidarity and resistance against talks about talks. Most whites believe that the state should unleash its full security powers against the resistance movements. We are convinced that your violent revolution cannot succeed. Or do you actually want a scorched earth?"

Mbeki, unperturbed by our emotion, started to explain: A three-hour discussion had been held with Hani. He *was* repudiated. But the ANC had a big problem with its command structures and control mechanisms. There was also another problem: the issue of training. The training of soldiers outside of South Africa was good, but the training inside South Africa less so. Moreover, in other countries ANC soldiers received political as well as military training. Inside South Africa it was limited to military training. Hence things could go wrong, as could also happen, and did happen, with even the South African Defence Force and the South African Police.

According to him matters were also complicated by the self-defence units that were being established in black townships by mainly the youth. The ANC, Mbeki admitted, was worried that things might get out of hand to such an extent that a situation of "violence for violence's sake" could develop. Meetings about this issue were being planned in Lusaka. They would also be attended by people from South Africa. The ANC accepted that if the internal violence spiralled out of control, it would have serious policial consequences. As Mbeki put it: The "supremacy of the political leadership" would be undermined and it would be increasingly difficult to establish a united black front. The standpoint of the political leadership in Lusaka was unequivocal: "Violence is not an alternative to mass political struggle."

Every effort had to be made to prevent a situation of violence for violence's sake.

The discussion then took an unexpected turn when Mbeki said that the ANC would be prepared to abandon the violence option if the political struggle yielded negotiation results and also proved to be effective in bringing about a nonracial constitutional dispensation. Terreblanche, De Klerk and I sat bolt upright when he said: "Violence can become unnecessary." In fact, a cessation of hostilities was something that could be negotiated. But there had to be a strong commitment to a meaningful process that would lead to a nonracial democratic settlement. His view, I realised that night in my bedroom, represented an unequivocal recognition of the negotiation option. He, Pahad and Trew had accepted that dialogue with "the enemy" was essential. I wrote in my notebook: "We are all in the same boat. Willem (de Klerk), Sampie (Terreblanche) and I accept that sustained informal dialogue is the only route to an official negotiation process. We have to do everything possible to build increasing support for the negotiation option within our spheres of influence. PW Botha and his government must be swept along by a pro-negotiation tide. Consensus within Afrikaner circles on conditions for negotiations and especially the way in which 'white fears' should be dealt with, is a high priority."

Mbeki also broached the question of the Sharpeville Six. Death sentences for political prisoners, he argued, raised the political temperature among blacks. He put forward a proposal: the ANC was prepared to hand over some of the South African agents that had been captured in exchange for the commutation of death sentences for political prisoners. The ANC had already held discussions with the Dutch government in this regard. But there had been no reaction from the South African government. Mbeki referred specifically to the case of Olivia Forsyth in Angola. The Zimbabwean government also held South African agents in its prisons. The ANC had declared its willingness to hold discussions about this sensitive issue without seeking any political gain. The message from South Africa, however, was: President PW Botha's standpoint is that no agreements must be entered into with the ANC. In the meantime there was dialogue by means of intermediaries about the ANC's position in Angola, with the ANC prepared to move its camps elsewhere.

The issue of prisoner exchanges featured prominently in subsequent discussions. There was clearly a hope on the part of the ANC members that such
a move would expedite the settlement process. Thabo Mbeki told me privately: "The issue of amnesty will also have to be addressed. It will have to
top the agenda for dialogue with the South African government." In 1989
he repeated this point and requested me to convey a message in this regard
to the NIS. He also informed me briefly: "The exchange of prisoners between South Africa and Angola-Swapo in September 1987 in Maputo can
serve as an example." Wynand du Toit, who had been captured in Angola,
was released at that time. Also Klaas de Jonge, who had spent more than a
year in the Dutch embassy in Pretoria after seeking refuge there to avoid
being captured by the police. There was also a Belgian citizen, Helene
Pastoors, who served a prison sentence in Kroonstad on account of her political activism against apartheid. Kobie Coetsee had objected very strongly to her possible release. Eventually more than a hundred captured soldiers of the fighting parties in Angola were released. Mbeki said: "It's a way
to end hostilities and build trust. If South Africa and Angola could do it,
why not us? After all, we belong to the same country." I said half-heartedly,
because I believed that this was not yet possible in South Africa: "I'll pass
on the message." On a subsequent occasion he also raised the possible exchange of another South African spy, Odile Harrington, who was detained
under deplorable conditions in Harare after an extremely unprofessional
and naive spying attempt.

It was evident at that stage that Mbeki, a driving force for negotiations
together with Tambo, was even anxious to hold direct informal discussions
with government officials about the release of Nelson Mandela and his
"controlled reintroduction into South African society". This willingness
had much to do with the fact that someone like Mbeki already knew about
the talks with Mandela and his clandestine "sightseeing trips" around the
Western Cape. The ANC did not want to be excluded from this process.
Hence the release of Nelson Mandela was of prime importance. Also that
of other political prisoners. The ANC maintained consistently: the release of
political prisioners had to be a prelude to the unbanning of all liberation
movements. It was the one issue that Mbeki stressed repeatedly. At some

stage he said: "We need to act in a manner which will not complicate his release." And he inquired: "How can we facilitate the process?" Some of the participants asked: "Maybe an international mediation team should be put together?" I said: "Definitely not!"

Sampie Terreblanche raised a thorny issue during the dialogue session: Mandela's release could be wrecked by the conditions of violence and unrest that prevailed at local levels and around municipal elections. Mbeki, Pahad and Trew all took notes. Mbeki, somewhat pessimistic, said that the unrest was not going to stop, and conceded indirectly that the Lusaka ANC didn't have control over what happened at the grassroots level. He also admitted for the first time that Mandela had given an indication of what he and Coetsee discussed. And he was adamant: the ANC was even prepared to conclude an informal agreement with government officials. I told myself: "We're moving! The ANC wants to talk to government representatives. Even if it's only about Mandela's release. The ANC, too, knows that negotiations are inevitable. The civil war is drawing to an end."

Time and again Willem de Klerk, Sampie Terreblanche and I brought the ANC back to the harsh South African reality. Our approach was direct and to the point: ANC-inspired violence was counterproductive. It fuelled right-wing resistance and the securocrats' obsession to crack down brutally with the full security powers of the state. We conceded: Blacks' political and extra-parliamentary power gave them a veto right. Nevertheless, Terreblanche contended, the weakening economy stimulated the growth of right-wing resistance among whites. Agricultural debt in particular was causing serious problems. This debt was escalating, and the farmers were up in arms. Mbeki was less pessimistic. He reckoned that alliance-forming processes would resolve our political and economic dilemmas. He referred to the South African Rugby Board in this regard, and said that the South African Rugby Union should not "run away" but rather seek common ground. This point became an important issue: What sort of common ground should be sought? On what? By whom? Mbeki, always the arch-optimist, suggested that we had to promote *all* processes that could lead to settlements. And processes existed where "islands of nonracial cooperation" were already being created. These had to be identified and supported. One such process, he stressed again, was that of the South African Rugby Board. He wanted to know whether a process of building consensus between black and white on "some basic principles" was possible. Such a consensus depended not only on the South African regime and the ANC. It had to be ratifed by parties, churches, businesspeople, trade unions and other organisations. It had to be based on the greatest possible participation of "the people". Mbeki admitted: the NP regime was a key player. This could neither be denied nor wished away.

Sampie Terreblanche once again set the cat among the pigeons: Land and the question of land reform were immaterial, he contended. What mattered was the redistribution of opportunities. He was right in this. After 1990, and more so after 1994, affirmative action became a major political policy position. The ANC government of course developed an obsession about land reform. Years later this would be responsible for great political uncertainty as well as a grotesque record of failed land-reform projects. At this dialogue session, however, the ANC was more interested in the weal and woe of the NP than in Terreblanche's important point. This interest was premised on the express assumption that the ANC would have to settle with the NP and the government of the day in the end. It was an important assumption, since it acknowledged the NP's position of power and that an armed seizure of power by the ANC was not around the corner. Negotiation was the only option.

The idea of *negotiations as the only option* was a position that had developed over time. In the case of the ANC the decisive push factors were the changes in the Soviet Union, the success of the Angola-Namibia settlements, and the escalating black-on-black violence. From our first meeting, and notably during this Mells Park meeting, another accent could also be heard: Can *any* government govern a ruined economy? Can a war be waged against poverty if the civil war reduced everything to ashes? This economic and developmental angle on the situation in which South Africa found itself gradually came stronger to the fore in the discussions about the future. Late one night during the Mells Park meeting, Pahad and I agreed: The only hope for South Africa was an end to the civil war in the country and the lifting of sanctions. "The ANC," Pahad said philosophically, "can't satisfy the rights and expectations of the poor with nothing. The madness must stop."

Willem de Klerk gave the ANC hope. He remarked prophetically: "We are currently in a semi-dictatorship, even though there is an expansion of socioeconomic development for blacks. It's really an attempt at co-optation. The NP, however, is a transitional party that will be phased out over the next five to ten years and will disappear eventually." Mbeki, Pahad and Trew looked at him sceptically. To them the NP was, as Pahad put it, "invincible". The discussions helped to explode the myth of the NP's invincibility. We then talked at length and incisively about the issue of a transitional stage. Thabo Mbeki was outspoken about the need for such a stage, which he also advocated later during the Codesa process. What he said in this regard was very illuminating: "A process must take place which will take us away from the old South Africa. This process has to be based on all of us thinking together and acting together. If we succeed in doing this, it will change the issues, questions and fears."

The discussion about the necessity of a transitional phase brought us to a consensus: acceptance of a transitional phase. It would help to establish a pro-negotiation culture and to allay white fears, particularly Afrikaner fears. I listened attentively to Mbeki, and realised that he was not simply flying a kite. This was something he had pondered for a long time. I suspected, too, that he had not yet raised this idea in broad ANC circles. It was not clear whether he had already given thought to mechanisms whereby the idea would be given institutional and political form. We didn't discuss possible mechanisms during the meeting either, but I wrote in my notebook: What does he mean by "acting together"? Will he perhaps return to this point at a later stage in the dialogue process? I realised that he had hit an important nail on the head: a political alliance with an eye to the future would build trust and allay fears. The objective and substance of this, I told myself, would make or break our country's future.

Terreblanche responded to Mbeki's point. In his opinion, reform in the sense of real transformation was not yet on the agenda of the government or the majority of whites. Because the government felt threatened by the right-wing Conservative Party of Andries Treurnicht, a former church leader who later became an NP leader and also a cabinet minister, the Botha regime had embarked on a propaganda campaign in an attempt to ward off the right-wing resistance. Besides, there was another problem: creeping poverty and a deterioration of the country's economic situation. He was of the view that the disinformation being spread by the Botha regime had to be countered by a programme to re-educate the whites. Pahad was visibly astounded when Terreblanche asked Mbeki: "What role can the ANC play in the re-education of the whites?" Mbeki didn't reply to this question. Our discussions were of course held at the time when the resolution of the Namibia-Angola conflict was in the offing. We devoted a good deal of time to this issue during the dialogue session. Britain, the US and the Soviet Union had faith in South Africa's good intentions as far as the resolution of this conflict was concerned. According to Aziz Pahad, the ANC knew full well that such a settlement would have great implications for the South African civil war. There would be increased pressure on negotiation, and Namibia's constitutional model that was to be negotiated would be held up as an example. The NP government and the ANC should not let that happen. We had to find our own route to full democracy. The ANC was also prepared to move its training camps from Angola to advance the process of settlement – even as far as Ethiopia. Mbeki endorsed what Pahad had said. So did we Afrikaners.

During the discussion, Mbeki maintained that Margaret Thatcher was tired of Botha's manipulations. She preferred to participate in a growing and coordinated Western oppositional role against apartheid. Relations with other Western countries and even with the Soviet Union were more important to her than those with South Africa. From what he had heard, Thatcher considered the progress of reform in South Africa to be "inadequate and pathetic". In any case, she had strong feelings about Nelson Mandela's release and the unbanning of organisations such as the UDF. And she sought "peace in the region". Mbeki said, not gloatingly or bombastically, but as a factual statement: "The tide has turned strongly against the Botha regime. Thatcher's attitude towards the Botha regime is going to harden." Later, when we talked privately, he said: "We'll sort out our problems in our own way. The British can't get involved. Tell that to your friends in Pretoria. We don't want foreign intermediaries. And report to me what they think." I reported later: "Barnard agrees with you."

During the dialogue session a long discussion was devoted to the ANC's constitutional guidelines. In his introduction, Aziz Pahad focused especially on the process that had been followed in the drafting of the guidelines. The legal department of the ANC had embarked on the process more than a year earlier. Various working documents were compiled and discussed during internal seminars. As an organisation, the ANC wanted to be fully prepared for eventual constitutional negotiations. The guidelines would be discussed as widely as possible, also within South Africa, so that an inclusive consensus on basic principles and values could crystallise. I jotted down a note to myself: "What is happening in the government's department of constitutional planning? And what progress has there been with the Afrikaner Broederbond's initiative that was started in 1986?"

The Afrikaner interlocutors wanted to know what the consensus-seeking process would look like. Pahad seemed somewhat unsure, and stated that the ANC and extraparliamentary role players would be involved. It had to culminate in a constitutional conference. Thabo Mbeki stressed the idea of a broad-based conference at which faith communities, business organisations, trade unions and the like had to be present. At some stage he used the term "constituent assembly". Tony Trew emphasised the necessity of a devolution of power. Then hastened to add: "Devolution of power doesn't necessarily mean a federal state. The ANC won't abandon the idea of a unitary state."

Willem de Klerk then raised the issue of "white fears". The group found it difficult to hold a meaningful discussion on this topic, which cropped up time and again like a shadow in all our meetings. Terreblanche contended that the ANC's intention to implement nationalisation was one of the reasons for "white fears". He also thought that the ANC's notion of a "developmental state" had not yet been clearly articulated. Terreblanche was in favour of a "promotional function" for the state; the country needed lots of jobs and high economic growth. Mbeki concurred with this point. It was as if we all knew intuitively that a political settlement process could not succeed independently of the economy, but were hesitant to subject this issue to too much scrutiny. I started to suspect that this was for good reason: it was the one area where serious disputes could arise in future. Even within the ANC.

"White fears" related directly to this. The protests and resistance from anti-apartheid circles were not just about political rights, but also about socio-economic rights – about political *and* economic injustice. As Mbeki put it: "The struggle is not only about the right to vote."

I came to realise very early in the dialogue process that the question of "white fears", more than hardline ideological convictions, was a major obstacle to a negotiated settlement. And I also accepted that this issue would have to be defused in cooperation with the ANC. There is indeed a specific relation between peace and fear. If fear is high, particularly among an elite or ethnic group, the prospects of a successful peace settlement are dim. That is why identifiable groups seek constitutional guarantees. Fear usually decreases when strong perceptions develop that a negotiated settlement, and particularly its constitutional outcome, would result in a better and more just constitutional dispensation and political process.

The Mells Park talks were a political tipping point. Terreblanche and De Klerk were at their best: articulate, to the point, and critical of both internal South African and ANC politics. It was a high-level and extraordinarily frank debate. The three ANC participants, too, didn't try to score propagandistic points. The discussion was problem- and solution-oriented, even though we had no mandate in this regard. There was strong consensus on another matter: conferences in the public domain were important and should be supported. But they were not enough or the only thing that needed to happen. Public conferences should also not hijack the attempts to get a settlement and negotiation process going. Lobbying in favour of stronger pro-negotiation positions that included support for the release of political prisoners and the unbanning of the liberation movements had to be done among influential networks, such as in the business sector. The ANC was also adamant: the organisation didn't want "outside mediation", especially not from Americans, the British, the Dutch or the Swiss. We all agreed enthusiastically with the outcome of the talks.

I later told Wimpie de Klerk: "Consensus is not just a dream. It becomes a reality as people start realising that there are bigger ideals and interests than narrow group-oriented issues. We're no longer talking as 'enemies', but as citizens of the same country and dreamers about a free, nonracial South

Africa." De Klerk replied: "Yes. If we work hard at preparing for a settlement, the actual process will go more smoothly and even more quickly." I
said, as an afterthought and an idea on which I would write a few rambling
paragraphs on the plane: "Willem, maybe we'll have to give credit to PW
Botha some day. Do you think the ANC and particularly Thabo Mbeki would
have started talking about negotiations if there had been a chance that they
could win the armed struggle? Did PW and Magnus's Total Strategy not
perhaps work after all, albeit unintentionally?" De Klerk replied: "I won't
tell other people about your question." On the plane, I didn't succeed in
structuring my thoughts about this matter coherently. I realised that it was
not a question that I liked.

# 7
## Flittwick: funeral for apartheid?

B arely three months later, from 17 to 19 December 1988, the fourth meeting of the unofficial Afrikaner-ANC dialogue group took place in Flittwick, Bedfordshire. Once again Mbeki, Pahad, Trew, Willem de Klerk, Terreblanche and I were the participants. At the Flittwick session, the agenda undesignedly took on the shape of the tip of a funnel. We had started off with a wide-ranging focus at our first meeting in 1987. Gradually the focus narrowed: releases and unbannings, and procedures and mechanisms to achieve these objectives in a way that would not heat up the political climate in the country. Eventually the focus became the creation of a climate that would be conducive to negotiations. It turned into a very intense discussion, although we started off bantering with each about the fact that 16 December was the Day of the Covenant, previously known as "Dingaan's Day", in South Africa. Pahad asked who in our dialogue group represented Piet Retief and who Dingane! I tried to mix the banter with seriousness and said that in our case the discussion was not about land, but about peace and reconciliation for all the rightful citizens of our country.[1]

I attended the meeting in Flittwick knowing that two pro-ANC groups from South Africa had visited Lusaka for talks during October: representative bodies of the Indian population group and of black soccer players. In the case of the former group, nine points were discussed: the political role and interest of the ANC in finding a "peaceful and lasting solution" to the South African crisis. Preconditions for this were the unbanning of the ANC, the release of political prisoners and the lifting of emergency measures. Other topics that were discussed included the armed struggle, communism, a post-apartheid economy, sanctions, the cultural boycott, religion, education and municipal elections. I realised: the majority of the Indian community would never accept the tricameral parliament, a variation of apartheid. They regarded themselves as part of the "oppressed". The soccer players shared the resistance to the apartheid system. Even rugby and soccer symbolised the racial divisions in the country.

The discussions at Flittwick had an underlying tacit subtext: the funeral of apartheid, with a farewell to a piecemeal or incremental reform process as prelude. It was in the bitterly cold surroundings of Flittwick, during a solitary walk to shake off my frustrations with the progress of the dialogue process, that I told myself: before one can bid "farewell to apartheid", one must first say goodbye to incremental reform. That day, with my ears burning from the cold, I deliberately and purposefully renounced the metaphor "farewell" and committed myself to another metaphor: "funeral".

As we sat chatting informally that evening in front of a cosy fire, I told Thabo Mbeki: "The NP and the ANC, together with other role players, must be the joint funeral directors for apartheid. Maybe then we'll start trusting each other." He looked at me and asked: "What you're really saying is that we should have a transitional period where we govern together and learn from each other?" Dumbfounded, I just nodded my head. As far as I can remember, it was the first time he talked about governing "together". This was not something that had crossed my mind at the time. Mbeki, true to his nature, said matter-of-factly: "It's something we need to think about. It will help to allay the 'white fears' to which you and Willem (de Klerk) always refer." He added ironically: "But of course we need to have the funeral first. You can't make funeral arrangements without a corpse." We both accepted that "transition" did not involve the gradual *phasing out* of apartheid measures. They had to be *abolished* before the formal negotiation phase of the transitional process.

The whole of November 1988 and the first three weeks in December were busy and even gruelling weeks. It was a juggling act to try to find a balance – and time – between my end-of-year university responsibilities and go-between roles. My family hardly saw me. On 28 November 1988 I had a meeting with Piet Müller of the magazine *Insig*. He had been one of the first Afrikaner journalistic explorers to venture on the road to Lusaka. And that as an employee of Nasionale Pers. As Piet Cillié put it to me in one of his cynical-ironic moments: "Along with the Bible and the Dutch Reformed Church, Naspers is a bastion of the Afrikaner." Adding as an afterthought as we enjoyed a late-afternoon brandy in his Crozier Street office in Stel-lenbosch:"You would of course call it an unholy trinity." His office building was next to that of the "philosophers", who were in turn next to Biblical Studies. Piet Cillié, from whom I learned a lot, was a master of irony. He enjoyed my quip that philosophy formed the balance between The Bible and *Die Burger.*

Piet Müller, whom I considered an exceptionally enthusiastic and far-sighted person, made me realise even better than before: incremental reform was a dead duck. There was neither the time nor the liberating vision for this approach. What we needed was *structural change, total transformation,* the death of apartheid and the birth of a new dispensation. After our conversation I had a different understanding of Thabo Mbeki's emphasis on a transitional process on previous occasions: *not* a phasing out of apartheid. On Tuesday, 29 November I also had an early-morning meeting with Koos Kruger and Hanna Langenhoven. Among other things, we talked about the scheduled dialogue session of the Consgold contact group in England. They ques-tioned me about the idea of a transitional process and what the ANC might put on the table in this regard if negotiations had to start. Kruger also want-ed more information on Margaret Thatcher's stance with regard to South Africa, Botha's reform initiatives and particularly the issue of sanctions. They also inquired about the interaction between her and US president George Bush in respect of South Africa and whether any clear picture and trend had emerged in this regard.

Fleur de Villiers turned 50 on 1 December 1988, and I went to London for a few days to attend her birthday party. Two days before my departure I had a meeting with British ambassador Robin Renwick at his request, and we had a long and incisive conversation. It became clear that the British government had lost all patience with PW Botha and was already specu-lating about "new blood". The brief visit to London confirmed Renwick's qualms about South Africa. In Thatcher circles, there was still the view that the consequences of comprehensive sanctions and disinvestment would be far worse than the injustices they were intended to protest against. Nor would these measures lead to radical political chance. Sanctions and dis-investment on their own would not bring about political change and the

end of apartheid. The South African government and especially the ANC
as the biggest liberation movement had to accept that a negotiated settlement was in the best interest of the country and all its people. There was
worry in Thatcher circles that the political gains of the Conservative Party
(CP) among white South African voters in cities such as Boksburg, Springs
and Pietersburg at the municipal level would result in a hardening of
attitudes among blacks.

The major concern, however, was that the NP would put on the brakes
politically to preserve its support base. According to Renwick, it was even
being mooted that British companies should terminate their interests in
CP-governed areas. A few days later I heard a similar view in London: "Let
them choose their own isolation. Make an example of these areas. Invest in
cities and towns that disregard or remove apartheid measures." For the first
time I started wondering whether civil disobedience among South African
whites and particularly businesspeople might not be the most appropriate
way to help break the back of the apartheid system. I was also told that there
was "fury" in Whitehall (London) about the embarrassment that the South
African spy Olyvia Forsyth had caused the British government. Her codename was Lara, or Agent RS407. I heard about her for the first time from
Patrick Fairweather, the former British ambassador in Luanda, Angola, who
had been promoted to assistant undersecretary of State, Foreign and Commonwealth Office.

Forsyth, who had studied at Rhodes University in Grahamstown, had
been recruited by the South African security police. At Rhodes, she posed
as a fiery activist and infiltrated leftist organisations, including the National
Union of South African Students (Nusas). She was sent to Angola to infiltrate the ANC. In 1988, however, she was caught out and landed in an ANC
prisoner camp, where she had a hard time. She managed to escape and sought
refuge in the British embassy. It became an enormous embarrassment for
the ambassador and for the British government. Eventually she was re-
united with her father in Britain, where she also settled. At one stage it was
claimed that she had been "turned" and then started spying for the ANC. But
Mbeki denied to me that this was the case.

Besides the conversations in Britain, there were also other shifts in the

British capital that were conducive to a negotiated settlement. The British role in the facilitation of a settlement should not be underestimated. For one, Thatcher had "adjusted" her attitude towards the ANC. Whereas she had previously equated the ANC to the Irish Republican Army (IRA), she said by the end of 1988 that the two could not be compared. The members of the IRA were entitled to vote. They could make their voice heard through the ballot box. The ANC did not have the right to vote, some of its leaders such as Nelson Mandela were still in prison, and the ANC and other organisations were banned. She also believed that President George Bush, who had succeeded her good friend Ronald Reagan, unfortunately had a "flexible backbone" when it came to sanctions and disinvestment as a means of pressuring South Africa. Her earlier more positive attitude towards President PW Botha hardened more and more.

South Africa's alleged involvement with Renamo really peeved her. Even the Helderberg disaster, when a South African Boeing crashed into the sea, raised questions on the part of Thatcher and her advisers that pointed to a growing distrust of the Botha government. In Whitehall there was still a critical stance against ANC-inspired violence. But the view that the ANC was a political organisation was increasingly being advanced in British government circles. After all, at that stage the British, like the Americans and the Russians, were the strong driving forces behind the settlement process in Angola-Namibia. An election in Namibia was the primary goal, with Swapo – who had fought side by side with the ANC in Angola against the South African Defence Force – one of the main participants. This context was a hefty political and moral boost for the pro-negotiation ANC.

★ ★ ★

The Flittwick dialogue session began with a sombreness that was not only due to the winter weather. Thabo Mbeki was not his former disciplined and businesslike yet friendly self. He did not seem to have much appetite for the discussions. He remarked half abstractedly to me that they (Lusaka, Tambo) had decided to bring "new blood" to the meetings. But first we needed to talk seriously, both privately and within the group, about the question: Where do we stand with the dialogue? Mbeki, not someone who sets much store by social gatherings and trivial conversations, was visibly impatient. He wanted me to give him signals of progress. I emphasised once again: "I'm just a go-between with no mandate or official status." He said, slightly irritated: "But you did create expectations on my part. That's logical after all. And human. Tambo and I seek clearer signals. There are too many confusing signals." He referred in this regard to all the "messages" he kept getting from Afrikaners at conferences and seminars. Yet the messages came to nothing. The only impression he got was that there were no Afrikaner opinion leaders left who supported apartheid. Even Idasa was not getting around to facilitating anything concrete towards what could become an actual settlement process.

I figured out immediately what the problem was. I realised that I had created scope for expectations when I told him about my Pretoria connection, and also understood that his knowledge of what was happening in Angola-Namibia and his many other contacts with leaders and with South Africans such as Idasa, Rosenthal, people from the South African Rugby Board, journalists and academics, inevitably created expectations. But that the real expectation in his mind was informal contact with official representatives of the South African government. He knew this was where the real key lay, and he sought clear indications that this contact process was being put in place. We talked it over and agreed that this issue had to be discussed within the group session as well, without giving any detail. It was, after all, at this time that Nelson Mandela was moved to the Victor Verster Prison and installed in a comfortable house equipped by Niel Barnard's people.

The subsequent discussions at Flittwick proceeded on a decisive note. It was agreed that the talks had *no* official status. It was merely a dialogue process, not negotiations. No one had any mandate on behalf of an organisation or, in the case of the Afrikaners, a supporting minister or government department. At one stage I was tempted to take the dialogue group fully into my confidence. Mindful of Fleur de Villiers's advice, however, I decided that this was not yet the opportune moment. There are no fixed rules as to when such an "opportune moment" arises. It depends on one's subjective evaluation of the situation, on the agreed objectives of the primary players, and especially on the quality of the relationship of trust that exists among all participants.

The parties to the dialogue agreed that it was worthwhile to hold these discussions. Dialogue was the front door to possible negotiation processes. Mbeki was also of the opinion that the interlocuters should invite at least "two new faces" for the next round. He felt very strongly that more effort had to be put into creating a climate that would be conducive to negotiations, for instance by releasing political prisioners, unbanning the liberation movements and internal organisations, and making progress with prisoner exchanges. We, the Afrikaners, supported him with great enthusiasm. I thought to myself: "How strong is the pressure that is being exerted from Moscow by President Gorbachev in this regard? Are Thatcher, Kohl and the Russian president perhaps working together?" Mbeki later referred to a meeting between himself, Tambo and Gorbachev.

During the morning tea break on the first day, Mbeki drew me aside and said: "Have you noticed that there is a decrease in violent actions in South Africa? It was a direct command from Lusaka. We are regaining control. Please convey that to Pretoria." My heart went out to Mbeki. For the first time he looked slightly vulnerable, as if he was trying to convince himself but seeking affirmation from me. I realised: the two of us needed each other. In a certain respect we were interdependent. The two of us were discovering, without being sentimental about it, that we faced each other not as "enemies", but as partners in a common dream of a peaceful future.

The discontent in ANC ranks during the first phase of the dialogue sessions had also been fuelled by other matters: the "small dividend" yielded by the ANC's meeting with "Doc" Danie Craven of the South African Rugby Board; the poor reaction to Idasa's conference together with Russian experts; the failure of attempts "on the part of a foreign government to establish contact between Lusaka and Pretoria". These experiences were examples of frustrated expectations, and also an illustration of the desire on the part of the ANC's pro-negotiation elements to make a breakthrough in the direction of official negotiations. Mbeki's reference to a "foreign government" related to the Rosenthal-Switzerland project. He had regarded this project with a measure of seriousness and hope. Rosenthal was desperate by this time. Firmly convinced that he had a mandate from Botha and Stoffel van der Merwe, he now wanted to have a meeting with Niel Barnard. He even left messages at Barnard's office. Two members of the NIS met with him, first Mike Kuhn on his own and later also together with Koos Kruger. Rosenthal hoped he could meet Botha personally via Barnard. He drafted a memorandum that he wished to submit to Botha. Early in November 1988 the memorandum was ready, and he and Kuhn arranged a meeting at the Holiday Inn in Pretoria's Arcadia suburb.

It became the stuff spy thrillers are made of! Rosenthal took all possible precautions in case something serious befell him. He met with the Swiss ambassador and informed him. He also gave copies of his memorandum, in which he explained the project, to Stoffel van der Merwe. Van der Merwe was of course extremely worried about the implications of all of this for his own future. After all, he was the one who had set something in motion for which he did not really have a mandate. Be that as it may, Kuhn and Kruger had a meeting with Rosenthal in the hotel room. The Swiss, excited about the key role they expected to play, talked to Rosenthal early in December 1988. Still believing that he (Rosenthal) had received a mandate of some kind from PW Botha, albeit through Stoffel van der Merwe, even the Swiss were convinced that they had to take the initiative to get the negotiation process off the ground. Rosenthal was also very encouraged by a letter written by the administrative secretary of Botha's office on 11 November 1988 in reply to Rosenthal's letter of 3 November 1988 and his memorandum. The letter stated that Botha was unfortunately too busy to give him a hearing, but that he had to liaise with Stoffel van der Merwe.

Whether Botha ever saw this letter of the administrative secretary as well as Rosenthal's letter and memorandum is highly doubtful. It seems more likely that confusion might have been involved here, or perhaps deliberate deception for whatever reason. Rosenthal and the Swiss, however, had reason to believe that they were on the brink of a great historic moment. On 6 December 1988, Barnard intervened in the political fiasco. He wrote that he had studied Rosenthal's "very interesting document" and taken note of the state president's letter of 11 November 1988. He appreciated Rosenthal's concern and his efforts to do something about "a most delicate issue". However, Barnard wrote, "I must ask you to desist from further action and to trust the judgement and capabilities of the relevant official instances." When

I found out later about these developments, I understood Mbeki's dissatisfaction during our meeting.

★ ★ ★

Thabo Mbeki told me privately about another matter that upset him: prisoner exchanges. In the grounds of the centre, while the weather was bitterly cold and dismal, he gave me a detailed account of the fate that had befallen the spy Odile Harrington. Harrington had been recruited as an agent for the security police around 1986. Her father was a medical doctor and her mother an artist. She was naive, but also adventurous. After her training she had been sent to Zimbabwe from where she was supposed to infiltrate the ANC. She presented herself as a political refugee, and was placed in a safe or transit house where she was monitored to determine whether her motivies were genuine. She did some stupid things, such as posting letters to her "handler" in South Africa from a post box close to the house. She was caught out and ended up in a Zimbabwean prison where she was subjected to extreme forms of humiliation.

This was one of the many occasions where Mbeki showed his heart. I was appalled at the atrocity both the South African and the Zimbabwean security services had committed against this naive individual, and was filled with an unprecedented combination of fury and disgust. Whenever I think of it today I get upset all over again, also because of my inability to have done anything about the situation. Mbeki asked me: "Can you do something about this? President Robert Mugabe himself has taken cognisance of it. There are also three other spies who have received death sentences in Zimbabwe. And then there is the McBride case in South Africa. If 'flexibility' prevails, we might come to acceptable arrangements." Mbeki, extremely upset, said: "It's a case we can do something about together. Mugabe is prepared to release her and a few other cases if South Africa closes down the radio transmitter in the north of the Transvaal that broadcasts anti-Mugabe propaganda to Zimbabweans." I made inquiries about this transmitter, with no success. Even people at ministerial level knew nothing about such a radio station. Many months later, with the help of Mof Terreblanche – a later participant in the dialogue group – it emerged that there was indeed such a transmitter. Ministers were deliberately kept in the dark so that they had the possibility of denial and could say "We didn't know", a typical manoeuvre in totalitarian states where accountability is of necessity on a very loose footing. I made the Harrington tragedy a very personal matter. She had been thrown to the wolves, I told Koos Kruger. "And now they deny any moral or political responsibility. It's a disgrace, and a blot on my own name." Kruger addressed me by my codename: "Gert, you need to distance yourself from this. You don't know the security police. There are bigger things you have to attend to." I did not listen to him, and during 1989 I continued with my efforts to do something about her situation together with Mbeki.

In the end President FW de Klerk was instrumental in helping to resolve Harrington's situation.

★ ★ ★

During the dialogue session we talked incisively about the political situation in South Africa. The so-called municipal elections had taken place in October. The possibility of a new party (the DP) was being mooted, and events relating to the Delmas Treason Trial had generated much publicty. This long-running trial had started in October 1985 and only came to an end in November 1988. "Terror" Lekota and Popo Molefe of the UDF were among the leaders who had been accused of intending to violently overthrow the state and of being surrogates of the ANC. They were found guilty, but a year later the judgment was set aside on appeal, on account of a technical problem. The commutation of the sentences of the Sharpeville Six was another talking point. It stood to reason that the ANC interlocutors were excited about the possibility of a new party. But the ANC members did not think highly of Denis Worrall. In their view, he was a prime example of a political opportunist. A few weeks before our meeting he had tried to make contact with the ANC in London, Mbeki said. The ANC, however, did not want to meet him. "Too liberal and English," said Pahad. Esther Lategan and Wynand Malan were rated highly. But not the PFP. It was "in collusion with big capital", Trew said with a wry smile. The following year, in April 1989, the PFP disappeared and the Democratic Party (DP) was born.

Thabo Mbeki raised a tricky question during our meeting: Will the party that is to be established, if it should get parliamentary representation, put the case of the extraparliamentary opposition in parliament? Will it say, under the protection of parliamentary privilege, what Cosatu and the ANC think? And, for example, raise the constitutional guidelines that have been adopted by the ANC in parliamentary debates? While looking at Willem de Klerk, he asked: "Will the new party merely engage in 'system politics', or help to promote the 'politics of the liberation struggle'?" We Afrikaners were at a loss for words. Willem de Klerk attempted a diversionary manoeuvre and referred to the government's idea of a more inclusive "National Forum" in which blacks would be involved. The normally dispassionate and rational Thabo Mbeki sounded annoyed. Such a forum already existed, he maintained: the extraparliamentary opposition. Instead of a forum, progressive whites should support the existing extraparliamentary movements. After this exchange Mbeki and his comrades did not seem impressed with the prospects of the yet-to-be-established new party. He told me privately: "Pretoria is the institution the ANC will have to talk to."

The NIS always took a great interest in what was referred to as the *profile* of the ANC interlocutors: their personal characteristics, the issues they felt strongly about, their habits and particularly their power of reasoning. At the Flittwick meeting I observed Thabo Mbeki closely. He was a good listener and thought before he spoke. Aziz Pahad was more spontaneous. Talked with his hands as well, especially when we socialised informally around good Scotch whisky and South African wine. During the formal meetings, Mbeki listened attentively and made notes, as I did. Before speaking, he would fill his pipe. This was a ritual that could take up to a few minutes. I soon realised that, on the one hand, it was intended to get his thoughts neatly and logically structured, and, on the other, to get his interlocutors' undivided attention. We usually sat watching on tenterhooks as he slowly and carefully filled his pipe. Everyone knew that what he would say would be authoritative within the broad context of ANC thinking and ANC policy. He spoke in a reasoned and very logical manner. Cut through the many words we used in the sometimes wide-ranging discussions and captured their essence. He also gave his views, always in terms of ANC thinking, ANC policy documents and prevailing international schools of thought. If anyone interrupted him, he listened patiently and then took up the thread of his argument at the point where he had been interrupted. He drank his whisky in the same way as he filled his pipe: unhurriedly, ritualistically.

At this meeting, Mbeki and Pahad briefed us comprehensively on attempts during the past two years (1987-1988) to get strategic clarity on the "broadening of the opposition against apartheid". Discussions in this regard were held with church leaders, community leaders, trade-union leaders, academics and businesspeople. Two questions were debated:

- How broad is broad? Should it also include, say, Inkatha and its leader, Mangosuthu Buthelezi? This organisation is not yet regarded as acceptable. There is good liaison and cooperation with Enos Mabuza and his party. He has already been accepted as part of the broad opposition against apartheid.

- Should parties that participate in the political system in parliament be included too? Should there not be selective participation in the system to undermine it from within? To render it unworkable? Can business organisations perhaps be mobilised, such as the Consultative Business Movement (CBM) of people like Christo Nel?

A broad-based conference around these questions had been planned to take place in South Africa, but the envisaged meeting had to be abandoned as a result of the bannings and restrictions imposed on various organisations. Pahad stated that they were now looking at the role churches could play. He looked at me earnestly and asked: "Do you think the Dutch Reformed Church will be able to play a role?" Sampie Terreblanche, Willem de Klerk and I looked at him in mute amazement. De Klerk said: "Well, luckily I'm not a member of the Dutch Reformed Church."[2]

Thabo Mbeki was never anti-Afrikaner during the talks. He accepted that the mediation and negotiation process primarily had to take place between the ANC and the Afrikaner regime. His second dream was: how could the ANC and the Afrikaners cooperate with each other to build a new South Africa and eradicate poverty?

He had an understandable obsession with the issue of poverty and socio-economic (racial) inequalities. This was to him the principal stumbling block on the path to lasting reconciliation and peace. Later, after he had become president, I supported him on his speech on South Africa's "two nations", the one rich and white, the other black and poor. At Flittwick he told me privately: "The contrast is the real problem. If we don't address that in an acceptable way in future, black people, once they have political power, will find any way whatsoever to gain access to wealth too." On this occasion he also said something that would cause me many sleepless nights: "Liberation from a dictatorship inevitably also entails corruption. South Africa's liberation will be plagued by corruption. People who have been oppressed and disadvantaged economically argue that they lost a great deal in the past. Hence they believe they are entitled to 'make up for it'." Later he elaborated on this point and referred to African states whose post-independence elites had enriched themselves at the expense of the poor. "South Africa," he said with passion in his voice, "must avoid this at all costs once the country is free: self-enrichment and corruption will be a betrayal of what the ANC has struggled for. But how are we going to redistribute wealth in a democratic state and progressively eliminate the gaps created by apartheid?" I could not give him an answer. In this conversation was the germ of something that would cause a serious crisis years later: affirmative action and the economic empowerment of disadvantaged (black) people.

In the discussions at Flittwick, the question of the release of Nelson Mandela and other political prisioners was once again dominant. This time it was not only related to the unbanning of all liberation movements, but also to the issue of violence as a means of furthering political objectives. The Afrikaner participants heard for the first time that there was a possibility of a "temporary suspension of the violence option". Willem de Klerk could not disguise his excitement. Mbeki said, rather vaguely, that the ANC might announce something in this regard in January 1989. I told myself: Mikhail Gorbachev's 'signal' has been picked up. Without his cooperation, the ANC is lost. And I told myself too: once the imprisoned leaders of the ANC and other organisations have been released, the violence issue can also be dealt with. The key was the release of political prisoners and unbannings.

I discussed this with Thabo Mbeki in private. He agreed with me whole-heartedly and asked: "Will you report that to Barnard?" I told him: "I'm just a go-between. If you say I can convey such a message, I'll do it." He replied: "Do it." When I talked to Koos Kruger about it, he said: "It's obvious, isn't it, that with this move the ANC wants to intensify domestic and interna-tional pressure on the Botha regime to release political prisoners. The ball is therefore in the Botha government's court." I said: "Yes. It's inevitable. The question is not 'if'. The question is 'when'." Kruger asked me why I believed that. I was reluctant to tell him. Thabo Mbeki had told me something pri-vately that I had assumed to be merely a speculative possibility. He did not say that it was confidential. The ANC had considered the idea of trying a sort of PLO (Palestine Liberation Organisation) option against "Pretoria" by the end of 1989 by declaring that it favoured negotiation and renounced ter-rorism as a way of achieving political aims. The ANC would then request a peace conference with "Pretoria" and use Angola-Namibia as an example. The British, the Americans, the Russians, Germany and France would sup-port this and exert further pressure on South Africa. Mbeki added: "The British and countries of the European Economic Community are already talking to representatives of the PLO. It's part of a process of legitimising the PLO."

I looked at him in astonishment and said: "I don't believe you." He re-plied unemotionally: "Between 1989 and 1990 the ANC will gain stronger international legitimacy as a liberation organisation. The Angola-Namibia settlement makes it inevitable. Those negotiations have sunk apartheid. Tell your contacts: the sooner we talk, the better." I was still sceptical. In a some-what paternal tone, Mbeki said: "The ANC's chief trump card is not the armed struggle. It's the political struggle – internationally and nationally. PW and Magnus can't win. Even if we have to move our military camps out of Angola, it will have no effect on the political struggle. The Nkomati Accord with Mozambique was just a temporary political and military setback for the armed struggle. We found other access routes. You can't imprison the dream of freedom or demolish it with cannons. Haven't you read Grams-ci?" With a helpless expression, I said: "I hear what you say. And I know Gramsci, the Italian communist whose ideas weren't locked up with him in a prison cell." I thought I could take the wind out of his sails: "As a *verligte* Afrikaner, I endorse Gramsci's views. We *verligtes* know what power and cultural hegemony are all about. It's time for you to pay more attention to the Afrikaner nationalists than to the liberalists." He laughed. "That's exactly what I'm doing. I know they are the people I may have to negotiate with some day." He trumped me: "The Botha government is seeking acceptability in the wrong places, such as PW Botha's visit to President Mobuto of Zaïre."

After this visit Mobuto had tried to arrange a meeting with Oliver Tambo. He was even prepared to travel to Lusaka to explain the meeting with Botha. Mobuto was keen to act as an intermediary between Botha and the ANC. Tambo refused to see Mobuto, however. PW Botha's state visit to Zaïre was a political gimmick. Mbeki, not one to mince his words in order to feign goodwill, said: "Africa and the ANC already have a veto right over what can and must happen in South Africa. There's not really much more your government can do to escape from the stranglehold in which apartheid has placed you. PW Botha knows this. But he doesn't want to accept the only gate out of his dilemma and open it wide. This gate is the release of all political prisoners and the unbanning of liberation movements. Are you prepared to convey this message in strong terms to National Intelligence?" I let on that I was enthusiastic about this message. Indeed, it had already been conveyed.

One thing became very clear during this dialogue session: the ANC had full knowledge of all interactions between the South African state and countries in Africa. Willem de Klerk said almost despairingly: "But do you think you are the arbiter of South African affairs?" Pahad asked: "Why not?" Mbeki then came out with a fascinating story that left us, the three Afrikaners, politically shell-shocked. "The British high commissioner in Lusaka and the ANC leadership are talking to each other. Messages are already being exchanged between Lusaka and London. The ANC representative in London will attend our dialogue group one day. There has already been contact between him and a senior British official." I suspected later that it had been my good friend Patrick Fairweather. The contact was not regarded as "official". The explanatory phrase used was "functional to the interests of the relevant parties". These outreaches had an important motive: Margaret Thatcher wanted to end off her career with a significant contribution in Southern Africa, such as facilitating a settlement process in South Africa. She especially felt strongly about the release of Nelson Mandela. In fact, it was said: "She has passed this stage and is looking beyond the release of Mandela." She went even further, and stated apropos of her frustrations with PW Botha's obduracy: "All degrees of patience with the RSA have been exhausted." And she was at that stage preparing herself for a trip to the frontline states. She was still refusing to meet Oliver Tambo, however, and was also disinclined to visit South Africa.

In the Flittwick discussions it became clear from the ranks of the ANC participants that the international consensus in favour of the abolition of apartheid had reached a peak. This perception had obviously given the self-confidence of the ANC representatives a great boost. The Afrikaner interlocutors were not on the back foot as such, but rather unsure of how and when the consensus could/should be acted upon. Our main argument was the question of "white fears", the nature of the transitional process, and issues such as affirmative action. To the ANC representatives, affirmative action was a non-negotiable given. The Afrikaner interlocutors supported it, but stressed the "how" aspect in particular. When the three of us had a post-mortem on the Flittwick meeting, we agreed that this gathering had highlighted one very specific issue within an international context: "The only way in which international recognition can come is on the back of majority rule," as Mbeki summarised it. This position was very far removed from that of the Botha government and its white support base. During one of our conversations, Möller Dippenaar made the valid point: "Surely the Botha government can't consider the release of Nelson Mandela and other political prisoners, and unban the ANC and other organisations, if there isn't a reasonable consensus on the political way forward. PW Botha and his party will *never* agree to black majority rule."

With this, delinking the process of releases and unbanning from prescriptiveness in respect of the constitutional negotiation process, such as the prior rejection of black majority rule, was on the table. Terreblanche was (prophetically) spot-on: "PW Botha first has to go." By 1988 the idea of black majority rule in South Africa was accepted in capitals such as London, Bonn, Paris and Washington. It just needed to be accepted in Pretoria.

In London and Washington it was stated plainly that once Namibia was independent "under a Swapo-controlled government", the writing would finally be on the wall for the "Botha-Heunis ethnic experiment". Patrick Fairweather made it abundantly clear that they were just waiting for Namibia's independence before starting to push on the "pressure points" in South Africa. Thatcher, given her strong pro-Mozambique stance, was incensed about British intelligence reports that confirmed the South African Defence Force's involvement with Renamo. Her question, which I passed on to the NIS, was brief and to the point: "Won't Magnus Malan also attempt to sabotage Resolution 435 on Namibia without PW Botha's knowledge in the same way that he and his hawks are sabotaging the Nkomati Accord?" This question placed the focus very sharply on the will and ability of the South African government to observe agreements.

Following the Flittwick meeting, Mbeki, Pahad, Terreblanche and I met in London in the company of Annemarie and my teenage daughter Liza in the flat Fleur de Villiers had arranged for us. Mbeki had a long conversation with my daughter who was guarded at first, but then gradually became more animated. After his departure she said: "Surely Thabo Mbeki can't be a terrorist? In *Die Burger* ANC terrorists are portrayed as black men with thick lips, knives, hand grenades and guns. He's not like that. He's well dressed, and he talked to me about maths." I understood for the first time how newspapers "create" perceptions. Liza never told her best friends about this historic meeting for fear that she would be victimised at school. Mbeki had asked Annemarie, who was an enthusiastic supporter and organiser of the Independent Movement, whether she intended joining the new party that was to be established. She said: "No, I'm going to join the ANC." Mbeki reacted swiftly: "You shouldn't do that. It won't be in Willie's interest."

★ ★ ★

By the end of 1988 the Rosenthal affair was still not resolved. During our meeting Thabo Mbeki only referred to it in passing in a private conversation and also mentioned Van Zyl Slabbert's name. I inferred that he and

Slabbert had discussed the Rosenthal-Switzerland initiative, and that my name had cropped up as well. I did not question him on this, however. According to Rosenthal, Slabbert was very positive about the Rosenthal initiative. By then he was aware of the activities of the Afrikaner-ANC dialogue group, and even sounded Mbeki out about the possibility of merging this initiative with the Rosenthal-Switzerland initiative. I was astounded when I heard this. Presumably it related to the misconception that the Rosenthal-Switzerland initiative had been officially sanctioned. Rosenthal kept Slabbert fully informed about his initiative. Still convinced that he had a mandate for what he was doing, and enthusiastically supported by the trusting Swiss, Rosenthal wrote a long letter to PW Botha on 14 December 1988. He referred to the Swiss government's willingness to provide a venue in Switzerland for a secret meeting between representatives of the South African government and ANC members. This meeting should preferably take place before the end of January, according to the Swiss. The ANC, Rosenthal wrote, was prepared to attend such a meeting. There were just a few questions to which they would like answers, which included an indication that such an initiative was regarded with seriousness, as well as possible agenda items.

It was at this point that Niel Barnard decided: enough is enough. Barnard, not one to mince his words when he thought pleasantness would not do the trick, wrote Rosenthal a blistering letter on 19 January 1989. He referred to his previous letter in which he had requested Rosenthal politely to desist from further action. Despite this, Barnard wrote, Rosenthal still persisted in his "inopportune initiative". Barnard objected to the fact that Rosenthal even mentioned the names of the people from the NIS who had talked to him as motivation for what he was doing. He wrote: "You leave me no alternative but to react very bluntly: The issue involved is of such a delicate and complex nature that the Government will certainly not pursue it through third parties." Then came the mortal blow to the Rosenthal-Switzerland initiative: "least of all with the connivance of a foreign power".

That the Swiss government had fallen for the Rosenthal-Van der Merwe story and had even set target dates, was one of the most remarkable political and strategic miscalculations of the 1980s. The same could be said about Thabo Mbeki and Van Zyl Slabbert. The only explanation for this that I could come up with was the despondency and sense of powerlessness experienced by many role players during that decade. Straws were mistaken for political lifebuoys. The Swiss contacts were left with egg on their faces. The NIS — and for this Barnard should be credited — did not try to capitalise on the situation or unleash PW Botha on them or even on Stoffel van der Merwe. There were more important matters on the agenda.

Barnard and the NIS were strongly opposed to what he sometimes referred to as "civil diplomacy": efforts on the part of institutions, organisations and individuals from civil society to bring the state and the ANC in contact with each other and get them talking. It was seen as "meddling" and an "irritation". Barnard and the NIS had no objections to public debate and even contact. What riled them, as Koos Kruger once put it, was the "arrogant claim" that "self-appointed organisations and leaders" could and should act as "intermediaries" between the state and "revolutionaries".

That was why one of the first "ageements" reached between the NIS and the ANC during their confidential Swiss talks (12 September 1989) was about the exclusion of persons and bodies that were "outside" the informal and formal settlement process. In the case of the conflict in South Africa, there was no chance or even opportunity for external parties to bring or force the South African government to the negotiation table. Pressure was exerted, of course, but without direct mediation. The same applied to the ANC, except that the pressure from Moscow was very effective. When the South African government and the ANC finally decided to settle, they pulled the other, smaller players into the dynamism and thrust of the unfolding process — albeit struggling and kicking in some cases. The two main parties to the conflict, the government and the ANC, however, wanted to control all facets of the settlement process. And they succeeded in doing that.

★ ★ ★

On the flight back to South Africa I reflected on our meeting and became aware once again of the symbolic significance that Afrikaners attached to 16 December. On numerous occasions I had delivered addresses at ceremonies commemorating the Day of the Covenant across the country and even as far as South West Africa (Namibia), and had witnessed the deep emotions evoked by this day. I wondered about something that caused me a great deal of worry: "Have we made any progress since the frontier wars and my ancestors' long and arduous trek in search of freedom and better chances in life? Will we ever be able to integrate the story behind the Day of the Covenant and the Voortrekker Monument in the psyche of an apartheid-free fatherland in a manner that would not promote political divisions?" I made up my mind to ask Mbeki what he thought of Afrikaner monuments such as the Voortrekker Monument, and what the thinking of a black majority government would be with regard to Afrikaners' symbols and statues and the names they had given to towns and streets.

But I neglected to ask him these questions. After he had become president, I was confronted with them when I was appointed as a trustee of the Freedom Park.

# 8

# PW Botha in political decline

By the end of 1988 South Africa was stuck in a severe strategic impasse. There was indeed a strong international consensus on a way out of this impasse, but Botha and his government were intransigent. His and his government's conditions for a settlement process, especially the public renouncement of violence as a political weapon and the position of the SACP, were non-negotiable. It has to be emphasised, though, that the blame for the impasse should not be laid solely at Botha's door, albeit that the final responsibility rested with him as state president.[1] The majority of his cabinet and caucus supported him strongly. So did his electorate. Politically, they clung obstinately to the syndrome of "This is our country". The propaganda of the Total Onslaught, with the Soviet Union and the SACP topping the bogeymen list of all the many dangerous enemies, was very effective among most Afrikaners. Hence the popularity of Magnus Malan and his military.

Nelson Mandela, who had been involved in more structured talks with Coetsee, Barnard and Co since early 1988, was also growing increasingly impatient during the last months of that year. He did not want to talk only to Coetsee and Barnard, but to President Botha himself. His transfer to the Victor Verster Prison had created expectations on his part, too. At one point he told Barnard: "Botha is the one with the real power. Not you. I want to talk to Botha." Moreover, the black-on-black violence alarmed him and he was not getting any younger. Despite the ANC's official position that the regime had to initiate dialogue about a settlement and not the ANC leadership, he was prepared to take the risk to talk to Botha. When the initial dialogue initiative was leaked by a warder to Mandela's fellow prisoners, Walter Sisulu, Raymond Mhlaba, Andrew Mlangeni and Ahmed Kathrada, the latter in particular was appalled. Sisulu was not excited either. Mhlaba and Mlangeni were supportive. Mandela, informed of events in the Soviet Union, the possibilities that had been opened up by the settlement process in Angola–Namibia, and the pugnacity of the young crocodiles in the muddy ANC pool, knew that strong strategic initiatives were required to launch a settlement process in South Africa. He acted like a visionary leader. A Moses figure. And he accepted responsibility for his initiative.

In January 1989 Mandela started drafting a memorandum to President PW Botha. By March the document was ready to be submitted to Botha. It is important to note that the Mandela memorandum and its contents had neither been cleared nor discussed with the leadership of the ANC. Barnard, who by that time had held numerous discussions with Mandela, was well aware of the tenor of the memorandum. A facet of the memorandum that thrilled me when I eventually got to read it was the acknowledgment of the reality of group fears. Mandela was, however, adamant about the issue of majority rule in a unitary state. Thabo Mbeki later told me: "This is what we fought for."

Mandela was not in favour of group rights, a political pet of Botha's and initially also of his successor. But he acknowledged the fears of whites with regard to majority rule in a unitary state. It was an issue we had been talking about in the Afrikaner-ANC dialogue group since 1987. The memorandum stressed something that had become a consensus in the dialogue group as well: structural or constitutional guarantees to prevent that majority rule would result in the domination of members of minority groups. "How" was the big question. Botha clung very firmly to the idea of (ethnic) group rights. He disliked the word "apartheid" and was in his own way morally uncomfortable with racial discrimination. His distinction between "discrimination" and "differentiation" was an attempt to express this discomfort. He had strong feelings about groups. At a meeting of the Broederbond committee that had to look at a new constitutional dispensation, which had been chaired by Gerrit Viljoen and of which I had been a member, Piet Cillié asked Botha about black people's political rights. He had replied: "There are no black people. Only black nations." I once put it to Thabo Mbeki: "Whites have reason to fear the possibility of black revenge and retribution on account of their privileged position under apartheid." He did not like this remark one bit. This possibility of revenge, I argued, would be part of apartheid's legacy for a very long time. It is significant to note that when a shortened version of the memorandum became known, Govan Mbeki was apparently very quick to get on his political high horse. He did not even want UDF people to visit Mandela in the Victor Verster Prison.

* * *

In January 1989, while Nelson Mandela was working on his memorandum, fate intervened: PW Botha suffered a stroke. Even some of his supporters wondered in whispers whether this was perhaps "divine intervention". His grip on political power was weakening. His opponents inside and outside the NP started doing political calculations for different reasons. Most of his political friends and colleagues began to look at other sources of power and influence. The central question was: what will happen when the Great Crocodile is out of the way? Rumours that this had not been his first stroke even started doing the rounds. An earlier, less serious stroke had supposedly been kept from the public. The rumours probably arose when Botha, according to what someone told me, had once been examined late at night because of a twitch in his cheek.

Botha was under enormous pressure in this period. Margaret Thatcher, who used to support him subtly, was personally furious with him. He realised that he had been painted into a political corner. He was thoroughly aware of the strong international consensus on the conditions for a political settlement in South Africa. Reform measures he had instituted, had created high expectations and had boosted the international consensus. Botha knew that this consensus had to be responded to in a way that would not bring about a bloodbath in South Africa. He was unable to respond creatively, however, because he clung to *his* control over the process, the idea of incremental progress, and *his* view of groups that convinced him of the necessity of a form of partition.

National Intelligence, with Barnard and Louw the key figures, became increasingly concerned. The NIS had a specific plan for extricating the country from the strategic impasse. For that, the NIS needed the cooperation of not only the president but also the State Security Council (SSC) and the cabinet. The president was the chairman of both these institutions. There were also other interested parties: parliament, the South African Defence

Force, the Police and especially the Security Police. The right wing, I was assured on one occasion, was dangerous, but not strategically decisive. General Constand Viljoen, my informant told me, would be a key person in future.

Should PW Botha retire for health reasons and a new president be elected, the settlement strategy might be scuppered or deferred for a long time, depending on who the new leader was. This wait-and-see situation became very tense. On the other hand, it was said in some NIS circles, a change of leadership might be just the right medicine. In fact, Mike Louw was of the view that there would be no progress towards a negotiated settlement with PW Botha at the helm. Botha lacked the mental elasticity that would be required, according to Louw. Within the NIS the debate about the national security situation and feasible strategic options increased. All intelligence services worldwide work with a hierarchical process of collecting, processing, evaluating and integrating information. The person who ultimately gets the result of this process on his or her desk, and who has to evaluate the memoranda, must himself/herself be an expert with strategic abilities. He/she must be able to assess whether the results of the process and the importance of the memoranda that landed on the desk are, in fact, of strategic security significance. Rash scenarios and unsubstantiated information can lead to serious fiascos. I, for one, never doubted the ability of Barnard, Louw, Spaarwater, Dippenaar and Hanna Langenhoven to take well-considered strategic decisions. Numerous memoranda were put aside.

Following Botha's stroke, the top management of the NIS accepted that a change of leadership at the highest level was only a matter of time. After all, PW Botha had done something that was fate-determining for his political future, especially for someone who was besotted with power: he resigned as national leader of the NP on 2 February. Thus the man who had advanced from overzealous party organiser who had broken up many meetings of the erstwhile United Party to the powerful position of chief leader of the NP and president of the most prosperous state on the African continent, took a decision in February 1989 that would make his political downfall only a matter of time. Possibly he had pinned his hopes on finance minister Barend du Plessis, a loyal Botha supporter, to replace him as national leader. This might have been a political lifebuoy for Botha. Du Plessis, a former teacher, was not exactly popular among many business leaders.

Botha might also have had something else in mind: time and energy to have a firm and more direct political hand in the initial phase of the inevitable settlement process. He liked control. In fact, Niel Barnard, who arranged the meeting between Botha and Mandela on 5 July 1989, had persuaded him with the argument that Botha's name would be immortalised in history if he were to meet Mandela and get more directly involved in the initial phase of the settlement process. And it was also in May 1989 that the NIS requested me to meet Thabo Mbeki privately in London to pave the way for direct contact with the NIS. Botha, however, had miscalculated. In the battle for the chief leadership of the already struggling NP between Chris Heunis (constitutional affairs), Pik Botha (foreign affairs), Barend du Plessis (finance) and FW de Klerk, De Klerk triumphed over Du Plessis by eight votes out of a total of 130 NP members of parliament. De Klerk, a skilful and seasoned political strategist, had also outmanoeuvred Treurnicht in the conservative Treurnicht rebellion against Botha (1982). He was, as his brother Wimpie once put it to me, "both skilled in and intoxicated by the game of power".

It is instructive to take a brief look at the Treurnicht saga. My contact with people from the NIS expanded with time to incisive discussions on a variety of themes. Conservative politics in South Africa and the ultraright resistance frequently came under the microscope. In the eyes of many conservative Afrikaners PW Botha was not only a liberalist, but also a sellout. Even Koos van der Merwe, who later became an MP of the Inkatha Freedom Party, rebelled against Botha at the time. The tricameral parliament and the interpretation on the part of some NP supporters and *verligte* Afrikaners that it could lead to forms of power-sharing and even one government in the same country, triggered a split. Treurnicht was the chief spokesman against the idea of shared rule. Harsh words were spoken at an NP caucus meeting on 24 February 1982. A motion of confidence in Botha was supported by 100 caucus members and opposed by 22. Treurnicht, leader of the NP in the (former) Transvaal, believed he could mobilise support in those quarters. De Klerk saw through his plan, however, and persuaded Treurnicht to

first convene the executive council of the Transvaal NP. Without Treurnicht's knowledge, De Klerk invited Botha to attend the meeting. On 26
February, Treurnicht lost with 36 votes against 172. De Klerk's path to the
top was open.

Like Treurnicht seven years earlier, PW Botha found himself on a down-
ward slope politically after February 1989. And once again it was De Klerk
who proved to be decisive. De Klerk had his own political aspirations. As
a party that was hierarchical in both its thinking ("The Leader") and its
organisation despite a federal appearance, the NP was heading for an inevitable crisis. The ANC and the UDF, with internal problems of their own,
were jubilant about these developments — albeit that De Klerk was generally believed to be politically very conservative. It was argued in some ANC
and UDF circles that De Klerk's conservatism was a political bonus: it would
further consolidate resistance against "the system". Botha was of course still
the chairman of the influential and powerful State Security Council (SSC),
the central nervous system of the militarised apartheid state. Thabo Mbeki
was dumbfounded when I told him that De Klerk was not part of Botha's
inner circle. It was a bonus point for De Klerk, someone who on account of
his legal background had a certain respect for the idea of the rule of law —
albeit that he had hidden this particular light under an apartheid bushel for
a very long time. As tends to be the case with retrospection and memories,
many years later De Klerk was very negative about the SSC that had usurped
the cabinet's responsibilities. The SSC, it should be remembered, had not
been Botha's brainchild. It had been instituted as far back as 1972 by his
predecessor, BJ Vorster. John Vorster, a prime minister who doubted his own
leadership abilities, had not made much use of the SSC. Botha eventually
recreated the SSC in his own image, as a centre of coordinated power, a government ruling the government. To my knowledge, no one within Botha's
sphere of influence had protested against this. Especially not his ministers.

The SSC, with its great variety of supporting organisations that had been
cast over the country like a carefully woven web, was Botha's principal instrument of power. I, too, nearly found myself in trouble with this organisation at one point. It was reported that I was suspected of being a courier for
the ANC. This was not completely untrue. I once handed a personal letter by

Professor Johannes Grösskopf of SU's journalism department and his wife Santie to Thabo Mbeki to pass on to their son Hein. He had fled the country and was accused by Botha's police minister Adriaan Vlok, among others, of being implicated in bomb blasts. The Grösskopfs were being terrorised by the Security Police. When I heard about it, I offered to take a letter to their son with me on a trip abroad. General Johan Coetzee of the Security Police shielded me at the time. I knew him, and had a lot of respect for him as an individual. Apropos of the courier suspicions, he had stated: "The professor won't involve himself in subversive activities." When I later told him the story about the letter, he laughed heartily and said: "You think I don't know about everything you got up to? But you weren't guilty of subverting the state. Not even when you talked to Thabo Mbeki."

It was from about September 1988, as a result of the many conversations about political issues, that I gained a better understanding of the primary objective of intelligence work: insight into processes and trends, and not just people, so as to be able to give strategic advice to the state and its government. In Hanna's words: "Prof, we gather and study information in order to understand trends better, to try and manage them, and to take countermeasures with new strategies in good time if the state is threatened." Few things became as clear to me as the fact that an open society and a democratic state cannot exist without good intelligence services. Democracy creates opportunities for subversion. Even terrorism. Möller Dippenaar once remarked drily: "Proffie, the Security Police and the guys from Military Intelligence want to know who is going to plant a bomb where, so that the person can be caught or eliminated in time. We want to know that as well, of course, but we are more involved in the war of ideas." On one occasion someone quoted a statement that stuck in my mind like an inflammatory slogan: "Intelligence is knowledge of the enemy." There were few words I heard as frequently during this period as the word "enemy". This was not a word I had heard from my mother and father, and later in my theological studies, with reference to human beings. It was only used in a religious sense to denote "the Evil One".

Between 1985 and 1988 two competing and contrasting positions crystallised within the South African state: those of the fighters and the peacemakers; the gunmen and the negotiators. With the securocrats and the military having an inside track with PW Botha for many years, the gunmen were the power behind the throne. And their capability was excellent. One evening during a sociable braai at the Old Observatory in Pretoria, someone from the military sphere related to me in detail how they had managed to crack secret codes. Some foreign governments even made use of their services. He remarked: "Not much is told to the political leaders. They want to be able to say 'we didn't know'." The possibility of denial, of being in a position to absolve themselves by washing their hands in innocence, had been a planned manoeuvre. It was in this period that accountability eroded even further and state-sponsored hit squads, funded by taxpayers' money, were given free rein to target "enemies" of the state. Despite speculative press reports as well as a multitude of rumours in the public domain, officially a very effective iron cordon of silence was thrown around this matter. The chances that Botha was completely ignorant of what was happening were extremely slim. As "father" of the militarised system, he knew its inner workings like the palm of his hand. Presumably he was never briefed "officially", which is a rule of the game of the cordon of silence. FW de Klerk, like most of his cabinet colleagues, definitely did not know. The real question, however, is rather: did they suspect it, and what did they do about their suspicions? After all, as members of the cabinet they were collectively accountable. Given their fear of Botha, presumably they lacked the courage to ask the right questions. Thabo Mbeki and I also sometimes discussed the use of violence and death squads on both sides of the political battlefield. Our consensus was that we were extremely concerned about this, and that it had to be made redundant.

Like the NIS, Mbeki and I later speculated about what the consequences of Botha's stroke and his relinquishment of the role of NP leader might be for South African politics. De Klerk's speech on his acceptance of the position of chief leader was scrutinised from all angles, as were some of his subsequent speeches. The NIS was not a lackey of the state or the ruling party that parroted official propaganda, although this facet sometimes filtered through in presentations I attended. The notion of the Total Onslaught and the Total Strategy was salient in this regard. This was once explained to me at the Old Observatory as a core doctrine of PW Botha's security policy that was above criticism. However, critical noises within the NIS were not unusual or taboo. Neither was debate, especially among the research staff, which was encouraged in my presence. But the Total Onslaught and the Total Strategy had set certain parameters within which the NIS had to operate. Botha, a former minister of defence, was totally enamoured with this doctrine.

This issue became a central debating point during 1989 apropos of De Klerk's advance to the political top. There was consensus in the circles in which I moved: De Klerk accepted that South Africa was stuck in a strategic impasse. Would he be capable of leading the country out of this impasse, given his obsession with group rights? Exposed to the discussions with Thabo Mbeki, Pahad and Trew, I repeatedly defended the view that the NP's anticommunism and De Klerk's idea of group rights stood no chance of being taken seriously either in a pre-negotiation preparatory phase or in the negotiation process itself. These positions should rather be taken off the table beforehand. It gradually emerged from the discussions that the involvement of the SACP would be a bigger problem than the NP's notion of group rights and group protection. The NP's constituency, I was told, had been indoctrinated "to the marrow" with anticommunist propaganda. I realised that the "myth of the enemy" had become an absolute and even last justification for Afrikaner power and Afrikaner self-preservation.

There was also another, institutional reason for De Klerk's conservative image. He had been included in the NP government's cabinet as a minister in 1978 and served in various portfolios. In 1982 he became NP leader in the then Transvaal. This was a powerful position. Then, in 1986, he was appointed chairman of the ministers' council of the "white" component of the tricameral parliament. Hence he had to exercise leadership over "white affairs" (interests). This institution, from which black Africans were excluded, was in many respects a time bomb that was waiting to explode. [2]

The news of PW Botha's stroke, his abdication as leader of the NP, and FW de Klerk's election provoked a sense of frustration in me that I was unable to cope with at first. I thought to myself: Our country is heading for more bloodshed. The fermentation processes in the direction of a negotiated settlement are going to be slowed down by a leadership struggle within the NP. The dialogue initiative between Coetsee, Barnard and Mandela, and that of the Consgold group, will stall. On 1 March 1989 I wrote in my diary: "Dancing like frenzied people on the edge of the abyss." The same day I had a meeting with Kruger. The next two days I had to deliver lectures at the NIS headquarters on "Mutations of Marxism" and "Euro-Marxism". I told Kruger: "A cloud of dejection is hanging over me. The possibility of dialogue about negotiations with the ANC is dwindling. At times it feels as if my mind is swaddled in a thick blanket of panic. I don't know what to do. I want to write something for a newspaper, but I don't know what." Kruger seemed unperturbed: "Gert, you have to be your own person. Write something to clear your head. I trust you. Just don't cause unnecessary trouble."

On 5 March 1989 an article of mine appeared in *Rapport* under the heading: "Talking to the ANC". The subheading read: "The rest of the world doesn't regard the ANC as a terrorist organisation, and in future the focus will fall increasingly on dialogue between the RSA and the ANC. " I concluded the article with: "Bullets and gunpowder may well be a last resort at times. But instead of resolving political problems, they exacerbate them in most cases. In short, the time has come for serious new reflection and initiatives." I got a phone call from Kruger: "You're sticking your neck out too far. It can be chopped off. And you go too far when you say it's time to at least have a discussion about the issue of the renouncement of violence. This is something that should be discussed very informally, not in newspapers. But you're the one who said it. Stand by your convictions." The following month, during the meeting of the Afrikaner-ANC dialogue group, I discussed the article with Thabo Mbeki. He said: "We [the ANC] know what you think. You don't need to make public statements. You have more important work to do."

How strong the international consensus was, came home to me during a conference at Wilton Park in Britain between 7 and 10 March 1989. It took place after Botha's stroke and his resignation as head of the NP. Without anyone raising it blatantly and directly as an important agenda point, there was an unspoken consensus: Botha is on the way out. The question was when, and what the political consequences of his departure would be for the inevitable settlement process. A central question, too, was how the conservative FW de Klerk would respond to the international consensus on a settlement. This question cropped up repeatedly in the private conversations during the conference. The views on De Klerk's will and ability to produce a breakthrough were predominantly negative.

The theme of the programme said it all: "Namibian independence as a dynamic element in the search for a regional settlement in Southern Africa and peaceful change inside South Africa". When I saw the guest list, I told Fleur de Villiers, who had also been invited: "The game is up for apartheid." Among those present were people like Chester Crocker of the US, who had played a decisive role in the settlement process in Angola–Namibia. He noted that the "human factor" had made a significant contribution to that settlement process. And he explained: "The negotiators discovered that they could work together, that they could understand each other, that everyone could gain something, and that the US and the Soviet Union were also in agreement about how the process had to be conducted." Franca Van-Dunem, Angola's justice minister and a former law professor, related how he and the South Africans had communicated with each other in Dutch and Afrikaans at times.

Patrick Fairweather (Britain), Enos Mabuza (South Africa), Dikgang Moseneke (South Africa), Yuri Yukalov (Soviet Union), Van Zyl Slabbert (South Africa), Pieter de Lange (South Africa) and representatives from Japan, Mozambique, Zambia, Botswana, Zaïre, Tanzania, Nigeria, France and Canada were among the conferees. On this occasion black South Africans did not threaten to walk out because of the presence of representatives of the South African government, such as Sheila Camerer. The request from Lusaka's pro-negotiation circles had been: "Take part." Chester Crocker asked me: "How many months before Afrikaners start talking directly to the ANC?" I said: "I don't know. It depends on too many things that aren't yet clear." He looked at me with a slightly cynical smile: "Opportunities for negotiation require strategic timing. And the right players. Botha's not a player. He's a loner. Stake your future on De Klerk." I understood then what he had meant by his emphasis on the "human factor". Also his view that neither the US nor the Soviet Union could be prescriptive. They could only "facilitate".

From Wilton Park the focus of consensus-seeking shifted to Bermuda, where the well-known Washington-based Aspen Institute presented a Southern Africa Policy Forum for members of the US Congress and other invited guests. It was held at the Lantana Colony Club from 27 March to 1 April 1989. The conference was not intended to be a debate on the different views and positions on South Africa, but a forum where explanations could be provided and information exchanged. According to Dick Clark, the director of the institute, Congressmen and -women had to be put in a position to take informed decisions. Clark managed to get together a very interesting group of people that included, among others, Paul Sarbannes, William Gray and Howard Wolpe of the Democratic Party. Constance Morella and John Danforth were among those who presented the Republicans. Nancy Kassebaum (Republican) and Ted Kennedy (Democrat) were unable to attend, but gave their support to the dialogue project. The theme was: "South Africa – From conflict to resolution". Helen Suzman of the Progressive Federal Party, Koos van der Merwe of the Conservative Party and Piet Coetzer of the NP were among the people from South Africa who attended. Fikile Bam of the Legal Resources Centre in Port Elizabeth, Frank Chikane of the UDF and the South African Council of Churches, Sam Mabe of the *Sowetan* and Van Zyl Slabbert of Idasa were some of the speakers. There were also other prominent South Africans, such as Willie Breytenbach, Oscar Dhlomo, Geert de Wet, Helen Zille, Johan Maree and Ntatho Motlana, who would later become my chairman on the board of Metropolitan Life. At the Urban Foundation I had developed an exceptionally enriching relationship with him and learned a good deal from him. Johan Maree, Helen Zille's husband, came from the Free State. I had met him years before at the University of Sussex. Together with Peter Hain, he had been instrumental in making a nightmare of the Springbok rugby tour that was captained by my good friend Dawie de Villiers.

Bam had to speak on the theme "Through black eyes: South Africa today", and my topic was "Through white eyes: South Africa today". The conference was abuzz with excitement because the ANC, led by Thabo Mbeki, was due to arrive later. Mbeki would give a brief overview of the conflict in South Africa from the ANC's perspective. The news about the ANC's attendance had caused a panic before the conference: What should be done about Stoffel van der Merwe, a minister of the Botha government, who was one of the invited speakers? PW Botha, then still president and chairman of the State Security Council, made an arrangement: the NP's attendance had to be downgraded from a government level to a party level. Ministers were not allowed to attend conferences at which ANC representatives were present, but a party representative could attend. However, this person had to fly out of the country as soon as the ANC flew in! They could share the airspace, but not the ground.

Piet Coetzer, who was at that stage the federal information director of the NP's Federal Council, the highest federal office in the party, was asked to attend the conference. Stoffel van der Merwe had summoned him to his office in the then Verwoerd Building in Parliament Street. Van der Merwe briefed him on the developments and said that Coetzer had to attend the Bermuda conference. Coetzer was also informed of the Coetsee-Barnard-Mandela "exploratory talks" by Van der Merwe. He said: "Later today you also have to talk to the president about your participation in the conference." Coetzer met Botha for about ten minutes. The president gave him no directives or detail about what he had to say at the conference. According to Coetzer, the following request by Botha was very illuminating: The ANC should renounce violence as a means of futhering political objectives. Probe them. If they are prepared to suspend violence as a means of furthering political objectives in order to start formal dialogue and eventually negotiations, it would be of great value. Coetzer never had any doubts that this was a "signal".

The Bermuda conference was the first public platform where Mbeki and I appeared together. But we only talked to each other in the privacy of my room. Fikile Bam, with whom I could speak Afrikaans and whose sister, Brigalia Bam, has meant a lot to me personally over the years, asked me at some stage: "Do you and Thabo know each other?" I said yes, but added: "Don't ask me how." It's not always possible to conceal a personal relationship of trust in public for strategic reasons. It often caused me severe inner conflict. This conflict nearly reached breaking point in Bermuda.

There was also another very personal and emotional reason for this:

Bermuda was one of my remembrance symbols of a (lost) freedom struggle, the first on our continent, that my fellow Afrikaners had fought against British imperialism. Visible evidence of this was the more than 140 graves of adult and young Boer warriors on an island of Bermuda. The visit to these graves was a profound emotional experience for me. "What an inhuman thing for so-called civilised people to do to others," I told myself. "To put prisoners of, say, the old Transvaal on a ship and transport them to Bermuda." Then it struck me like a Transvaal thunderclap as I stood beside the memorial stone: "But we as Afrikaners did not learn from our own experiences. Apartheid was another abominable form of colonialism and imperialism." Koos van der Merwe of the former Conservative Party (CP) was also responsible for drama. He was intensely interested in the history of the Boer prisoners of war on Bermuda and we were able to buy some of the artefacts they had made during their captivity. But he did not "fly out" when the ANC "flew in". As a result, the CP expelled him.

Fikile Bam came up to me where I stood at the memorial stone. He said: "I think I'm beginning to understand you. You're standing at the graves of your ancestors. Maybe one day when our country is free, we should gather the bones of our ancestors in foreign countries, such as Angola and Bermuda, and bury them at the Voortrekker Monument. Then we call it the 'Freedom Monument'." We walked away pensively, in silence. At the boat, I helped Helen Suzman to get on board. I wanted to tell her: "Helen, thank you for what you have done for our country, for its people and for me." I neglected to do that. Many years later I served on the board of trustees of the Freedom Park, the post-apartheid government's commemorative symbol of the new South Africa. Barely a stone's throw from the Voortrekker Monument. And we could not reach consensus on the names of the dead that should appear on the memorial wall. The day that I wrote my resignation letter, I cast my mind back to my visit to Bermuda and the Boer graves. Told myself: "I'm resigning for your sakes."

★ ★ ★

Meanwhile FW de Klerk was doing his political homework. As leader of the NP he swiftly expanded his political networks in the corporate world as well as internationally. He was not only a good speaker, but had also mastered the rules of logic much better than PW Botha. And he was not in the habit of losing his temper. The contrast between him and Botha gradually increased, as did the rift in the relationship between them. None of my contacts in the diplomatic world believed that Botha could survive politically. At a dinner in June on the 18th floor of the Naspers building in Cape Town, at a meeting of the Urban Foundation in Johannesburg and in conversations with NP parliamentarians there was an unspoken consensus: PW's political days were numbered.

There was another consensus as well: If De Klerk believed that incremental reform could resolve the political impasse, he, too, would meet his political Waterloo. De Klerk, one of his *verligte* fellow NP members told me, was very critical of the haphazard way in which reforms had been introduced thus far. In his view, there was a lack of vision and a clear plan. My informant expressed the hope that De Klerk would come up with something drastic to break the deadlock. When I told this to Washington Okumu of the Jubilee Initiative, he was sceptical. He asked: "Is De Klerk's critical attitude not perhaps due to the fact that he has realised that the haphazard reforms have unintentionally undermined a keystone of the NP's policy, namely group rights? Surely that's the real crisis in South African politics: the NP's attachment to its notion of group rights." I decided not to answer him. Only said that there was a process of settlement in the works that was surging ahead inexorably and that would leave the NP's set notion of group rights as driftwood in its wake. At that stage, of course, I had no way of knowing how the ANC intended to accomplish that.

# 9
## "Watch this space": the NIS makes a move

The year 1989 was one of South Africa's most historic years from a process perspective. In the course of this year the momentum of the international consensus, along with internal political processes, triggered a number of initiatives that would ultimately lead to the collapse of apartheid. This applied not only to the apartheid government and the formidable system of power and supporting organisations that had been built up over many years, but also to the ANC. The flame of the revolutionary hope of an armed seizure of power in South Africa was extinguished in 1989. A few hotheads desperately fanned the ashes in search of revolutionary embers. It was a futile stunt.

The start of the year saw a new phase in our lives for me and my family. Annemarie and I moved into a house next to the Goldfields student residence as resident wardens. Although it was reserved for blacks, generically, the residence at least accommodated both male and female students. The funds for its construction had been provided by the gold company Goldfields, a subsidiary of Consgold. Goldfields' intention to help establish a nonracial culture by means of this residence was thwarted. The SU rector Mike de Vries, who aimed to build beacons of nonracial hope on the campus, found his way blocked by apartheid walls, represented among others by FW de Klerk and later mainly the *verkrampte* Piet Clase, education minister in the House of Assembly in the then tricameral parliament. De Vries was even threatened with the downscaling of government subsidies.[1]

On Monday, 17 April 1989 I had a meeting with the British ambassador Robin Renwick. He was informed about the Afrikaner-ANC dialogue group in broad terms and more than once gave me good counsel. On that occasion I was on my way to England for another meeting of the dialogue group and wanted to check a few matters with him, including the effect of Botha's downscaled political position. Renwick was positive about De Klerk and remarked prophetically: "Even De Klerk can no longer hold out against world opinion on a settlement in South Africa." We also discussed the up-coming meeting of the Afrikaner-ANC dialogue group and possible agenda points. It was a great advantage that I had personal relations with the US, German and Dutch ambassadors as well. They were instrumental in keep-ing me well informed about the positions of their respective governments with regard to the conditions for a negotiated settlement, the urgency of a settlement, and especially who the main players in the process had to be.

In February 1989 two other meetings took place, one in Harare, Zim-babwe, and the other in Lusaka, Zambia. From 31 January to 4 February legal experts from South Africa held a conference with members of the ANC and Zimbabwean legal personalities on "The Role of Law in a Society in Transition". At this meeting the ANC's draft document on constitutional guidelines was discussed. There was consensus on the role of law prior to and after the start of a transitional period, the need for a new constitutional or-der, a bill of rights and an independent judiciary. The second meeting (on 24 February) focused on sport and mainly the consolidation of South Africa's isolation in this regard. This particular sanction, it was argued quite justly, hurt South Africa severely.

Between 21 and 24 April 1989 the Afrikaner-ANC dialogue group met for the fifth time, again at Mells Park. As soon as we were on our own, Thabo Mbeki asked: "When do you think the official dialogue can start?" I replied: "I don't know. It all depends on Niel Barnard." He said: "I've heard a lot about him. People often talk about him. Afrikaners from South Africa say he's an enigma. I'd like to meet him. We must involve Jacob (Zuma) in our discussions some time. He's involved with the ANC's intelli-gence service. MK has its own intelligence service, like Magnus Malan has his."[2] As brother of the new NP leader FW de Klerk and a participant in the dialogue, Willem de Klerk was inevitably the focus of the ANC members' attention. Mbeki, Pahad and Trew intimated that they were convinced that FW de Klerk would succeed PW Botha as president. The question was when and how. Late one night after a convivial dinner and everything that went with it, Pahad tried to assure me in a serious tone: "The ANC, too, has a problem. Oliver Tambo is not getting any younger. Nelson Mandela's in jail. We also have to start looking at successors." There was consensus at the meeting that the NP was embroiled in a fierce succession battle. The outcome of this battle would later determine the dynamics and rhythm of the negotiation process.

I thought to myself that while a new leader would no doubt be able to exercise choices, the internal and international context would constrain his discretionary powers. "Shoot-to-survive" was no longer an option. Thabo Mbeki stressed repeatedly during our private conversations: "It's of no real consequence who wins the succession battle in the NP. There is an international consensus on the conditions for a genuine negotiation process and the constitutional objective of a nonracial, democratic unitary state. The only question is what mechanisms and procedures should be used." The session of April 1989 once again brought it home to me unequivocally that the settlement process would primarily be a process between Afrikaners (the NP) and the ANC – the main parties to the conflict and in the South African constellation of power. Willem de Klerk, and that must be said to his credit, went out of his way on this occasion to boost his brother's image, using his formidable oratorical skills. His contrasting of his brother with PW Botha and the securocrats was excellent, and not far-fetched either. FW de Klerk, at that stage a conservative politician, did not suffer from a lust for power. He had respect for the dream of the rule of law, albeit in a limited way. Neither the majority of the NP nor Botha understood the first thing about this dream. It was true, though, and I say this reluctantly, that Willem de Klerk was his brother's superior intellectually. This caused certain tensions between the two.

At times Willem de Klerk's positive image of his brother created the impression that he was speaking on behalf of his brother, who was at that time still only the chief leader of the NP. His tactic was clear: he wanted to provoke Mbeki, Trew and Pahad. He spelled out four possible options for his brother:

- Little change, if any;
- A conservative shift to the right;

- A progressive shift to the left, but in calculated phases so as not to cause political resistance among whites; or
- Drastic and radical changes.

Willem de Klerk chose the third option as the most likely possibility. In his view, his brother was a pragmatic politician. He was conservative and wanted to keep "his people" with him. FW accepted that drastic change was inevitable. It would be "against his instincts", however, to summarily reject the racial model on which the NP's political thinking and incremental reform initiatives were based. He was not likely to topple this pillar of the apartheid temple abruptly. Willem explained bluntly: "The NP, as well as Botha himself, is threatened by mounting right-wing resistance among Afrikaners in its power base. A protracted and bitter power struggle will fuel this right-wing tendency. There is also uncertainty among Afrikaners about their future within a government system that accommodates blacks. As chief leader of the NP and as potential president, FW de Klerk won't be able to get too adventurous politically. The continuing violence in the country is in any case not conducive to an acceleration of the reform process." De Klerk's accentuation of right-wing resistance was a good tactical point. Rightists, and their influence in the Permanent Force and the Citizen Force, were a major source of concern for the ANC.

I watched Thabo Mbeki closely and saw his hope for the future sinking more and more. He asked me later: "Do you agree with him?" I said: "Yes, those are the four options. But which possibility becomes a reality will depend on what happens over the next six months. FW de Klerk will be forced to face choices of which he doesn't have the faintest notion at present. Like you and I, too. We are participants in a process. The strength of our hope and the exploitation of strategic opportunities might be factors that help determine De Klerk's choice." He regarded me sceptically and asked: "How long do you think we have to wait? Patience has limits."

The general election that was due to take place later that year was obviously an important talking point. I mentioned to Mbeki that De Klerk and his supporters would try beforehand to keep PW Botha out of the election campaign. One of the Afrikaner participants was of the opinion that the election had to take place before November, the month in which elections for a Constituent Assembly were scheduled to be held in Namibia. A good showing by Swapo would fan right-wing resistance in South Africa. Terreblanche, a committed supporter of the new Democratic Party (DP), was very optimistic about this party's election chances. It could mobilise even enough votes to replace the Conservative Party as the official opposition and to pressurise the NP with regard to its group thinking and lack of progress with talks about South Africa's future. He also reckoned that the internal protest movements would build up new steam in the run-up to the election. Mbeki later told me privately: "If Sampie is right, De Klerk, if he became president, would be in a very good position. He'll be able to move faster, because the DP will support him."

In the discussion that followed, it was inevitable that we had to focus on the question as to when the time would be ripe for the two contending parties to start talking directly to each other. By then the conditions set by both the ANC and the NP had been clearly defined for some time, with the release of Nelson Mandela one of the non-negotiable conditions on the part of the ANC. For Botha and his government, the insistence on a renouncement of violence by the ANC was of prime importance. Naturally, none of the participants at our meeting had the mandate or power to give any authoritative view in this regard. This was a matter the contending parties themselves had to discuss. But the Afrikaner-ANC dialogue group did manage to make an important contribution: even though there were conditions on the table on both sides, nothing prevented the contending parties from holding informal and confidential discussions about this very issue and jointly finding ways of addressing it officially. Mbeki said at one stage: "Maybe Nelson (Mandela) should only be released after FW (de Klerk) has taken over." Willem de Klerk, Sampie Terreblanche and I were shocked. Later I discussed this with Mbeki. He was clinical: "Botha is in trouble politically. His time is past. Mandela's release shouldn't be exploited to rescue Botha politically. Don't underestimate his obsession with power and publicity."

Once again the negotiated independence of Namibia came up for discussion. For the ANC, an ally of Swapo, it was of great political significance that this process should run smoothly. A relatively calm and nonviolent transition to majority rule on the basis of the democratic constitution would be a huge bonus for the ANC. It would be instrumental in allaying uncertainty in some international circles and profound doubts among whites in South Africa. An incident between South African troops and Swapo guerillas, who had blithely crossed the ceasefire line in the north of the country, had led to serious questions about Swapo's ability to control their guerillas. The South African troops, who had anticipated the invasion, mowed down many guerillas. The crisis was averted, however, and the peace agreement survived. Mbeki asked: "When can direct talks begin?"

The NIS had warned me: Don't make any positive noises about international mediation in the resolution of the South African conflict. There were determined efforts in this regard, as in the case of the Rosenthal-Switzerland episode. At one stage the pro-negotiators of the ANC also had contact with representatives of the Dutch government. There were people within the Reagan administration who wanted to play a mediation role, not to mention the American Democrats. Many were keen to plant their mediation flags in Pretoria. Michael Young undoubtedly wished to do not only himself a favour, but also his country. He suggested quite subtly at the meeting that Britain and Margaret Thatcher should play a mediation role. The term that was used was "international mediation". I told myself, also in light of my views on the Anglo-Boer War: "The British want to colonise again. Can't they leave us alone? We'll sort out our problems on our own." Later I talked to Aziz Pahad about this. He failed to understand my problem, because he knew nothing about my perception of the Anglo-Boer War. The majority view in the group was that Thatcher could play a mediation role. I thought to myself: "She can exert pressure. Even meet FW de Klerk. But it's 'we' who have to learn to trust each other and who have to mediate and negotiate with each other." I mentioned this to Mbeki. He said: "What are you going to do about it, because I agree with you."

This Mells Park meeting was particularly significant to me. It was dialogue at its best, without a trace of mistrust, even when we discussed the thorny issues of violence and group rights. There was an explicit desire that we (Afrikaners and ANC members) should find a way of taking joint responsibility for the future. This type of commitment is an important building block for the creation of trust and confidence, as it symbolises a shift from the notion of "the enemy" to the notion of "partners". The partnership model represents a suspension of one's perception of the other as an alien and an enemy. I looked at Mbeki, Pahad, Trew, De Klerk and Terreblanche, and wrote half amazed in my notebook: "We're not even 'friendly enemies', because we trust each other with the future even though we have no idea what it will look like in five or ten years' time. We're sitting here discussing Botha, Mandela, De Klerk, Tambo, the violence in the country, the release of political prisoners and negotiations as if we're playing for the same team. We accept that our country is being consumed by conflict, and that a scorched earth is not in anyone's interest. And we share words like 'peace' and 'reconciliation' with each other."[3]

It was also on this occasion that I once again confirmed Mbeki's bona fides as a negotiator. From various quarters, even within the NIS, the question was sometimes posed: "Isn't Mbeki simply co-opting credulous Afrikaners for his future plans? Is it not just a case of him using 'negotiations' in order to achieve what MK didn't manage to accomplish: a political takeover of the South African state?" My response to this was unequivocal: "Mbeki is striving for a settlement process. He does have a constitutional proposal in his briefcase, but he has no guarantee or ability to dictate the outcome of the process. It will be determined by the ruling power elite in South Africa and other participants in the process."

The opportunity to do something about this arose during May 1989. The NIS contacted me. The request took me completely by surprise: "Get in touch with Thabo Mbeki. Request him to travel to London where you and he can meet in private. No one else must know what you talked about." I literally trembled with excitement. I knew intuitively that this was the real deal, and even experienced an emotion of fear. Should I get involved in something that would compromise me so deeply that everything that was morally important to me might go to ruin? I also told myself: "Oom Koos, Möller, Hanna, Maritz, Niel and the other NIS people that I have met and come to know aren't moral 'shysters'. They are people of integrity that perform an important, though admittedly an extremely complex, function."

Later I would realise why the NIS had taken the initiative. PW Botha's time was running out. Mandela's memorandum had been passed on to Botha in May 1989. He wanted an appointment with the president, and had received an indication that it was in the offing. All of this made direct contact with the exiled leaders of the ANC inevitable. The Coetsee-Barnard-Mandela dialogue channel was no longer enough. It was impressed on me that Mandela knew nothing about the NIS initiative. I had to stress that to Mbeki. Hanna, someone for whom I would gladly go the extra mile, remarked with a smile: "Prof, we know that you have all sorts of involvements and interests in London. Surely you can think of many good reasons why you should travel to London."

I made the necessary arrangements, and decided with almost excessive emotion that Mbeki and I would meet each other in London on Wednesday, 31 May 1989. It was Republic Day, I reasoned. What could be a more symbolic day for conveying an important message to an ANC leader?

By that time I already knew what the message was: "We (the NIS) want to start talking officially to the ANC. The talks are obviously exploratory and confidential. We would like a telephone number." The NIS gave me the codename the person would use when contacting Mbeki: John Campbell. As it would turn out later at the first official meeting, Mbeki was accompanied by Jacob Zuma. Mbeki's codename was John Semelane. It became a mad rush to get everything organised for the meeting in London. There was not much time. On Wednesday 24 May I spoke to Robin Renwick, the following day to Koos Kruger, and later in the week to Professor Mike de Vries. Luckily, lectures ended for the winter holiday on Friday 2 June.

I had arranged beforehand with Michael Young that Mbeki and I would meet each other in a room at the offices of British American Tobacco (BAT) in London. Young was at that stage involved with this company. The irony of the situation was not lost on me. The Rembrandt Group, with whose founder Dr Anton Rupert I had a long and instructive association, was a major competitor of BAT. Rembrandt would later sell its tobacco interests and some of its buildings to BAT. Rupert, who had started out in the 1940s with very little corporate muscle, but an ambitious dream, was strongly in favour of a negotiated political settlement of the South African conflict. And a room of BAT, without the BAT management being aware of it, became the address for a momentous meeting. Michael Young, too, was unaware of the purpose of the meeting.

As usual, I travelled to London on a South African Airways flight. My appointment with Mbeki was scheduled for eleven o'clock on the morning of 31 May. In the taxi on the way to BAT's offices I was assailed by growing anxiety: Would he keep the appointment, given the risk he was taking and his notorious overfull agenda that often made him arrive late at meetings? Would he cooperate and give me what I was looking for? Would he grasp that "the hour had come" and that it was the state that was finally taking the initiative officially to enter into dialogue with the ANC in exile?

The meeting was top secret. In sensitive pre-negotiation talks confidentiality is unavoidable, and a condition for the initiation of the political process. It prevents parties to the conflict from exploiting the internal tensions in their own ranks, as was the case with the NP and the ANC, for their own political gain. Moreover, it fosters a certain commitment to respect each other's integrity and to build trust. It also prevents what I call naive optimism and idealising political daydreaming: "Liberation is just around the corner." It is a fact, after all, that pre-negotiation initiatives in situations of deep-rooted conflict not only provoke resistance on the part of some, but also create expectations on the part of others. And nothing is as destructive as frustrated expectations. That is why all states have classifications and gradings regarding secrecy and confidentiality.

Mbeki and I met just after eleven in a luxurious BAT lounge. Michael Young accompanied us. We exchanged a few platitudes: "How was the trip? What's the weather like in Lusaka? And in Stellenbosch?" In a hurry and excited about the message I wanted to pass on, I had to exercise patience. At last Young left the room. British silver and a delicate porcelain tea service waited for us on a table. I am a dedicated coffee drinker, even in the morning. Mbeki poured the tea and I tried to enjoy drinking it. He was evidently at home in this British cultural ritual. I offered him the silver plate with biscuits and made small talk. I did point out he and I were meeting here in BAT's lounge on Republic Day. He showed no emotion about this historical commemoration day, and said: "You Afrikaners' Republic Day!" I replied: "Of course. It's *my* day. Maybe one day we'll get a date on which we can celebrate together. But you understand, don't you, that today is a symbolic day for me?" He nodded his head.

Our interaction since 1988 had established a strong personal facet. We had to learn to trust each other, given the sensitive nature of the talks and our agreement that they had to be kept confidential. We also discovered very soon that we had much in common: the literature that interested us; the music we appreciated; that which we hoped for; the values that were important to us. And he, too, loved philosophy. In fact, I once told him that he was perhaps a better philosopher than he was a politician. At a point during our tea session I noticed that he was getting restless and even withdrawn. That was how I had come to know him. Time was precious when there were important matters on the agenda. Then one should not socialise or indulge in small talk. He was in any case bored by superficial conversations. Besides his personality and his more intellectual attitude towards life, even as a child in the former Transkei, I often wondered whether his exposure to the leadership of the old Soviet Union and East Germany had not played a role as well. Those states had been rigid societies. Strict hierarchies were maintained. "The Leader" was the key to the future. As in the apartheid state. You also couldn't show too many ordinary human emotions. It was a sign of weakness. Especially when, on top of that, you had to live as an exile in foreign parts and constantly had to look over your shoulder for fear that a rival or an apartheid killer might stab you in the back. In such circumstances it was a tough task to preserve Crocker's accent on the "human factor". If one adds to this the fact that many ANC leaders had been trained directly or indirectly by the Sovier Union's KGB or the East German Stasi, the issue of the undermining of the "human factor" even assumes catastrophic forms.

Slightly irritated, he asked: "Why did you come here? You're talking about issues we already discussed during our April meeting." I was ready for this moment, and said: "Yes, that's true. But there are implications that we need to clarify further." The NIS had advised me not to convey the message in a place that could be bugged. "Do it in a pub," was the serious advice. "And try to get a table in a corner." I wondered at the time why a tree in a park might not also be a suitable spot. Mindful of the NIS's advice, I had brought along two hand-written notes in my briefcase. One was very brief: "The walls have ears. And sometimes the ears have ideological walls." Many years later Mbeki took a great delight in poking fun at me in public on a few occasions by saying that when I gave him this message, he realised that I was a "true Afrikaner". Afrikaners were well acquainted with bugging.

The second note was longer:

- A very senior person from the National Intelligence Service would like to make contact with you in order to explore the possibility of future talks and agenda points. I am convinced that the intention is honest. It has been authorised at a very high level. Only a few people know about this. Strict confidentiality is expected. It is guaranteed as far as Pretoria is concerned.

- I need a reliable telephone number from you where you can be contacted in person. You will receive a call from someone called John Campbell. This person will discuss logistics and other issues with you. I don't know when he will call. I was asked to assure you that the person who will liaise with you does not want to play any games. It would also be appreciated if you should respond positively.

- I would like to emphasise the sensitivity of this issue. And also the necessity of confidentiality. I am convinced that you can regard this initiative as serious and well-meant, even though I have not been informed of any detail or objectives. I suspect, though, that the initiative also has something to do with Nelson's (Mandela's) position. And with the issue of "talks about-talks" and negotiations.

I had added with a big NB:

- Sampie and the others don't know about our meeting. My trip was reported as "academic".
- I requested very specifically not to be involved in possible talks between you and the NIS – or even to arrange meeting places and dates. Hope you understand. I must maintain a certain distance even though

there is a good relationship of trust between me and the NIS. If a meeting should take place between you and the NIS and you are not satisfied about the seriousness and honesty of the NIS, I would appreciate it if you would inform me in this regard. As I have told you before, I will protect your integrity and position.

When I saw his irritation, I handed him the notes, stood up, and said I was going to the bathroom to give him an opportunity to read them. On my return to the BAT lounge we talked about our next dialogue group meeting, agenda points and people we needed to invite in future, particularly from the business sector. At some stage he said that he also had other business to attend to in London. Maybe we could get together again if there should be an opportunity to do so. We went to say goodbye to Michael Young, walked out of the building and shook hands before going our separate ways. A little while later we met each other in a London pub, The Albert, as I had arranged with him. Fortunately, there happened to be a corner table available.

While we had a beer, I again conveyed the NIS's request to him. I emphasised: "The hour has come: the door is unlocked. And you have a hand on the bolt." He wrote something on a scrap of paper and handed it to me. At the top was written in Afrikaans: "Only Willie". Underneath that, the telephone number where he could be reached in person. There was emotion in his voice when he told me: "Oliver Tambo has said: 'Will the ANC get the signals right that the NP leadership sends out regarding negotiation?'" Mbeki paused for a while, then asked: "How do I know that it's not a trap?" The old distrust between the ANC and the Afrikaner regime resurfaced, despite the fact that he knew about the Coetsee-Barnard-Mandela talks. I became somewhat annoyed, and said that I trusted Niel Barnard and his team. Even managed to get in a dig: "You'll find more trust in Pretoria than in New York, Paris and Dakar. Barnard and his team are engaged in a process. Not a sensational event." Later, to moderate my reaction, I made him a promise: "I give you my word of honour that I'll keep my ear to the ground. If I hear anything that sounds fishy, I'll let you know. I'll also draft a document on all our talks, including today's discussion, and have it kept in a safe to which a trustworthy journalist friend of mine will have access. If anything should happen to you or me, she will make the document public." He said: "Let's go outside." Thinking of Aggrey Klaaste, I said to him: "It's never too late to talk." He then reconfirmed that I could give his telephone number to the NIS. I repeated the codename. We said goodbye. And he looked at me with humour in his eyes: "Maybe next year you and I will meet in Stellenbosch on 31 May, and not in London. Do you think we should keep the name 'Republic Day'?" Almost as an afterthought: "I trust you." Years later he would often refer to my undertaking in the presence of his fellow ANC members.

On my way to the house of my journalist friend Fleur de Villiers and her mother, I marvelled at the spring green of a tree in a little park. And I told the tree on this 31st of May 1989: "Trust between adversaries *is* difficult, but possible! Sometimes more possible than between bulls in the same kraal that are all roaring to be heard, to be recognised and to gain influence. But what do you know, tree, of this kind of tragic rivalry among people? After your winter you adorn yourself with your spring finery, unhindered. Provided, of course, that you don't die a natural death or are chopped down. Because all living things are doomed to die. Fortunately, not all ideas and memorable events." I thought of Dr Anton Rupert's words: "Trust is a risk. Distrust is a greater risk."

Lee Blessing's *A Walk in the Woods*, a highly acclaimed US play about disarmament, was being staged in London at the time, with Alec Guinness in the role of the Russian and Ed Herrmann playing the American. Fleur de Villiers, her mother and I went to see it. I identified very strongly with the story and it became a window through which I looked at the Afrikaner-ANC dialogue group's contribution. In the play, the two arms-control negotiators were sworn enemies who met each other in the woods as concerned individuals and came to an understanding about future peace. I stayed in London for a few days to gather information on examples of political mediation between governments and liberation movements at Chatham House and the International Institute for Strategic Studies, and wrote a report on this topic during my return flight to South Africa in which I said: "Negotiation is merely a part of a more comprehensive process ... a process that is known as 'trust- and confidence-building' and wherein common ground and differences have to be clarified." I stated that the NP was ill-equipped for both this process and for official negotiations. Nonetheless, in my view people such as Gerrit Viljoen, Dawie de Villiers, Stoffel van der Merwe, Tertius Delport and Leon Wessels could make a difference. So too could officials such as Niel Barnard, Mike Louw, Niel van Heerden and Fanie van der Merwe. With regard to Dawie de Villiers, I wrote: "One of his great assets is that he is able to gain people's confidence and knows how to hold a good discussion."

On Monday, 5 June I addressed a conference of the Anglo Alpha company in Johannesburg. The theme was "Socioeconomic trends and future scenarios for South Africa". I had to exercise discipline not to let anything slip about my meeting with Thabo Mbeki in London. Fleur de Villiers's advice to me not to violate trust and act as if you know more than others, stood me in good stead on this occasion.

# 10

## Tea party at Tuynhuys: Botha
## meets Mandela

A fter the excitement of 31 May 1989, the big wait began. On the one hand, for the meeting between the two "paramount chiefs" in the lapa of our internal politics, namely Botha and Mandela. Botha was still president of the country. But FW de Klerk, chief leader of the ruling party, was in charge of the party's policy-making processes. And Botha, should he remain in office for a long while still, would have to implement NP policy. On the other hand, there was the telephone call to Thabo Mbeki that the NIS had to make at some or other time with a view to a meeting. There were time pressures. The Botha-Mandela meeting was determinative for the Mbeki meeting. And then there was also the looming general election later in the year on 6 September 1989, with FW de Klerk and a growing number of NP MPs breathing down Botha's neck.

To make matters worse, the Mass Democratic Movement (MDM) remained politically active. The broad-based network could not be banned. Political unrest continued. So did deaths and black-on-black violence. The high levels of political intolerance in the insurrectionists' own ranks were particularly alarming. The political activism and resistance against the regime also became a tale of atrocities and brutal acts of violence, like the notorious necklace killings that were strongly condemned by people like Archbishop Tutu. It was a case of the revolution devouring its own children. In this period I frequently pondered something Thabo Mbeki once said to me in passing: "Incremental reforms fuel revolutionary activism. When last did you read De Tocqueville? And Hegel and Marx on dialectical relationships?" I understood once again that an oppressive system could not be reformed. It had to be drastically transformed. Incremental reforms confirmed to oppressed people that they were disadvantaged and had the moral and political right to revolt. Botha's reforms weakened certain pillars of the apartheid system, but they also fuelled activism, forced him to declare a state of emergency, and led to all kinds of other draconian measures and security actions. He and his securocrats were stricken with a political blindness: The activists, the ANC and the communists wanted to seize all power by revolutionary means. Botha thundered: "I don't negotiate with a gun to my head." His reform project eventually ground to a halt. I often thought: "The road blockades of the police are symbolic of Botha's and the NP's psychological obstacles."

The state of emergency, which had been declared in July 1985, was of course still in force. It was also supported by FW de Klerk, in 1985 leader of the Transvaal NP and from the beginning of 1989 the NP's chief leader. In 1998, in *The Last Trek: A New Beginning*, he looked back on this and justified his position. In his opinion, the state of emergency had compelled the revolutionaries to develop a more realistic view of the balance of power between them and the government. I don't disagree with this view, but he is too apodictic. There were also other, more important factors: the prevailing international consensus, the stronger position of the negotiators vis-à-vis the fighters in the ANC, Tambo and Mbeki's diplomatic victories, and the pressure exerted by influential heads of state. The tide had turned in favour of a negotiated settlement. The ANC knew that it had nothing to lose in this process.

Coetsee, but mainly Barnard, succeeded in persuading Botha to meet Mandela. By then Barnard was already firmly convinced that a negotiated settlement was strategically inevitable. He also accepted that Mandela's role in such a settlement would be of key importance, albeit that Mandela was not at that stage an elected leader of the ANC. He knew, too, that Botha was on his way out, but wanted to involve him in the further preparations for the settlement nonetheless. It would in any case confront Botha's successor with a political given that could not reversed. The strategically minded Barnard was already thinking much further ahead than a meeting between Botha and Mandela. He had not requested Mbeki's telephone number without good reason. There were, however, a few matters Barnard and the NIS still had to settle. One of these was official sanction for the dialogue with Mbeki, preferably by the State Security Council and not merely in the form of personal approval by Botha. Barnard always had a very correct and professional relationship with Botha, yet also displayed a certain empathy towards Botha and his wife. Botha had a lot of respect for Barnard. He once remarked to me: "Barnard is a decent person." According to Barnard, he had told Botha that he could lose nothing by meeting Mandela. Even if the meeting went wrong, Botha would be remembered as someone who had at least tried to expedite progress. And if the conversation turned out to be positive, it would be the start of South Africa's settlement politics. History would recognise Botha for this. Barnard, together with his good friend General Jannie Geldenhuys and Neil van Heerden, had been deeply involved in the Angola-Namibia settlement process. He was Botha's eyes and ears on this mission. Much was learnt from this process.

What happened in Angola-Namibia not only boosted the international consensus on a settlement process in South Africa, but also brought home to Barnard and his team that time was no longer on the side of Botha and his government. In one respect, however, Botha was a major obstacle: his anti-communist sentiments had assumed a religious quality. I thought at times that these sentiments, rather than his dictate that Mandela and the ANC had to renounce violence, were the strongest emotional and political obstacle. Botha in any case associated violence with communism and the Soviet Union. This was not unjustified. There was the Cuban involvement in Angola. They had put pressure on his good friend Jonas Savimbi and had given Swapo a military capability.

But that was not the actual reason. Botha had a grudge against the Soviet Union. During our conversation about Chester Crocker to which I referred earlier, Botha had been very firm in his view that the ANC was a surrogate agency of the Soviet Union. The ANC, he believed, had been transformed into a violent revolutionary movement by the Soviet Union and the Stalinists. Without Soviet support, the ANC would have got nowhere. Accordingly, he regarded the Soviet Union as the real source of all the unrest and violence in South Africa. I partly agreed with Botha about this. The ANC's goal of a revolutionary takeover of power was the direct result of the influence of the Soviet Union, then still enmeshed in the Brezhnev doctrine's centralist and totalitarian aspirations, and the KGB's and the East German

Stasi's dreams of power. In fact, one should understand the political conduct of Chris Hani, Mac Maharaj, Siphiwe Nyanda and even Lindiwe Sisulu from that perspective. And although Mikhail Gorbachev had consigned dreams of this kind to the political scrap heap, Angola-Namibia had kept them alive in the revolutionary circles of the ANC. To them, "takeover of power" was the real dream. Maharaj and Nyanda did not infiltrate South Africa in 1988 and establish Operation Vula in order to start a democratic peace process.

Botha was almost panicky about the possibility that the communists would get a foothold in South Africa. It would endanger the future of "my people", was his argument. To him, Mandela's loyalty to the communists was a flashing danger signal. It was never clear to me whether Botha had read Mandela's memorandum. I am reasonably sure, though, that he had at least been briefed thoroughly on it. Mandela's declaration of loyalty to the SACP would have been a bitter pill to him. Indeed, in the later dispute with De Klerk and Barnard about Barnard's destruction of the secret recording that had been made of Botha's conversation with Mandela, it was particularly his warning to Mandela against communism that featured prominently.

At a later stage, after the ANC and other organisations had been unbanned and were participating in the settlement process, I personally experienced Botha's bitterness about the SACP's position as a fellow player. Through my mediation, Zanele Mbeki, Thabo Mbeki's wife, appeared at a conference of Dutch Reformed Church ministers in the HB Thom Theatre in Stellenbosch. Zanele, a devoted Christian whose parents had been spiritual leaders in the Johannesburg township of "Alex", addressed the ministers. Her presence caused a highly upset Botha to say during a telephone call from his home in Wilderness: "The Mbekis are communists. Now they've taken over my church, too." Botha took as gospel the propaganda of his Total Onslaught and Total Strategy that had mainly been aimed at the Soviet Union and the communists.

The historic meeting between President PW Botha, the Great Crocodile of the regime, and Nelson Mandela, the global Great Icon of liberation dreams, took place on 5 July 1989. According to Neil Barnard, it lasted from ten o'clock in the morning until just after eleven. It was 35 days after my meeting with Thabo Mbeki in London. None of my good friends in the NIS had informed me of the planned Botha-Mandela meeting in advance. I heard later that it had been classified "top secret". Mandela was literally smuggled into Tuynhuys from the parking garage via an elevator. He was a "politician from an African state," it was stated at the well-guarded gates to the grounds around the complex. The security men at the gate were impressed: a convoy of cars, five in all, transported the Great Icon into the grounds to meet the Great Crocodile. The guards were, of course, unaware of the identity of the "African leader" sitting in the middle car of the convoy in his smart tailored suit. Arrangements for the suit had been made by the prison's tailor, who had taken his measurements beforehand. Mandela was also decked out in a new shirt, ties and shoes. He had been told to be ready at six o'clock that morning for the trip from Paarl to Cape Town. The knot in his tie had been redone by a warder because his own tie-knotting skills had grown rusty in prison.

It was striking that much effort had gone into making him look dignified. "Like a leader and not like a prisoner," according to an NIS source. Mandela's later remark that all of this was an indication of how much the officials feared Botha, is in my view an incorrect reading. It was rather a case of Mandela being given recognition by people who had accepted that a new political dawn was breaking through the darkness of apartheid, and that he would play a role in it.

Getting Mandela into Tuynhuys, via Roeland Street which was renowned for its notorious apartheid-era prison where Tony Trew had also been detained, was a meticulously planned operation that had started in the early hours of 5 July. The security measures that had to be taken for the trip by the NIS, in close cooperation with "IB", an expert in security arrangements regarding the transport of VIPs, were executed with military precision. Apart from the possibility of a right-wing assassination, the measures were aimed at preventing the South African Security Police and Magnus Malan's Military Intelligence from getting wind of the visit. In fact, even the policeman guarding the house in the grounds of Victor Verster Prison had to be evaded. With the exception of two people, "IB's" team of about ten members were unaware of the identity of the VIP. "IB" himself drove the car in which Mandela and Barnard travelled. As he put it to me: "Drivers have to be carefully selected and well trained. They, too, have eyes and ears, and know what is discussed inside a car." The trip from Paarl to Tuynhuys and back was potentially highly dangerous. Even Jack Viviers, PW Botha's communications right-hand man, had been kept in the dark. He felt very affronted about this.

On the way to PW Botha's office, Barnard noticed that Mandela's shoelaces had come undone. He stopped Mandela, knelt down and tied the laces. This "kneeling episode" understandably gave rise to much symbolic speculation. It was even claimed that when Barnard knelt in front of Mandela, he suddenly realised he was kneeling before a future president. A simpler and more likely explanation is that Mandela, who didn't have shoes with laces in prison, had unlearnt the art of tying laces. Barnard did the logical thing: he bent down and tied the laces. In my dealings with him, I had came to know Barnard as someone with a sense of common decency – even though he could cross swords with people in a blunt and even brutal way.

There were two salient similarities between Botha and Mandela: both had a will of iron; both despised cowardice and turncoats. And of course both of them passionately loved their fatherland, patriots par excellence. There were dissimilarities, too: Botha was a political incrementalist, a piecemeal reformer, and fiercely anticommunist. His craving for power was not just a personal quirk. He was also willing to give his all for "his people" (=Afrikaners). Mandela was a passionate political transformer: all (nonracial majority rule in a unitary state) or nothing, with at most temporary transitional measures. The notion of group rights irked him inordinately because it reminded him of apartheid and oppression. And Mandela respected his friends over many years, such as the communists. If one juxtaposes Mandela's memorandum to PW Botha with the policy documents and pronouncements of the NP and its leadership from the beginning of 1989, the meeting between Botha and Mandela was actually a historic miracle. To Botha, the three primary issues of group protection, renouncement of violence, and the position of the communists were political gospel. In this period he developed yet another obsession with regard to the communists: Joe Slovo, who in his eyes was evil incarnate. One of the bitterest pills for him to swallow after his retirement was seeing Joe Slovo, red socks and all, at Groote Schuur, in a group photo that had been taken during the first formal talks between the government and the ANC in May 1990.

Botha's meeting with Mandela went off exceptionally well. He even posed for a photograph, despite having initially expressed his concern to Barnard about what "his people" would say if he talked to Mandela. The conversation was friendly and relaxed, but not incisive; Mandela's important memorandum hardly came up for discussion. Barnard did not want to raise contentious issues. He only sought a meeting, a political icebreaker. Naturally Botha, true to form, had instructed Barnard beforehand to record the conversation in secret. Besides wanting to listen to the conversation again afterwards, he mainly wished to protect himself against criticism if the meeting should leak out. Barnard did so very reluctantly. That was not what he had agreed with Mandela. When I heard the story, I thought of Mbeki's reaction to my worries about bugging. Mandela did bring up one very sensitive issue. He requested Botha to release his good friend Walter Sisulu, who was advanced in years, on humanitarian grounds. Botha didn't respond directly, but said instead that Barnard had to attend to this request. Barnard, not one to tiptoe around thorny matters, spoke bluntly to Mandela on the trip back to Paarl. Sisulu's release was not something that he was either able or willing to attend to at that stage. The political climate in the country was very tense, and an election was just around the corner. Mandela retorted that Barnard was an official and that he had to implement the president's requests. Sisulu was eventually freed by President FW de Klerk on 15 October 1989. It's not always easy to focus, as the NIS did, on a bigger strategic picture at the expense of more individual or incidental moral issues.

Viewed symbolically, the group photo that was taken at the meeting was truly historic: the leader of the apartheid state, in the person of the Great Crocodile, appears on a photograph with the Great Icon of the liberation movement, Nelson Mandela. Everyone seems to be in a particularly good mood. Niel Barnard stands between the two leaders, almost as if he has to define a distance between the two. Kobie Coetsee stands next to Botha. Next

to Mandela is General Johan Willemse, commissioner of prisons, and someone who played a massive role in thawing relations with Mandela and senior
political prisoners. Ters Ehlers from Botha's office had taken the photo of
the cheerful group. Many years earlier HF Verwoerd, South Africa's great
apartheid ideologue, had not even bothered to acknowledge a memorandum sent to him by Mandela. In 1989 Mandela again sent a memorandum
to an apartheid leader, and ended up posing for a photo with this leader.

This photo nearly caused great consternation, I was told. Latish in the
evening during a function at a game farm in the north of the country the
following day, Botha was full of bravado and wanted to be the centre of
attention. He was surrounded by his closest colleagues and people he believed to be loyal to him. He declared that he had something in his pocket
that would astonish them all. With all the eyes of the intrigued onlookers
on him, he produced the photo of the cheerful group at Tuynhuys. Some
of those present were shocked when they saw it. One told me afterwards:
"While we're fighting the terrorists, Botha is chatting quite cosily to their
leader."

Barnard had organised the meeting between Botha and Mandela in great
secrecy. The NP cabinet members, who had been waiting impatiently for
PW Botha to vacate his presidential chair, were caught off guard. Barnard,
not someone who tries to explain decisions about power and strategy with
moral justifications, owed Botha this surprising historic event. He also knew,
of course, that once this meeting became known nationally and internationally, there would be no turning back. Botha's successor was compromised. Hereafter, all that remained to be talked about was the timing of the
release of Mandela and other political prisoners, and the parameters of the
settlement process that lay ahead. Botha could not be a part of this. With
the tea party in Tuynhuys, his time was over for good. The tea party was,
however, one of the most significant events in South Africa's settlement
history, as was Mandela's memorandum to Botha.

Barnard's relationship with Botha soured at a later stage. By then Botha
had already retired to Wilderness, but he hadn't lost his fighting instincts.
De Klerk, then the president of South Africa, thought it fit to invoke Botha
and declared that he was simply pursuing Botha's policy. Which was, in my

opinion, not altogether untrue. When Botha met Mandela at Tuynhuys, he had in effect confirmed Mandela as leader, indirectly ratified his release, and acknowledged the necessity of settlement politics. He was just not the person who would or could carry it through. Be that as it may, Botha blew his top about De Klerk's claim and demanded the secret tape recording from Barnard. Barnard said that he had destroyed it personally, because it had been wrong to make the recording. The only record he had was the notes he had made. Then Botha really went ballistic. His rancour against De Klerk, and eventually also the NP, knew no bounds. It grew even worse during the hearings of the Truth and Reconciliation Commission (TRC). Conservative and aggrieved Afrikaners who enthusiastically embraced his resistance to and statements about the TRC, among other things, reinforced him in his rancour. He died an embittered man.

When Botha died, Thabo Mbeki, then the president of the country, phoned me and asked whether he should attend the funeral. I encouraged him to do so by saying: "Your liberation, mine, and that of all South Africans became unstoppable the day Botha and Mandela talked to each other like good and civilised South Africans. That meeting was a leap into the potential new South Africa." I appreciated it greatly that, despite criticism, he attended the funeral. Botha had begun leaving some of the apartheid train's important carriages behind in the form of the scrapping of certain laws. But he was either unwilling or unable to consign the locomotive with its remaining carriages to the political scrapyard. When he met Mandela, the target became set on the boiler of the apartheid locomotive: group rights as understood by the NP. This boiler, I once told Mbeki, would be responsible for hot steam among Afrikaners for many years to come.

Meanwhile I started growing anxious about the possibility of a meeting between the NIS and Thabo Mbeki. This was a matter with which I should not concern myself, I was told. There were still a few issues that needed to be settled. From 27 to 29 July 1989 I attended a meeting of the Jubilee Initiative in Britain. I tried to say as little as possible and avoided speculating about the future for fear of giving the game away. Botha's meeting with Mandela and the leadership battle within the NP were major talking points, along with the unrest and violence in the country. My good contact in government circles told me on 13 August 1989 that a make-or-break situation had arisen between Botha and his cabinet. My contact said: "D-day has come. Botha has no support left in the cabinet." FW de Klerk led the rebellion on 14 August, a cold, wet Monday morning. They had been summoned to Tuynhuys by Botha apropos of the Kaunda affair. The Zambian president had announced that he would meet De Klerk on 28 August. Botha was furious, and complained that he had not been consulted about this. Whether this visit had been a calculated move on the part of De Klerk and Pik Botha is not verifiable, but it was indeed likely. The date scheduled for the meeting, 28 August, was barely a week before the election. A visit to Kaunda, the leading president of the frontline states, would be an enormous political bonus for De Klerk in the West, among blacks, and in the ranks of progressive whites. Moreover, it would take place shortly after Botha's earthshaking meeting with Nelson Mandela. The rebellion happened seven days before the ANC's Harare Declaration on negotiations. It was perfect timing on the part of the ANC.

The planned visit of De Klerk and Pik Botha to President Kaunda became the last straw in the ongoing power struggle. The meeting in Tuynhuys started at eight-thirty in the morning and was opened with a prayer by the then minister of minerals and energy Dawie de Villiers. We had both studied philosophy and theology. De Villiers, who was a good speaker, endeavoured to create an atmosphere of calm and reconciliation with his prayer. Botha had respect for him, even though he later rejected De Villiers's attempt at reconciliation at Die Anker, Botha's house in the village of Wilderness, and more or less showed De Villiers the door – along with the gift De Villiers had offered him.

The meeting with the cabinet lasted about three hours. Botha was calm at first. As tends to be the case in politics at this level, the ministers started off by singing Botha's praises. He was a great leader who had done much for "his people". Botha listened to all of this without interrupting the eulogists. They were filled with appreciation and admiration for him, they assured him. Botha, who detested hypocrisy, waited patiently for the eulogists' "but", especially when they began raising their concerns about his health. They thought that it would be in his own interest and also in the interest of the country and the party if he took a holiday. Maybe he could appoint an acting president until after the election. It was a way of saying: your time is past. Finally, Botha exploded as only he could.

His wrath was directed mainly at De Klerk, national leader of the NP and potential president. It became a severe confrontation in Afrikaner ranks between a leader of the government and the members of the cabinet or inner core. This face-off was another clear indication of what Sampie Terreblanche called the crumbling of the NP. It was a further phase of the process of the erosion of power and institutions within Afrikaner ranks following the events around the Independent Movement. Botha fulminated emotionally against De Klerk. He accused him of cowardice for raising his (Botha's) health as an excuse. He challenged De Klerk and asked whether he thought he, Botha, was incapable of thinking for himself. Why didn't De Klerk say so openly? De Klerk protested. Botha, true to type and showing no impairment of his attacking and mental techniques, asked De Klerk why, then, he was insinuating this with a smile on his face and a dagger in his hand. At one stage he even declared that De Klerk needed to put his relationship with God in order. Magnus Malan, one of Botha's good friends and in control of the military facet of the Total Strategy, also walked away from Botha. He would later be known as the "Brutus" of this episode. Botha, without a single supporter in a cabinet he himself had appointed, refused to designate an acting president. He took the right decision and resigned as president. De Klerk had won the power struggle. He was appointed as acting president on 15 August 1989.[1]

The NIS was prepared for these developments. On 16 August, a day after De Klerk had been sworn in as acting president, he chaired a meeting of the mighty State Security Council (SSC). This had been Botha's real instrument of power. De Klerk did not know this environment well because there was an inner circle from which Botha had excluded him. Besides, De Klerk was a rule-of-law person – admittedly not in the full sense of the term. One of the items on the agenda was a carefully formulated motion from the NIS (number 13 of 1989). It stressed the need for gathering and processing more information on the ANC. That the objectives, alliances and rapprochement possibilities of the ANC's leaders and groupings had to be explored.

To this end special direct actions had to be undertaken, mainly by means of the NIS.

De Klerk, who was not informed of the track-two contact processes that had been taking place for quite a while, and especially not of the meeting of 31 May, supported the motion. In fact, the NIS had no alternative but to compromise him in this way. Botha was out of the picture, and a new president would take over the reins of government after the upcoming election. The NIS could not afford years of painstaking preparation for a negotiated settlement being put on the back burner. "Colleague Möller" told me: "Proffie, time is of the essence. Particularly in politics. We don't have many options left." With the NIS's motion adopted by the SSC, the NIS now had a mandate for a personal meeting with Thabo Mbeki. Most members of the SSC, including De Klerk, were blissfully unaware of this implication. I, too, didn't know when the first meeting between the NIS and the ANC would take place. I had been waiting for a signal since 31 May 1989. Mbeki had also been waiting, but more patiently than me, as I would discover later. He was schooled in what I once referred to as the "politics of patience". Also called "timing", which is crucial in political processes. Finally, the wait was over.

Möller Dippenaar drew my attention to the irony. On 15 August 1989, a day before De Klerk presided over a meeting of the State Security Council as acting state president, and a day after PW Botha had departed for Wilderness, De Klerk delivered a typical election speech. He lambasted the ANC and declared that the NP's attitude towards the ANC had not changed. The NP would only negotiate with people who did not engage in violence to achieve political objectives. The ANC disqualified itself. A day after this speech, he accepted a motion that unlocked the gate to negotiation with the ANC. But he was unaware of this at the time.

# II

# "Archenemies": the political ice
# is broken in Switzerland

The entire country as well as foreign governments with an interest in South Africa had high expectations after PW Botha's departure. Especially the US, Britain and the Soviet Union kept a watchful eye on developments. With the UDF and other organisations still banned, the Mass Democratic Movement (MDM) continued the struggle with heightened passion and energy. The MDM specifically targeted the election that was due to be held on 6 September 1989. It was slammed as a political scam that was only intended to strengthen apartheid's ideological obsession with ("white") group rights and would not advance democracy. The Rev. Simon Adams of the "coloured" Volkskerk in Stellenbosch declared at a mass meeting at the University of the Western Cape: "Six September will retard everything."

It was impossible to ban the MDM. The movement had no clear structures with an executive, and was rather a widely extended network of mobilised energy. Everyone knew, however, that this energy source was representative of the UDF, Cosatu and other banned organisations. As Jan Steyn of the Urban Foundation remarked ironically and aptly: "How do you ban energy?" There was little doubt that the renewed zeal with which the internal resistance had flared up would impact the post-Botha regime. On 2 August 1989, even before Botha's departure, the MDM embarked on a series of protest marches. These were aimed mainly at apartheid in hospitals, on beaches and in respect of public transport. Around three million people participated in a strike against the election of 6 September. The power of the state and its government, which was locked in an internal power struggle, was challenged. It became a riotous affair, with the security services having their work cut out for them. In my view, the protests during the first half of 1989 had also played a role in the cabinet's rebellion against Botha. Innovative leadership was required. In the circles of the intelligence service it was asked whether the MDM, in cooperation with the ANC, might be planning a "Leipzig option", with reference to East Germany where a peaceful mass movement had brought down that country's communist dictatorship with burning candles in the streets.

Meanwhile there had been a brilliant political move on the part of the ANC. Early in 1989, and particularly after my meeting with Thabo Mbeki on 31 May 1989, a small group within the ANC had started working intensively on a more focused document on constitutional negotiations. This took place under the leadership of the president of the ANC, Oliver Tambo. The militants in the ANC were not really briefed on it. By then there had of course been a debate and policy documents on constitutional issues within the ANC for a considerable time.

Thabo Mbeki was the real driving force behind the latest document. Mbeki had an important objective: he wanted to lobby to gain the support of the Organisation for African Unity (OAU), thereby compromising the militant revolutionaries. He knew that President Kenneth Kaunda supported a negotiation option, and also wanted to have an advantage over the NP government by having a document on the table that would reinforce the existing international consensus. After all, this consensus was something that he had worked for.

The NP, which was preparing for an election for the tricameral parliament (white; coloured; Indian), had neither the time nor the capacity for serious reflection on the preparatory phase of negotiations. Even though 1989 was the ANC's "year of mass action", Mbeki's real priority was a well-developed strategic plan for negotiations. The Harare Declaration was unveiled on 21 August. It was a strategic coup for the ANC. The only institution that had been prepared for this was the NIS. But there was not much they could do in public, as there was an election that had to take place first. Thabo Mbeki knew, however, that when the day came for him to talk to the NIS, there would be a document that had already been publicised and widely accepted. He could afford to wait. Besides, shortly before this declaration, on 19 August – my birthday – a very significant meeting had been held: the one between the ANC and the Congress of Traditional Leaders of South Africa (Contralesa).

Within the NIS contact group we speculated a lot about the possible outcome of the election. There were divergent opinions. Some reckoned that the Conservative Party (CP) with its avowed racially oriented policy would make strong gains. The manner in which PW Botha had been dumped, it was argued, was likely to alienate many conservative whites from the NP. Another view was that the Democratic Party (DP) would do well. Many Afrikaners, especially the new generation, were eager to see an end to the conflict in South Africa. Many of them had done military service in Namibia-Angola. They asked: "For what? In Angola we lay side by side with coloured and black people in the trenches. Now that we're back in South Africa, we're supposed to use separate entrances again." Someone from the NIS was even more forthright: "Apartheid is fatal for Afrikaners." We reached a kind of consensus: if both the CP and the DP were to do well, the NP would sweat blood. Its absolute majority could be in jeopardy.

In the event the DP fared reasonably well, but the CP stumbled. The majority of white voters gave their support to De Klerk's leadership. I realised that most of the voters had accepted that a new dispensation was imminent. They just didn't know what this dispensation would be; in fact, there was not even unambiguous clarity about policy. Hence they had put their faith in a new leader, FW de Klerk, albeit that his image was at that stage quite conservative on account of his interpretation of group rights. Everyone was also convinced that the good showing of the DP in contrast to the old PFP was a political bonus. It would not only keep the NP on its toes, but provide De Klerk with a buffer against right-wing resistance if he should wish to act more progressively.

The cruel harshness of the South African political reality was illustrated shortly after the election: the Namibian advocate and Swapo member Anton Lubowski was assassinated in Windhoek. His death caused a national and international uproar, with many fingers pointed at Magnus Malan and his military. From these circles it was alleged that Lubowski had worked for the military. Others claimed that while this might perhaps have been the case initially, he had undergone a political conversion and became an ANC mole. He had to be killed to keep his mouth shut. His assassination highlighted once again in blood the moral and political quagmire in which South Africa had become bogged down. All my subtle and less subtle inquiries among some of my contacts about this murder came to naught.

This assassination happened on the same day as another very significant event: the meeting on the evening of 12 September between Mike Louw and Maritz Spaarwater of the NIS with Thabo Mbeki and Jacob Zuma of the ANC. It took place in the Palace Hotel in Lucerne, Switzerland, without the knowledge of the Swiss government.

The meeting in Lucerne had been deliberately planned to take place after the election and before De Klerk's inauguration in Pretoria on 20 September. I had not been told about it beforehand; Mbeki informed me afterwards. The NIS was anxious that a claim had to be staked for negotiations in the rapidly shifting political landscape. Nelson Mandela, too, was impatient. The resistance in the country had become endemic. There was a need for political momentum in the process that was already under way. De Klerk had not been briefed beforehand about the meeting of 12 September. In the wake of the election, he also had other weighty matters on his agenda. The police had fired on a group of protesters in a coloured community near Cape Town and several people were killed. Eruptions of rage followed. Church leaders such as Archbishop Tutu and Allan Boesak declared that enough was enough. They were at the forefront of a planned action to lead a massive protest march through the streets of Cape Town. My friends in the NIS predicted trouble. Should the protest march be banned, De Klerk would pay a price. If the march should proceed despite a ban, as they suspected would be the case, and the police were to intervene harshly again and fire on people, De Klerk would be slated internationally as another Botha.

De Klerk, however, took an excellent strategic as well as moral decision: the planned march was not banned, but cooperation was mediated with its clerical leaders. They succeeded in leading an estimated 30 000 protestors peacefully through the streets of Cape Town to the city hall. This was one of De Klerk's most audacious decisions, to allow the anti-apartheid activists to protest peacefully. Nationally and internationally he was seen to distance himself from Botha's iron-fist approach. He had signalled to the leaders of the protest march that his door was open to them. There was no need for them to kick it down.

Shortly afterwards I learnt reliably that someone else had also played a role in this decision: Johan Heyns, a professor in dogmatics from Pretoria and a leading figure in Dutch Reformed Church circles. As I mentioned before, in 1987 he had declined an invitation to participate in the Afrikaner-ANC dialogue group. Heyns had talked to the church leaders who were organising the protest march, and also to De Klerk. At that stage Archbishop Tutu was opposed to holding discussions with De Klerk, but Heyns had access to the church leaders. People like Boesak and Tutu were gatekeepers. Most Afrikaners and the Botha government detested these leaders; they were routinely demonised in parliament and in the Afrikaans media. But they were influential, extremely competent and leadership icons in their own right, not revolutionary militants. Heyns had facilitated a decision that was of great strategic importance. When I heard the story, I told myself: The future of South Africa in general and Afrikaners in particular will be determined significantly by committed facilitators. They are the people who have to pave the way for negotiations.

Hereafter the question on everyone's lips was: What is De Klerk going to do about the conflict in South Africa? There were two upcoming events in October that highlighted the importance of this question in red: Namibia's independence and the Commonwealth conference. The Commonwealth was fed up with the struggle of getting a settlement going in South Africa and highly irritated with Margaret Thatcher's lukewarm attitude towards sanctions. I met the British ambassador Robin Renwick on 13 September 1989 to discuss these and other matters with him, including Mandela's anticipated release. These issues had also been talking points in Lucerne the night before. The process of settlement that had already started unfolding, had to be accelerated. Dramatic initiatives that had to produce exciting and hopeful moments were required.

Among such initiatives, the meeting on the evening of 12 September was an important marker in the history of South Africa's transition. Barnard, who was fairly open with Mandela and referred to him respectfully as "the old man", had kept Mandela in the dark about the Swiss project – "Project Flair", as it was called. Barnard later admitted that this was the one issue that he had neither discussed with Mandela nor asked permission for. By then he and Mandela had had many discussions and had come to know each other well. In fact, Barnard sometimes spoke in Afrikaans and Mandela in English. Mandela welcomed this, as he was keen to establish a good relationship with Afrikaners. At an early stage in their talks Mandela had pointed out to Barnard that the NIS should not contact the leadership in Lusaka behind his back. That was *his* prerogative. Presumably Mandela wanted to control the tentative dialogue project himself and put his own stamp on it. He did not know Thabo Mbeki, and in all likelihood he did not trust him either. Mbeki was a very loyal Tambo supporter. Tambo's wife, Adelaide, was Mbeki's second mother. He even prepared meals in the Tambos' kitchen on occasion. There was also another, more fundamental reason, something that Mbeki often questioned me about: What were the real motives behind Botha and Coetsee's tentative overtures to Mandela, and, especially, what was Barnard's game plan? Mandela and Mbeki shared an important reservation about the talks about talks: Was the project not perhaps a strategic plan to isolate Mandela from the external wing of the ANC, sow division and doubt, and antagonise mainly the militants within the ANC? The initial negative reaction to a shortened version of Mandela's memorandum, even on the part of someone like Allan Boesak, was an indication of how strongly the winds of mistrust were blowing.

The ANC leadership in Lusaka was also divided on what should be understood under settlement and negotiation. Maharaj and Nyanda's infiltration to launch Operation Vula had been authorised by Tambo. This project was still steeped in the revolutionary dream of a violent seizure of power. Personally, I also believed that Mbeki's and Mandela's fears about a "divide-and-rule strategy" on the part of the Botha regime were not completely groundless. Botha liked divide-and-rule. But Botha, and particularly Coetsee, Barnard and the members of their team, had already realised in 1988 that such a strategy would not work. This was one of the reasons why Barnard took the initiative in 1989 to ask for the reliable telephone number. It was argued that time was not on the side of the South African government. Their power base could weaken, which would have a negative effect on their bargaining power. They had to negotiate from a position of strength. This point was made repeatedly by Barnard and the NIS. It was not a moral point, but a strategic one: in the inevitable settlement process, the government should not be on the wrong side of the power equation.[1]

Mandela, for his part, could not quite grasp Botha's anticommunist position. Mandela and even Thabo Mbeki mainly used two arguments in their reasoning. One was the loyalty argument: The ANC and the SACP had come a long way together. There were solid historical and personal ties. Slovo played a huge role in MK, as did Hani. They were fighting for a common cause. The second argument was of a different kind: Botha and his government had been prepared to negotiate with communists in Mozambique (the Nkomati Accord) and in Angola-Namibia. Why not also in South Africa itself? Barnard once answered this question in his typically blunt, one-sentence style: "South Africa is not Mozambique or Angola-Namibia." When I informed Mbeki about this, he said: "Barnard has a point, but we can't exclude the SACP from a settlement process."

By this time there were already rumours circulating that the NIS had put out feelers to exiled ANC leaders and sought contacts. Some of these rumours even cropped up within British and US intelligence circles. This was understandable. The NIS had good relations with the Zambian intelligence service and the services of a few other African countries. Barnard, like Spaarwater, sometimes travelled in Africa. There tends to be contact between intelligence services. What there was no contact about, however, was the issue of how, when, and by whom a negotiated settlement in South Africa had to be initiated. The British did manage to "find a trail" in Lusaka of the meeting between me and Mbeki in London on 31 May. In Tambo's inner circle, together with the Mandela talks, there was undoubtedly a real expectation after May 1989 that something more dramatic could happen. After May, Mbeki could also be reached telephonically by "John Campbell". The first meeting was preceded by telephonic contact. The shrewd British had identified this "trail" in Lusaka without, however, being able to establish the detail of its implications. They would not have leaked it anyway, because Britain had an interest in a settlement process.

Since 1988 Barnard, true to his character, had planned the whole project in minute detail with key colleagues of the NIS. Nothing was left to chance. They even gave thought to seemingly non-essential issues. Mandela's transfer to a comfortable house in the grounds of the Victor Verster Prison was handled by the NIS, who had furnished the house. Mandela, accustomed to prison cells, had to be exposed to a lifestyle within the totally different environment of a residence. According to Barnard, he even had to learn how to work with money. There were security considerations, too: right-wing fanatics could attempt to harm him.

The NIS had also planned the entire process in clearly defined phases. In Barnard's view, the first phase was crucial: the gathering and evaluation of information.[2] Among other things, the NIS needed to know how Mandela thought and felt about certain issues. The phase of trust-building inevitably arose from this first phase. Both parties had to experience that they were not engaged in a political game. According to Barnard, it was only after this that a third phase could kick in: exploratory talks about future possibilities and options outside the confines of a rigid win/lose model. The fourth phase, a key phase, followed hereafter: transfer of the dialogue process to more, yet well-controllable interlocutors. The ANC-Afrikaner dialogue group was of course involved in all these phases in an unofficial way. There was no direct contact between the NIS and the group, and especially no feedback from the NIS about the course of the process. Formalised transfer occurred, however, with the meetings in Switzerland.

The first official meeting between people from the ruling elite and leaders of the exiled ANC on 12 September 1989 represented the start of Barnard's fourth phase. Switzerland was chosen for the meeting although the Swiss had sponsored Rosenthal and Barnard had referred to that as "connivance of a foreign power". The choice fell on Switzerland because the NIS officials, as South Africans, did not require visas. Louw and Spaarwater were accompanied by three other NIS members who had to reconnoitre the terrain and would act as watchdogs. The two travelled on passports that identified them as Michael James and Jakobus Maritz. Everything was done very professionally, as could be expected from a good intelligence service. They flew from Zürich to Lucerne and checked into rooms 338 and 339 of the hotel, a suite with a lounge. The two NIS officials who attended the first meeting were senior people with many years of experience. Louw was Barnard's deputy and had migrated to this post from within the NIS over time. According to

Louw, he preferred to operate in a small-group context. He relied strongly on his instincts and possessed a very good strategic sense. He succeeded Barnard as director-general of the NIS in the 1990s, after Barnard became director-general of constitutional affairs.

Maritz Spaarwater, an old hand in the NIS, had very good high-level contacts in Africa that he had acquired on his frequent travels in the rest of the continent. He had contact with President Kenneth Kaunda of Zambia, for instance. While Louw had an instinctive-intuitive personality and sometimes came across as shy, the tall and lithe Spaarwater was a bundle of energy and a person with an exceptional sense of humor. At that stage he was the chief director of operations, which involved among other things that he had to exercise control over the security arrangements for the meetings. As the talks progressed, the emphasis on security increased and became more challenging. (Later, ANC leaders had to be literally smuggled into the country, for example on 21 March 1990. The unbanning of the ANC did not yet mean indemnity against prosecution.) Louw and Spaarwater were a good team, the right one at the right time.

The other three members of the NIS team awaited the arrival of Mbeki and Zuma at the Geneva airport. They wanted to make sure that the pair were not accompanied by other ANC members, and that everything was going according to plan. In fact, the trio followed Mbeki and Zuma to Lucerne. The two ANC leaders travelled in a car driven by an ANC representative in Switzerland. There was no one else, not even a single security guard. Mbeki and Zuma arrived in Lucerne early in the evening, casually inquired about the room numbers of James and Maritz at the hotel's reception desk, took the elevator and walked to the suite where the NIS men were waiting for them. Mbeki related later that he and Zuma had learnt how to live with fear and even the possibility of death. They were all too aware of the South African government's well-trained and highly effective soldiers and agents. But by then he also knew that time was running out rapidly for the ANC's sponsorship by the Soviet Union. He and Zuma *had* to talk to "the enemy". This was not a moral decision, but a strategic one.

Louw and Spaarwater on the one side, and Mbeki and Zuma on the other, were understandably both excited and tense.

Louw and Spaarwater had left the door to their suite open as a kind of welcome and assurance of good intentions to the ANC visitors. Thabo Mbeki, someone who gives a lot of thought to how thorny situations should be handled, spoke first as he entered the suite. It was a typical Mbeki ice-breaker: "Here we are, the terrorists, and for all you know, damned communists too." Masters of irony and humour know how to defuse tension. Their own as well as that of the opposing party. As I mentioned elsewhere, this was also one of Spaarwater's strengths. The four men talked until long past midnight. The agenda for the dialogue had been determined long before the meeting by issues that constituted a consensus in the public arena by then: the necessity of a negotiated settlement, Mandela's release, the state of emergency with its bannings, the violence option, and the ANC's alliance with the SACP. As in the case of the Afrikaner-ANC dialogue group, it was agreed that this particular dialogue should be exploratory and aimed at clarification: talks about talks. Barnard was really just seeking an assurance that the ANC was ready to talk and to negotiate. By that time policy documents had already been adopted in Lusaka. Louw and Spaarwater were given this assurance.

There was also a second agenda on the part of Louw and Spaarwater: would-be facilitators and mediators within and outside South Africa that offered their services and over whom the NIS had no control. Barnard had an aversion to the involvement of third parties. This was not something that the government could allow. He maintained consistently that the government was the only role player vis-à-vis the other parties to the conflict. Louw's advice to Mbeki was to get rid of everybody who wished to play an intermediary role. Only direct dialogue would lead to progress. Mbeki agreed with this view. At the time, the NIS was still of the opinion that the ANC's meetings with Afrikaners were part of a deliberate effort to drive a wedge in Afrikaner ranks and widen divisions. This stance was largely responsible for the reservations about an intermediary role for Idasa and its two leading figures, Alex Boraine and Frederik van Zyl Slabbert.

As is to be expected when it comes to the retelling and rethinking of extraordinary historic moments, this memorable meeting gave rise to a good many anecdotes. One is about what Mbeki is said to have remarked to Zuma in Zulu on their way to the suite: "It turns my stomach to think that in a few seconds we'll be meeting two archenemies." This anecdote captures the essence of the prevailing political feelings and perceptions. "Archenemies" suggests something in the past that impacted so destructively and fundamentally on people's dignity, self-esteem and rights that even the possibility of peace was lost. The disciplined Mbeki, who never allowed his personal resentment and anger to come in the way of his goal, reacted in a typically human manner in the anecdote. The meeting was indeed historic: between archenemies. The first outreach action. At the same time, too, a giant leap towards peace. What was primarily intended as a clarification of positions, became in reality also an unofficial declaration of intent: "We have to make peace with each other and among ourselves." How strong that intent was, is proved by the fact that within six months Nelson Mandela was released, the ANC and other organisations were unbanned, and the peace process started in earnest.

Among the considerable number of reasons to which the success of the Lucerne meeting can be attributed, I would like to single out the following:

■ PW Botha had been an encumbrance. While the NIS had been argu-ing for a long time that Nelson Mandela was not the problem but in reality part of its solution, Botha had stubbornly dug in his heels: Mandela, his attitude towards violence and the SACP, was the real problem. The NIS's position in this regard was a great assurance to Mbeki and Zuma, as was the knowledge that the ANC, together with Mandela, had to be part of the solution.

■ The discovery by the "archenemies" that they were in agreement about the necessity of a peace settlement and also about the most important conditions for such a settlement.

■ Discovery of each other as fellow South Africans. In the case of South Africa this facet of the process played a major role without it lapsing into mawkish romanticisation. In reality, however, peace processes never happen outside of personal relationships, or as Hannah Arendt would say, the ability of people to forgive as well as to enter into new convenants with each other. Louw, Spaarwater, Mbeki and Zuma did not talk to each other as "enemies", but as (potential) partners in a new project for the future.

Five days after the meeting in Lucerne, on 17 September – three days before De Klerk's inauguration – Louw and Spaarwater met the new president in Tuynhuys. While he had hardly had time to get used to his presidential chair, he already had to take important decisions, as in the case of the protest march a few days earlier. And as someone put it to me: "Botha's ghost still hung heavily over the chairs, desks and other artefacts of Tuynhuys. It had been his castle, the place where he met Mandela." It was here that Louw and Spaarwater gave a report-back on their Lucerne meeting to the unsuspecting De Klerk. De Klerk, at first astonished and then annoyed, asked where they had got the mandate, as he had not been briefed on this. Louw, unperturbed by De Klerk's attitude, put the State Security Council's resolution of 16 August 1989, where De Klerk had been the acting chairman, on the table. De Klerk, equally unperturbed, told Louw and Spaarwater to continue with their report and tell him everything. In a wink he had changed the hot potato he had been handed into a ball with which he could run.

This was De Klerk's strength. His political instincts enabled him to spot strategic opportunities. De Klerk recognised the possibility of taking the political initiative. This decision was a political tipping point. It made his speech of 2 February 1990 possible. It should also be remembered that the meeting with Louw and Spaarwater took place three days before his inauguration as president: when De Klerk sat listening in the church to the emotion-laden "sermon" of his good friend the Dopper minister Pieter Bingle about new ways that would have to be explored, with reference to Jeremiah 23:16 and 22, he knew about the ANC's meeting with Louw and Spaarwater. Few people in the audience were aware of it.

I never thought that De Klerk had experienced some kind of political Damascene conversion. Such an explanation looks for drama where there was none. He took a strategic decision. And he didn't really have a choice, because there was a prevailing international consensus. He *had* to ask: "How can I take and retain the initiative within such an environment?" It was not a moral decision. The morality only came later as a retrospective justification of something that could not be reversed. With Botha's incremental approach in tatters, something else was required to grab the initiative: doing the unexpected and the dramatic in order to comply with the prevailing international consensus. It was not uncalculated either. It was not a question of succumbing to pressure, but rather a case of making the pressure manageable and giving whites, particularly Afrikaners, the opportunity to be co-partners in a new dispensation instead of pariahs.

On 31 May 1989 Thabo Mbeki had asked me a blunt question in London, namely to what extent the NP's and especially FW de Klerk's notion of "group rights" would be an obstacle to a negotiated settlement. I had reckoned that it was an important issue, and would therefore have to be high on the eventual negotiation agenda. In other words, not something that should be decisive in a pre-negotiation phase. At that stage, shortly after De Klerk's election as NP leader in February 1989, his position was still unequivocally that a nonracial society was not possible in a multiracial environment. He was also of the view that domination by an ethnic majority was just as unacceptable as domination by an ethnic minority. He even referred to the Nazis in this regard. To the ANC's relief, however, De Klerk ran into difficulties as early as March 1989. The South African Law Commission sank the judicial acceptability of his notion of group rights in a working paper. Mandela and Mbeki were delighted.

On 15 October 1989, barely three weeks after his inauguration, De Klerk made a dramatic move. This was something that Louw, Spaarwater, Mbeki and Zuma had discussed: releasing political prisoners in order to create a climate that was conducive to negotiations. Early on Sunday morning, 15 October, police cars parked in front of the houses of six ANC political prisoners who had been sentenced to lifelong imprisonment. Walter Sisulu was one of them. All six were released. So was Jafta Masemola, who had founded the PAC's military wing. By then Sisulu had spent 26 years in prison. Some of Sisulu and his wife Albertina's children were also in prison or banned from participation in political activities. Another son and daughter were in exile. Soweto was in a state of joyful commotion about the releases. The ANC's and particularly Thabo Mbeki's insistence that the releases had to be managed by "the people", was respected. At a gathering in the Holy Cross

Church that evening, Sisulu made a very conciliatory speech in which he stressed the necessity of a democratic system and also said that a black or a white person could become president in a democracy. To all intents and purposes, the ANC now had a voice in the streets of Soweto, in the press and in the public domain. Margaret Thatcher, too, was very pleased. The releases took place a few days before the Commonwealth conference in Kuala Lumpur in Malaysia. De Klerk was riding a wave.

Thabo Mbeki could not stop this wave. He was the leader of the ANC delegation to the Commonwealth conference. It led to a diplomatic flurry: he and his delegation had been booked into the same hotel as Margaret Thatcher. She was dead set against the idea. The host country had no choice but to make alternative arrangements for the ANC. Mbeki, who in any case held Thatcher in low esteem, was convinced that the Iron Lady had been averse to sharing a hotel with "terrorists". He experienced her attitude as an insult.

## 12

# Front-page news in the *Sunday Times*

On Friday, 29 September, after I had arrived at Mells Park for our next meeting, I received an urgent late-night call from South Africa. It was my friend Tertius Myburgh, editor of South Africa's biggest Sunday paper, the *Sunday Times*. He had been informed of the dialogue project in broad terms, mainly to be of assistance in the event of leaks to the press. Myburgh sounded upset. Someone had leaked details of the project to journalists of the *Sunday Times*; it was considered a major news story, and he was unable to stop it. I had to prepare myself for a front-page report on Sunday, 1 October 1989, in which the names of those attending our meeting would be revealed. Myburgh said I could accept that the information had been made available from within the dialogue group itself. Years later he would confirm that a journalist who had ties with the Afrikaans weekly paper *Vrye Weekblad* had obtained the information from someone in the dialogue group. It had then been passed on to the *Sunday Times* as a scoop. He advised me to exercise damage control.

We had managed to keep the project secret and out of the media for two years. Myburgh later provided me with a copy of the newspaper report. The first thing I did was to call the su rector, Prof. Mike de Vries, in London. He was supposed to attend our meeting for a while as an observer, but I advised him to cancel his trip to Bath on the Saturday. Then he could at least say, when the report appeared on the Sunday, that he had not been present at the meeting. It would have been an embarrassment to him. I also informed Mbeki and the other participants who had arrived by then. They were unperturbed. It was Saturday, we didn't have to respond immediately and had time to think until Sunday. We arranged that the ANC, through Thabo Mbeki and the ANC representative in London, would deal with any queries directed to them. I would issue a statement on behalf of the Afrikaners and stress the unofficial nature of the dialogue group.

Our meeting took place less than three weeks after the NIS-ANC meeting in Lucerne. Besides De Klerk, Terreblanche and me, the Afrikaner side included some new faces: Louis Kriel of the deciduous fruit industry, who knew all about the effects of sanctions; Ebbe Dommisse, the designated chief editor of *Die Burger*; and Ernst Lombard, a Stellenbosch minister from the Dutch Reformed Church (DRC). The ANC had specifically requested to make contact with someone from the ranks of this church.[1]

Willem de Klerk did not initially attend our first session. He was restless, unlike how I had come to know him, and there were reasons for this. Shortly after FW de Klerk's inauguration on 20 September, I was visited by someone from the NIS. The next meeting of the dialogue group had already been arranged for the weekend of 30 September to 1 October 1989. My NIS visitor seemed ill at ease. The NIS, he said, did not interfere as far as invited participants were concerned. There was a big problem, however: Willem de Klerk was the brother of the new president, FW de Klerk, and he was extremely uncomfortable about his brother's participation. It could cause unnecessary embarrassment. Willem de Klerk had already been invited and all the logistical arrangements had been made, but I undertook to speak to him. It was up to him to decide whether he wanted to withdraw, I told him. Willem de Klerk was unwavering: he was going to attend the meeting. He called me later and said: "Dr Niel Barnard contacted me. He would like me to withdraw for my brother's sake. There are too many political risks." I emphasised again: "The decision is up to you." And added: "Thabo appreciates your contributions, he respects you and won't abuse the changed situation." He attended the meeting in the end.

After our arrival at Mells Park on the Friday, De Klerk and I went for a walk in the grounds. Now that his brother was president of the country, he said, he had to find a new way of dealing with their relationship. He felt very strongly about the necessity of unofficial dialogue with the ANC-SACP, the release of political prisoners, the lifting of the state of emergency and a free democratic election. He was going through a personal crisis, too. We talked for a long time and agreed to stress one point throughout: "Give FW a chance!" I also told him: "You are FW's brother. Not his political factotum." I arranged for a taxi and encouraged him to go to Bath for a while, to visit the Roman ruins and to try and clear his head. I had already been to Bath on several occasions and could tell him about the history of the ruins and which sites he had to visit.

Jacob Zuma was a new ANC face. By then I had heard much about him and knew that he was in charge of the ANC's intelligence service. He and Mbeki were very spontaneous with each other and I assumed that they were good friends. We all arrived at the estate on Friday, 29 September and, as was customary, we were treated to an exquisitely prepared dinner in true British style. We spent a social evening in each other's company without an agenda, exchanging views and chatting about everything under the sun except political issues. The businessman Louis Kriel had brought along boxes of South African fruit, to the delight of the ANC participants, the fruit boycott notwithstanding. While the NIS never dictated to me about who should be invited, I did inform them before each meeting who the participants from South Africa would be. Koos Kruger had not been impressed with my list of Afrikaners. Too many and too diverse. It would make it more difficult to exercise control over what was said afterwards, he claimed. Kruger, dutiful servant of the state, was also very unhappy about Willem de Klerk's participation. "Too sensitive now that his brother is our country's president. The ANC will think that he speaks on behalf of his brother. And he may act like that, too." He was particularly concerned about the presence of "the press". I promised that I would give a full report on the discussion, and also informed Thabo Mbeki accordingly. Mbeki asked: "But don't you do it in full for all our sessions? Surely you can't be a reliable go-between if you filter discussions?" I failed to reply immediately, and said eventually: "It's not a question of filtering, but rather a responsibility to distinguish, even as a go-between, between reason and emotion, sense and nonsense, the real issues and diversionary manoeuvres."

The Afrikaners were indeed a diverse group. They had just come from an election where the NP had had the knives out for people like Wynand Malan, Sampie Terreblanche and Willem de Klerk. That was probably the reason why someone had spoken confidentially to the journalist who leaked the story. Ebbe Dommisse was the designated chief editor of *Die Burger*, a newspaper that had gratified many readers and angered others with its cartoons about Malan and Terreblanche.[2] Kriel had only one main focus: circumventing and combating sanctions, which he was doing with great success. I wanted the ANC participants to get a sense of the diversity among Afrikaners. The ANC considered the presence of the businessman Kriel and the editor Dommisse an important addition, because they brought different perspectives to the table. Through Ernst Lombard, they could for the first time gain some understanding of the tensions that existed within the DRC as well. It was news to them, as this church was a bastion of apartheid in their eyes. Mbeki, Zuma, Pahad and Trew interacted with the Afrikaners as if they were old acquaintances. When I mentioned this to Pahad, he said: "But you *are* old acquaintances. You are Afrikaners."

Naturally, the ANC participants knew about the Lucerne meeting. It created a positive attitude on their part. The Afrikaner interlocutors had not been informed about it; at that stage it was an extremely delicate and secret track which could be very negative for the peace initiatives if it had to leak out. Mbeki and I did not discuss it in detail either. He only confirmed that the meeting had gone well, and that there was now a path forward. I tried to worm details about their discussions out of him, and was most frustrated because I failed to get any. As could be expected, the ANC was very interested in the Afrikaners' interpretation of the election. We discussed this on the Saturday. There was a remarkable consensus among all the participants that the election had been a turning point. The conservative FW de Klerk was in a strong political position, greater numbers of English-speakers had voted for the NP, and the voters sought change even though they did not exactly know what form it should take. The ANC argued that the Democratic Party (DP) had a significant role to play as facilitator in a settlement process. It was not a potential leading party, though. The NP had the power. The DP, however, could strengthen De Klerk's position if he were to take a progressive leap. But could he and would he do so, given the nature of the NP's election campaign that had been more geared to the threat posed to them by the Conservative Party (CP) than to a progressive future?

Willem de Klerk, who arrived late because he had spent the night in Bath, was at pains to explain his brother's important leadership role on the road ahead. He was a supporter of the Democratic Party (DP), but accepted that the settlement process would take place primarily between the NP and the ANC. He surprised me. The expedition to Bath had done him good because he didn't speak of "my brother", but of "the president", the leader of the NP. He made a point that he substantiated from the literature on the subject: In times of dramatic political change processes, a leader with a conservative image has a competitive advantage over one with a liberal or leftist image. Such a leader is more likely to succeed in initiating progressive turns, managing resistance on the part of conservatives, and inspiring and mobilising the centripetal forces. I watched my ANC friends. They nodded approvingly. The three newcomers, Dommisse, Kriel and Lombard, also concurred with this view. Dommisse remarked at a later point in the discussion: "The crux of the matter is a settlement between Afrikaner nationalism and black nationalism. The new generation wants to negotiate." No one disputed his standpoint.

On one issue, Willem de Klerk did not mince matters: the racial basis of the NP's policy and how "the president" understood group rights. This was the big political hot potato that still needed to be dealt with, because it required more than just a smoother style than PW Botha's. It was at this stage that a measure of reserve surfaced again among the ANC members: Will FW de Klerk do what many people hope he will do? Jacob Zuma later placed the question on the table: "What exactly is FW's agenda?" Louis Kriel responded quickly – too quickly, because he wanted to talk about sanctions: "To further the process of change that already exists. We're waiting for positive reaction from your side." Zuma did not answer him.

In the course of the weekend, it was also Zuma who singled out two issues apropos of the focus on FW de Klerk's future leadership: the position of the CP; and De Klerk and the security forces. The ANC always had a certain fear of right-wing Afrikaners. They were seen as "dangerous" and "tough", even later by someone like Moeletsi Mbeki who had thought of Afrikaner men as people with close-cropped hair in khaki shorts and long socks that drove around in bakkies with their rifles at hand. He was flabbergasted when I introduced him to farmers in Ceres shortly after his return to South Africa. Hence the urgency in Zuma's voice when he inquired whether the CP would negotiate and what the attitude would be towards "white self-determination" in future. The Afrikaner interlocutors believed that the CP's capacity to mobilise Afrikaners was very limited. Dommisse did think, though, that right-wing resistance, even armed resistance, could come from the ranks of smaller rightist groups. Zuma's question as to whether FW de Klerk would be able to control and even transform the military and the security police, was harder to answer. We all realised that this answer would be of central importance in the period ahead. If the South African Defence Force and MK did not accept the process and help to protect it, the suspension of restrictive security measures could create opportunities for severe chaos and bloodshed. Mbeki and Zuma were particularly worried about the military wing of the PAC, the African People's Liberation Army (Apla), which was not well organised and disciplined. Meanwhile, the rumours about and evidence of state-sponsored hit squads and destabilisation actions were increasing.

"We have a history of blood," observed Zuma, who hailed from Natal, in a dispirited tone. Like Klaaste's "It's never too late to talk", this became another refrain in my mind. He made a second observation that also followed me like a shadow: "Africa has a disease. There are too many 'one-man shows'. And a lot of corruption. Military coups give Africa a bad name. How can the military be controlled?" No one had an answer. We knew that our discovery of each other's humanity and responsibility for the future was not the norm. Conflict between ethnic groups was a reality in South Africa.

We devoted much time to the *Declaration of the OAU Ad Hoc Committee on Southern Africa on the Question of South Africa*, the Harare Declaration of 21 August 1989, which had been adopted a few days after PW Botha's fall. Mbeki and Zuma were the main speakers. Mbeki talked with a calm conviction in his voice, without any written notes. He was, after all, the father of the document in which the conditions for a settlement were spelled out with an international consensus, and I knew that there was very little FW de Klerk would be able to do to nullify this consensus or to get the basic guidelines of the document changed. At one stage Mbeki looked at Willem de Klerk and asked: "Do you think FW believes there's a lot of time for a settlement?" De Klerk replied: "I don't think so. Most of his party members and many of his ministers think so, though." He paused and then continued: "I think FW knows the sooner he settles, the better his position would be. It will weaken if he waits too long."[3]

Zuma supported Mbeki's emphasis on the Declaration. He was articulate when it was his turn to speak and avoided intricacies. At one stage he made a good point: the document was also intended to defuse white fears, such as the notion "that we are only interested in a revolutionary takeover of power. We want to show that this is not the case. We are interested in a negotiating process." In addition to that, the Declaration wanted to define the "main issues" from the ANC's perspective: "We South Africans never really had the opportunity to discuss these issues that we have to talk about." The Afrikaners were pleasantly surprised by this reasonableness, especially when Zuma stated that the document had also created an opportunity: How should one go forward from here? To Mbeki, the big question was: Is the government ready and willing to become involved in a settlement process? And what can be done to ensure that the process is conducted according to agreed rules of play? The old mistrust resurfaced: Will the government be prepared to discuss the document?

Though it sounded like a wish, it was in reality a challenge. I knew that the NIS had already studied this document intensively. Mbeki, as if he were reading my thoughts, said with conviction in his voice: "The document is a proposal. Not a directive."

The discussion on "mutual trust" that followed was long and intense. I was astonished at the honesty with which views were exchanged. I told Mbeki later that frank discussions were, of course, a form of trust-building. Hell doesn't *have* to be other people, I stressed with reference to the French philosopher and Marxist Jean-Paul Sartre. He only laughed in agreement.

Dommisse, Kriel and Terreblanche felt strongly about the issue of sanctions and the fact that "lifting of sanctions" would only come up for discussion after the expected conclusion of the negotiation process. It was then that Mbeki, supported by Zuma, Pahad and Trew, very honestly and sincerely put on the table their seriousness about a negotiation process as well as their understanding of its complexity and delicacy. Mbeki made a point that he and I had already talked about previously: there are different phases in the process of settlement. The first phase, that of contact, talks about talks and clarification of positions, includes both informal and formal facets, as do all the other phases – for instance, the active negotiation process itself. There were, as I often told myself, both unformalised and formalised rules of engagement; unofficial and official agreements. Mbeki explained this distinction on the basis of what he called the policy (theory) and the practice.

Theoretically and in terms of policy, the ANC was committed to sanctions. They could only be lifted by way of a formal resolution once the negotiation process at least proved to be "irreversible". In practice, however, it could be agreed that there would not be a deliberate drive to push for sanctions. The US, he informed me later, would hold off from further sanctions. During a meeting with the US State Department it was emphasised that sanctions would not be lifted, but that a wait-and-see approach would be followed for at least six months. The same explanation was given with regard to the highly emotional issue of violence, namely the ANC's armed struggle. Ernst Lombard delivered a short address on this topic and gave an exposition of the DRC's position in a calm and dispassionate manner. He related how vehemently the DRC was opposed to the ANC's use of violence as a political instrument, but never used the word "terroristic". He also explained the DRC's powerful anticommunist campaigns that had been waged over many years, and said that peace and reconciliation had to be achieved in the country as soon as possible. While there were signs of a new approach, however, the DRC was not yet a leading light in this regard.

We returned repeatedly to the contents of the Harare Declaration. This Declaration, I realised, was the ANC's "foundational text". It also became the Afrikaners' "foundational text" in the sense that we were compelled to respond to it. The government did not really have such a text or road map at that stage. The document stated that "if discussions start to take place", a number of things could happen informally, such as the "suspension" of hostilities. This could then be formally negotiated later; the Harare Declaration envisaged that "after the adoption of the new constitution, all armed hostilities will be deemed to have formally terminated". At this meeting, therefore, the ANC was prepared to undertake that the bombs would stop exploding once they were convinced that the first phase of the settlement process was on track. Mbeki, supported by Zuma, Pahad and Trew, stated pertinently:

"Put yourself in our shoes. There is mistrust. In fact, a history of mistrust and a history of broken agreements." He referred again to Mozambique and Namibia in this regard, and even recalled John Vorster's "give me six months".

Mbeki was very specific: "To safeguard our interest in view of the history of our region, we are of the opinion that informally and in practice we can suspend violence and things like that, but not formally. That is something that can come at a later stage." One of the problems the ANC had with a formal agreement on an immediate suspension of hostilities was how something like that could be monitored. Who would have to monitor the ANC? And who the South African Defence Force and the South African Police? These were questions that would have to be thrashed out thoroughly by the parties to the conflict. It could not be done by international bodies. Linking up with this point, Zuma said: "The government has everything on its side. We have very little. We can't give up on the little muscle we have." The "muscle" to which he referred comprised sanctions, South Africa's isolation, and international support for the ANC. Consequently, Zuma said, the ANC would refrain from publicly recommending to foreign governments not to isolate South Africa. The ANC would not push for further isolation, however. He asked: "If the isolation stops and the government says, 'go to hell!', what can we do then?"

He subsequently made a strategically strong point: "The South African problem is a political problem and it needs a political solution. In getting a political solution the South African government should not be unchecked. Isolation, and sanctions and international pressure are the methods by means of which a check can be kept on the government." To which he added: "Time is limited." What struck me during the discussion was the ANC interlocutors' attitude that it was a matter of urgency to talk to the government. This was undoubtedly closely connected with President Mikhail Gorbachev's pressure on the ANC and the rapidly changing situation in what was then still the Soviet Union. And then there was the issue of the UDF/MDM that was increasingly becoming a protest movement in its own right. Both Mbeki and Zuma were clearly nervous about this. Let alone the envisaged election of the ANC's National Executive Committee that was due to take place by the middle of 1990. There was an explicit aversion to the Pan-

Africanist Congress (PAC) on the part of the ANC members. The attitude towards the Azanian People's Organisation (Azapo) and the National Council of Trade Unions (Nactu), however, was positive. After all, these organisations agreed with the ANC's stance on negotiations.

Mbeki spoke about Mandela and his position, an issue that surfaced repeatedly in all the discussions. Oliver Tambo, even after his stroke in August 1989 and his admission to a Swedish clinic, was still the elected president of the ANC. Within the formal structures of the ANC, Mandela's highest rank had been that of a provincial leader in Transvaal. In MK, though, he had held a high position. It could not be taken for granted that Mandela was the next president of the ANC; he was only a possible candidate that could be elected in a democratic process. Zuma emphasised that if Mandela was released, he had to be able to say "this and this will happen going forward". In other words, he had to be allowed to exercise public leadership in order to prevent the eruption of chaos in the country in the wake of his release and the unbanning of organisations. Such chaos would give the military and the police a reason for a violent crackdown. It would also prejudice the ANC's international standing and its negotiation goal.

Mbeki stressed that Mandela needed to have clarity on what he would be allowed to do and what exactly his role would be. The government should not release him uninformed and in a vacuum, as had been done in the case of his father Govan Mbeki. Hence it was better for Mandela to be released under FW de Klerk than under PW Botha.

Pahad raised the question of sanctions. Waving his hands as usual, he put forward the familiar ANC mantra: pressure on the South African government. There was a "but", though: if there were clear signs that the process of political negotiations was under way, the socioeconomic process could also get off the ground. A frowning Terreblanche regarded Pahad very sceptically. The next day (Sunday) Terreblanche returned to the issue of sanctions. He stressed with both hands and emphatic words: "Once the settlement process starts, a clear signal *must* be sent out that can get the economy moving. We dare not wait with that."

I saw that Mbeki was making notes. He had already spoken about "obstacles to rapid change" earlier in the weekend: the South African Defence

Force; the South African Police; the CP; and "white" fears. Mbeki's central argument was that South Africa was, politically and economically, a high-risk country. This placed an extremely important responsibility on De Klerk: He had to convince the international world and the extraparliamentary opposition in a very powerful and resolute manner of his integrity with regard to the settlement process. He had to prove in particular that he understood the high-risk situation and had found a way of dealing with it. Mbeki referred especially to the bankers in this regard. They were nervous. Financial sanctions were biting. Hank Cohen, a senior official of the State Department of the Bush administration, had conveyed this message to Mbeki: "Sanctions are working. We will mark time. If there is no progress with a settlement process in South Africa in the next six to nine months, we'll come up with more stringent measures."

Mbeki subsequently put it very clearly: "We're no longer going to listen to promises. What should the message to bankers be?" He was accommodating, nevertheless, and understood that De Klerk could not lift the state of emergency immediately. He even expressed the view that De Kerk was already making the state of emergency redundant in practice by opening up the political process and allowing protest marches. Mbeki reckoned, however, that De Klerk could accelerate this informal process. "He can take a stronger lead on Monday (2 October). If De Klerk said: Here are a few things that I have done, let's sit down and talk about violence and sanctions too, we'll accept it. We seek clear signals. Not promises."

A salient aspect during the two-day-long sessions was the ANC leadership's insistence on being informed of when Mandela would be released and playing a role in the handling of his release. In my view, there were two reasons for this: on the one hand, the external wing's fear that the release would be used to drive a wedge between this wing and the internal protest movement, and on the other, the genuine concern that Mandela's release would lead to uncontrolled and anarchic chaos unless there was strong solidarity within the protest movement about the manner in which the release had to be dealt with. Mbeki's standpoint was unequivocal: "The way in which he acts during and after his release will determine the release of all political prisoners and the trend of the negotiation process." Zuma also made a point with which I agreed wholeheartedly: "The way of speaking and that which is said in public, will be crucial."

The meeting once again devoted time to the role of Margaret Thatcher. With Bush having succeeded Ronald Reagan as US president, she could no longer rely on support for her anti-sanctions stance. In her own ranks, too, there were people who had started nipping at her political heels. She had been in power too long. Thatcher was vehemently opposed to Renamo, an organisation she considered "a bunch of bandits". Besides, the oil pipeline was Zimbabwe's lifeline. Her patience, which was limited in any case, had started running out as far as South Africa was concerned. She sent a clear message: if the SADF, with Magnus Malan, caused trouble again, she and Britain would wash their hands of South Africa. This was instrumental in sealing Malan's fate as a future role player. She had in the meantime also been told by President George Bush that the Bush administration wanted to establish a certain level of contact with the ANC. Bush did not let himself be intimidated by her. And then there was President Gorbachev, too. It was not only the political situation in South Africa that had changed drastically; so had the global and international context. Unlike Botha, De Klerk understood this. At the conclusion of the meeting, there was consensus that the international world had to accept that South Africans had the right and the duty to resolve their own political problems. The spirit of goodwill that prevailed was captured well by Thabo Mbeki: "We are listening to what FW is saying. We want to be confident that all participants are serious and not playing games. The way in which the ANC deals with (Mandela's) release must also be a signal. The other side must also feel confident."[4]

On Sunday, 1 October 1989, the last day of our meeting, the *Sunday Times* proclaimed on its front page that a meeting between "the Broederbond and ANC leaders" was taking place that day "at an undisclosed venue in England". The newspaper was in its element. Some of the Brothers, it was said, were people with ties to the new minister of constitutional planning, Dr Gerrit Viljoen, who had been given the task of spearheading negotiations with blacks over a future constitution. Apart from Lombard, the names of the participants at the talks were also mentioned. The article stated that one of the ANC officials at the talks would be the chief of information, Thabo

Mbeki, "a moderate who is widely tipped to be successor to the ailing Mr Oliver Tambo". It added: "Mr Mbeki, who cannot be quoted in this article, made a number of conciliatory remarks in a recent TV debate on the BBC."

My comment, which I had been asked for beforehand, was reported correctly: "My movements are my own concern and I don't have to report to anybody." With the assistance of Ebbe Dommisse, I drafted a statement in the form of an article for *Die Burger* which was made available after the appearance of the *Sunday Times* article. It read as follows:

A discussion about views on a peaceful solution to South Africa's problems in which a group of South Africans and the ANC were involved, took place in England over the past weekend. It formed part of a series of academic discussions that have been going on for a number of years.

A spokesman for the group of South Africans, Professor Willie Esterhuyse, issued a statement about the discussion yesterday after inaccurate reports on it had appeared in South Africa.

Professor Esterhuyse made it clear that the discussion had not been held on behalf of either the government or the Afrikaner Broederbond. As a matter of fact, he is not a member of the Broederbond.

The rector of Stellenbosch University, Professor Mike de Vries, was at no stage involved in the discussion.

"Other South Africans and I have been participating in discussions with the ANC on our own responsibility for a few years now. We are doing so on our own behalf and not on behalf of anyone else. These are nothing more than exploratory discussion opportunities, and we consider it unnecessary to issue public statements constantly in this regard. It is regrettable that some individuals and institutions were prejudiced," Professor Esterhuyse said.

One of the members of the ANC group was Mr Thabo Mbeki. Dr Willem de Klerk of Johannesburg was among the group of South Africans. Mr Ebbe Dommisse, assistant editor of *Die Burger*, who is holding discussions with opinion leaders while on a trip to Europe and the US, attended the discussion by invitation as an observer.

The dialogue group agreed that we all had to stick to the same story. Thabo Mbeki, who would inevitably be in the spotlight on account of his position and public profile, would deal with media inquiries together with the ANC's representative in London. I told Mbeki: "Well, our decision about how the leak should be dealt with is the first negotiated settlement between the ANC and Afrikaners. And it wasn't even difficult!" Mbeki retorted: "Yes, but we had a common 'enemy', the 'English press'!" We did not know it then, but at our next meeting in February 1990 we would reach another negotiated settlement.

The leak caused something of a stir in the British media in particular. *The Daily Telegraph* (3 October 1989) reported that while the ANC had confirmed the dialogue session, they denied that the delegates from South Africa represented the "influential Broederbond organisation". The London representative of the ANC stated that the discussion had promoted mutual understanding. It had dispelled misapprehensions about the ANC. He said: "People who come expecting to find bushfighters, their faces twisted in terror, in fact find sensible human beings who care about the future of their country."

The *Financial Times* had interesting commentary under the heading "Inching across the South African divide" (3 October 1989). The paper even used the Afrikaans word "*toenadering*", which was described as a term that was rich in political significance but had no exact equivalent in English. The nearest translation was "coming closer together". The two journalists who wrote the article, Michael Holman and Jim Jones, quoted a diplomat to whom they had spoken, who referred to "talks about talks about talks". I have always had a strong suspicion that this diplomat was Robin Renwick, the British ambassador in South Africa. This phrase had been deliberately chosen both to indicate that there was no question of negotiations and to protect us from political embarrassment in the event of a leak. It was, after all, an informal, unofficial process. Renwick was informed about it. The *Financial Times* also dragged in the issue of the Broederbond. In this case, too, a few Afrikaans words were brought into the English language: "*broederbond*", "*boere republiek*" and "*volk*".

The article in the *Financial Times* was important in one respect: it spelled out the drivers that were going to accelerate the pace of progress towards the conference table. The first driver was the establishment of common ground between Washington and Moscow on a strategy with regard to Southern Africa. The second was the meeting between PW Botha and Nelson Mandela in Tuynhuys. A third driver was insufficient foreign capital for South Africa and the negative effects of trade sanctions. These factors, together with the resurgence of internal protest and the role of Cosatu, were putting great pressure on the system.

Thabo Mbeki also reacted to the leak. Mbeki stressed that the discussions were unofficial. He stated emphatically: "The people who attended were not representing anyone except themselves. They were not representing the Broederbond, and they were not representing the government." He was supported by the ANC's representative in London. An ANC representative even made the point that the ANC would not meet with the Broederbond as an organisation. "It's possible that some were members, but this was a meeting with Afrikaner intellectuals, not the Broederbond." Mbeki stood to lose much if the perception should arise that he was talking officially to the Broederbond. The ANC hawks had their knives out for him. Chris Hani was on his high horse again. During a meeting of the National Working Committee on 13 October 1989 he objected vehemently, especially because he and some of his comrades had not been informed of the discussions.

FW de Klerk, newly inaugurated as South Africa's president, also issued a statement in Pretoria on 2 October. He distanced himself and his government from the discussion in the strongest terms. De Klerk expressed the view that the ANC exploited talks of this kind in order to conceal their true nature as a revolutionary organisation. He declared that his government had been neither directly nor indirectly involved in the meeting. *The Daily Telegraph* (3 October 1989) presented the statement to its readers under the headline "Pretoria attack on Afrikaners' talks with ANC". The headline of *The Independent* (3 October 1989) read: "De Klerk gives ANC talks the seal of disapproval". Not many days after De Klerk's statement, I gave a report-back of my meeting with Mbeki and his comrades to the NIS.[5]

# 13
# A new covenant: 2 February 1990

A fter the Mells Park meeting, from 2 to 3 October 1989, I attended a meeting of the Jubilee Initiative. The *Sunday Times'* informant had known about this meeting, too. The Jubilee participants were both worried and thrilled. Washington Okumu expressed his concern, but also his excitement about the disclosures: Would it be possible to continue with the project now it had been revealed in the press? It was a "miracle of God" that Afrikaners and the ANC were talking to each other, he reckoned. I was not so certain about it being a miracle, and said: "Miracles don't happen by themselves. You have to work to make them happen. That's why the Afrikaans term for 'miracle' (*wonderwerk*) also includes the word 'work'." Everyone seemed impressed. I said the leak had been a blessing in disguise. It had made it possible for me and Mbeki to appear in public together in future. The dialogue project would not be called off. Good damage control had been done.

Walter Kansteiner, an official of the US State Department, was present at the meeting. He stated that a meeting between President George Bush and Oliver Tambo had been cancelled as a result of Tambo's illness. Bush, he maintained, found the ANC's negotiation plan acceptable and was opposed to a Resolution 435 for South Africa by outsiders. He also told us that President George Bush wanted to raise his reputation among black voters in the US and establish a good image in Africa by taking a more conciliatory approach to the ANC. According to Kansteiner, it was said in Bush circles that Thatcher's days were past and that the US would adopt a stronger position in respect of a settlement process in South Africa. Hank Cohen of the State Department would play a role in this regard. Whereas Chester Crocker had planted his flag over settlement processes in Angola–Namibia, Cohen was keen to plant his in South Africa. Such a role would, however, be facilitative with regard to the process that had to be initiated and managed by South Africans themselves.

Plans were rapidly being devised in the US to give the ANC a good public profile, prompted by the Botha-Mandela meeting. The "turning point in Namibia", as Chester Crocker once put it, had opened up new challenges and possibilities for Southern Africa. In fact, it was accepted that a settlement was inevitable and that the ANC with Nelson Mandela would be one of the main players in this process. The US did not want to be left out in the cold. One such initiative was that of Dick Clark's Aspen Institute, which had organised the Bermuda conference. I met Clark again in Cape Town on 9 October 1989. He had held a conference on the Southern African region in Switzerland in the meantime. Members of the US Congress strongly supported his initiative, he told me.

Another initiative was a conference organised by the Africa-America Institute (AAI) in Tarrytown, New York, during the first week of November 1989. Mbeki and I had to share a session on the "new regime" under De Klerk and his thinking about the road ahead, with the theme being: "A climate for negotiations?" We arranged with each other that we would take part, but not talk about the activities of our dialogue group. We had accepted long ago that the British and US intelligence services knew about it. The big question at the centre of this conference was whether "a climate for negotiations" existed in South Africa. The Harare Declaration was of course known in the US by that time. Meanwhile De Klerk was making all kinds of positive noises and had released a few political prisoners, but he had still not met Mandela. My secretary, Lulu Botha, had to plan carefully to get me to New York in time for the conference. She was for many years an important "go-between" in the arrangements for the Afrikaner interlocutors' involvement in the dialogue project.

The conference was attended by a large number of people, including participants from South Africa. The hall was packed. Before the start Thabo Mbeki introduced me to the ANC's representative in Washington, Lindiwe Mabuza, a friendly, plump woman. We greeted each other in African style with a hug. I had purchased a blue check silk-lined jacket in New York in order to look respectable and smart. Mbeki was a natty dresser, and I did not want to compare unfavourably with him. Both of us wore a white shirt and a tie. I told him: "I see you're also wearing a white shirt. So 'white' is not out!" He laughed and replied: "It all depends on what you're going to say today." I was extremely tense. I knew this was going to be a make-or-break appearance for me. There were not only expectations among members of the audience, but also opposition to my presence, especially on the part of some of the South Africans. One of them, a well-known liberal, had asked me sceptically in Afrikaans: "And what are you doing here?"[1]

I was the first speaker, and defended the standpoint that it was premature to say that a climate for negotiations existed in South Africa. South Africa was at best at the start of a pre-negotiation phase. The De Klerk government was making a sincere attempt to build trust and confidence. It was accepted, for instance, that a settlement of the conflict in South Africa could not exclude the ANC and the MDM. The real question, though, was how to facilitate the process, identify the phases thereof, and design a strategy that at least the most important parties would go along with. The release of Nelson Mandela, and especially his future role, as well as the unbanning of the ANC and other organisations, would eventually form part of a structured process of creating a climate for negotiations. A major stumbling block was how to deal with discriminatory legislation, particularly the "Unholy Trinity": group areas, population registration, and laws pertaining to land and property rights – legislation that had guaranteed white political dominance. The withdrawal of the security forces from black townships was another stumbling block. I explained, too, that the De Klerk government followed a two-level strategy: actions at the formal level; actions at the informal level. The latter included the building of contacts over a wide spectrum, as well as an effort to get "unsigned protocols" established between important role players and parties.

After my address, to which Mbeki had listened attentively although he was very familiar with my interpretation of the De Klerk government's open-door approach, he stood up and walked towards me. He removed his ANC lapel badge and pinned it onto the lapel of my expensive new jacket. His voice came with dry humor over the microphone: "The professor has given a good exposition of the ANC's position." The audience was astonished at this friendly interaction. He whispered in my ear: "The Americans are shocked. They have strange ideas about Afrikaners. And they don't know that we know each other and have been talking to each other for a long time."[2] Then he delivered his speech, calm and reasoned as always. He, too, was of the view that it was too soon to talk of a climate for negotiations. There were too many things that still needed to happen, such as the release of Nelson Mandela and other political prisoners, and the unbanning of the ANC and all political organisations. He also devoted much attention to the issue of violence and sanctions. The suspension of the armed struggle and sanctions as a precondition for negotiations was not an option for the ANC. Regarding group rights, he drew a very clear line in the sand: "It is our view that De Klerk is committed to the notion of groups and group rights. What he would be negotiating for is the survival of a system based on the notion of groups. If the National Party came to negotiations saying the notion of groups is non-negotiable, and therefore we must produce a constitution which is based on groups, then of course negotiations could not take place. That would be an affirmation of apartheid." The audience strongly agreed with this view. I realised that Mbeki was making a powerful, emotive point: The notion of groups was directly linked to apartheid. Whoever wanted to talk about groups and group rights would first have to get past that. He was also the soul of reasonableness: The ANC could not expect the De Klerk government to first accept the Freedom Charter before negotiations could take place.

Our speeches subsequently appeared in *Africa Report* (November-December 1989). We were able to speak the way we did because we had by then already gone through a lengthy informal dialogue process. Mbeki was also in direct contact with the NIS by that time. The lapel badge episode nearly landed me in hot water on a later occasion. On Wednesday, 8 November 1989 I presented a course in business ethics at the University of Stellenbosch Business School. I wore my new jacket. In the course of my lecture, I noticed that the students in the front row were restless. One asked: "Professor, could you explain the badge on your jacket to us?" I looked down, and realised that the ANC badge Thabo Mbeki had pinned to my lapel was still there. I had the presence of mind to say: "Oh, this? It's a good friend's way of trying to get me into trouble." I removed the badge, put it in my pocket and carried on with the lecture.

There was a good discussion at the AAI conference. The attitude of the conferees was predominantly pro-ANC. Mbeki played the leading role in the carefully planned and well-orchestrated AAI conference. The platform had been prepared for him, I realised after a conversation with one of the organisers. Mbeki and I also had a few conversations during the conference. He was in a hurry for further meetings with the NIS to take place as soon as possible, and said at one stage: "The longer FW waits to send out a clear and directional message of hope, the more the political and violence pressure in South Africa will intensify. How and when is he going to defuse it?"

De Klerk was, of course, already hard at work to get his own strategy in place. In December 1989 these plans started to take shape during a *bosberaad*. The NIS, abreast of everything, was not yet ready for a further meeting. There was an understanding, though, and informal contact.[3]

Mbeki and I, like many others, knew that the steps that had to be taken to create a climate for negotiations were not the real problem. De Klerk could take those steps "tomorrow", he observed more than once. The problem was the unrest and violence in the country, the ANC's commitment to the armed struggle, and the possibility of a white backlash. These topics surfaced time and again in our conversations. At our previous meeting in England, Mbeki had said at one point: "We don't need to have peace in order to talk about peace. One talks about peace precisely because there isn't peace." He knew, too, that the ANC's violence option was a growing cause of concern in the international community, even among the "friendly" audience at the AAI conference. On this occasion, therefore, he went out of his way to argue that the ANC had been in favour of peace since its founding in 1912. Walter Sisulu, who had spent 26 years in jail, made the same point after his release by De Klerk in October 1989: "We call on the rank and file of all organisations to work together for peace. The ANC has consistently throughout its history been committed to the politics of peace and negotiations." According to the ANC it was the government that had been unable or unwilling to hear this voice, personified by former prime ministers such as DF Malan, Hans Strijdom and HF Verwoerd, who had failed to respond to the ANC's letters. As was known, the NP had been invited to the "Congress of the People" at Kliptown where the Freedom Charter was adopted.

In 1989 violence, and the rationalisation thereof by the ANC and people like Sisulu and Mbeki, was of course directly related to what the ANC was confronted with: the township wars and black-on-black violence. Mbeki used a very convincing argument in this regard: if the ANC would be allowed to function like any other political party, the violence could also be dealt with. It became a matter of great urgency to him. I was not optimistic that this would happen soon, though. Despite all the positive signals, there were still too many complex stumbling blocks. The NIS had had only one meeting with the ANC. The election had instilled hope that things would change under De Klerk. I considered his open-door approach and willingness to talk to be something very positive. He had not yet met Mandela, however. Willem de Klerk and I had positive expectations of the future, but none of them included the possibility of what Sampie Terreblanche referred to at Mells Park as a "dramatic symbolic gesture, a quantum leap".

My NIS contacts were not helpful either as far as announcements or snippets of information about future developments were concerned. Even Mbeki, when he asked me at the AAI conference what I had "heard", seemed disappointed when I said: "Nothing." Barnard and the NIS were of course accustomed to playing their cards close to their chests. It was their job. They had not even briefed PW Botha fully on all the talks. As early as 1988 the feeling in those quarters had been that the chance of a settlement was a one-in-a-thousand opportunity, and that neither Botha nor anyone else should be allowed to wreck it. By December 1989, though, I detected positive indications among my NIS contacts that De Klerk was "the man for the hour". A senior member even said that it was "fortunate" that Chris Heunis, Pik Botha and Barend du Plessis had been defeated earlier that year.

De Klerk's political confidence grew apace after his inauguration. Möller Dippenaar was of the view that the fall of the Berlin Wall shortly after De Klerk became president had been a decisive moment in the growth of his confidence. He knew that Mandela and the ANC, and especially also the communists in the ANC, would be on the back foot and less demanding and militant than before.

De Klerk met Mandela for the first time on 13 December 1989. Unlike the convivial Botha-Mandela tea party, this meeting was much more substantial. Naturally De Klerk had studied Mandela's memorandum to PW Botha. The NIS also had a well-prepared profile of Mandela and his standpoints by that time. At this meeting, Mandela raised the thorny issue of group rights. This was after he had given a lengthy account of how a black colleague of his had crossed paths with De Klerk at the time when the latter was still a lawyer. Mandela, true to his habit of creating a good personal atmosphere, recounted that his colleague had spoken with appreciation of De Klerk. Mandela, too, expressed appreciation of De Klerk: Politics was in his blood, and he descended from a line of leaders. It was unclear whether Mandela intended to mellow De Klerk with these remarks or whether instead he spoke very honestly, as one leader to another. What was unmistakable, however, was his fatherly tone. He was, after all, twenty years older than De Klerk. Hence he felt confident to broach De Klerk's, and the NP's, most cherished notion: group rights. He advised De Klerk to abandon this idea. It sounded like a "modern" version of apartheid.

De Klerk, presumably surprised and taken aback by Mandela's self-confidence, replied that group rights was a way of dealing with white people's fears, particularly regarding black domination. When Mandela explained that, on the contrary, the notion inspired fear and antagonism on the part of black people, De Klerk defused the matter with his assurance that this was something that would be open to discussion. Mandela was satisfied. Group rights were to remain a central issue throughout the settlement process. While Mandela did appreciate the fact that De Klerk was a good and intelligent listener, the meeting, however, did not mark the beginning of a stable relationship of confidence and trust between the two men.

What very few people knew at the time, and which I had no inkling of either, was that De Klerk was already mapping out a path to 2 February with the help of a reliable team. As I was told only after his far-reaching speech of 2 February, this had been a long, incisive and intense preparation process that was not only aimed at developing a strong consensus between himself, his advisers and senior government officials, but also at achieving maximum international and national impact. The Rubicon debacle had been a good lesson in the destructive consequences of a poor speech about South Africa's future coupled with inept communication. My NIS contact told me after 2 February: "The substance of the speech not only had to be a political triumph. It also needed to be a communication triumph." The speech itself, and everything surrounding it, was the product of a well-planned team effort over time – it was neither a miracle nor an individualistic, spur-of-the-moment impulse to play to a large gallery. It had been an ambitious project, executed by committed and capable people.

When I learned more about the detail of the process at a later stage, I asked myself: "How was it possible that nothing leaked out beforehand?" Mike Louw reckoned that the confidentiality of the project had been an essential condition for its success. The participants knew that. They had also been wholeheartedly committed to the project. To all of them, including De Klerk, it had become "the right thing" to do, more than merely a strategic decision, as I had been inclined to regard it. There was, if I may bring in Hannah Arendt, not just an acknowledgement of the failure and injustice of apartheid, but also the willingness to enter into a new "covenant" with the previously oppressed. De Klerk's historic speech not only created a climate for negotiations, but also a new "covenant". Up to the last minute, though, there were serious disagreements about the SACP. Magnus Malan in particular was strongly opposed to the party's unbanning. He had, after all, waged war against the communists' Total Onslaught. Niel Barnard, who was very close to the drafting of the speech, took a different view. Unbanning had to apply to all prohibited organisations. It would bring the SACP into the settlement process and expose the party to public criticism and assessment. The SACP was actually the ANC's problem, not the government's. The evening of 1 February, De Klerk attended a birthday party of his friend Fanna Malherbe for a while before putting the finishing touches to his speech and going to bed in a confident frame of mind.

Apropos of public comment and right-wing resistance, within the ranks of the NIS we often debated the question as to whether De Klerk "had no alternative". Rightists were up in arms about the unbannings, especially in respect of the SACP. According to them, the SACP had been a major reason for the Total Strategy and why young men were sent to Angola to keep "the communists away from our borders". Along with all the other risks De

Klerk took, this was one of the most serious; anticommunist sentiment was embedded in emotions that extended beyond politics and included cultural and religious dimensions as well. The long-standing article of faith of the Afrikaans churches and Afrikaner cultural organisations that South Africa was a "Christian state", couched in Calvinistic terms, also melted into thin air on 2 February 1990.

In light of this, had his decision been unavoidable, or had it been a well-calculated choice? The ANC, and notably Thabo Mbeki, were convinced that international and national pressure had left De Klerk with no alternative. At the AAI conference Mbeki had told his audience, the majority of whom conspicuously signalled their agreement: "The impact of the struggle is very gravely underestimated. The political struggle, the armed struggle, and sanctions have obliged the regime to move. It has had to move. Look at the release of the eight political prisoners on the eve of the Commonwealth conference. The reason is obvious." On Mbeki's part, it was a shrewd strategic position to take at this high-level conference. He was especially intent on motivating the audience: "The struggle must continue, the pressures must continue."

Be that as it may, De Klerk's speech, given the circumstances, was the right speech at the right time, a historic moment in South Africa's history, for which De Klerk earned well-deserved credit. It is indeed correct that he could have taken a different decision had he wanted to. But he chose not to do so. He wanted to break out of the "cycle of violence" towards "peace and reconciliation". The time and the conditions were ripe for such a move.

The speech had a dramatic impact on the ANC, and not only because the organisation had insisted on prior notification of matters such as Nelson Mandela's release and the unbannings. There had been expectations on the part of ANC leaders that De Klerk would create a climate for negotiations in an incremental fashion. Many Afrikaners had thought so too. I, for one, had believed that De Klerk, given his political cautiousness and conservative roots, would not have the courage to take what Terreblanche referred to as a quantum leap. De Klerk proved the ANC and many other people wrong. In particular, he proved that he did not fear the rightists and would not allow them to dictate politics. With a single speech he brought about every-

thing that was required to create a climate for negotiations: the unconditional release of Nelson Mandela, the unbanning of organisations, and
the return of exiles.

Mbeki, too, was caught off guard by the timing and magnitude of De
Klerk's announcement. There was nothing in the speech from which the
ANC or the UDF could extract any political gain. De Klerk was the man of the
moment. The ANC also did not know exactly when Mandela would be released. De Klerk kept the ANC guessing. Shortly after De Klerk's speech,
Mbeki told me that he and Van Zyl Slabbert had discussed the nature and
implications of De Klerk's announcement at a recent meeting between them.
A view that was put about subsequently that Mbeki had, as it were, turned
pale with fright on hearing De Klerk's announcement and had asked un-
certainly: "What do we do know?", was excessively dramatic. He might have
been wrong-footed by the timing and scope of the announcement, but he
was by no means uncertain. Indeed, in October 1989 I had already returned
from England with a message from Thabo Mbeki to the NIS: "Unban one,
unban all."

Four days after De Klerk's announcement, on 6 February, Louw and
Spaarwater were at the Palace Hotel in Lucerne for another meeting with
ANC representatives. The arrangements for this meeting had been made beforehand with the historic announcement of 2 February in view. This time
Mbeki was accompanied by Aziz Pahad, one of the permanent members
of the Afrikaner-ANC dialogue group. The issues on the table were clearly
defined and had been ratified by De Klerk's speech: How to implement all
of this? How do you go about getting people who were being hunted by
the security forces and were wanted by the police for all kinds of offences,
safely into the country? Mbeki had raised the issue of indemnity with me
on an earlier occasion, as well as the question as to who would be considered
political prisoners. It was the start of a tough bargaining process. Of give
and take. Working committees were eventually established to get the official
"talks about talks" off the ground and thrash out thorny issues in a small-
group context. These committees were even given special names: Alpha
(Mandela's release); Charlie (talks at the political level); Delta (contact between the NIS and the ANC's intelligence services); Bravo (prisoner releases)!

Two weeks later another meeting took place in Switzerland, this time at the Bellevue-Palace Hotel in Bern; the Swiss intelligence service had apparently started showing an interest in the meetings in Lucerne. Niel Barnard and Fanie van der Merwe, who were involved in the talks with Mandela, also attended the meeting. Everyone travelled under false names. Joe Nhlanhla, who would be in charge of the new South Africa's intelligence service in later years, represented the ANC together with Mbeki and Pahad. Fanie van der Merwe, an official and a legal expert, was an illuminating addition to the team. Within the civil service and during the PW Botha era he had devoted much attention to constitutional models. In 1988, together with Barnard and Louw, he became a member of the team that conducted more structured discussions with Nelson Mandela. Van der Merwe was present at all phases of the settlement process, including, for instance, the negotiation of the Groote Schuur Minute, the Pretoria Minute and the DF Malan Accord. He was a key person at Codesa 1 and Codesa 2, and established a special understanding with Mac Maharaj in particular. The two of them played a huge role in the process that led to the Truth and Reconciliation Commission being given constitutional status. During the official negotiation process, Van der Merwe was instrumental in steering De Klerk and his government towards acceptance of majority rule in a unitary state. Years later, he would have a hand in launching the first talks between the Irish Republican Army (IRA) and the Loyalists, in South Africa.

The Bern gathering became an important and fairly intensive meeting, with the return of the exiles high on the agenda. A high-risk decision was also taken on this occasion: a big meeting should take place inside South Africa, in which the National Executive Committee (NEC) of the ANC and the government had to be involved. Serious disagreement then arose about the position of Joe Slovo of the SACP. This was something I had realised early on in the Afrikaner-ANC dialogue group: Slovo's possible participation would be a red-hot potato. He was, after all, the embodiment of the Total Onslaught. Slovo's participation immediately made Barnard's hackles rise: Slovo could not attend the envisaged meeting, he maintained. He was not acceptable. Mbeki, however, dug in his heels: Slovo was a member of the ANC's NEC. No Slovo, no meeting.

Mbeki contended that the government could not dictate to the ANC about who they included in the delegation. Barnard phoned his president, FW de Klerk, in South Africa. He was equally adamant: Slovo was not welcome. As head of state, he could not allow the leader of the SACP into the country. By this time Barnard was more conciliatory. After he had spoken once more to Mbeki, who had again stressed that the government could not prescribe to the participating parties who should be included or omitted, Barnard made another call to De Klerk. The principle should be that each party could designate its participants autonomously. If the government wanted to designate, say, Eugene Terre'Blanche, the ANC could not object. It was an important breakthrough.

Two weeks later the fourth meeting of the contact group was held in the Noga-Hilton in Geneva. Hereafter the launch committee, which had been put together in Bern, could begin with its activities inside South Africa.

The NIS, who had a lion's share in everything, experienced anxious hours. Indemnity was a big problem. Legislation was required for this, and it was being deliberately delayed by some of De Klerk's conservative parliamentarians. The second problem was even more serious: members of the state's hit squads and right-wing militants. Incidents that could sabotage the sensitive and still fragile process had to be avoided. The NIS had to include such threats in its intelligence focus. It was an extremely complex and sensitive matter. In fact, early in 1990 I realised that the success of the settlement process would depend to a great extent on effective intelligence work. Barnard and his team were more than equal to the task. Fortunately, the NIS was able to provide safe houses to the leadership of the exiled ANC and also make transport and other arrangements. The NIS had the necessary funds and capabilities at its disposal to deal discreetly and professionally with such a delicate operation. And the exiled leadership trusted the NIS.[4]

The ANC representatives, Jacob Zuma, Penuell Maduna and Gibson Mkanda, travelled from Lusaka to South Africa by plane on 21 March 1990. They would be assisted by two internally based members, Mathews Phosa and Curnick Ndlovu. This committee, which had been agreed on in Switzerland, was tasked with planning the first public meeting between the De Klerk government and the ANC in conjunction with the NIS. It was a very delicate planning meeting that had to take place in the utmost secrecy. Louw and Spaarwater met the ANC contingent on the runway. Spaarwater, who gave me the impression he relished this type of operation, had to help with smuggling the visitors unnoticed past customs. They were first taken to a safe house and from there to a smallish hotel north of Pretoria, the Hertford Hotel. Because there was no official indemnity yet, this visit had to be controlled very strictly. By then there was already an unspoken but well-functioning agreement or compact between the NIS and the exiled leadership (Zuma, Maduna) to respect each other's bona fides. The NIS kept its word.

Jacob Zuma tells an anecdote about one of his visits. On that occasion he was transported by Basie Smit, then head of the security police, in a government car from the airport. Smit would resign in 1994 when De Klerk's Goldstone commission of inquiry implicated him in the possibility of pro-Inkatha destabilisation actions against the ANC from within the security services. Smit settled in comfortably next to Zuma in the car, while in the eyes of the police the latter was still a terrorist who had to be caught or eliminated. Like other ANC visitors, Zuma was taken on a sightseeing trip through Pretoria by car. Among other attractions, Smit took Zuma to the Voortrekker Monument, the prime symbol of the Afrikaners' struggle for survival and freedom – in that case against the Zulus, Jacob Zuma's ethnic-cultural home.

# 14
# Cricket, economic posers, and Mandela released

It is remarkable how often coincidence plays a role in delicate and informal track-two contacts. Such "coincidences" may occur on the personal or on the more impersonal level. Pahad and I, for instance, had a connection: the Desai family of Roodepoort near Johannesburg. Kobie Coetsee and Pieter de Waal had been fellow students at the then University of the Orange Free State. Father Theodore Hesburgh, the dialogue broker who brought the Russian Vasily Emelyanov and the American John McCone together to reach an agreement on nuclear disarmament after many years, had been good friends with Emelyanov and Leonid Zamyatin, who later headed the Soviet news agency Tass. This "impossible friendship" (what Westerners could or would be friends with communists?) prevented a possible Armageddon. "Coincidence" has many facets and is related to networks, but there are also unplanned, unpredictable and unregulated incidents that assume historic-dramatic dimensions at a specific moment. This is usually described as something that happens "at the right time through the right people", albeit that it was unplanned.

Long before De Klerk's speech of 2 February 1990, it had been agreed that the dialogue group would meet at Mells Park from Friday, 9 February to Sunday, 11 February. The timing was a "fortunate coincidence". No one had had an idea of what would happen before this weekend. At the request of the ANC participants, it had also been agreed that this session should represent mainly Afrikaner business leaders. The business sector, Mbeki stressed repeatedly, would have to play a key role in the transition to an inclusive democratic dispensation as well as thereafter. It was an aspect to which he returned time and again: "Without the cooperation of businesspeople and without a growing economy, we will struggle with the democratisation project." I recall that he once told me more or less the following: "The political process of transition to an inclusive democracy with international status should not be too difficult. We would be able to manage that. The socioeconomic transition process, though, is the more complex issue. There is terrible poverty, and the legacy of apartheid is visible everywhere. There are also high material expectations on the part of the oppressed. The gap between rich and poor is massive. How are we going to integrate 30 million blacks, mostly poor, in an economic process that is currently controlled by a rich, white elite? The right to vote isn't going to be our problem. Socio-economic rights, access to the economy and a share in South Africa's natural resources, including land, will be the real issue. You can't eat the right to vote. You can use it, however, to achieve socioeconomic rights. Afrikaners, given their history, ought to understand that."

The economy had been a talking point in all our discussions, from the basement talks in 1987 to the meeting in September/October 1989. There were mainly two reasons for this: the stranglehold of sanctions and the limited ability of businesspeople to expand; and the realisation among all the participants that a settlement would have no chance of sustainable success if the economic engine didn't start firing on all cylinders. Mbeki, who had studied at the University of Sussex and knew much about economic matters, had remarked over and over during the talks and in our private conversations that businesspeople needed to be involved in the dialogue project. The question, though, was: when, and who? De Klerk's election made it easy to answer the first part. Whereas Botha had tried to co-opt businesspeople to support his plans, De Klerk wanted to cooperate with them. He had a better understanding of the importance and functioning of the free-market economy than Botha. He was not only a proponent of the rule of law, albeit within the limits of his group-rights thinking, but also a free-market advocate with a good grasp of the crucial role of businesspeople in the development of the country. He had even received "lessons" in this regard from business leaders such as Wim de Villiers from the Sanlam/Gencor stable and people from Barlow Rand, and businesspeople were brought into his cabinet. It was also De Klerk who persuaded Jan Steyn of the Urban Foundation to launch a state-supported developmental initiative in February 1990.

The big question was who should attend further talks at Mells Park. The

258 — CRICKET, ECONOMIC POSERS, AND MANDELA RELEASED

ANC participants wanted to talk to Afrikaners from the business sector.[1] Not to English-speaking businesspeople. This preference was something I only understood later. What interested them in this regard was not just Afrikaners' close proximity to the centre of political power, but also their past. As Aziz Pahad put it to me, they had to pull themselves up by their own bootstraps after the Depression. And before that, they had had to deal with the aftermath of the Anglo-Boer war. Blacks could learn a lot from Afrikaners. How were Sanlam and Volkskas started, for example? Where did Anton Rupert come from? And the Sasols?

I decided to invite only people from the Sanlam stable and not individuals from rival groups. This would guarantee confidentiality. My contact in this regard was Willem Pretorius, a friend and kindred spirit who also lived in Stellenbosch. Pretorius, the managing director of Metropolitan Life insurance company, was in all respects the soul of integrity. The two of us had already cooperated earlier in efforts to make it plain to business leaders that apartheid was on its deathbed and that a negotiated settlement was the only alternative. He was immediately enthusiastic and suggested Marinus Daling, the head honcho of Sankorp and also Sanlam, as a possible participant. Daling was more than willing to participate as long as it remained confidential "and the government doesn't cause trouble". We decided to invite one of his senior colleagues as well, a brother of Minister Barend du Plessis: Attie du Plessis. I knew him, and never ceased to wonder at his immaculate appearance and shiny shoes. Du Plessis was hesitant and first wanted to consult Daling and his brother, but gave us the green light shortly afterwards.

I was keen to involve the financial press as well and invited Gert Marais, the editor of *Finansies en Tegniek*. Like a journalist smelling a good story, he agreed at once. (At his request I later ran a column in *Finansies en Tegniek* for a long time, which was a significant experience in my life.) The ANC had specifically requested the participation of someone who could talk about the stock exchange, a topic of which they knew nothing. I had to find a person who would fit in with the Sanlam group and decided to invite Mof Terreblanche, a stockbroker with close ties to Naspers and Sanlam. Decisions of this kind, within the context of an unofficial and confidential track-two process, are not always easy. Fleur de Villiers had given me good advice in this regard: The interest of the dialogue project and the needs of the "other party" in the project are the decisive factors.

Thabo Mbeki was convinced that the modernising South African economy and the rise of Afrikaners in the economy had played a crucial part in the erosion of apartheid ideology. We were in agreement that there was a clash between the centrifugal political force field of apartheid and the centripetal force field of a modernising econmy. He remarked that PW Botha's abolition of the notorious influx-control measures had not been a moral decision. It had been a strategically inevitable decision in the interest of the modernising South African economy. Besides, he added, Afrikaners had migrated to middle- and higher-income brackets. They were no longer the Afrikaners of 1948. Sanctions hurt them. Nor did they like their country being a global pariah.

On Thursday, 8 February 1990 I flew from Cape Town to Johannesburg and from there to London. Owing to my aversion to long queues, I am in the habit of boarding flights early. On that occasion I was one of the first passengers to board the plane. A little while later I was approached by an air hostess, who inquired whether I was Professor WP Esterhuyse. My presence was required urgently in the VIP lounge. Someone from the airport management would escort me. She did not say what it was about. I replied that we were due to depart in 15 minutes, and I had to catch a connecting flight to London. She reassured me – our flight would be delayed. My escort informed me that Minister Pik Botha wanted to speak to me urgently. On our arrival in the VIP lounge, he called the minister's office. Pik Botha was as friendly and charming on the telephone as only he could be. After apologising for the inconvenience, he explained that he had to take part in Ted Koppel's world-famous TV programme *Nightline* later that evening, together with Thabo Mbeki. Could I please arrange with Mbeki that the discussion would be conducted in a gracious and civil manner?

He knocked me for six. I had been under the impression that my visit to England with the business leaders had been kept under wraps. Botha said: "Just use the phone in the lounge."

I called Mbeki in London and conveyed the request to him. This was the first time that an ANC leader would engage in a discussion with an NP cabinet minister, and on a high-profile programme at that. Mbeki kept quiet for a moment before replying: "Tell Botha I'll address him as 'minister'." And then, with a chuckle: "Tell him that when the ANC takes over the government, I'll make him my deputy." I called Botha and conveyed only the first part of the message to him. After that Botha and Mbeki often talked to each other on the phone. I later watched a recording of the programme and also discussed it with Mbeki. One of the things he said in the course of the conversation became anchored in my mind like a beacon light: "We are at the beginning of a process," with the goal being "a political settlement to end apartheid". A facet of this process had been our talks since 1987.

On Friday, 9 February 1990 we all gathered at Mells Park. As usual, Michael Young saw to it that we arrived on time in comfortable, chauffeur-driven cars. The meeting had been arranged prior to De Klerk's speech of 2 February 1990, and a sense of great excitement and expectations prevailed among the Afrikaners. And naturally a good dose of confidence too, because De Klerk had unlocked the door to negotiations. I was the only person in our group who had held discussions with the ANC before. As was to be expected from dedicated businessmen, they were sharply focused on what affected their business interests most profoundly: sanctions and nationalisation. These issues had to become history as soon as possible. This was a high priority, one of them said. When Nelson Mandela would be released, was almost an afterthought.

With De Klerk's speech barely a week old and having been analysed worldwide for pointers as to what would happen when, our dinner that Friday evening took place in a very good-natured spirit. On the ANC side, Thabo Mbeki, Aziz Pahad and Tony Trew were once again present. A new addition to their ranks was Joe Nhlanhla, who had been involved in the ANC's guerilla activities and would occupy an important position in the ANC's government elite after 1994. Also present was someone from the ANC's London office, who did not say much. Mbeki was his charming self, smartly dressed as always. Aziz Pahad, the jovial member of the ANC's team, went out of his way to put the business leaders at ease. It was not really necessary. In South Africa, they were used to luxurious settings and symbols of success and wealth. Nhlanhla looked at all of us searchingly and with a brooding expression. I felt strangely attracted to him. I knew a little bit about his background and wondered whether, and how, I could get past his eyes to reach him. He was not as friendly and jovial as Jacob Zuma, but rather aloof. About a week after our meeting, together with Mbeki and Pahad, he would hold talks in Switzerland with Louw, Spaarwater, Fanie van der Merwe and Niel Barnard, the head of the NIS.

Mbeki, who had travelled to Britain from Switzerland where he had met with the NIS, divulged nothing about the NIS meeting. He only told me later: "There was good progress. From now on things will move very quickly." We all talked about De Klerk's speech. Everyone realised that a new era with difficult challenges was at hand. There was consensus that De Klerk had done a brave thing. It was a turning point in our country's history, albeit that we did not know exactly what it would involve. Willem Pretorius told me privately: "After this, De Klerk won't be able to prevent black majority rule in a unitary state. White dominance and white political influence are over. De Klerk may not realise it today, but that is what will happen."

After dinner, we assembled in a comfortably furnished smoking room/library. A fire was burning merrily in the fireplace. In line with agreed practice, we steered clear of serious and contentious topics and instead talked about general matters and shared interesting personal details. The intention behind the Friday night gatherings was to allow participants to socialise and to foster a feeling of solidarity. The atmosphere was relaxed, and the business leaders and ANC members could learn more about each other. After all, they had never spoken to each other before. First meetings between traditional "enemies" are usually ceremonial and artificially friendly. This is necessary, but not of material importance. One should not be too sentimental about this, but rather regard it as a sense of "common decency" before the start of the chess game. I was astounded, however, by the ease and openness with which people talked and the conspicuous signs of goodwill. Daling told me: "We (the businessmen) will be able to work with these guys." He asked: "I suppose not everybody in the ANC thinks like them?"

Around ten o'clock that night, Mof Terreblanche asked Mbeki a question that caused the latter to stiffen visibly. Terreblanche, who was a sports fanatic, inquired whether the ANC could not do something to get the protests and unrest surrounding the rebel cricket tour, led by the British player Mike Gatting, under control. He lived near the Newlands cricket grounds, his children went to school in the area, and things were becoming unsafe. Terreblanche was a close friend of De Klerk's. The rebel tour was a big headache for the government and put great pressure on measures to maintain public order. Besides being a circumvention of the sports boycott that was supported by Western governments, the tour was also an emotional and effective mobilisation focus for the MDM. There was great anger in these circles.

Terreblanche's question made me go cold with shock. I glanced at Joe Nhlanhla and imagined that his eyes had grown darker and his expression even more brooding. Pahad was always quick to defuse a tricky situation. He and I said almost simultaneously that we should perhaps discuss the matter even though it was delicate. Terreblanche, also a jovial person but a newcomer to the dialogue group, was of course blissfully unaware of the somewhat loaded atmosphere. Daling, who disliked long stories but rather sought solutions, said immediately that we had to find a way of defusing the situation around the cricket tour. South Africa, he maintained, had more important things to attend to than a rebel tour. Mbeki nodded his head in agreement. Nhlanhla too – even with a gleam in his eyes. He, Pahad and Mbeki knew by then what had been discussed with the NIS, and that further talks would be held in Switzerland in a few days' time.

It turned into an intense, very honest and no-holds-barred discussion – in fact, a negotiated settlement of an extremely delicate problem. The rebel tour was, after all, the focus of a nationally organised protest movement from the ranks of the MDM under the leadership of the activist Krish Naidoo. There was money at stake, too: the rebels were being paid handsomely, and a second tour was already on the agenda. As a result of the sports boycott, playing opportunities had to be "bought" for South African cricketers. The ANC members explained the reasons for the sports boycott. It formed a good introduction for the following day's planned discussion on sanctions. Mbeki made his point calmly, but I knew he was inexorable: Apartheid, the government and those who were advantaged had to be hit where it hurt most.

Isolation was a major weapon. If the settlement process in South Africa were to get under way, certain boycotts could be relaxed gradually.

Daling, who took the lead and wanted to move towards a solution, said that Sankorp had good links with the well-known legal personality Michael Katz. Katz, in turn, had ties with the South African cricket governing body and Dr Ali Bacher. In Daling's view, the present tour should be shortened and its second leg cancelled. Sankorp would carry any costs that might be involved. Pretorius, Terreblanche and the other Afrikaners were openly enthusiastic. Mbeki looked surprised at first, and then declared that it was not a bad idea. There were bigger issues that required attention than well-paid rebels. He turned to Pahad and told him to call Sam Ramsamy, who spearheaded the ANC's highly successful sports boycott against South Africa from London. Pahad had to brief him on what had been agreed. Ramsamy, in turn, had to brief Krish Naidoo. Naidoo and Bacher should confer with each other in Johannesburg that same weekend, and come to an arrangement as to how they would implement the agreement.

Naturally the business leaders, Mbeki and the other ANC participants didn't know at the time that Mandela would be released that Sunday. Pahad, a passionate cricket fan, had one request: once the sports boycott was lifted, the first official match should be against India. That country was one of apartheid's fiercest antagonists. Du Plessis was asked to liaise with Michael Katz. He was busy on the telephone until far into the night, a bitterly cold one. It was long past midnight when he managed to get hold of Katz and informed him of the dialogue group's decision, for which there was of course no official mandate. As Du Plessis put it: "For me personally it was highly stressful; the instruction could boomerang." Du Plessis later played a key role in the formation of Business South Africa and in other talks after 1994 to foster institutional unity in the business sector.

That this initiative was taken during the weekend of Nelson Mandela's release, but without the group having known about this on the Friday night, was a particularly fortunate conjuncture. It undoubtedly made the meeting and conversation between Bacher and Naidoo easier and turned Sunday, 11 February into an exceptionally special day. Early on Saturday, 10 February I received a message from South Africa. Our group should watch television later that afternoon: De Klerk was going to make an announcement. Terreblanche received a smilar call from another source in Pretoria. On Sunday, 11 February Mandela was a free man. South Africa's cricket liberation, too, started on that day. The rebel tour was cancelled as had been agreed, and the demonstrations against the remaining four matches were called off. In England, where we had our meeting, the cricket world welcomed the decision. But the big news, of course, was Nelson Mandela's release.

The story of the cancellation of the rebel tour did not begin in South Africa, but in the country where the leader of the rebels hailed from. And it had started when Mof Terreblanche spoke out of turn while we were chatting sociably over good South African wine and Scotch whisky. On 10 November 1991 South Africa's national cricket team played its first international match after the sports boycott. It took place in India! The sports boycott was over. So were the demonstrations against South African sports teams. Pahad's wish had been granted, and this match became a symbol of South Africa's welcome into the world.

After breakfast on Saturday, 10 February we gathered formally in the seminar room. It was the first time that we allowed photographs to be taken, including a group photo. Two vexed issues were on the agenda: economic sanctions and nationalisation. Two of my sons, De Waal and Friedrich, had arrived from London and sat apart from us, listening to the discussion. It was a frank but tough discussion. Understandably, the business leaders were impatient to see sanctions lifted. A South Africa without apartheid needed a growing economy. Their argument was that De Klerk's speech of 2 February had removed the need for sanctions.

Mbeki and the rest of his group, however, were adamant: The negotiation process had not started yet. To the ANC, economic sanctions were a major instrument of pressure and a weapon. The lifting of sanctions, like the issue of violence, was part of the envisaged negotiated settlement. It could not be a condition for the process. Besides, the ANC was sure that the international world would wait for a signal from the organisation before lifting sanctions. As an afterthought, they said this did not rule out the possibility of a relaxation of certain sanctions being put into effect informally. This could only be discussed, however, once other conditions had been met: visible releases of political prisoners, especially Nelson Mandela; the return of exiles; definite arrangements about the rules and mechanisms of the negotiation process. The business leaders did not seem thrilled. Their focus was on the economy, not on political issues. The ANC's focus, on the other hand, was mainly on the political process. We arrived at an understanding of sorts nonetheless: A negotiated political settlement and the establishment of a democratic state would have to be buttressed by a sound and growing economy. Poverty alleviation and job creation would be a keystone for socio-economic stability. Some or other time the business sector would have to be involved in the settlement process. The ANC members were also very optimistic about the likelihood of a "dividend" after the fall of apartheid. I even got the impression that they believed there was a right to such a dividend.

The issue of nationalisation became a major bone of contention. Some of the ANC interlocutors clung doggedly to the letter of the Freedom Charter. The mines were the prime target. Also agricultural land. The business leaders were strongly opposed to this notion. They advanced two arguments: investor confidence would be undermined; and the state and state-owned corporations were incapable of creating jobs and wealth. The expertise to achieve this was to be found in a dynamic free-market system. The gulf between the two parties was wide. I realised that the favouring of whites by the apartheid system had also sabotaged the credibility of the free-market system among blacks, and that it would take long to change the distrust of, and even resistance to, a free-market system. Thabo Mbeki then repeated something he had said before: the ANC was neither communist nor socialist, but essentially a social-democratic organisation.

Few of the businessmen understood what he meant when he observed that the Freedom Charter did not envisage a socialist state, but a developmental state. However, the (re-)interpretation of this foundational document of the ANC was not at that stage on the agenda of the ANC's internal debate, in any case not in the period following Nelson Mandela's release and during and after the 1994 election. A developmental state would later become Mbeki's passion when he took over as deputy president and then as president of the country. Mbeki was never personally in favour of nationalisation. His notion of a "soft" developmental state, built on negotiated partnerships with the private sector, had been a conscious attempt to avoid a "hard" developmental state, in other words, a state that has a finger in every pie and believes that it can drive the economy.

The issue of restitution surfaced. There was a strong consensus on the part of the ANC members that apartheid was solely to blame for poverty and socioeconomic inequalities. Political and economic power had been deliberately monopolised in the hands of whites. Apartheid was the concentration of power for the sake of white domination on all fronts. That was why economic sanctions hit so hard. Hence the question was: Given the advantages it had enjoyed in the past, what was the private sector going to do about the socioeconomic harm suffered by blacks? And what was the responsibility of the state in this regard?

The businessmen were visibly uncomfortable. I threw in the phrase "restitutive justice" as opposed to "retributive justice". It made no impression. Everyone knew intuitively that this issue would gain more and more prominence in future. Pretorius referred to the "damage" and "legacy" of apartheid. I told Mbeki that whites in general and Afrikaners in particular would find it very hard to accept, or even acknowledge, the notion of collective responsibility for apartheid. Daling, Pretorius and Du Plessis felt very strongly about skills development and the creation of training opportunities. The three of them, together with people such as Dr Motlana, Advocate Dikgang Moseneke and Franklin Sonn, would later become the driving force in launching Metropolitan Life as the first big corporate empowerment action. I was on the board of Metropolitan at the time.

After lunch we reassembled in the seminar room and tried to sum up the main points of the morning's discussion. We also identified problem areas. This was something that the dialogue group managed to do very openmindedly and unemotionally during all our discussions, which was in my view one of the great plusses of the dialogue process. It was especially the case at this meeting. The talks focused less on the past and more strongly on the future. As he and I had agreed beforehand, Terreblanche interrupted the discussion at one stage and said that we should adjourn to the television room: De Klerk was going to announce that he would release Mandela the following day (Sunday). The group was dumbstruck, particularly the ANC members. Pahad remarked: "There he does it again, pulling the rug from under our feet." The ANC had long insisted that Mandela's release should be discussed with the ANC leadership in advance. They had also requested to be informed of the date of his release.

Once again De Klerk and his advisers had done the unexpected, in the hope that the element of surprise might guarantee him and his government the initiative in the entire settlement process. We adjourned to the television room and listened to De Klerk's speech together, Afrikaners and ANC members, many of us with tears in our eyes. Afterwards we were in a joyous mood and drank champagne. It became a festive occasion of intensely experienced brotherhood and camaraderie. De Klerk's risk-taking was lauded from all sides. Everyone speculated: What would Mandela look like? How would the masses react? Mbeki was constantly on the telephone, to Lusaka and also to South Africa. A massive gathering was being organised on the Parade in Cape Town, where Mandela would deliver his first public speech in 27 years. Mbeki told me that the big question was how the excited crowd would conduct themselves, and whether the ANC/MDM and other organisations would be able to ensure an orderly state of affairs.

We accepted that our talks had come to an end. Late that evening a British TV station tracked me down. They offered to send a car to transport me and my two sons to London for a TV interview. The TV journalist asked whether I perhaps knew where Mbeki was, as he would like to get him to participate in the interview as well. He would arrange for me and Mbeki to watch Mandela's release together. Mbeki, who stood next to me, shook his head to indicate that I should not reveal his whereabouts. I advised the journalist to call the ANC's London office. An appointment was arranged for Mbeki at the TV studio. On the Sunday morning we all departed for London. It became an amusing situation. My two sons and I enjoyed the luxury of being fetched by car while the rest of the group, including Mbeki, had to travel by train. It was a very cold day. Willem Pretorius had a bottle of Kirsch with which they tried to ward off the cold.

Mbeki, Aziz Pahad, my sons and I met again in a London TV studio. We did not talk much but sat watching the events unfolding at Victor Verster Prison, where an excited crowd was waiting for Mandela to make his first public appearance in 27 years. Mbeki remarked half matter-of-factly to Pahad: "I wonder if he's going to look very different from the photos we have of him?" I told my two sons in Afrikaans: "Watch Mbeki when Mandela appears. You'll be able to conclude from that whether you have a future in South Africa." We already knew that Mandela, accompanied by his wife Winnie, would walk out of the house in which he had lived on the grounds of Victor Verster. He had insisted on being released there, and not in Pretoria as the government had wanted. It took longer than had been anticipated, and the five of us could not hide our impatience. At last Nelson Mandela made his appearance, with Winnie at his side. Mbeki pulled calmly on his pipe and said eventually: "Now there is hope for the country. Now there will be peace."

Shortly afterwards we were called for the TV interview. As we walked to where we had to sit, I remarked to Mbeki, with the first landing of a human on the moon in mind: "A few steps out of prison. A huge leap forward for our people." He looked at me, smiled slightly and said: "Thank you, comrade. We will meet in Pretoria."

# 15
# Swan song in England

D e Klerk and his advisers had undoubtedly taken the wind out of the
ANC's sails on 2 February 1990. To reinforce the initiative that had
been captured with this move, De Klerk did something very risky: he invited Mandela to Tuynhuys and, without Mandela having bargained on
that, simply stated that he was going to release him. The announcement
would be made on Saturday, 10 February. Mandela, I was told later – it was
also confirmed in his autobiography – was not happy at all with this pro-
cedure. He had wanted time to prepare himself for his release. In fact, he
told De Klerk that he needed a week for this and that he did not want to be
released in the north of the country, but at the grounds of Victor Verster
Prison. He believed that De Klerk had acted in an authoritarian manner.
Although the two later came to a workable understanding, there was little
trust between them from that day. This trust deficit increased over time,
giving rise to a situation that is described in the literature as "low trust" (as
opposed to "high trust"). De Klerk and his advisers gained only a short-term
advantage from the way they organised Mandela's release. The longer-term
damage had not been factored in. Journalists were informed of Nelson
Mandela's release before he himself knew about it. This was an ill-considered
strategic mistake.

Mandela's insistence on more time to plan his release made sense. He had
to deliver a speech in front of an international audience. Massive crowds
would be waiting to welcome him, and order would have to be maintained.
The ANC/UDF wanted to have a hand in the process. His release, a momentous
international event, was, as Möller Dippenaar aptly summed it up, an "enormous security risk". Also for De Klerk. What would happen if the crowds
got out of control?

Mbeki and I, like millions of others, watched the historic release in Paarl
on television. Mandela, who was due to deliver his first public speech after

27 years in prison and as the world's best-loved political prisoner from a balcony of the Cape Town City Hall to a crowd on the Parade, was nearly five hours late. Winnie, who had to fetch him at the Victor Verster Prison, had also arrived late. The ANC/UDF would help ensure that order and security arrangements were in place. Security personnel from the state were, however, inconspicuously present among the crowds. One of them told me later about the anxiety, and even dread, on their part; the ANC/UDF's hastily made arrangements were not up to scratch when it came to controlling the surging mass of people. The delirious crowd just about swamped the car in which Mandela and his wife were transported, as well as other cars in the convoy. Mbeki and I watched the subsequent events in Cape Town on television in different parts of London: he in the company of his ANC comrades, and I with my Afrikaner dialogue partners in a hotel.

There was chaos on the Parade. Mandela could not get to the balcony. Rioting even erupted, and the police fired. As I watched the shambolic events, I started doubting whether the dream of peace would ever become a reality. But I did not feel at liberty to express my doubt to Mbeki. If I had, it might have created the impression that I, as a white Afrikaner, had reservations about the ability of black people to govern South Africa effectively. Mbeki, who once told me that the well-known African-American politician Andy Young had said the ANC would prove one day that blacks were capable of governing a sophisticated country, had an understandable sensitivity in this regard. To him, this was a facet of white racism and the explicit as well as implicit confidence in "whiteness" and the "qualities of excellence" it symbolised.

Mandela eventually had to deliver his speech with a pair of borrowed spectacles. He read it out while prominent figures from the ANC/UDF occupied the balcony. It was never clear to me who all had had a hand in the drafting of the speech. A growing sense of disappointment enveloped me like a dark cloud as I sat listening to his words: a declaration of protest and resistance, steeped in ANC/UDF rhetoric; enemy-against-enemy, despite a somewhat oblique reference to De Klerk's "integrity". Two weeks later, after a conversation with someone from the NIS, I realised that the manoeuvre on the part of De Klerk and his advisers to throw an unprepared Mandela in at the deep end, had paid off. Mandela's first public appearance was actually a political fiasco. The rhetoric had been directed at his supporters, not at the broad South African society and the international world. Had De Klerk and his advisers perhaps intended to expose the emperor's lack of clothes?

The following day, in the company of Archbishop Desmond Tutu, it was a totally different story, as I heard from a journalist friend who had been present. Mandela was his true self: peace seeker; conciliator; moderate ; non-racial. The journalists were astounded by his conciliatory attitude towards the Afrikaners and their fears in particular. The "leftists", I was told, were upset. They had hoped that Mandela would be more aggressive, but on this occasion he spoke positively about De Klerk, said that he could be trusted to go the full distance on the road ahead, and even stated that he, Mandela, was not a communist. However, the nationalisation of mines, as envisaged in the Freedom Charter, had to be considered. The NIS, some of whose members had held talks with Mandela over many years, was highly satisfied with the moderation Mandela displayed on Monday, 13 February 1990. This was how they had come to know him. But, as someone remarked: "He is now among his people, and a public figure. Will he be able to withstand the militants' pressure? Will we manage to create a middle ground?"

If there are indeed "lessons" to be learnt from history, there was something I realised only too well during these times: Freedom does not necessarily bring peace. It opens up possibilities for new power struggles. No one understood this risk better than De Klerk and his security advisers. From 1990 onwards, black-on-black violence reached the proportions of a full-scale civil war. Between 1990 and 1994 many people died in the township wars and unrest in rural areas, notably in the former Transvaal and of course in KwaZulu and Natal. In these areas it was mainly the ANC supporters and the (traditionalist) Inkatha supporters who battled each other. Shots ringing out and hordes of people armed with sharpened pangas and assegais taking to the streets in a theatening manner became "normal" events.

Inkatha was on the back foot after Mandela's release. Who could really compete with Mandela, who had been appointed as deputy president of the ANC to assist the ailing Tambo? The NP government, desperately looking for black supporters, were particularly well-disposed towards Inkatha and its leader, Dr Mangosuthu Buthelezi. So, too, were the military and the security police. Everyone knew that white support alone would have no significant impact at the first one-person-one-vote election. The ANC-Inkatha conflict led to a extremely bloody situation in KwaZulu and Natal. It was soon rumoured that the government's security forces were supporting Inkatha. If the blood of martyrs provided the seed for the growth of the church, as is said in ecclesiastical circles, one might say that many bags of seed went into the start and growth of our democracy.

We had an example of this in April 1990. De Klerk and Mandela eventually agreed that the first talks between the government and the ANC would take place on 11 April 1990. By that time a lot of work and planning with the help of the NIS had gone into the process. Towards the end of March, however, a protest in the black township of Sebokeng near Vereeniging, where De Klerk had deep political roots, ended in bloodshed when police fired on protesters. Several people were killed and around 400 were injured. In protest against the police action, Mandela called off the planned meeting. De Klerk moved swiftly, and appointed a judicial commission of inquiry. The subsequent report found that the police had fired too quickly and that their use of force had been immoderate and disproportionate. They had not been trained in crowd control. According to the iron-fist approach of apartheid, bullets and batons were the only resort, as "colleague" Möller put it.

On 2 May 1990 the government finally met the first delegation from the ranks of the ANC, including Joe Slovo, at Groote Schuur. Mbeki later told me that he wondered what Cecil John Rhodes and Hendrik Verwoerd would have made of the group assembled around the polished table. De Klerk's team, which he had already announced on 29 March 1990, comprised Pik Botha, Gerrit Viljoen, Dawie de Villiers, Kobie Coetsee, Barend du Plessis, Adriaan Vlok, Stoffel van der Merwe and Roelf Meyer. Nelson Mandela's team caused a great deal of surprise: Joe Slovo, Beyers Naudé, Thabo Mbeki, Alfred Nzo, Walter Sisulu, Ahmed Kathrada, Joe Modise, Ruth Mompati, Archie Gumede and Cheryl Carolus. In certain conservative Afrikaner circles it was whispered that Naudé was a member of MK. Someone from the ANC group wondered whether the meeting perhaps contrasted with the one Piet Retief attended in Dingane's kraal!

Meanwhile the violence in the country had become a huge headache for the NIS. I was asked to advise them on two issues: Mandela and the PAC.

Regarding Mandela, at that stage the leader of the internal ANC, there were mainly questions about his position within the ranks of the organisation's National Executive Committee. Oliver Tambo was ill. He was an important unifying factor between the external and internal wings of the ANC. Could Mandela fill that role? Could Mandela, given his many years in prison, exercise strong leadership in an organisation that was transforming itself from a resistance movement into a political party? The NIS also wanted to know whether Mandela would be able to help create a measure of unity in black ranks. Or would the power struggle in black ranks intensify? Moreover, there was another, bigger problem. Many exiles had to return to the country. The NIS, in cooperation with its ANC dialogue partners, had already made logistical and other arrangements in this regard. A major issue, however, was how these "exiles" were to be integrated with the "inziles", particularly at the leadership level. What would Mandela's role in this be, and was an ANC conference and election of people to leadership positions likely to happen soon? It was accepted that the ANC had the sole mandate to manage the integration process. The NIS could only provide assistance. A conference and election, however, would be decisive. These were all very pertinent questions, and we discussed them in detail. Our conclusion was that Mandela was the key figure and that his leadership role would grow very quickly.

The PAC did not elicit any enthusiasm. One concern was the possibility of continued violence on the part of the PAC's military wing. No one believed that African states would continue to support the PAC financially and militarily. Neither would the Organisation for African Unity. There was little chance of the ANC and the PAC cooperating, given that they were involved in a power struggle.

In the meantime FW de Klerk and Nelson Mandela had embarked on trips to convey to the world the message of the peace initiative of the South African government and the ANC, as it had started to take shape at Groote Schuur. Möller Dippenaar of the NIS told me: "De Klerk and Mandela are the only ones who are travelling. These two are the political heavyweights in the ring." De Klerk visited several countries. His key point was that the settlement process was irreversible. Mandela's trip was a triumphal progress the like of which the world had not seen for years. In the US, where he met President Bush, about one million people turned up in New York to pay tribute to him. He met Margaret Thatcher as well, and the two of them had a good discussion. The somewhat aggressive relationship that she had had with Tambo and especially with Mbeki, belonged to the past.

In April Mandela also delivered a short speech at London's Wembley Stadium. It was at this venue where his birthday had been celebrated in exuberant fashion the year before, when he was still in prison. On the stage, with the ANC's well-known flag as backdrop, he stood in front of the podium flanked by Winnie Mandela and Adelaide Tambo. Archbishop Trevor Huddleston, one of apartheid's fiercest archenemies, stood to the right of Winnie, gesticulating while he spoke to Mandela. To many Afrikaners, including the clergy, Huddleston was the incarnation of a spiritual leader who had been taken on tow by evil political propaganda. The event was a triumph: Mandela at his most charming *and* implacable. The crowd of around 170 000 people were enraptured by his words: "Our first simple and happy task is to say thank you. Thank you very much to you all. Thank you that you chose to care, because you could have decided otherwise. Thank you that you elected not to forget, because our fate could have been a passing cause." He then demonstrated his resoluteness and implacability when it came to apartheid. "Together we must pledge to continue our united offensive for the abolition of the apartheid system. The apartheid crime against humanity remains in place. [...] Therefore do not listen to anyone who says that you must give up the struggle against apartheid. Reject any suggestion that the campaign to isolate the apartheid system should be wound down." The ANC was opposed to any "reward" for Pretoria as a result of the "small step" that had been taken, such as the unbanning of the ANC and other organisations, and also his own release. "The reward the people of South Africa, of Southern Africa and the rest of the world seek, is the end of apartheid and the transformation of our country into a nonracial democracy." I heard Thabo Mbeki's voice at the Mells Park session of February 1990, diametrically opposed to the businessmen's view that De Klerk had abolished apartheid on 2 February and that sanctions had become unnecessary.

I was in London from 6 to 10 April and experienced the excited expectations prior to Mandela's visit to the British capital at first hand. His speech, I later explained to my NIS friends, had made a very clear point: No adjustments to the system, but total transformation. We agreed that the constitution that was to be negotiated would therefore be of key importance, as it would lay down the norms for the transformation process. We acknowledged that there was still a world of difference between the ANC's notion of transformation and the NP leadership's understanding of the term. Someone remarked: "The NP leadership haven't yet given much thought to it." I mentioned that transformation would mean a managed revolution, a radical structural change for South Africa. It would also have a drastic effect on value systems. Without saying it to each other, we realised that Mandela's objective on behalf of the ANC ("the end of apartheid and the transformation of our country into a nonracial democracy") would be the major political hot potato in the process that lay ahead. Mandela, who had visited Oliver Tambo in a Swedish clinic in March 1990, would have cleared all of this with Tambo. The actual revolution, and not bloodless either, had in fact started after his release. There are always unintended consequences in settlement processes within a society that is at war with itself. The euphoria of 2 February 1990 and 11 February 1990 had hampered thorough consideration of the possible unintended consequences of these two momentous events in our country's history.

From 23 to 27 May Idasa presented a conference in Lusaka on the future of the military and defence forces in South Africa. Chris Hani was the person everyone wanted to speak to. A huge photograph of a friendly and smiling Mandela hung on the wall. John Nkadimeng, a member of the NEC, started off the first session. We whites were all very impressed: "We are about to build a new civilization in South Africa. A united, nonracial democracy. We all know that our country has many graves and tombstones. War is the continuation of politics through other means." The new defence force, he said, had to be a "symbol of unity" and "a keeper of democracy". Chris Hani spoke, too: "South Africa is a country which has shown the desire to move towards a spring of hope." The discussions covered a number of issues: the Groote Schuur Minute that had been signed by the De Klerk

government and the ANC; the continuing violence, particularly in Kwa-
Zulu and Natal; a cessation of hostilities; and the process ahead. There were
more questions than answers. At least it was an honest dialogue that focused
on the most important points, I told myself, not merely a getting-to-know-
each other function or a slanging match.

Thabo Mbeki, who attended the conference later, told me: "The road
ahead is uncertain, slippery and full of potholes. Don't be too idealistic." We
also met at his flat, where I met his wife Zanele for the first time. He told
me about the attempt by the South African Security Services to assassinate
him in his home. We listened to Russian church music, which we both loved.
As we prepared to tuck into our food, Zanele said: "We must first say grace."
She then asked for a blessing on the meal. She put me to shame. I had never
imagined that people at the heart of the ANC's struggle would say grace before a meal. With my roots in a patriarchal Afrikaner farming community,
I was also not used to the woman of the house taking charge of this ritual.
During the meal we discussed the next meeting of our group at Mells Park.
It would be our last meeting in England.

We met on the weekend of 29 June to 1 July. In August 1989, the month
of Botha's political demise, Consgold had been taken over by Lord Hanson's
group, which continued financing our talks, together with British Airways
which provided some of the air tickets, and Standard Chartered Bank's
Patrick Gillan. It was summertime in Britain, and for the last time I savoured
the walks among the parklands, trees and forests. I always stopped at a specific spot to admire the facade of the stately group of buildings. Like before,
we visited the village of Mells on a few occasions to enjoy a typical English
beer at the local pub. The dialogue group comprised Minister Dawie de
Villiers, Willem de Klerk, Willem Pretorius, Attie du Plessis, Mof Terreblanche, Thabo Mbeki, Aziz Pahad, Joe Nhlanhla, Tony Trew and me. By
that time the Groote Schuur talks had already taken place. De Villiers sits
next to Mbeki on the photo that was taken at our last session. Joe Nhlanhla,
the only other participant besides Mbeki who wears a jacket, stands next
to De Klerk.

Before our meeting there was already growing irritation with Mandela
on the part of some senior government representatives, especially after his

speech at the Wembley Stadium. In their view he spent too much time travelling, failed to devote enough attention to a speeding up of the settlement process, employed delaying tactics, and did not take action on behalf of the ANC to address the violence in black townships. It became clear from numerous conversations why government representatives were impatient. De Klerk had taken the political initiative on 2 February 1990 and again with Mandela's release. This was a huge bonus. This bonus was being squandered, however, with the ANC and Nelson Mandela buying time to reposition the ANC strategically inside the country and also being the pivot of excited interest, focused on Mandela, internationally. Meanwhile De Klerk had to govern the country and his ministers had to continue with their normal duties. The ANC, a master when it came to the game of time, could afford a more leisurely approach. Besides, Nelson Mandela had to be introduced to the world after 27 years in prison. Oliver Tambo was not in good health either. Time was on the side of the ANC.

With this realisation in my mind, I looked forward with great interest to the Mells Park talks. At his home in Lusaka, a little more than a month before the Mells Park meeting, Mbeki had already briefed me on the "expectations" of the government. He had stated in his usual calm and diplomatic manner that these expectations would have to be "discussed". Black people, too, had their own expectations. De Klerk and his advisers would also have to listen to those. Our dialogue group meeting started off with the usual pleasantries and an exchange of impressions about the "new era" we had entered. De Villiers and Mbeki were very comfortable with each other, like good colleagues. Mbeki, who sets great store by being treated with dignity, told me: "Dawie is a good man." He knew that De Villiers and I were old friends. In our interaction we experienced something of our common South African identity and our connectedness to a continent that was also soaked in blood. At one stage I wondered whether we would succeed in seeing the peace process through. South Africa, I told Pahad, was different from all the other countries in Africa. It had a large white population, and the Afrikaners had long since ceased to be settlers. They were white Africans. Pahad agreed enthusiastically. We were all suffering from post-11 February euphoria.

We devoted plenty of time to what we called a "review" of the process since Nelson Mandela's release. The state of emergency, instituted by PW Botha, had been lifted in June 1990, except for Natal which had become a battle front. The participants in the talks between the government and the ANC, Dawie de Villiers and Thabo Mbeki, briefed us in general terms on progress, problems and prospects. Within the Afrikaner-ANC dialogue group Mbeki had stressed repeatedly that an interim government had to be in charge of the transition to an election for a "constituent assembly". During our meeting of 29 September to 1 October 1989, after the first meeting with Louw and Spaarwater in Lucerne, he even contended that the democratisation process at the level of political institutions that had to be involved in the negotiation process needed to take place before the first inclusive election. The argument for this, still steeped in mistrust, was that the apartheid government could not be allowed to control the process. My counterargument was that a distinction, as in the case of sanctions, should be made between formal rules and informal rules of engagement.

I was in favour of the government's position that the existing system of government should be adapted so that some form of continuity and, in light of the high levels of violence, political stability could be guaranteed. The serious question, in my view, was how it could be ensured that the process would have institutional integrity. I reckoned, probably too idealistically, that a culture of trust between leadership figures would enable us to smoke the peace pipe throughout. At that stage there was of course still the expectation on the part of certain segments of the governing elite that a veto right and mechanism should be built into at least the transitional system.

Our last meeting differed from all the previous meetings in one important respect. It did not focus on possible solutions to the country's political impasse. This time the focus was sharply on what had happened between February and the end of June 1990 and what could be done to support, where necessary, the formal process that had already started. We acknowledged that we had no official mandate. De Villiers and Mbeki were not present in their capacity as formal participants in the process. It is never possible, however, to keep the formal and the informal totally separate in processes of this kind.

During the formal session it was Willem de Klerk who took a strong stance against the slow pace of progress with the process. I don't know whether De Klerk had discussed this with his brother, because I never managed to get a definite "yes" or "no" from him in this regard. De Klerk came across firmly, almost aggressively. In his opinion, Nelson Mandela's criticism of the government for dragging its feet was actually applicable to himself and his leadership. It was the ANC that was dragging its feet, travelling around and making conversation. De Klerk went even further, and said that the power struggle within the ANC was the cause of all the problems. This was a very sensitive issue. Within the NIS as well as among people close to FW de Klerk this power struggle was noted and seen as, on the one hand, a reason for the violence in the country, and on the other as a weakness within the ANC.

By that time De Klerk's security and intelligence services knew about Operation Vula – the brainchild of Mac Maharaj, Ronnie Kasrils and Siphiwe Nyanda. Maharaj and Kasrils's subsequent explanation that they had intended to take out an insurance policy in case the De Klerk government failed to keep its word about a negotiated settlement, was not in my view the real reason behind this project. Be that as it may, Maharaj and his militant conspirators were arrested in July 1990. Nelson Mandela persuaded De Klerk not to continue with prosecution. Thabo Mbeki, who was not a comrade of the revolutionary dreams of Maharaj and Co, was his usual disciplined self when he answered Willem de Klerk. The white participants in the dialogue were very despondent about the bloody violence in black ranks. The general feeling was that the ANC leadership, including Mandela, lacked the capacity to bring it to an end. In white ranks, the NIS assured me, there had been a swing to the right as a result of the violence. People were starting to say whites had been sold out by the De Klerk government.

Mbeki convinced me: Mandela, too, was running huge political risks among his people, especially the new generation. He still needed to establish his leadership. There was a rolling revolution of rising expectations. "The people" were impatient; they wanted to acquire their political rights and a share of the economic cake immediately. They did not understand the need for a process that required time and patience. Pahad added that it was incorrect to claim that the ANC did little or nothing to address the violence. They were holding talks with Inkatha, the PAC and Azapo. The events of 1976 and what happened thereafter, however, had left very deep scars. There was a lot of pent-up anger in the townships. He reckoned that there were elements in the security forces that were fomenting this anger, which was an accusation Mandela had also levelled at FW de Klerk. Later it would emerge that there had indeed been instigation on the part of elements in the security services. Taxpayers' money had even been channelled to Inkatha to protect this party's power base. It was my personal view that the ANC revolutionaries welcomed the violence. They were hoping for an authority vacuum that could be filled by them.

Mbeki, in a sincere attempt to emphasise the ANC's goodwill in respect of the process, pointed out that the ANC leadership referred very specifically to De Klerk as "president". This was an ANC decision and had special symbolic significance. In the past, no ANC member would have addressed an apartheid head of state or minister by his official title. After all, they had no moral credibility. But the ANC leadership had decided to acknowledge De Klerk's role and position in the process and to confirm thereby that there had to be continuity within the state and government during the transitional process. The followers of the ANC, however, had not yet taken this step. A big problem with an acceleration of the process, he continued later, was who had to be present at the formal negotiating table.

As could be expected, the economy came up for discussion. The businessmen's major concern was once again the issue of nationalisation. On his international trip Mandela had defended the notion of nationalisation, as contained in the Freedom Charter, in Sweden. He had also advocated the continued isolation of South Africa. This contrasted with the stance of spokespersons of the De Klerk government who were of the view that De Klerk deserved recognition from the international world in the form of a "reward", for example the lifting of sanctions. At the time of our meeting at Mells Park the Groote Schuur Minute was already well known. It committed the government and the ANC to a peaceful process of negotiations. The parties had also agreed on a commitment to stability and the resolution of the climate of violence and intimidation. Mandela's implacability regarding nationalisation unfortunately resulted in the weight and integrity of the Groote Schuur Minute being called into question in wide circles. [1]

De Villiers, who had been involved in the Minute, explained the government's economic policy: the economic priorities were growth, jobs and poverty alleviation. That was the reason for the establishment of the Independent Development Trust under the leadership of Jan Steyn. The De Klerk government also believed that the private sector had been neglected and that everything possible had to be done to streamline cooperation between the public and private sectors. Privatisation of state corporations was already being considered. Privatisation and entrepreneurship were the key to success, not nationalisation. Hereafter Mbeki again emphasised his standpoint about a mixed economy, as well as something he had stressed repeatedly at previous meetings: a political settlement would not be sustainable without the cooperation of the private sector and a dynamic economy. [2] He told me later that there was no consensus yet within the ANC on a future economic policy. The political struggle was predominant. The ANC was actually a coalition with conflicting economic ideas, albeit that Gorbachev had upset the communists' and socialists' applecart. An ANC-led government, he continued, would have to give very serious attention to labour legislation. The ANC's mass support came from the working class, after all. He also mentioned the necessity of black empowerment, which would later become one of his major policy objectives. The business leaders who were present were once again impressed by his moderation, even though he dug in his heels regarding the immediate suspension of sanctions. Sanctions were an important instrument of pressure for the ANC, but the matter could be discussed further after Nelson Mandela's return from his overseas trip in mid-July, he declared, thereby concluding this particular discussion.

We also devoted attention to several other issues. The most important of these was the mechanism that should bring the process to a new constitution and an inclusive election. The government and the ANC still held different views in this regard. It was common cause in the dialogue group that the Namibian model could not serve as an example. There was consensus that South Africa was a sovereign state. All the participants also agreed with the ANC's objection that an inclusive election could not take place under the supervision of the De Klerk government. The idea of an Independent Electoral Commission was born here. Mbeki even maintained that a kind of state council, with power being shared between the government and relevant parties, could be instituted as an interim measure. There was a strong consensus in the group about the desirability of interim measures. With regard to the transformation of the South African Broadcasting Corporation, the consensus was even enthusiastic. Thabo Mbeki also insisted that the military-controlled *Radio Truth*, which broadcast propaganda to Zimbabwe and infuriated Robert Mugabe, had to be closed down. This was done eventually.

On Sunday, 1 July we departed for London. Dawie de Villiers and Thabo Mbeki travelled in a separate car in order to talk privately. The government and the ANC met again on 6 August 1990, this time in the Presidency in Pretoria. The meeting resulted in the Pretoria Minute, which paved the way for talks of a more exploratory nature. The departure from Mells Park had been fraught with visibly suppressed emotions. We found it hard to say goodbye to each other. It had been our last meeting in England, but we promised each other that we would get together again in South Africa if the need for unofficial and informal dialogue should arise. I told Mbeki in Afrikaans: "Thank you. It was good to get to know you." He embraced me – an African custom that took me some time to get used to – and said: "We'll meet again in South Africa."

# 16
# Back in South Africa:
## talks *must* continue

On 28 April 1990, after more than 27 years in exile, Thabo Mbeki arrived back in South Africa together with other ANC members. The ANC team stayed in the Lord Charles Hotel in Somerset West, near Stellenbosch. I told my Goldfields students: "How ironic! The ANC gives publicity to a hotel with a name that commemorates British colonial history with its imperialist lust for power!" A member of the residence committee trumped me: "It's a sign of hope. Things *can* change for the better."

Anglo American put the historic Vergelegen estate at the disposal of the ANC for their caucus meetings. Vergelegen is a beautiful wine estate in the Helderberg basin at the foot of the majestic Hottentots-Holland Mountains. The original owner at the beginning of the eighteenth century, the Dutch governor Willem Adriaan van der Stel, was also a businessman with a sharp eye for opportunities. The view over False Bay, where the ships of the Dutch East India Company passed on their way from the East to the refreshment station at the Cape, is still a spectacular sight. Van der Stel's farm could provide all the ships with supplies. Mr Badenhorst, my history teacher, used to say that the early Dutch settlement at the Cape had two frontiers, the one man-made and the other geographic: the hedge planted by Jan van Riebeeck, and the mountains in the huge basin next to the bay. The settlement, he told us, *had* to expand. Development meant expansion, and hence also conflict with the indigenous people. As I understood it at the time, Vergelegen was a development node on the frontier; a growth node of civilisation this side of the wilderness that lay behind the mountains.

In 1990 the ANC's first caucus meeting after the organisation's return to South Africa was held in the picturesque surroundings of Vergelegen with its ancient camphor trees, Cape Dutch architecture and lawns. In May 1998 Thabo Mbeki referred in a speech to the Afrikaans poet DJ Opperman's verse play *Vergelegen*, thinking of his first visit to this historic farm of a governor who had been recalled after a revolt against his leadership. Opperman's line *"Maak die honde los / Daar's goeters in die bos"* (Let loose the dogs / There are things in the forest) captivated him.

This "farm on the frontier" was a political metaphor: the conflict between early settlers and the indigenous population transformed into a conflict between white and black, rich and poor. After hundreds of years, the "frontier" was still in place.

The Groote Schuur Minute, the first official "frontier crossing" between the Afrikaners and the ANC, was signed between 2 and 4 May 1990. This Minute, like the Pretoria Minute (August 1990) and the DF Malan Accord (February 1991) that followed, was an important beacon of light and not merely ceremonial.

Mbeki's first address in South Africa was the Carlton Court Hotel in central Johannesburg. On the recommendation of Van Zyl Slabbert, Mbeki and his wife Zanele moved into a comfortable penthouse flat in Van der Merwe Street, Hillbrow. It belonged to Jürgen Kögl, a businessman. The realisation that South Africa had entered a process of radical change sparked off a great scramble among white business leaders at the time. Suddenly their old, established political networks and direct telephone links with the apartheid regime's leadership were in question. The businesspeople were in search of new telephone numbers, new contact persons and new addresses. In certain cases it became a somewhat ludicrous spectacle: capitalists genuflecting before socialists, communists and revolutionaries.

As of 1990 Pretoria was no longer the only symbol of political power. The ANC eventually established a head office at 54 Sauer Street, Johannesburg. But what a struggle to master the art of good office management: telephones rang endlessly with no one bothering to pick them up, appointments were either not kept or started late. I said to Mbeki on one occasion: "If the ANC can't even run an office, how does it intend to run the country?" He did not seem impressed with my remark.

Tokyo Sexwale, though, impressed me. He had told me that his office telephone was not allowed to ring more than twelve time before being answered. That proved to be correct. I was instrumental in arranging a meeting between him and business leaders in Auckland Park, Johannesburg. He arrived promptly at the agreed time. Everyone was impressed by his reasonable and conciliatory speech. The venue was barely a stone's throw from Die Eike, the headquarters of the secret Afrikaner Broederbond. The institutional and organisational nerve centre of Afrikanerdom was situated in that building. The interaction with the business sector was indeed new and difficult territory. As Sexwale put it to me: "We have to take cognisance of the tension between white expectations with all their vested interests, and the aspirations of blacks." He noted that apartheid was not only a matter of racial discrimination. It was interwoven with and embedded in something else that the Afrikaners had inherited from the British colonialists: oppression in order to benefit the ruling class economically. I realised that this would be a major obstacle on the road to nation-building, reconciliation and peace.

During this time I mentioned to Zanele Mbeki that the Cape had been described in two ways by the white seafarers from Europe: Cape of Storms and Cape of Good Hope. Zanele, a committed Christian, reckoned that the hope of millions of people in South Africa and internationally would help to create reconciliation and peace in our country. To me, this became a key for trying to understand South Africa's road ahead: a dialectic between hope and despair.

Despite all the unrest and turmoil following February 1990, the process of settlement continued. It was actually mind-boggling. On 6 August 1990 the second meeting between the government and the ANC took place in Pretoria, and the Pretoria Minute was signed.

From the outset there had been tension between De Klerk and Mandela. They were very different personality types with distinctive histories. There were also other, more fundamental political-ideological differences. One was the issue of group rights versus the ANC's unswerving commitment to ordinary majority rule in a nonracial unitary state. On this matter, the two were sworn political adversaries who had to find a way of working together. Mandela later wrote in his autobiography (p 604), with the memories of his interaction with De Klerk during the long and arduous negotiating phase still fresh in his mind: "To make peace with an enemy, one must work with that enemy, and that enemy becomes your partner." Meaningful peace processes between historical enemies indeed relate to forms of cooperation that were previously considered "impossible" because there are good and pressing reasons for such cooperation. De Klerk and Mandela needed each other.[1]

To what extent this partnership was simply pragmatic and not sufficiently based on trust and confidence, is debatable. The NP and the ANC were engaged in a power struggle with each other during the negotiating process. This was compounded by Mandela and the ANC's accusation that De Klerk was not doing enough to end the violence. When the allegations about state-sponsored Third Force activities and especially the support to Inkatha turned out to be correct, the political fat was in the fire. Someone from the NIS told me: "It doesn't really matter what De Klerk says about this. Mandela and his supporters, the majority of people in the country, don't believe him." This credibility gap would never disappear. One evening at his home, Thabo Mbeki convinced me that something was rotten in the country. In between all the countrywide forms of political violence, he said, there was also another form: a distinct pattern of violence that erupted as soon as there was progress with the settlement process. "It's intended to sabotage the process," he said. I, who had been worried for years about black-on-black violence, the township wars and the intolerance, was reprimanded: "The violence is much more complex than you think. There is right-wing and state-sponsored violence that wants to wreck the process. De Klerk and his government refuse to acknowledge this. Why not? Does it suit his negotiating plan?"

When De Klerk became president, there was an important chink in his political armour: a lack of experience and information with regard to the complex security apparatus he had inherited. The manipulations within this system and its "operational activities" were sophisticated and very well concealed. Without his knowledge, many crocodiles were bred and unleashed on "the enemy". The day Sexwale addressed the meeting in Auckland Park, he asked me: "Is De Klerk in control of his security services? Does he know about the underminers in his own ranks?" At first I was at a loss for words, and said in the end: "De Klerk and Mandela have the same problem." The Pretoria Minute of 6 August 1990 was, as Thabo Mbeki put it to me, "a big breakthrough on the road to a negotiated settlement". The ANC undertook, for instance, to suspend all armed actions. This was a personal victory for De Klerk. Thabo Mbeki was also of the view that ANC-inspired military actions were not conducive to a climate for negotiations. In these times of unrest and violence he was even more in favour of negotiations.

Operation Vula, which was exposed in July 1990, had undermined the ANC's claim to the moral high ground internationally. The disclosure of this project and the arrests of the conspirators were a huge embarrassment to the ANC. The organisation and its leaders had to try their best to do damage control. Joe Slovo, who was very close to the Vula conspirators, including Mac Maharaj, then came up with a plan that helped De Klerk: the suspension of the ANC's armed struggle after nearly 30 years. Slovo, together with Mandela who was initially reluctant, persuaded the rest of the ANC leadership. The Swiss ambassador, with whom I had good contact for quite some time, asked me at one stage: "Can the ANC ever be trusted, with so many revolutionaries in key positions?" De Klerk and his security advisers wondered about this too. I told the ambassador: "The question is not really whether the ANC can be trusted. It is rather whether the ANC has the capacity to keep the revolutionaries in check and to live up to undertakings." I even wondered prophetically: "Would the ANC *ever* be able to curb the violence? Is it not inevitable that a revolutionary spirit ends up devouring its own children?" The problem, I realised later, was that South Africa was enmeshed in a kind of "war transition". Both organised and unorganised forms of violence were important driving forces. Violence had assumed systemic features and become part of the societal system and culture. Not even iconic figures such as Mandela and Tutu could turn it around.

The Pretoria Minute brought hope, but not peace. The parties agreed, though, that political prisoners would be released in a phased manner. This was a key condition, as had also been highlighted in the Afrikaner-ANC dialogue process. But even Mandela and Buthelezi's joint campaign for peace did not achieve much. On 12 February 1991 a third preparatory meeting between the De Klerk government and the ANC took place at the DF Malan Airport outside Cape Town. It culminated in the DF Malan Accord, which focused very strongly on the combating of political violence. The principle was accepted that in a democractic society no political movement or party should have a private army. The Accord had no significant impact on the violence in the country. The state's security forces were increasingly implicated in the violence, and Mandela did not spare De Klerk his anger about this.

The ANC was also not well organised between 1990 and 1991. This was partly understandable. The exiles had to return, the ANC/UDF alliance had to act in an integrated manner, the Lusaka office had to be closed down, and a new leadership (National Executive Committee) had to be elected. The internal challenges the ANC had to grapple with gave De Klerk and his team an inside track. Nonetheless, some in the ranks of the NIS believed that the sooner the ANC sorted out its internal problems, the better for the settlement process and South Africa. If matters dragged on for too long, De Klerk and the NP's bargaining position would weaken. In July 1991 the ANC's first official meeting as a political movement took place in South Africa after more than 30 years. The elderly Alfred Nzo, the ANC's secretary-general who had indicated that he would not be available for another term, addressed the meeting on the organisational state of the ANC. I heard beforehand that he had been asked not to mince matters or aim to please the delegates with reassuring platitudes. Nzo, who was not the most dynamic speaker, let fly with gusto. He was in a position to do so because his diagnosis had been discussed with the core leadership in advance, and this was his last appearance as secretary-general. The diagnosis could not be worse. He confirmed what Thabo Mbeki had told me a few weeks earlier: "The ANC cannot try to dominate the settlement process with mass action. It has to be an organisation that sits down at the table with clear objectives and strong leadership. We *have* documents." Nzo did not spare his comrades: The ANC had become a prisoner of populist rhetoric and slogans, and would lose the leadership position it occupied at present.

I heard later from my ANC contacts what had been the primary reason for Nzo's stance: De Klerk and his government were used to divide-and-rule. They wanted the process ahead and the constitutional guidelines to be determined by designated representatives of existing political groupings. The only way in which the ANC could prevent this ill-considered group approach, was to get its own house in order as soon as possible. I was sceptical of this claim and thought that it was based on unfounded mistrust. Be that as it may, the meeting elected Cyril Ramaphosa as secretary-general. Within a short time he knocked the ANC into shape institutionally and organisation-ally. Through a clever move he also managed to get himself appointed as the ANC team's chief negotiator and Mbeki sidelined while Mandela, Mbeki and Zuma were travelling overseas. At a dinner with friends, where De Klerk was also present, people only laughed when I said in reply to a question: "Cyril is a man of iron."

Thabo Mbeki and I kept in touch during the political winter of 1991. In England he had repeatedly raised the issue of a general amnesty in our conversations. I regularly conveyed this message to the NIS. Back in South Africa he kept hammering on it. This was a matter to which Minister Kobie Coetsee was supposed to attend on behalf of the government, but which he did little about. What was happening, said Mbeki, could confound things like amnesty. Aziz Pahad phoned me later and asked whether the three of us and someone from the business sector could perhaps meet to discuss the road ahead, with a possible role for the business sector. I contacted Marinus Daling. He recommended Attie du Plessis. Daling also undertook to arrange that our group could meet in the Bankorp building, not far from Sauer Street. The offices had already been vacated, but he would make arrange-ments with Piet Liebenberg for a table, chairs and refreshments. It was a huge venue. There were neither people nor furniture on that particular floor. I told Pahad: "The place not only looks God-forsaken. It's also been for-saken by people – a dismal environment. Might this be the kind of future you and I avoided talking about over many years?"

We sat down at the table. Four people who had talked on many occasions and shared their expectations of the future. Thabo Mbeki, Attie du Plessis, Pahad and I. I made a note in my diary: "Can this quadrumvirate help to blast open bolted doors with battering rams?" Mbeki and Du Plessis were cool-headed and dispassionate. Rationality triumphed over emotion. My emotions were turbulent: "Once again we're dancing like frenzied people on the edge of the abyss." It became a long and incisive discussion: How can the settlement process get back on track? Mbeki was implacable:"Ne-gotiations are the only option." He looked at me:"Talk to Niel Barnard.We'll talk within our own ranks. Informal and unofficial contact is now more necessary than ever.We *must* keep the informal and unofficial talks about negotiation alive."

There was a second issue too:Were there other ways in which the busi-ness sector could play a role? We decided to hold a bigger meeting about this over a weekend. It was organised for 10 and 11 August 1991, a Saturday and Sunday, at Gencor's Magaliesberg conference centre in the vicinity of the Hartebeespoort Dam, not far from the venue of the Afrikaner Broeder-bond where I had attended my last national AB meeting in 1987. Marinus Daling's Sankorp office made the arrangements. By 6 August 1991 I had received provisional confirmation of their attendance from MichaelYoung, MofTerreblanche (broker),Willem Pretorius (Metropolitan),Attie du Plessis (Sankorp), Marius Smith (Metropolitan), Kobus du Plessis (Sankorp), Louis Geldenhuys (broker) and Emile Linde (Sanlam). Leon Wessels andWillem de Klerk would "pop in". From the ranks of the ANC,Thabo Mbeki,Jacob Zuma, Aziz Pahad and Tony Trew would attend. Some participants cried off at the last minute, including Zuma andYoung.The ANC participants were joined by Penuell Maduna. Our gathering took place just after Magnus Malan had been replaced by Roelf Meyer as minister of defence.This was regarded as a positive sign.

We stayed at the conference centre on the Saturday night.That evening around the braai fire we talked very personally and intensively about the necessity of salvaging the dialogue process.As in the case of all informal track-two mediatory talks, the atmosphere created by unspoilt nature, a star-spangled sky and firelight was conducive to honesty and openness.We re-discovered our common South African identity. Mbeki said:"We are all part ofAfrica."The consensus was that the dialogue process *had* to continue.The business sector *had* to provide expertise and funds, without being intrusive. An institutional framework had to be created within which the business sector could operate in a way that would ensure the success of the setttle-ment process.We were imbued with new hope and inspiration when we left that Sunday.[2]

With South Africa caught up in waves of bloody violence and a negotiating process that could not get off the ground, something remarkable happened in September 1991 that put the country back on the settlement track:
the National Peace Accord. I remember Hanna's sigh of relief when this
Accord was signed. The National Peace Accord was a lighthouse in the rough
seas of our Cape of Storms. Religious leaders, business leaders and members of civil society organisations played a decisive role in the Accord. De
Klerk had not been enthusiastic at first. Some of the organisers who went to
see him, John Hall, Frank Chikane and Theuns Eloff, did not get support
from him. Hall later stated in an interview that De Klerk had been "arrogant and tough". Earlier, in May 1991, he himself had arranged a conference
that was boycotted by the ANC. Mandela had called De Klerk's conference
"pointless". According to Mandela, De Klerk knew full well who was responsible for the violence and how to put a stop to it. In De Klerk's view, it
was the task of his government and the state to ensure security and peace.

The Accord had two major consequences. One was the institution of a
commission of inquiry into the prevention of public violence and intimidation. The other was of decisive importance: the launching of a process
that I like to refer to as the broadening and deepening of the reconciliation
process by civil society at the grassroots level. This involvement on the part
of the business and civic communities provided a much-needed impetus to
the settlement process. The politicians later became less enthusiastic about
the Accord, and in time it unfortunately came to an end.

On 29 November 1991 the first Convention for a Democratic South Africa (Codesa) was held in the vicinity of the international airport outside
Johannesburg, then still known as Jan Smuts. The Afrikaner Weerstands-
beweging (AWB), the Herstigte Nasionale Party (HNP), Azapo and the Black
Consciousness Movement (BCM) did not attend. During one of our dialogue
sessions in England Thabo Mbeki had said that while the process had to
be inclusive, it could be disrupted by the presence of too many "fringe organisations". In the end there were ± 300 delegates. The meeting, as one of
my NIS friends put it, "produced a strategic catastrophe". Under pressure
from his inner circle and some advisers to show strong leadership and to
prove that the NP had muscle, De Klerk launched a scathing attack on the

ANC and Mandela. Mandela retaliated in a similar vein. Mbeki told me later that Kobie Coetsee had warned him of the possibility of a confrontation. But Mbeki did not know exactly what it was all about, and was in any case not directly involved in the process. After this it was hard going to get the settlement process in motion again. The construct of "the enemy" – from the De Klerk government's perspective on the one hand, and from the ANC's perspective on the other – predominated. Following the "strategic catastrophe", weeks became months before the process revived.

The De Klerk government also had to contend with serious difficulties in its own ranks. It was the by-election in Potchefstroom in particular that set off the political alarm in Afrikaner ranks. Potchefstroom had been a secure NP seat since 1915, except for the period when it was held by the United Party (UP) from 1938 – the year of the symbolic Oxwagon Trek – to 1948 – the year of General Jan Smuts's (UP) fall. Potchefstroom was also the university town where De Klerk had his academic and religious roots. It soon became clear that the NP stood a good chance of losing this important seat. There was great concern in NP circles. Even before the election Dawie de Villiers, a minister in De Klerk's cabinet, decided to talk to FW de Klerk. He took along a fellow minister, Barend du Plessis.

De Villiers came with a proposal: if the Conservative Party (CP) won the seat, De Klerk as national leader of the NP should immediately call a referendum among white voters before the ultraconservative CP with its cheerleaders could get into their stride. De Klerk accepted this proposal. De Villiers was also of the view that the referendum question should specifically seek a mandate for negotiations. Pik Botha, when he was briefed about this later, reckoned that a second referendum should be promised, which would test white voters' support of the negotiated constitution. This would give white voters a kind of veto right, which was an issue some NP supporters felt strongly about. De Villiers objected to this on the basis that, in his view, a mandate for negotiations was also a mandate for the outcome of the process. In the event, the CP won the seat. On 24 February 1992 De Klerk announced a referendum among white voters to seek a mandate for the negotiating process. Members of his caucus were unhappy because he had not consulted them beforehand. There was no need for him to do so.

The referendum, which took place on 17 March 1992, planted a clear beacon of hope and expectation: 68,7% of the white registered voters voted "yes" to the question "Do you support continuation of the reform process which the State President began on February 2, 1990, and which is aimed at a new constitution through negotiation?". This masked the beginning of the end of large-scale rightist resistance. Voters to the left of the NP mostly voted "yes".

During the night of 17-18 June 1992, a day after the commemoration of the Soweto uprising, a thunderstorm of despair once again broke over the country: the massacre in Boipatong, which left 45 people dead. Four days later Mandela announced that the ANC was suspending the negotiation talks. The blame for all the blood and misery was again squarely put on the shoulders of the De Klerk government. The ANC leadership, as is still the case today, did not find it possible to look for some of the reasons for black-on-black violence in the lust for power that also obtained in black politics. In its investigation of the Boipatong massacre the Goldstone Commission found no evidence that the De Klerk government had fomented the political violence, but this was of little consequence as far as black perceptions were concerned. It was from this date that the bargaining power of De Klerk and his government visibly started to decline. The massacre made headline news around the world, and the De Klerk government became like an athlete who has to participate in a competitive race with an Achilles tendon injury. In one night the diplomatic gains of De Klerk's international visits, also to African countries, were for the most part wiped out.

Mandela took the initiative and addressed the angry residents of Boipatong on 21 June. He undertook to request a special meeting of the UN Security Council. With the aid of the OAU and the zealous contributions of Thabo Mbeki, Joe Modise, Tebogo Mafole and Stanley Mabizela who held talks with OAU delegates in Dakar, almost exactly five years after the Dakar conference, the Security Council adopted Resolution 765 on 16 July. Former US secretary of state Cyrus Vance was sent as a special envoy to South Africa. I met him a few times through a common American friend, Wayne Fredericks. Vance's report resulted in Resolution 772 on 17 August: a UN Observer Mission (UNOMSA), comprising 50 observers, should be sent to

South Africa. Mandela had pulled off a coup for the ANC's diplomatic strategy, which was aimed at limiting international support for the De Klerk government and putting pressure on De Klerk.

Meanwhile more than 50 000 protesters marched in Pretoria on 5 August 1992. Nelson Mandela was passionate and even fiery in his support of the mass action that threatened to sink the settlement process once and for all. Some saw the mass action as an alternative to negotiations, with the dream of a seizure of power resurfacing. Black people confirmed that Mandela was the political leader in the country. Ramaphosa even declared that the ANC had taken over Pretoria and would also take over De Klerk's office. I told my NIS contacts that we were experiencing "woeful political times". The ANC Youth League held a kind of trial on the Parade in Cape Town where Mandela had delivered his first public speech, and sentenced De Klerk to lifelong imprisonment. Fortunately, a personal track-two interaction developed between Ramaphosa and Roelf Meyer to salvage the continuation of the negotiations. This second track was crucial. But the waves of violence failed to subside. The Boipatong massacre, which had involved Inkatha hostel-dwellers, spurred ANC militants on to launch counterreactions, their dream of a seizure of power far from exhausted.

During a march near the Ciskei capital Bisho on 7 September 1992 the militants, with Ronnie Kasrils and thousands of whipped-up supporters, broke through the barriers that were intended to keep the crowd out of Bisho. The defence force of this black "state" that had been carved out of South Africa fired on the anarchic crowd. Twenty-eight protestors died. Luckily, Kasrils and Ramaphosa were unharmed. Ramaphosa and Meyer had meanwhile maintained their track-two contact and continued talking to each other, holding more than 40 discussions within the space of a few months. During these turbulent times I still had contact with my friends and acquaintances in the NIS. We accepted that the settlement process was on a knife edge. "We're staring into the dark abyss of endemic violence and chaos," I noted pessimistically. "It's not a Leipzig option, but a Vietnam. That's where ANC militants learnt their power games." There was another worrying consensus among us: De Klerk and his government were losing ground. His ability to manage the settlement process was eroding. I found solace in something that President Kenneth Kaunda had given me with regard to the conflict in South Africa when I was his guest for a weekend shortly before his defeat in Zambia's 1991 general election: the Lusaka Manifesto's (1969) call, "We would prefer to negotiate rather than destroy, talk rather than kill."

Even before the breakdown of the Codesa talks (May 1992), the notion of a Government of National Unity had been mooted. Thabo Mbeki had raised it on several occasions as his personal standpoint. Nelson Mandela had also spoken along such lines at a meeting in Stellenbosch (1991). Joe Slovo, always the astute strategist, worked out the detail of the notion during the period of turmoil and published the proposals in the October edition of the *African Communist*. A heated debate erupted in the ANC between the advocates of negotiation and the militants. That it was Joe Slovo who had proposed the so-called "sunset clauses" and not Mandela or Mbeki, was a masterstroke. In November 1992 the ANC's NEC adopted the proposals as ANC policy. Thus the NP was forced into a political corner, its notions of entrenched provisions and power-sharing on its own terms a thing of the past. This opened the door to further concessions. A dramatic paradigm shift, away from race-based political benefits and entrenched guarantees towards nonracialism, was required.

On 2 October 1992, against a backdrop of mounting questions in the international world and in ANC ranks about the De Klerk government's will and ability to prevent "dirty tricks" on the part of elements in its security services, I participated in a discussion on "Public Accountability: Dealing with Security Intelligence" at the South African Military Intelligence College in Pretoria. I had to speak specifically on "The Intelligence Service and Public Accountability: A Philosophical Perspective". A speaker from the ranks of civil society made a strong point: "There is alienation between the state and the media. The state has increasingly found it necessary to prohibit access to information and conceal certain actions. Ill-equipped reporters have even been fielded to assist in this regard." I was very impressed by General-Major CRJ Thirion. He made the point that Military Intelligence had been politicised, which was a serious problem. He also predicted that international terrorism would increase, and stressed the need for a good military intelligence service. During the "Night of the Generals" in December 1992, Thirion, together with 22 other officers, were, for all practical purposes, fired by De Klerk. The allegations against him were never tested. De Klerk probably wanted to prove to Mandela that he was in charge of the state and had the will and authority to tackle wrongdoing head-on. Whether he succeeded in this aim, however, is another question.

A tragic incident stunned the country in April 1993: the assassination of the charismatic Chris Hani by right-wing fanatics during Easter. The attentiveness of a white woman led to their arrests. This helped in some way to cushion the impact of this cruel deed on black people. Something remarkable happened after Hani's death: a memorial service was held for him at the well-known Dutch Reformed "Student Church" in Stellenbosch. It was a powerful signal. My business friends, my NIS contacts and I were on tenterhooks. We acknowledged that South Africa could sink into an inferno of rage and bloodshed. But Nelson Mandela rose to the occasion and demonstrated the quality of his leadership. In one of the most amazing visionary leadership initiatives I ever experienced, he managed to avert the eruption of an inferno. With that, he in effect took over the political leadership of the negotiating process.

A major reason for the decline of the De Klerk government's political and moral authority was undoubtedly the poor handling of the amnesty issue, a matter that Thabo Mbeki had highlighted as a priority during the talks in England. The De Klerk government had considered it a trump card that they would be able to use against the ANC, but instead it became a trump card in the hands of the ANC once evidence of the state's Third Force activities, hit squads and all, started to emerge. There was on one occasion even a stormy cabinet meeting on the amnesty issue during which De Klerk asked Kobie Coetsee to leave the meeting so that they could talk privately in De Klerk's office.

An issue that was closely connected to the thorny problem of amnesty was that of political responsibility for wrongdoing that had taken place and on which ministers had not been briefed. According to what I was told during this time, a motion to accept political responsibility was discussed at a meeting of the De Klerk cabinet. It received very little support, the advice of a legal expert notwithstanding. In terms of how Jamshid Gharajedaghi (1999) describes ways of dealing with this type of political conflict, the government chose the route of "absolve": absolving itself from responsibility. This option was a huge bonus for the ANC's claim to the political and moral high ground.

Codesa 1 and Codesa 2 came and went, necessary and important stations on the road of our country's search for peace between bitter and sworn enemies. De Klerk and Mandela, who were the two main antagonists in this complex and emotional drama, did not really like each other and did not really trust each other fully either. They had to work together, however, in what I called an impossible partnership. The eyes of the world were fixed on South Africa. The majority of South Africans yearned for peace. Advocate Dikgang Moseneke, who had come from the PAC and always respected me by speaking Afrikaans, once told me with reference to this period of our history: "Our country was tired of violence. Especially in the townships. Everyone lived with fear." Later, in the Mbeki era, he would become a respected judge.

FW de Klerk had to brave many head-on winds. I received a call from one of my NIS contacts: "Prof, I've got bad news. Your mentor, Prof. Gerrit Viljoen, has buckled under the pressure and has to retire as minister of constitutional affairs and chief negotiator. What are we going to do?" I was totally dismayed. The ANC, and Thabo Mbeki in particular, had the utmost respect for Viljoen. There was high trust in his intellectual abilities and integrity. In addition, he had worked extremely hard and studied all documentation. De Klerk lost other cabinet ministers too: Barend du Plessis (finance) left; Stoffel van der Merwe (information) retired from politics abruptly. Adriaan Vlok (law and order) had already been demoted in 1991. Likewise Magnus Malan (defence). Vlok, it must be said to his credit, indicated in 1994, when De Klerk was still president, that he would apply for amnesty. Then, shortly before the election, came the bombshell of Inkathagate: the relevation of the state's support to Inkatha in an attempt to stymie the ANC's advance. Thabo Mbeki phoned me and said: "I told you so."

The news of Inkathagate was one of my most shattering experiences since the start of my involvement in the track-two talks in 1987. Mbeki, who was not given to gloating, was acutely aware of my feelings about what I liked to call the "historically and religiously inculcated integrity" of Afrikaners, apartheid notwithstanding. My ANC contacts respected my attitude in this regard and always referred to Beyers Naudé as an example. I felt betrayed, a victim of a naive perception of Afrikaner leaders and politicians. It was also then that I accepted something that may sound contentious: De Klerk and his government's position at the negotiating table had been undermined by the so-called "unconventional" actions of his security forces and services. When these actions leaked out, and even Magnus Malan had to be moved, the security apparatus was effectively taken out of the settlement process. De Klerk was militarily emasculated and without bargaining power.

I was neither formally nor informally involved in the negotiating process that resumed in earnest on 1 April 1993. On the government side, Roelf Meyer became the crucial person in the process that unfolded. According to someone from the NIS, he had been "converted" from all notions of group rights and protective measures for groups. The road that had to be followed was majority rule in a unitary state with a constitution that protected individual, cultural and other rights. "The constitution is what counts," Mbeki told me as well. By then I had long since walked away from the NP's notion of group rights and minority vetoes. I had other questions: "How can we create a nonracial political culture that will respect the negotiated constitution? Will the institutions that have to guard the constitution be sufficiently strong and independent? Will civil society and whites be able to play a role in this? Is the dream of nonracialism achievable? Surely this is what sustainable peace and reconciliation in our country will mainly be about?"

To what extent the NP and the government's negotiating team were equal to their task, is one of the questions being asked in Afrikaner circles today. Some people even make the astonishing claim that the rightists were right. How the rightists in Afrikaner ranks would have done it differently and better, however, is not explained. That the ANC government has failed in important respects since then does not prove the rightist Afrikaner standpoint "right". Many people's fears have been realised, though. In this regard

De Klerk also comes in for unfair criticism on certain points. To be sure, he did underestimate Nelson Mandela and his team. And his focus on the process and that of other members of his team was not always as desired. But Roelf Meyer's after-the-fact story that De Klerk had supposedly told him as far back as December 1989: "We are the liquidators of this firm," was not – as Meyer claims – a green light for black majority rule. This was not what De Klerk had wanted. It was rather a contest that he lost. The question is: Was there any way De Klerk could have won this contest? With what, and with whom?

After 1 April 1993 the negotiating process raced ahead like an express train. Black majority rule became inevitable. The rest is history, with the election in April 1994, a year after the resumption of the process, *the* big event in South Africa's woeful history. It was a "turning-point date" that ushered in a totally different political dispensation from what had obtained since April 1652 when Jan van Riebeeck landed at the Cape and a fort was built and hedges were planted to keep the "barbarians" out. Annemarie and I stood in the "mixed" queue of voters at Stellenbosch University's DF Malan Centre to cast our ballots as part of an inclusive electorate for the first time. The coloured man in front of me, someone I happened to know, asked me as we entered the voting station: "What's under that blanket over there?" I hesitated before replying: "It's the statue of Dr DF Malan." He gave a belly laugh: "From today we're covering all your apartheid symbols with blankets."[3]

My NIS contacts and people close to De Klerk soon informed me: "De Klerk won't make the grade in the Government of National Unity." His problem, one of his colleagues told me, was that he saw Mandela as an opponent and himself as a potential president. He expected the NP ministers in the cabinet to caucus with him beforehand so that they could jointly plan strategy to oppose Mandela and the ANC. I was dumbfounded. He was working with a fierce adversarial model, I told my source, not a partnership model. There was no way he could survive. Moreover, De Klerk was being urged on by conservative Afrikaner commentators to walk out of the Government of National Unity. He yielded to this pressure.

The failure of the Government of National Unity was a great loss for South Africa's future. This was not what Nelson Mandela and Thabo Mbeki had wanted, as Mandela confirmed to an NP minister when they flew together to Durban to defuse a thorny situation there. The person De Klerk had earmarked as his successor was easy prey for the ANC's political crocodiles. Hereafter the established institutionalised Afrikaner community crumbled at a rate that was astounding. The reason was obvious: the disintegration of the NP's power and influence on which the Afrikaner community had depended, and a total inability to think innovatively and differently about the institutional future of Afrikaners. Like the Afrikaner Broederbond, not even the once powerful and influential Dutch Reformed Church escaped the ravages of a new era. This is aptly symbolised by the fate of a former landmark in the vicinity of parliament, the DRC Synod Hall. It has been converted into shops and a luxury hotel.

The New South Africa inherited a dialectic that stems from the 1980s: the dialectic between hope and despair. Thabo Mbeki was acutely aware of this dialectic. It stood to reason that his focus was mainly on the question as to how hope could be generated within the previously oppressed masses. He also knew that unfulfilled hope was the seed of revolution. He himself was a victim of this at Polokwane. Can this dialectic be steered in a more positive direction after 18 years of liberation? Towards a country of Good Hope?

# 17
## The New South Africa:
## a tension between hope and despair

This book is about a process in which many people took part and which created great and exuberant expectations as time went on. The question as to whether all the time and effort that was invested in the process has been worthwhile – whether the transitional process has been successful – is often asked today. And this question is asked not only by whites. I encounter it regularly among coloured, black and Indian South Africans too. It is a question that deserves attention, even though it can be addressed only in broad terms in this chapter.

Very few people had sceptical questions about the need for a settlement and whether the timing was right. The majority of whites was in favour of a negotiated settlement, as was confirmed by the referendum. In many places in the country I personally experienced their hope and expectation that this process would lead to sustainable peace, justice, equity and stability, even though a small number of whites were sceptical. Shortly before the 1994 election and particularly afterwards, however, questions began to arise about the content of the negotiated agreement. In time I myself started asking many questions about the implementation of the settlement agreement, the administration thereof, and especially the way in which the important project of the transformation of the state and its institutions was being manipulated. The spirit and intentions of the agreement were gradually sabotaged at this level. Be that as it may, the decision in favour of negotiation to resolve the conflict that had carved deep divisions through our country and among its people over decades, had been the right decision.

After the 1994 election the flame of hope and confidence in the future burnt very high, mainly inspired by an individual: Nelson Mandela. He had become the embodiment of the dream vast numbers of South Africans had of a South Africa that would be free from racial conflict, political megalomania and severe poverty. Stellenbosch University (SU) awarded him an honorary doctorate at a special ceremony in October 1996, which I had helped to mediate together with the then rector, Andreas van Wyk. We could not afford a situation where he would refuse or respond in the same vein as Mamphela Ramphele, who on an earlier occasion had told me and the rector at the time, Mike de Vries: "Not yet the time." Mandela's reaction, after consultation with his advisers, was that he would consider it an "exceptional honour".

It was an event of great symbolic significance, barely six years after his release. A friend of Mandela's who had been with him on Robben Island and later in Pollsmoor Prison, drew my attention to the reconciliation symbolism: DF Malan, BJ Vorster and PW Botha, former apartheid leaders, had been chancellors of SU. De Klerk had received an honorary doctorate in 1992. And SU used to pride itself on the fact that six white prime ministers were alumni of the university: Smuts, Hertzog, Malan, Strijdom, Verwoerd and Vorster. It was indeed a sign that a new era had dawned and that a choice had been made in favour of inclusivity and reconciliation. No one could imagine, however, how difficult and complex the road ahead would be. Many people were blinded by a euphoria about our so-called miracle and naive views on reconciliation.

It is not possible to discuss all the factors that thwarted a successful transition process. I will only point out a few. The first of these emerged in the same year that Nelson Mandela received an honorary doctorate from SU: the failure of the Government of National Unity. In many respects this was a political disaster, a body blow to the brains and experience trust on which the settlement agreement had been predicated. De Klerk had the experience and ability to help facilitate a well-functioning constitutional state. He seemed to lose interest in continued participation in the implementation of the settlement agreement and withdrew from the Government of National Unity. With that, the possibility of dealing with the fears and interests of whites at a high level was amputated from the body of the settlement agreement.

The second factor that has had a negative impact on our transition process is the high levels of violence in the country. The many case studies of transition processes generally emphasise that crime and violence, combined with poor socioeconomic conditions, impede a successful transition. The transition to a democratic dispensation is not simply an *event* (such as a free, inclusive election), but a *process* that may take a long time. Success is neither guaranteed nor can it be taken for granted. Transitions are complex and comprise a political facet, an economic facet and a social facet, which includes building and maintaining social capital. A culture of violence impacts directly on all these facets because it undermines public confidence.

South Africa is prey to its complexity and network of deep-seated fault lines to an extent that is matched by few other countries in the world. In such a situation, reconciliation and peace can never be merely the absence of visible, direct violence. Also not merely "safety and security". Ethnic, socioeconomic, political and structural violence has taken on too much of an intertwined, endemic and systemic character over time, as in the case of corruption which has long since ceased to be "random" in South Africa. As far back as 1990 the question arose: what will the consequences of the protracted and deep-seated direct as well as structural violence that has maintained an iron grip on our country for so long, be for future reconciliation and peace processes? There were two national attempts with distinctive institutions to answer this question: the National Peace Accord (of September 1991), and the official Truth and Reconciliation Commission (TRC) under the leadership of Archbishop Desmond Tutu. The TRC afforded people the opportunity to tell their stories. We were able to hear and experience exactly how dirty many hands in South Africa were as well as how strong were the desire for knowledge of the truth about our past and the will to reconciliation. But the TRC could not bring about sustainable reconciliation and peace. The process has remained provisional. We are still writing a large part of our history in blood.

Our reconciliation and peace process since the official and moving election of 1994, which demonstrated that our country also contains a Cape of Good Hope, currently looks extremely threadbare in light of the prevailing culture of violence. We are still a frontier country with "things in the forest" (to quote Opperman). But this frontier now runs through cities, towns, communities, streets and even families. We have transformed from an authoritarian, race-based minority government to an inclusive constitutional democratic dispensation. This transformation, however, was neither a transformation to sustainable, visible institutional and personal images of reconciliation and peace, nor a transformation to a nonracial dispensation, free from mainly socioeconomically driven forms of violence. We also have severe forms of violence against women and children, visible symbols of our tattered reconciliation and peace process after 18 years of inclusive democracy.

It is a tragic reality, but indisputably a clearly recognisable face of our country: the ANC government has failed to get direct and structural violence in the country under control. We have democracy and freedom, but not safety. The kind of violence we experience and the brutality that accompanies it even seem to be getting worse. Socioeconomic inequalities, in other words, structural violence, have reached grotesque proportions. It contrasts with the obscene forms of materialism and self-enrichment that are promoted by the ANC leadership. What we are experiencing in the so-called post-apartheid era illustrates that freedom does not necessarily establish a culture of peace, nor does it automatically foster reconciliation.

The third factor that poses a grave threat to the process of transition to a stable yet dynamic democracy and that has already caused great damage, is the ANC's transformation of the state and particularly the view that has taken root since their Polokwane conference: that the state is a tool of the party and the party, in turn, is the seat of all power. The Polokwane conference was a turning point in this regard. The Mandela dream of an inclusive, nonracial democracy was destroyed there as a result of the power struggle between two former friends: Thabo Mbeki and Jacob Zuma. All movements eventually undergo power struggles. The ANC, which was initially an inclusive "broad church" movement, was doomed to this. The question was not whether, but when the power struggle would erupt.

The mainstream within the current ANC supports the notion that the state is the party. When an Afrikaans newspaper announced against lampposts after Mbeki's humiliation at Polokwane: "Thank you South Africa", it was also a writing on the wall: Welcome to a party state.[1] Movements contain disparate tendencies and ideologies in their ranks. The ANC, as a collective liberation movement, could comfortably accommodate Christians, atheists, Muslims, Stalinists, Marxists, democrats and humanists. This diverse "faith community" had a common "enemy". And when this "enemy" (apartheid) disappeared, competition was inevitable. This competition also acquired a reference point at Polokwane: not the pragmatic developmental state of a Mbeki, but a "hard" developmental state, a state that wields both the political and the economic sceptre.

The power struggle within the ANC is not only about who wields the political sceptre, but also about who wields the economic sceptre – who shares in the economic wealth. This is where the real struggle manifests itself: not nonracialism, but instant wealth; material compensation for the struggle for freedom; total control. Hence the Stalinist obsession with power on the part of a certain ANC clique. This power struggle has intensified after Polokwane.

The current erosion of public confidence relates to an increasingly negative perception and experience of the state and its institutions *in practice*, in other words, the *state in action*, regardless of what the constitution may say. What is the case in South Africa in this regard after 18 years of democracy? States in action can be classified roughly into four main categories:

- *Successful states*. They are not necessarily democratic in the usual (Western) sense of the word, but they perform well economically, have institutional ability and capacity, excel with regard to education, entrepreneurship and training, and possess social capital and cohesion.
- *Fragile states* show signs of institutional decay, serious bureaucratic failures, skills erosion, corruption and significant policy differences. They do have a reasonably vibrant civil society, certain insitutions still function well, and the notion of "law and order" features strongly in the public domain, in certain state institutions and on the part of some leading figures. Organised crime and syndicates have started to gain a foothold, however.
- *Failed* or *dysfunctional states* have fallen victim to systemic corruption: corruption that is produced and entrenched by the system itself. This kind of corruption is destructive and counter-productive. The poor are the major victims in such a state. The rich barricade them-

selves, while the hard-working middle class feel vulnerable and disillusioned. The working class is a suffering, marginalised class. Service delivery, for example, becomes patchy and unpredictable. A leadership vacuum develops, which is filled by authoritarian figures that take over and have links with syndicates.

■ *Criminal states* exhibit two variations. In the first variant the crime syndicates have infiltrated the state so effectively that they dictate the functions of the state for all practical purposes. In the second variant the state has abdicated as state, and has itself become involved in criminal activities. A state-controlled and state-driven "criminal economy" develops.

South Africa is admittedly still a constitutional state under the rule of law, but by far not a successful state. It is currently a very fragile state with competing positive and negative trends. Certain departments do excellent work. Others fail to make the grade. The constitution still prevails in many crucial instances, despite signs on the part of the ANC of administrative-political circumvention through "cadre deployment". Anti-corruption institutions still do their work fearlessly, albeit that many of the big fish manage to evade the net. The post-Polokwane ANC is at present a political sponsor of what is known as transactional leadership: support and loyalty are not based primarily on a shared vision, values and policy objectives, but on agreements (transactions or deals) that are entered into to buy votes. Cadre deployment is a good example of this, as is the rise of "tenderpreneurs". It is self-evident that transactional leadership opens the door to corruption and promotes the possibility of opportunistic compromises. It is transactional leaders that convert fragile states and uncertain democracies into criminal states.

There is also an assault on the independence of the judiciary, with President Jacob Zuma having publicly announced the ANC's agenda: The courts cannot be allowed to restrict the political will of the majority, as expressed in ANC policy. The Constitutional Court is in the party's sights too, with the ANC's secretary-general Gwede Mantashe and a deputy minister, Ngoako Ramatlhodi, the political underminers in this regard. What we see in these and other examples is not only an attempt to shift the negotiated goalposts for good governance and the rights of civil society so as to suit the ANC as political party. It is also an attempt to establish a political culture in which generally accepted ethical norms, as they exist within democratic societies, can be negated for the sake of the elite who are able to manipulate the votes of the majority. The end result of this is the implosion of those ethical standards that are vital for order, stability and justice in any democratic society.

We have enough reasons to be in despair about the influence of the post-Polokwane ANC's transactional leaders, even though our transition process has brokered, strengthened and also institutionalised important democratic forces and values. The role that the constitution and the Constitutional Court have played in this regard, and continue to play, can only be described as excellent. The ANC's political transactional leaders are understandably aggrieved by this, as it places limits on their ability to manipulate and play power games without restraint. A common characteristic of unbridled transactional politics is fierce assaults on and undermining of politically independent institutions, including the media. Committed transactional leaders do not like watchdogs that oversee their doings. To them, accountability and responsibility are irksome encumbrances. If they succeed in their assaults, the result would be an amalgamation of state, personal and party assets. This super transaction is the most salient feature of an authoritarian state with authoritarian leaders.

Pressing problems such as endemic violence, the HIV/Aids pandemic, systemic corruption, the education crisis, imploding service delivery and the enormous socioeconomic gap which owes much to the ANC's ineffective leadership, need to be tackled urgently with workable policies and plans. These problems are currently confronted with a bigger crisis: the increasing elitist control of the state by the ANC and the concomitant creeping nationalisation of all sorts of things. There is even a bid to nationalise information. But this is not, as is the case with education or service delivery, the result of poor policies and inept leadership. It is a deliberate, well-planned and politically inspired "coup", an assault against the state as institution as it has started to take shape constitutionally after 1994. What is in jeopardy, is our constitution and our dearly bought democracy. As a populist ploy aimed at mobilising the poor in particular, the post-Polokwane ANC has revamped the term National Democratic Revolution to serve as the banner under which this assault on the constitution, our democracy and the independent facets of our state is being conducted.

This revolution, should it succeed, would not only undermine all forms of constitutional accountability through the appointment of people who are politically compromised and part of the post-Polokwane transactional culture. Eventually it would also radically restrict, on the authority of the state, the formal spaces for public debate, criticism of policies, disclosure of reckless politicial conduct and the names of incompetent leaders, the right to be heard, and even the ability to protest and be in opposition in all sorts of ways. What is at stake, is the kind of democracy for which Albert Luthuli, Oliver Tambo and later Nelson Mandela struggled. The post-Polokwane ANC is betraying the legacy of these and other leaders. Their National Democratic Revolution has no connection with the dream of eliminating the legacy of apartheid. On the contrary, it relates solely to a different dream: complete control over the state and its resources; control and wealth at any cost.

Does this mean to say that the transition process has failed altogether and that once again, as in the violence-torn 1980s, we have reason only to despair? Are there no signs of a tipping point in the direction of a more hopeful post-conflict dispensation and a practical experiencing of our country's constitutional ideals and values? Has Luthuli House already annexed the state and its institutions to such an extent that even Albert Luthuli's ideals and values have landed in a political dustbin? The answer is a qualified no. There are many signs of a tipping point, provided that one accepts that creative processes of renewal and democratisation are never one-time or dramatically game-changing events. They are still *processes*, with a few dramatic events that give them a stamp of popular acceptability.

The most important signs of a possible tipping point and reason for hope are the following:

First: A growing body of black opinion leaders and eminent "elders" who are in revolt. Luthuli House and President Jacob Zuma are losing the moral and intellectual soul of the ANC. Whether populism will rescue the ANC, is an open question. In this regard the ANC is going down the same road as the former National Party in the last decade of its rule. Just more rapidly, but with the same degree of political arrogance. As was the case with the National Party at the time, it happens less and less frequently that religious, moral, intellectual and business leaders give their unqualified or even qualified support in public to the ANC, its ability to govern the country and its policy practices. The ANC party leadership who single out the media as the major scapegoat for this alienation, are in fact admitting indirectly that they have lost a significant battle: support from the black leadership of civil society — especially those with broad public credibility. This alienation has resulted in a huge public gain: the refusal by many black opinion leaders to let Nelson Mandela and his legacy be hijacked by ANC opportunists and populists. The same goes for the legacy of Albert Luthuli and Oliver Tambo.

The list of impressive names in this regard is getting longer, with a number of black journalists leading the field. Respected intellectual leaders such as Mamphela Ramphele, George Bizos, Njabulo Ndebele, Barney Pityana, Jonathan Jansen and many others do not beat about the bush. A religious leader such as Emeritus Archbishop Desmond Tutu is today even a role model among Afrikaners who caricatured him during the Truth and Reconciliation Commission hearings. Allan Boesak, a source of inspiration within the former UDF, has long since turned his back on the ANC leadership. Not all black, coloured and Indian people support the new ANC leadership. Many refuse to genuflect before the president and his political commissars.

This sign of a possible tipping point should be read together with the recent diagnostic overview of Minister Trevor Manuel's National Planning Commission. The well-argued overview highlights nine serious challenges confronting the country: high unemployment; the substandard quality of education for poor black South Africans; problems relating to infrastructure; the unsustainability of economic development based on intensive dependence on natural resources; the continued marginalisation of the poor as a result of spatial challenges (spatial apartheid); an ailing public health system that is faced with a massive disease burden; uneven performance of public services; corruption; plus the deeply rooted divisions in South African society, which are not only based on race.

This diagnostic report is one of the most important documents we have at present, even though its reception was extremely disappointing. The anticipated debate failed to materialise and was submerged by more sensational reporting on "incidents". It is nonetheless a significant document, as it represents an official and public consensus – across party-political, ideological, class and racial divisions – on where South Africa stands in 2011–2012. There is actually little disagreement about this diagnosis. The question is, though: What to do about the diagnosis? Manuel's commission recommends an "effective social compact". Such a compact would of course still have to be brokered and negotiated, because it cannot be dictated. How the process should be launched is therefore important. There is also the question: Is it accepted that our country is experiencing a serious "state of disease" and that a partnership approach is indispensable? That cooperation, and not cooptation, has become the name of our developmental and survival game? To put it more specifically: Is the ANC hotheads' obsession with a National Democratic Revolution an answer to the Planning Commission's diagnosis? And how can the obsession be "transformed" by black and white democrats? When will black and white opinion leaders, intellectuals and democrats, in a nonracial manner outside of party divisions, become a respected choir instead of individuals crowing loudly on their respective dunghills?

Second: The protests about poor service delivery, even accompanied by varying forms of violence. This unrest can no longer be blamed on the legacy of apartheid. It is the direct result of ANC-generated inability, nepotism, corruption, lust for power, cadre deployment and "criminal" incompetence. The transition process has failed catastrophically at many local and community levels. This affects civil society directly. The scenes of an ANC government having to deploy the police to suppress riotous protests in townships illustrate the magnitude of this failure. The police won't quell this unrest. It will continue and probably intensify.

There is an important reason why this issue should be seen as a sign of a possible tipping point. The struggle for political freedom, heroic and necessary as it may be, is only one side of the coin when it comes to sustainable democracy. There is also another side that has to guarantee the genuineness of the coin: the entrenchment of freedom in processes, institutions and value systems where a culture of relative peace and justice prevails. Without that, the reconciliation dream becomes a form of romanticised delusion and is ultimately sabotaged by what is called the justice and equity gap. This gap is embodied in the experience of growing numbers of people that there is no justice and equity in political and social practice.

A lecture (in 2006) by Mary Anderson of the University of Notre Dame in the US left a profound impression on me when I related it to South Africa as I sat listening. It helped me to understand something of the above. In her address "False Promises and Premises? The Challenge of Peace Building for Corporations" (in: *Peace through Commerce*), Robinson stated: "Peace cannot be mined, manufactured, outsourced, hired, contracted, bought or sold. Peace is essentially a political process, not an economic one." In the final analysis, lasting peace and reconciliation in deeply divided and conflict-ridden societies rest on "political arrangements in which people have confidence". Those concerned need to have confidence that the agreed arrangements would result in predictable and acceptable processes "for redressing injustice and unfairness when it occurs". Anderson hits the nail on the head. In my view, this erosion of confidence in processes and institutions for narrowing the justice and equity gap has gone from bad to worse after Polokwane. Two salient failures need to be emphasised:

- The inability and even reluctance to reverse the slide to systemic corruption in a resolute and effective manner.
- The implosion of numerous local government institutions on account of inability, the lowering of management standards, a lust for power, and self-enrichment. Well-functioning local authorities are crucially important to efforts aimed at establishing lasting peace processes in previously conflict-ridden societies. After all, these institutions have a direct bearing on the success that is achieved in eliminating systemic injustices. In local contexts, peace and reconciliation translate into bread-and-butter issues: jobs, housing, clean water, the experience that one's quality of living is improving and that social services can be relied on. If there is no visible progress in

meeting basic needs, national commitments to peace and reconciliation mean very little.

There is a further fatal political complication. In all societies that have been exposed to prolonged and deep-rooted conflict, one finds two intertwined claims on the part of former strugglers in the so-called post-conflict dispensation: They believe that they know everything about democracy. They struggled for it with their blood, after all; they are entitled to a reward. On the other hand, those who used to profit from the system, particularly if they were members of a privileged ethnic minority, tend to be quick to wash their hands in innocence. Many of them experience apropos of the above claims that *they* have now become the victims of the justice and equity gap. To them, reconciliation means that the past should be left behind and forgotten. As they put it, they "just want to go on with their lives".

Riotous protests within local communities are indeed a source of concern, but the phenomenon may also be read positively: an expression of poor people's legitimate claim to meaningful intervention with regard to the justice and equity gap. Many of the current protest actions represent civil coalitions, in other words, cooperation in order to place a common interest or grievance on the agenda of the authorities regardless of the participants' party-political sentiments. As disorderly as some of the protests may be, they also send out a positive signal: a rupturing of the culture of slavish tolerance and loyalty on which political parties feed like parasites. In South Africa, the expectation that those who are discontented should "make representations" or "protest peacefully" has lost much of its credibility and persuasiveness in poor communities.

To use the title of Mary Anderson's address: It is a sign of hope that many of those who are used as voting cattle by the ANC have finally noticed the post-Polokwane ANC's accumulation of "false promises and premises" – notwithstanding the fact that many of them have grown up in the ANC's sphere of influence. It is this "notwithstanding" that can motivate a civil society to engage in creative actions. I regard it as a sign of a tipping point. It is after all *their* dreams, and not the dreams and desires of whites, that are being betrayed by the current ANC leadership. Their vision does not include a practical form of nonracial justice. What we are likely to see more of in future are public demonstrations that express people's experience of betrayal. This experience usually results in new forms of violence.

The post-Polokwane ANC has not only demonstrated an inability to lead South Africa into a post-conflict dispensation as was promised, but has also created new, serious conflict that can no longer simply be described as apartheid's legacy. This is apparent from the socioeconomic structure of South Africa: a pyramid with a very broad base. Right at the bottom, at the base, are those who struggle to survive. They make up an "underclass" that live on the scraps. After them come the informal entrepreneurs who try to make a living in one way or another, whether it be from hawking cigarettes on the streets, meat from informal, unregulated butcheries, copper from electrical conducting wire, stolen cellphones, organised micro-crime and other uncontrolled business transactions. Together with the bottom layer of our socioeconomic pyramid, they represent about half of our population. They are not only getting younger, but are overwhelmingly black and coloured. Whether they can be pacified permanently by populism and empty promises, is an open question. But a more important question is: How can this reality motivate *and* mobilise the leadership of our country to come up with workable developmental projects?

Third: There are good indications of a realignment in our politics, including growth points for effective opposition politics. The latter have been sprouting in white ranks from as far back as 1990. With his exit from active politics and later the disappearance of the once mighty and seemingly indestructible National Party, De Klerk unintentionally promoted the realignment of opposition politics by preparing the demise of the National Party. His successor was no match for the ANC's political manoeuvres, with Thabo Mbeki regarding the dissolution of the "party of Verwoerd" into the ANC as a very special political achievement. This put the possibility of opposition politics on a different and new track: the DA with Helen Zille as its current leader — someone whose footsteps through many stations also refer back to the days when Helen Suzman of the Progressive Federal Party (PFP) had the "Nats" seething with rage at times. This process of the realignment, reorientation and reorganisation of opposition ranks is still under way in a wider circle.

The muddle in which the ANC finds itself at present is a gain for the DA in particular. After all, the ANC's current crisis is not a temporary one. As a "congress movement" consisting of a coalition of conflicting ideologies, interests and personalities, the end of its political problems is not yet in sight by a long chalk. The Malema phenomenon should therefore be seen in the context of the ANC's unstable political congress culture and the dominance of transactional leadership. Never before has the ANC leadership's authority been challenged so blatantly and over such a long period. Whatever may happen around this authority challenge in future, the ANC of the Mandela era will not arise again. Along with it the notion that the ANC is the only party capable of governing the country, a view that even held sway in international circles after our so-called "miracle", has fortunately also bitten the dust.

In the emerging and established black middle class and its intelligentsia there is a growing discomfort about, and at times even resistance to, the kid gloves with which the ANC handles internal conflicts. Those who have advanced through merit to where they are today – and there are many of them – have a vested interest in a full-fledged democracy and a state that does not dictate economic activities. In fact, it is in these quarters that the dream of nonracialism flourishes strongly. And they are also the ones who understand that the views of Julius Malema and others on, say, agricultural land, will jeopardise food security within a matter of a few years. The political hegemony and bonds of power that existed in struggle times have started to erode in the post-Mandela era.

A fourth beacon of hope can be found in an observation made by Paul Cluver, prominent wine farmer and thinker: South Africa is not postcolonial Africa where leaders cling to their positions by hook or by crook. (A good example just across our country's Limpopo River is Robert Mugabe of Zimbabwe.) Not even the post-Polokwane ANC with its transactional leaders would find it easy to lead South Africa into this kind of political quagmire. The right and possibility of leadership and regime change has been bred too strongly into our country's body politic. Even in the days of apartheid this right and possibility existed. Thabo Mbeki, too, accepted this tradition and did not enlist the aid of the military to stay in power. Admittedly, there are disturbing signs. The current ANC leadership do not accept the right of opposition unconditionally, and consider the ANC to be the only true and legitimate standard-bearer of democracy. In a political culture of transactional leadership there is little, if any, understanding of the necessity and importance of opposition politics. Despite worrying signs, however, it is also the case that there are still many honourable, genuine and visionary democrats within the ANC who have developed a strong resistance to the transactional politics and obscene self-enrichment of their leaders.

There is an additional hope-inspiring reality. Besides the constitution and the Constitutional Court, construction work on a society wherein democracy can flourish and citizens' rights remain on the national agenda, is continuing in yet another way: the activities of the network of nongovernmental organisations (NGOs) that is embedded like a giant nervous system at national, regional and local levels. In light of the antagonistic discourse from the ranks of the Afro-racists, I would like to emphasise: Whites play a significant role in this network and its branches. Not because they are white and therefore arrogantly assume that they have the leadership skills and ability to do so, but because they care about the country and its people. Fortunately, the political uncertainty that is in my view being created deliberately by the Afro-racists does not deter these whites from making a difference in our country by working at the dream of a better life for all. Thereby they, too, are celebrating the legacy of an Albert Luthuli, an Oliver Tambo and a Nelson Mandela.

Nevertheless, we need to acknowledge that South Africa is still an "uncertain democracy" in 2012 and will remain so for a long time to come. This premise, which is embodied in the battle between hope and despair, confronts us with a fundamental question that has hung over our conflict-ravaged country for many decades: How can we move towards more sustainable peace, and broaden and deepen our uncertain democracy in the process? And how can our civil society play a decisive part in this? For an answer to these questions, it is useful to dwell briefly on some of the lessons learnt during the Afrikaner-ANC dialogue process in the 1980s.

Firstly, the Afrikaner-ANC dialogue group took as our point of departure something we called our basic assumption:"Our country is deeply divided and stuck in a deeply rooted conflict. Let's try to reach consensus on the nature of/reasons for the conflict as well as on the road ahead."There was a directional question:"Are we prepared to accept joint responsibility for this and not to lapse into mutual attributions of blame?" Such a question neutralises techniques of denial and the transfer of blame. All political mediation stands or falls by it.This is an exercise "enemies" cannot embark on in public from the outset, because all politicians are programmed to play to their audience on a public platform. For this reason successful cross-cutting partnerships aimed at resolving deep-seated problems never start out on a public stage.

Secondly, we rapidly achieved a consensus:"We need each other.We are interdependent.We *cannot* oppose each other as enemies forever.We have to learn from each other as 'concerned South Africans' and get rid of the notion of the 'enemy'." Alliances, functioning partnerships and sustainable peace and reconciliation are impossible without such consensus. One of the most remarkable outcomes of the Afrikaner-ANC dialogue process was that the myth of the enemy dissolved so quickly and we discovered each other as human beings. Unless dialogue succeeds in transforming the construct of the "enemy" into Martin Buber's "I become through my relation to you", reconciliation and peace are not feasible.

Thirdly, the dialogue and interaction process was multidimensional.The track-two model was differentiated. A great number of concerned people participated in it, their central focus being: what should be done to resolve our country's "hurting stalemate"? A decisive factor was the involvement of leaders who were able to deliver results. Daling/Du Plessis and Mbeki/Pahad, for example, could deliver with regard to the rebel tour. Mbeki/Zuma/Pahad/Nhlanhla and Louw/Spaarwater/Barnard could deliver on their interactions. De Klerk and Mandela, despite serious problems between them, could deliver an election. Complex reconciliation and peace processes require people who are capable of delivering. Our dilemma at present is that there are few, if any, track-two initiatives. Recognition and especially material reward ("What's in it for me in return for my efforts?") have become the rule at higher levels. At lower levels it is often different.

A problem in this regard, though, is the reluctance and sometimes even inability on the part of political leaders to accept track-two interactions .[2] They are often so geared to power, influence and recognition that interventions outside of their control are not always welcome. This is one of the reasons why track-two interactions have to take on an informal and private character. Even the now defunct Peace Accord, an initiative that did not start off as a public declaration but first went through a thorough preparatory phase, did not enjoy immediate support. Besides, today the state with its president and particularly Luthuli House reckon that they are the only agent of peace and reconciliation, and do not acknowledge that reconciliation and peace processes need to take place multidimensionally on vertical *and* horizontal levels. They also do not accept that a wide variety of role players need to be meaningfully involved. Neither a party nor the state can monopolise reconciliation and peace processes. Nowhere in history has the state been able to do this. The reason? Reconciliation and peace go to the heart of civil society, nationally, at regional level, and locally. This is the real context of reconciliation and peace processes: civil society. Not the presidency. There was consensus within the Afrikaner-ANC dialogue group that peace and reconciliation can only be meaningful if *experienced* as such within civil society.

We have reached a point in our ailing transition process where track-two talks have become imperative. Without such dialogue, Minister Trevor Manuel's Planning Commission's recommendation of an "effective social compact" to combat the nine diagnosed disease conditions our country suffers from will become simply another idea that ends up on our growing sociopolitical scrapheap. The foundation of an effective social compact is, after all, trust and confidence. We have an excellent example of such a compact from which much can be learnt: the Peace Accord. It was an accord, led by leaders from civil society, which was not only absolutely representative but also, like a carefully woven web, extended from national down to mainly local levels.

The organisers of the accord were symbolic of the nonracial dream cherished by many South Africans. Inclusivity was the watchword. It was acknowledged at the time that the negotiation process had stalled, mainly on account of high levels of political violence, and that civil society had an interest in the continuation of the process. The role of the business sector should be mentioned in particular. In light of this experience, it should be asked: How can the concerned and critical forces in today's civil society, as well as those who have already raised their voices in public, make a stand in a nonracial manner? Do they want to? Can they? And about what? For this to happen, a considerable number of second tracks first need to be carved out and reliable stepping stones laid down in the boggy political terrain. There is a growing nonracial consensus on what has gone wrong in our country. All that remains is for important facets of the consensus to find a public, nonracial address. And that is why interpersonal and interracial contact and dialogue have become imperative.

We need a new peace accord that can foster not only a culture of respect and trust, but also consensus on the nature of our country's central problems, the role players that need to be involved in solutions, and how we can move forward. This dream of a comprehensive and sustainable process of peace requires a mustard seed: meeting points and dialogue between improbable participants that would result in partnership projects capable of powerfully inspiring people's hope of a better life for all. [3]

# Epilogue: Track-two negotiations and the value of secret talks

"What manner of beasts are these Afrikaners?"
This was the question in the mind of Thabo Mbeki, at the time still a prominent exiled ANC leader and an enemy of the apartheid state, when he attended the Afrikaner-ANC dialogue group for the first time in Ashford, England, on 21 February 1988. He spoke about this more than 20 years later, on 30 May 2009, after a private screening of *Endgame*, a dramatised version of this secret dialogue process and the impact it had. *Endgame* is neither fiction nor a documentary. It is a "faction" film, a mixture of factual and fictitious elements. We watched the film in the company of family members and a group of mutual friends. Memories were recalled and questions asked. The film and our discussion had a common focus: peace between enemies *is* possible. Enemies *can* learn to trust each other. This does not happen spontaneously, however, but as a result of a laborious learning process in which timing plays a significant part.

Mbeki told us that evening that he had already met Afrikaners on several occasions prior to his first participation in the dialogue group. In July 1987, for instance, there was the much-publicised Dakar conference in Senegal, where he was one of the main players. As important as the Dakar conference was, in February 1988 and for two years thereafter he held talks in a small-group context with Afrikaners of a different kind: people who were close to the centre of the establishment. The Afrikaner participants at the February 1988 meeting included Sampie Terreblanche from Stellenbosch University, Marinus Wiechers, an authority on constitutional law from the University of South Africa (Unisa), and me. Wiechers subsequently assisted in the drafting of the Namibian constitution and later became rector of Unisa. Stellenbosch University was known at the time as the intellectual birthplace of many leaders of the ruling National Party.

Terreblanche, an authority on economic history, was also a prominent political analyst and social critic.

To Mbeki, the dialogue project was as much a novel experience as it was for the Afrikaners who took part in it - a journey of discovery without a compass or road map. In time he would meet many "beasts" of the Afrikaner species and even come to know some of them well.

This book describes, against the backdrop of Mbeki's question about the "other", the events in which I, a number of other Afrikaners and members of the ANC were involved in England between 1987 and 1990. My account of these events is neither a historical document nor an academic report, but a narrative: *my* version of how *I* experienced and remember the events in question. There is a text, though: *my* notes and minutes. Thabo Mbeki and Tony Trew also made notes.[1] So did Michael Young, who was involved with the Consolidated Goldfields (Consgold) company that helped to launch the project. As in the case of all texts, interpretation inevitably occurs. My interpretation focuses on a central question: What enables historical enemies in situations of pervasive conflict to start trusting each other? What caused Mbeki's question to be answered within the dialogue group in such a manner that the political construct of "the enemy" was neutralised? How can historical enemies learn from each other in such a way that peace processes become a reality? How does one develop sustainable trust and confidence that make negotiated settlements and even coalitions possible in situations of deep-rooted conflict?

The sporadic commentary from academic and other circles on the Afrikaner-ANC dialogue group's unofficial involvement in the first phase of the setttlement process has been varied, ranging from strongly positive to strongly negative. It has to be assumed that the film *Endgame*, based on Robert Harvey's book *The Fall of Apartheid*, played a role in the critical comments of some, including writer Breyten Breytenbach (*Rapport*, 16/05/2010) and academics Heribert Adam and Kogila Moodley. They were all good friends of Frederik van Zyl Slabbert's and are extremely dissatisfied with Thabo Mbeki, who in their view turned his back on Slabbert as time went on.[2]

Breytenbach and Adam/Moodley rate Idasa's Dakar conference highly and view the Afrikaner-ANC dialogue project, which also started in 1987, as if it were in competition with the Idasa initiatives. In a tribute to Van Zyl Slabbert after his death, Breytenbach even invokes a contrast with the "Esterhuyses and the National Intelligence of this world together with the "Gladdebekis" [a play on Mbeki's name and the term 'smooth talkers' in Afrikaans] (who) plotted in back rooms to ensure that state power remained in the hands of an undemocratic elite". Idasa was Van Zyl Slabbert's and Alex Boraine's attempt to do something about the deteriorating political situation in the country. It was a timely and necessary initiative, one of many. Within the public domain it was definitely an icebreaker, albeit that a kind of hyped-up Dakar cult developed over time.

In contrast with the critical comments on the dialogue group there were also more considered and positive assessments, as in the books of Allister Sparks and Patti Waldmeir, both seasoned journalists. Daniel Lieberfeld was one of the first academics who reflected dispassionately and analytically on the dialogue group's contribution. He had conducted interviews with me and other participants. Mark Gevisser's book on Thabo Mbeki, *The Dream Deferred*, and David Welsh's standard work, *The Rise and Fall of Apartheid*, provide valuable background information and interesting insights that are helpful in understanding the dialogue group's contribution.

It is, of course, a fact that there was competition between individuals and institutions in South Africa's white community for a ringside seat in the settlement arena. It was inevitable. The political crisis in the country was deeply rooted, and within the white Afrikaans-speaking community there was not a large pool of creative minds and courageous leaders. Disagreement about what routes should be followed to resolve the impasse was the order of the day. The battle in Afrikaner ranks between the so-called *verkramptes* and the *verligtes* was merciless. Moreover, those who wanted to change the system from within and those who attacked it from outside were regularly at each other's throats. A small number of Afrikaners supported the ANC. Critical diversity instead of conformity was a pattern among Afrikaner intellectuals.

My own approach was predominantly multidimensional: not either/or as far as ways were concerned, but rather and-and. In deeply divided societies where violence has become a pattern, an exclusive approach becomes part of the problem. This applies particularly when, as in South Africa, the notion of "the enemy" has led to armed resistance. In such cases "dialogue with the enemy" is viewed as treason by the ruling elite because it is a form of subversion. Among resistance fighters, too, dialogue is opposed as it is seen as an alternative to a military seizure of power. There is nothing as "romantic" as the idea of a military struggle for power. In such a situation, alternatives are usually slated as naive optimism.

A multidimensional approach may help breach this dogmatic position, even on the part of the ruling elite who in the case of the South African military were convinced that their bullets-and-casspirs approach had matters under control, albeit that hit squads had to lend a hand. It is true, of course, that even a multidimensional approach is a choice for an answer to specific questions: Can all other approaches be tolerated and accepted? Is dialogue taking place among all the leading lights in a search for understandings? Are some approaches destructive and should they therefore be neutralised? Surely not all approaches can be acceptable? On the part of both the government and the ANC there was, for instance, a fairly negative perception of the role that intellectuals and academics could play. This was a loss. Important research inputs, for example on the rights of cultural minorities, went to waste as a result.

Both Thabo Mbeki and I, without having explicitly agreed this with each other, refrained from making public statements about the dialogue project afterwards. We did not provide much detail in the few interviews that were conducted with us in this regard. Some commentators even wrote about the project without having interviewed us.

There were two main reasons for our approach. First, it was necessary to allow time for reflection before one could talk of the effects of this unofficial dialogue process on the official settlement process. The second reason was more important: avoidance of any controversy and confrontation between competitors in the post-1990 negotiation drama. Within the ANC there had already been controversy about the dialogue process prior to 1990, especially on the part of militants such as Chris Hani and Joe Nhlanhla. There was also Cyril Ramaphosa with his own political aspirations and manoeuvres to replace Mbeki as the initial leader of the ANC's negotiation team. Moreover, there was an election in the offing and high positions that had to be filled in a new government. Giving too much publicity to the dialogue project would have been unwise.

The term "transfer" is sometimes used in the debate on the role of informal, unofficial dialogue in the handling of deep-seated conflict and its effects on formal, official negotiation processes. The question, then, is *whether* a "transfer" took place from the informal to the formal, *how* it took place, and *what* was transferred. This question can be easily answered in cases where the interactions concerned and the players have been selected and operate within a predetermined game pattern. In such a case there exists a form of relatively official sanction – an agreement to participate in the game on certain conditions, for example confidentiality and the possibility of denial. Without such a sanction and access, "transfer" becomes hard to determine.

This issue is not new. We encounter it, for instance, in Greek mythology. The god Hermes was the "messenger" between Zeus and the humans, and *vice versa*. The term "hermeneutics" is derived from his name: the study of understanding and interpretation. Even Zeus had to trust Hermes. So did the humans. What this myth tells us is that "message-bearers" and "intermediaries" are inevitable, with the question being: Can the "message-bearer" be trusted, and how should the "message" be interpreted? This is why trust and integrity are among the oldest values in our cultural history.

How should the story that is told in this book be interpreted? Was there an academically grounded "theory" behind the talks from the outset? A clear strategy on the part of the Afrikaners and the ANC? At the start of the talks in 1987, little of this was present. It was rather a case of: "As political enemies, we want to learn from each other by talking to each other." In retrospect, it is possible to make theoretical sense of this. Besides what I read about the Vienna conference on nuclear disarmament and Lee Blessing's dramatised version of the events *A Walk in the Woods*, one book stands out. In 1988 I read a book that politically "transformed" my views on dialogue with reference to Martin Buber's philosophy: *Conflict Resolution: Track Two Diplomacy*, edited by J MacDonald and D Bendahmane. Joseph Montville contributed a chapter with an imaginative title: *The Arrow and the Olive Branch*. This was my "Aha!" experience. In 1981 in an article on "Foreign Policy According to Freud", Montville had made a distinction between official and government-inspired talks to resolve conflict (track one), and unofficial efforts by private individuals with influence to contribute to conflict resolution within a state or between states (track two).[3]

According to MacDonald and Bendahmane's book, official and formal forms of conflict resolution are perforce the primary strategic objective – the *first track* to a settlement agreement. This made a great deal of sense to me; after all, agreements require an official sanction. Good ideas are crucial, but people with a mandate are the ones who ultimately have to make decisions. How this decision-making process can be informed and influenced positively, is therefore an essential strategic methodological question. I prefer to talk about it as a question about positioning with a view to access to the decision-making process. All forms of positioning include both contact (access) and compromise. One may also put it by way of a question: are there possibilities within the fields of reference and experience of the contending "enemies" that can be utilised for the purpose of dialogue and settlement? It is in this regard that I am an advocate of multidimensionality. The advantage of an unofficial and nonpublic *second track* is that it cannot be abused to sow public dissension, something both the Botha government and the ANC were wont to do.

A second track is by no means an unusual phenomenon. The business world is an example of this. Many important corporate decisions start on the golf course rather than in the boardroom. Networks and reliable contacts play a major part in all track-two interactions, particularly in the political arena. Hence embassies do not host social functions merely for the purpose of conviviality. MacDonald and Bendahmane's reference to *Track Two Diplomacy* makes sense, although I prefer to steer clear of the term "diplomacy" and rather refer to words such as "talks" and "dialogue" in order to stress that sustained plans, objectives and outcomes are on the agenda in the dialogue process. The notion of an open democratic society implies a demonstration of an open dialogue even within a confidential track-two context.

Track-two talks are generally unofficial, unformalised and confidential.

Strictly speaking, such talks represent a footpath in a pre-negotiation phase. They are not themselves negotiations, because they lack a formal mandate and guidelines. They are, however, more than just briefing sessions and clarification of positions. Not getting-to-know-each-other functions. They are aimed at achieving consensus on political rewards as well as risks, determining agenda points, defining preconditions for track-one negotiations, and establishing common ground. The ultimate success of South Africa's laborious official, public track-one settlement process from 1990 to the election of 1994 was founded on the confidential track-two interactions between the government and the ANC both prior to and after 1990. Mac Maharaj, a major role player on behalf of the ANC in the post-1990 period, was adamant about the question of confidentiality during track-two contacts. And also about the naivety of academics who took delight in analysing anything under the sun, but did not have to make political decisions.

A very important methodological issue in this regard is how transfer can be effected from a second to a first track. Access by virtue of personal relationships of trust, acknowledgement of integrity, equal status and a good dose of self-confidence is crucial in this process. In the case of the Afrikaner-ANC dialogue group, the "transfer" to political elites was guaranteed – to Lusaka and to Pretoria. The dialogue group was a secondary transfer channel. The primary channel in the preparatory phase was the Coetsee-Barnard-Mandela connection and the NIS-ANC connection in Switzerland in 1989/ 1990. Once the formal negotiation process got under way there were several other informal channels, for example Meyer-Ramaphosa and Fanie van der Merwe-Mac Maharaj.

All track-two interactions between traditional political enemies comprise various facets that give them a multidimensional character. One facet, within the context of unofficial, informal and confidential interaction, is the role of intermediaries and reliable message-bearers. Who should they be, and what is their shelf life? This is also sometimes referred to as "quiet diplomacy". I prefer the phrase "reliable message-bearers". This go-between role differs from the roles of a facilitator, mediator or negotiator who assumes a more active position in the settlement process. The Afrikaner participants in the dialogue project were rather in remote-control contact with both the state and the ANC, the two main parties to the conflict. This type of role requires a high measure of trust and acceptance of the integrity of the message-bearer. Both parties to the conflict need to be satisfied that the messenger does not have an agenda of his own and therefore manipulates the message, but instead conveys it as accurately as possible.

Separating personal views and interpretations from "the message" was one of many challenging issues I had to deal with. An intrinsic danger of message-bearers is that their interpretation of the message may create misconceptions and wrong expectations. Even though message-bearers are not mediators or negotiators in the true sense, it may be necessary at times to play a limited mediatory role and suggest advice. A message-bearer also has to guard against being misused. In fact, very early on in my interaction with the NIS one issue was dominant in an unspoken and even intuitive way: Can it be assumed that messages that are being conveyed to each other and feedback that is given, are indeed reliable? Verification was difficult, if not impossible. Message-bearers have influence and also a position of power. Through Lieberfeld I encountered a reference to a remark by Paul Pillar in his contribution to *Psychological Dimensions of War* that shed light on this facet as I reflected on the talks: "The best agent for a peace initiative is one who is known to have access to his government's leaders and can convey their intentions accurately, but who holds no official position and thus can be disavowed if necessary."[4] Most of the Afrikaners who participated in the dialogue project were in such a position.

All of this, of course, raises an important moral question: What about the exigencies of democratic values such as accountability and transparency? Do the public not have the right to be informed of *everything* that affects their future? My own standpoint was that an answer to this question is determined by the nature of the process, which forms part of the bigger, broader and more far-reaching settlement process. This process inevitably proceeds in phases. Preparatory processes that have to culminate in a settlement of deeply rooted conflict are not subject to the requirement of transparency and disclosure. Hence the international acceptance of the notion of quiet diplomacy. Messages between sworn enemies about the possibility of a settlement are not necessarily in the public interest. The consequences and eventual reactions to these messages within an official first track, though, are decidedly in the public interest. Naturally, this position is not as easy and straightforward as it may seem on paper. I often wondered whether it had been a good decision to involve myself in the secret track-two dialogue project. The project also caused emotional tensions and raised doubts in my mind as to whether I was the kind of person who could play a positive role in it. Talking to sworn enemies may sound like an adventurous or even missionary endeavour. In the harsh reality of the South African political cauldron, however, such a venture was a totally different story.[5]

It meant a lot to me afterwards when Mike Louw, formerly of the NIS, replied as follows to Lieberfeldt's question as to why they had used me: "We trusted him, his instincts . . . We regarded him not as someone who had a rosy view of a meeting with the ANC . . . He was a trained person in political science and . . . his views were balanced. He could give you quite a clear report on the personalities that he spoke to, what he saw as weak points, strong points, how a person behaved under this or that circumstance."[6] Given the personal and political risks, however, things might also have turned out differently and very negatively. You don't get involved in interactions of this kind because you reckon that success is guaranteed or dependent on your input.

The NIS had a formidable reputation. The ANC feared this organisation more than they did Military Intelligence or the Security Police. Years later, during a reception in Pretoria after I had received the Order of Luthuli (Silver), Jacob Zuma, then deputy president of the country, confessed in his jovial way to Annemarie: "Thabo and I were petrified as we walked towards the hotel rooms of the NIS agents in Lucerne. We kept wondering: What if it's a trap?" The NIS was held in high regard internationally as an intelligence service. My decision was not a shot in the dark. Owing to my interests I was aware of the role intelligence services play in all states, notably in Britain and the US. From a strategic perspective I was convinced that while outside institutions like Idasa could indeed play a role, it was primarily an institution such as the NIS that would cut the negotiation knot for South Africa. My decision was a calculated risk that could have blown up in my face, and I was prepared to take full responsibility for it.[7]

The unofficial Afrikaner-ANC dialogue group's meetings were bilateral, with a core group that provided continuity and especially a "memory". A "memory" is of decisive importance in all exploratory talks. Michael Young of Consolidated Goldfields was an impartial chairman, the facilitator during the organised sessions. We assumed that he had his own contacts with the British government and its intelligence services. No third party was present directly as a participating party, which was something the ANC and the government felt very strongly about later during the official, track-one process. This matter was broached several times during the unofficial dialogue group's meetings. In 1984 the ANC took a strong stance against so-called independent mediators when British and South African academics proposed to bring ANC members and members of the National Party together "informally" for discussions "in their personal capacities". The opposition to mediation by outside parties related to the ANC's perception of what had happened at the Lancaster House talks on the independence of Rhodesia/Zimbabwe, which was reinforced by the later SWA/Namibia process. This also explains the failure of the attempt by HW van der Merwe of the University of Cape Town to play a mediation role in the early 1980s. The time had not been ripe either. Niel Barnard of the NIS was also very outspoken about outside intervention on more than one occasion: The government would not be prescribed to by the private sector, clerics, writers and academics. Least of all by foreigners. He and Mandela soon reached agreement on this issue during the prison talks, another "track". The interest of confidentiality played a huge role in this.

Although the ANC participants in our dialogue group took part unofficially in the track-two talks, they were prominent leaders and people who occupied official positions. The progress made with the dialogue process and the significance thereof were apparent from the new ANC entrants, such as Jacob Zuma and Joe Nhlanhla. The latter's involvement was a significant tactical move. He, together with Hani, had been highly upset about the dialogue process when it became known in Lusaka and objections were raised at the ANC's National Working Committee in 1988. Mbeki had not been present at the time. Nhlanhla eventually also attended some of the NIS-ANC dialogue sessions in Switzerland.

The Afrikaners, leaders in their respective occupations, were themselves very well networked with the ruling elite. Sampie Terreblanche, for instance, was an important opinion leader and popular speaker. He also had good contacts with foreign journalists. Willem de Klerk was a member of the executive council of the Afrikaner Broederbond. He kept this influential council informed. In addition, he regularly sent written reports to FW de Klerk and Gerrit Viljoen, a cabinet minister. I could talk to the National Intelligence Service. The Afrikaners, admittedly, had no official political position. But their professional and social networks within the sphere of the ruling elite were solid. PW Botha, the president at that stage, could not withdraw their passports. This was something with which he often threatened other people, and which he also did at times. The interlocutors were able to utilise the possibilities within the system without having to fear alienation or isolation. This is a great strategic advantage for any track-two interaction, and not only a question of good networks. There also had to be trust on the part of members of the Afrikaner and government elite that track-two explorers would convey information and intentions correctly. Participants had to be selected judiciously on the strength of their position and influence within certain networks. The transfer of the talks and the messages that emanated from them was not difficult within the above contexts. Such transfer fostered a shared narrative.

The meetings of the Afrikaner-ANC dialogue group were deliberately deformalised. They were not conferences but small-group discussions in ideal conditions, dialogue in the real sense of the word. There is little doubt that the settings, the informality and especially the acknowledgement of the equal status of the interlocutors had a dramatic effect on interpersonal relations and the sense of a shared South African identity. Experiencing this common identity in the dialogue situation and during our social interaction at the places where we met, particularly inside and outside the Mells Park estate, was new to us in all respects. The settings and social contexts enhanced these experiences, for instance in the traditional pub of the village of Mells where we often gathered. The "Ingelse", as we Afrikaners tend to refer to the English, regarded our group with curiosity. It was highly unlikely that Mells had many black visitors. At times the Afrikaners spoke "the taal" (Afrikaans). We laughed, because as South Africans we took great delight in confusing the "Ingelse" in Mells's pub. It was not merely a question of the mutual demonisation having lost its emotional and political force. The myth of the enemy had imploded as well, and was replaced by joking comments about the "Ingelse"! *They* became "the other". Personally, I put a very high premium on this experience of a shared South African identity and nonracialism. To me it was one of the major building blocks on the road to a sustainable and dynamic democratic dispensation, and it gave me much hope at the time.

Scholars have noted that track-two initiatives can influence official and formal track-one talks in various ways. One of these is that they encourage and sometimes even force political decision-makers to take negotiation possibilities seriously. On the part of the major parties to a conflict, there needs to be a realisation that there is a good *possibility* of a negotiated settlement. What plays a role in this, of course, is acknowledgment of the existence of a stalemate that hurts to such an extent that there can be no winners, as even John Vorster — a former South African prime minister — admitted with his prediction of a future "too ghastly to contemplate". But without purposeful and sustained dialogue, starting with a second track, such acknowledgment doesn't amount to much. In Vorster's case it was worthless. Neither the NP nor the ANC was willing or ready at that stage. Aggrey Klaaste, a former editor of the *Sowetan*, rightly pointed out that parties also need to have the conviction and will that "It's never too late to talk". In Vienna, Father Theodore Hesburgh personified this. He brought the American and Russian negotiators together so they could talk face to face.

I don't subscribe to the view that the widely accepted notion of a "hurting stalemate" was the only factor in the case of South Africa's acceptance of a negotiated settlement. (According to this theory, the ruling elite are more inclined to negotiate when there are signs that they are losing their power.) There were other driving forces too. The global power balance was changing dramatically. And there was a strong international pro-negotiation consensus. Moreover, there was a growing awareness among elements of the government elite and the ANC that a negotiated peace was the best option. This awareness was reinforced by discussions and actions that built trust.

Another factor that promotes the success of track-two talks is crucial: the transparency and openness with which the acceptability of certain positions, interests and proposals is discussed in exploratory talks. There has to be a willingness to find workable and acceptable compromises instead of generating confrontation. We called it "the search for common ground". Of course, this objective goes much further than simply attempting to "clarify positions" and "gather or provide information". The amount of discussion we devoted to "risks and rewards" was striking. Getting clarity on political risks and political rewards needs to happen swiftly in track-two talks. They tend to derail quickly if the participants indulge in moral indignation. Moral outrage is sometimes called for, but not when it comes to exploratory and track-two dialogue. This is one of the reasons why the ANC, despite their appreciation of the liberals' moral outrage against apartheid, did not want to involve them in the secret track-two talks about a negotiated settlement.

The unofficial Afrikaner-ANC dialogue group was not the only example of a track-two model. This model also had other, more public examples, as in the case of Idasa's public initiatives. These were mainly aimed at one facet of the track-two model: changing public opinion, especially among intellectual elites. There were other public initiatives too, undertaken by business organisations, institutions that associated with the ANC, and foreign governments and think-tanks, for example the United States South African Leadership Programme (Ussalep) and the African-American Institute (AAI). These initiatives took place within a limited domain. South Africa represents a unique historical case in this regard. The process was multidimensional on both the second and the first tracks. While the Afrikaner-ANC dialogue group was a nonpublic and unofficial track two with access to the track-one process, Idasa and numerous other contact groups were significant track-two actions in the public domain. These actions are referred to in this book because they were instrumental in bringing about an international consensus on the settlement process. There were even crosscutting contacts between all these tracks. Singling out one "case" as decisive is therefore a blinkered and one-dimensional approach to an extremely exciting and complex settlement process.

The Afrikaner-ANC dialogue group's initial objective was the clarification of positions – clarity on how the ANC leadership would react to various possible moves by the South African government. Hence much of the discussion focused on the release of political prisoners, such as Nelson Mandela, and the legalisation of banned organisations. For example, Govan Mbeki was released shortly after the first meeting. The "how" of the ANC's reaction to government initiatives was the directional question in the talks, and not so much who and what the ANC was. We did talk about ANC policy, of course, for instance regarding the violence option and the economy. The underlying focus, however, was on the way in which the ANC would react to certain government initiatives.

The Afrikaner-ANC dialogue group also had another facet: the *dialogue-within-a-dialogue* between me and Thabo Mbeki. These talks were exclusively bilateral and pertained to practical issues such as prisoner releases and possible official contacts. The multidimensional handling of the track-two model was continued in the interactions between the De Klerk government and the ANC from February 1990 onwards, especially when the formal negotiation process was launched and official negotiation teams were announced with committees that had to deal with specific issues. This track-two contact functioned from early on, with representatives of the De Klerk government and the ANC often socialising informally outside the conference room to discuss thorny questions. The NIS was present at many, if not all, of these interactions. Barnard was a key figure in this because the NIS had not only been involved in the process in all its phases since its inception, but also had a supporting research unit.

Within the ANC in exile, Mbeki was a strategic central nervous system: numerous "messages" reached him, whether they came from Idasa, business leaders from South Africa, the UDF, Cosatu, Enos Mabuza, Van Zyl Slabbert, Wynand Malan, the South African Council of Churches, Gorbachev, or whoever. This was a remarkable position within the ANC. He also knew what the militants in the ANC were talking about. The NIS was of course also a central nervous system, connected to both the track-two and the track-one talks. Afterwards, when I read the book by Louise Diamond and John McDonald on *Multi-Track Diplomacy: A Systems Approach to Peace*, I realised how people can understand and deal with complex problems without a theory, learning as they go along.

My book tells the story, from my own perspective, of what happened within the second contact track between 1987 and 1990. It is, of course, a story to which other people contributed. I refer to this as well, but my narrative reflects how *I* experienced and digested their interaction. My use of the phrase "Afrikaner-ANC dialogue" is not merely factual and historical. To me it also encapsulates an important political as well as a moral stand. From as early as 1985, but mainly from 1987 onwards, numerous inner-circle Afrikaners played an indispensable and crucial part in the preparatory phase of the official negotiation process. Their involvement was a considered choice.

Within the National Party and its supporting institutions there was also an ethically driven fermentation process at work that struck at the root of apartheid ideology and was supported by a growing, new moral consciousness. An important signal of this was the resignation from the National Party of Wynand Malan, an NP MP of the Johannesburg suburb of Randburg, in 1987. My accentuation of the role of Afrikaners during the preparatory phase relates to what I would like to call the moral liberation of many Afrikaners. This moral liberation and the ANC's dream of political liberation eventually encountered each other.

Patti Waldmeir, an American journalist with whom I had good contact, and author of the book *Anatomy of a Miracle*, flattered me when she wrote in the copy she gave me: "To Willie. The greatest seducer the Afrikaner side could have hoped for." While I find the metaphor "seducer" – in the political sense of the word – seductive, and she also used this metaphor to describe Thabo Mbeki, I prefer another metaphor to portray that which the Afrikaner-ANC contact group did: bridge-builders to peace. But even bridge-builders to peace have to resort to seduction at times. Leaders and decision-makers have to be helped to embark on a "love affair" with trust and confidence.

# Notes

CHAPTER I

1.  At times this sparked bitter wars of words, notably in Stellenbosch. In retrospect, these "wars" mainly symbolised a difference between an overemphasis on high moral liberal-democratic principles on the one hand, and strategy and tactics on the other. Naturally, there were also differences with regard to principles and ideology. Many *verligtes* were on the staff of Stellenbosch University. There were, of course, also *verligtes* at other universities and institutions. The then Potchefstroom University for Christian Higher Education, with the journal *Woord en Daad* (Word and Deed) a herald of renewal, deserves mention in this regard. This was where Willem (Wimpie) de Klerk's roots lay. The Stellenbosch *verligtes*, both individually and as a group, were outspoken, well known and involved in influential networks among the Afrikaner power elite whose political leader was President PW Botha, who hailed from the Cape.

2.  There was no love lost between moralists and *verligtes*. Egos undoubtedly played a part in this mutual intolerance, and competition between the two camps was fierce. At least it resulted in creative conflict, which enabled innovative progress and demanded strategically calculated thinking. I have always regarded conflict as the mother of creativity. Hence the *verligtes* opted for deliberate brinkmanship, in other words, the search for triggers for processes of renewal from within the ruling power elite with a view to either motivating this elite to think more progressively, or subverting them. As Sampie Terreblanche, a leading social-democratic *verligte*, once put it: "While the apartheid politicians are erecting their constitutional and other constructions, the *verligtes* are hammering at the foundations to see whether they can hold." Many *verligtes* also argued against resignation from the National Party, the Afrikaner Broederbond and other power institutions of Afrikanerdom. They wanted to be kicked out instead. This would have caused embarrassment for those kicking them out. *Verligtes* opted for calculated embarrassment.

3.  On the Stellenbosch campus there were prominent critics of apartheid who stood outside of the political system, for instance Johannes Degenaar (philosophy) and SP Cilliers (sociology). Despite the vilification to which they were subjected from certain circles, they had a huge impact on many students and people within the broader Afrikaner community. The classicist André Hugo, who later joined the University of Cape Town, should also be mentioned. Many years later Nico Smith (theology) became another critical voice. He resigned from the Broederbond and Stellenbosch University (SU), and chose to work and live in the black township of Mamelodi near Pretoria. And of course there was also a considerable number of critics-from-inside-the-system in Stellenbosch. They were vehemently opposed by supporters of the system within the NP, the Broederbond and SU. All these critics were closely watched by the Security Police. As I realised later, "Koos" had good reason to ask that we should meet at my house. The NIS, the Security Police and Military Intelligence competed with each other in Stellenbosch.

4.  That same evening he issued a statement to *Die Burger*. A senior journalist from that paper called me late at night, informed me about the statement, and asked whether I wanted to comment on it. I said no, but if it were published I would likewise disregard the confidentiality of the meeting, disclose everything, and also name the people who had participated. This caused consternation.

After numerous telephone calls the statement was withdrawn. I decided to resign from the AB. In later years Piet Marais and I managed to restore the good relationship we once had. When Esther Lategan stood against him as the Independents' candidate, he had to battle hard to retain his seat. And he was, after all, a member of the National Party's caucus, albeit that he and I were in agreement about many things.

5.  The focus in the literature on "white" contacts with the banned ANC was a mirror image of our country's stark racial divide with its deeply rooted racial conflict. Whites were by no means the only ones who beat a path to the ANC's door in Lusaka. Many black organisations did the same. This list reads like a "who's who" from the world of the oppressed shortly before and after the Dakar conference: the *Inyandza National Movement* of Enos Mabuza (March 1986), the *Congress of South African Trade Unions* (March 1986), the *National Union of South African Students* (March 1986), the *Southern African Catholic Bishops' Conference* (April 1986), the *National African Federated Chamber of Commerce* (May 1986) and the *Evangelical Lutheran Church in Southern Africa* (Northern Diocese – November 1986). They were later followed by the *National Council of Trade Unions* (May 1988), the *Natal Indian Congress* and the *Transvaal Indian Congress* (October 1988), the *National Soccer League and Soccer Association of South Africa* (October 1988), the *Lawyers Conference* (February 1989), the *International Campaign Against Apartheid Sport and the South African Non-Racial Olympic Committee* (February 1989) and the *Congress of Traditional Leaders* (August 1989).

6.  In the Epilogue I look back on the dialogue process and endeavour to make sense of it theoretically in the light of my own experience and with reference to some of the literature on conflict resolution. An academic theoretical reflection on the dialogue process, as a case study, might make an interesting contribution to the growing body of literature. My epilogue should be read as marginal notes for such an undertaking.

CHAPTER 2

1.  Rupert met Botha personally on 21 November 1985 with reference to Rupert's discussions the day before with the Swiss banker Fritz Leutwiler, who was mediating between South Africa and its international creditor banks. At a second meeting with Botha on 22 November 1985, Rupert and a group of businessmen briefed Botha on their conference with US business leaders in London on 11 November 1985. In a subsequent private letter to Botha, Rupert wrote that, if he had understood Botha correctly – that he would "rather be poor than yield" and that he was not prepared to say that he would "renounce" apartheid – he (Rupert) was "deeply concerned" about this attitude. Botha responded sharply on 29 January 1986. He wrote that he had found Leutwiler "wiser, stronger and more sympathetic than some businesspeople in my own country who are more interested in temporary profits than in the government's struggle for stability, also on their behalf." He added: "I gladly listen to advice from good friends. But I tend to ignore advice that does not sound genuine to me. Dr Kissinger also warned about this in his writings."

2.  The Urban Foundation, a brainchild of the business sector following the 1976 uprisings in black communities, was formed with the inspiration of Harry Oppenheimer, Anton Rupert and Jan van der Horst from the Anglo American, Rembrandt and Old Mutual stables respectively. During this time it was an important chisel that took on the granite rock of apartheid. The living conditions of urban black people, security of tenure and numerous other restrictive measures were on the agenda. The strategy was incremental reform, in other words, a focused reform of cardinal aspects of the apartheid system; the intention was not to reform the "system", but to replace it with another system over time by way of an evolutionary process without jeopardising stability. The Foundation's CEO Jan Steyn made me a member of his "negotiation committee". It turned into

a unique experience that was continued on a limited basis after 1985. The first thing Steyn did was to expose me to Soweto by means of in loco visits and talks with community leaders.

After the declaration of the state of emergency in July 1985, he asked me one morning in his office diagonally opposite the supreme court building in Cape Town: "What do you think is going to happen after the state of emergency?" He regarded me over his spectacles and answered the question himself: "These are all temporary measures to postpone the inevitable. But perhaps reason will triumph and we will avoid total chaos and anarchism." He and I once met General Johan Coetzee of the Security Police very early one morning in Coetzee's office in Pretoria. We discussed the security situation in the country and Steyn made a point that he felt very strongly about: "Some of the security actions are causing growing alienation between white and black leaders." The general paused before replying. I had got to know him earlier when I worked at the Rand Afrikaans University and we served together on a school committee. He also visited me a few times at my home in Stellenbosch. The general looked at me and said: "We're sowing dragon's teeth in this country. It will devour all of us." In terms of lobbying and opinion forming, particularly among businesspeople, the Foundation was the best organised and most effective locally based institution. Jan Steyn was someone with an exceptional vision as well as moral courage. We held talks with dozens of leaders and politicians from white, coloured, black and Indian ranks.

CHAPTER 3

1.  From 1987 onwards I read a great deal about the Charter. In government and security circles it was predominantly described as a socialist-communist document, with Marxist authors the primary drafters. The "father" of the idea of a Charter was not a communist, however, but an outstanding intellectual: Professor ZK Matthews, father of Minister Naledi Pandor. Reading the document with its poetic moments, one can accept that the drafters expressed the prevailing political sentiments and socioeconomic expectations of "the people" (= the oppressed majority). It included almost everything for everybody; "almost", because the Africanist line of thinking within the black community was not fully articulated. This line of thinking, particularly with regard to the land issue, was responsible for an internal element of tension, which is once again illustrated by the Malema saga regarding agricultural land and the mines. The Africanists did not like the Charter's understanding of nonracialism either. It is interesting to note that the Youth League of the ANC was strongly Africanist, as is still the case today. The apartheid state's reaction was predictable: in Desember 1956 the police arrested 156 people on treason charges, more or less the entire leadership of the ANC, including Luthuli, Tambo, Mandela, Sisulu and Matthews. The trial became a protracted affair that ended in nothing but international and national embarrassment for the state when all the defendants were found not guilty in March 1961.

CHAPTER 4

1.  It was instructive to experience, through what I read, the gap between (written) propaganda and academic literature and research. It is a tragic reality that good research does not easily find its way to policy planning and strategic development, on the one hand because researchers do not always have the ability to "translate" findings into policy and strategic contexts, and on the other hand because politicians and bureaucrats are averse to findings that may go against their perceptions of achievable policy options and political power. Knowledge is not simply power. Power is also a battle for "knowledge" that furthers ideological objectives. This is where the issue of propaganda comes in and the context in which Karl Marx spoke of "useful idiots".

2.  General Giáp, who became a legend in Indo-China and inter alia defeated the French at Dien

Bien Phu (1954), celebrated his 100th birthday at a military hospital in Hanoi, Vietnam, on 25 August 2011. He is regarded as one the world's greatest military strategists. On 30 April 1975 the US, too, had to throw in the towel in South Vietnam. Later in his life he became very critical of the communist party in Vietnam and wrote in 2006 that the party had become a "shield for corrupt officials". In a photograph taken on 2 November 1979, not long after he had met Tambo, Mbeki and Slovo, he appears with Muammar Gaddafi and Raul Castro.

3. Ury's follow-up to *Getting to Yes*, which he coauthored with Harvard psychologist Daniel Shapiro, was even more illuminating: *Beyond Reason: Using Emotions as You Negotiate* (2005). I read this book at a much later stage, and it helped me to understand the Afrikaner-ANC dialogue group's meetings better when looking back on them today. The authors identify five "core concerns": autonomy, affiliation, appreciation, status and role. When these concerns are taken into account and receive proper attention, they stimulate constructive emotions in negotiation processes. As I read this book I thought of Nelson Mandela, the charming and truly human leader who could sweep people off their feet despite having teeth as hard as steel. Fisher owed his special expertise to the fact that he not only theorised, but also engaged in mediation and negotiation in practice in order to test his theories and correct them where necessary. He was a practitioner scholar and not only wrote books.

4. Kelly distinguishes five types of constructs or frames of reference: *impermeable; permeable; pre-emptive; constellary; propositional*. The first, third and fourth constructs are conducive to exclusivity. In any mediation and negotiation process, therefore, the major challenge is: How can "the other" be de-demonised? Can another construct be developed to replace the mutual labelling of each other as "enemies"?

5. I could appreciate this objective of the Afrikaner-ANC dialogue group better when I listened to John Paul Lederach's lecture on "The Role of Corporate Actors in Peace-Building Processes" during a conference on *Peace through Commerce* at the University of Notre Dame in the US. It has been published in a book with the conference theme as its title (2008). Lederach, professor of international peacebuilding at Notre Dame's renowned Kroc Institute for International Peace Studies, describes peace processes as follows: "Peace building represents the intentional confluence – the flowing together – of improbable processes and people to sustain constructive change that reduces violence and increases the potential and practice of justice in human relationships" (pp 98-99).

6. The Freedom Park, situated near the Voortrekker Monument in Pretoria, is a state-initiated memorial in celebration of the coming into being of South Africa's inclusive democracy and the struggle that preceded it.

CHAPTER 5

1. The public outcry about the Sharpeville Six led to a further estrangement between PW Botha and Anton Rupert. On 17 March 1988, Rupert wrote a letter in which he asked Botha "humbly" if he could not "please commute the death sentence of the 'Sharpeville Six' in the interests of our children and grandchildren. We should at all costs avoid creating another six Jopie Fouries." (Jopie Fourie had been executed during the Rebellion of Afrikaners against the Smuts government. He became a heroic figure in Afrikaner eyes.) Botha, clearly annoyed, replied within days (on 21 March 1988). He wrote: "It was a shock to me to learn that you blithely compare the persons under sentence with Jopie Fourie. I must say that I was deeply disappointed after I had read your letter, but it proves to me once again how the best among us are falling victim to orchestrated propaganda against our country and a government which is trying to uphold civilised values in South Africa." Botha at least concluded his letter "With kind regards".

2.  The ANC especially feared the SA Citizen Force, which consisted of thousands of young conscripts. They were very well trained and did "border duty" in SWA/Namibia and Angola. They were also deployed in the township wars in attempts to maintain order. In addition, there was the established Commando system that operated mainly in rural areas as an organised volunteer corps. The activities of the End Conscription Campaign were directly connected with the ANC's tacit admission that the Citizen Force system was a major impediment to the realisation of the ANC's dream of a revolutionary takeover of power. Mbeki admitted to me that South Africa could not be equated with Vietnam, inter alia because of the South African state's militarised political culture and well-trained Permanent and Civilian Forces. On a visit to Lusaka in 1990 I got a very clear message: A black majority government will accept neither compulsory military service for young people nor the Commando system. "Too expensive and dangerous," Aziz Pahad told me.

CHAPTER 6

1.  The Fellowship Movement, a worldwide network, was non-ecclesiastical and not linked to any faith denomination. Its focus was sharply on leaders and how they could obtain personal support in terms of ethical values and virtues. "Virtue ethics" was a priority, linked with "ethics of care". In the 1980s this movement invited Buthelezi and me and a few other people from various parts of the world to a prayer breakfast with President Ronald Reagan, his vice-president George Bush, and members of the US Congress in Washington. In those days political leaders from other parts of the world were also invited to this event, at which seminars took place. Leaders from behind the Iron Curtain were among those who attended. President Kenneth Kaunda had a close association with the network, as did Dr Mangosuthu Buthelezi and Enos Mabuza.
2.  "Soft targets" were undoubtedly one of the biggest strategic miscalculations on the part of the ANC. In many parts of the world and especially among "people of faith" in South Africa it led to words such as "terrorism" and "undisciplined" taking root. Later it became not only a very delicate political and moral issue, but also a conundrum during the formal negotiation process: Which incidents of violence were "politically" motivated, and who should get "amnesty" on what basis? The Norgaard principles, which had been drafted by the Dane Carl Norgaard and were applied in Namibia to define political offences, were also adopted during the formal negotiation process in South Africa. De Klerk's interpretation of the principles was swept off the table by the ANC, for example in the case of Robert McBride. In 1986 he had planted a bomb in a Durban bar that killed three people and injured 69. The ANC, however, demanded the unconditional release of everyone the organisation regarded as "political prisoners" – regardless of what act of violence they had committed. A directional and guiding decision on violence was lacking.

CHAPTER 7

1.  I was wrong, of course. In situations of deep-rooted conflict where direct and structural violence prevails as a result of group-oriented discrimination and a violation of the demands of justice by a ruling (ethnic) minority, "ownership", and especially landownership, becomes an important political issue. The battle for land is as old as the hills, the valleys and the pastures. It is a highly emotional issue because it is not about land as a *productive asset*, but about land as a *political identity symbol*.
2.  The Dutch Reformed Church (DRC) and the NP were seen by the ANC and the UDF/MDM as ideological allies and a "conspiracy against the people". Among all the ecclesiastical contacts I had with black theologians and ministers from the so-called reformed tradition, not a single one disagreed with this identification. The DRC *was* institutionally the NP-at-prayer (for the preser-

vation of apartheid). While criticism of apartheid theology and apartheid practices that came from within the DRC was appreciated, there was not really a strong identification with it. Like the state's incremental reforms, the DRC's attempts at incremental reform were regarded with contempt. The manner in which the DRC responded to the now famous Belhar Confession reinforced the belief in a political conspiracy between the apartheid state and the apartheid church. The DRC became part of the enemy construct of the liberation movements.

CHAPTER 8

1. Botha took over as prime minister from BJ Vorster in September 1978, after much infighting and many public political clashes as a result of the Information Scandal that had erupted around the heads of Vorster and Connie Mulder (a minister). Taxpayers' money had been used generously for propaganda purposes. A newspaper had even been established with secret state funds: *The Citizen*. In 1983 Botha became executive state president within the tricameral parliamentary system which was instituted in that year after a referendum for white voters.

2. I was then still a member of the Afrikaner Broederbond, which played a huge role in the development of the tricameral parliamentary system. At one of our meetings in the Verwoerd holiday home in Betty's Bay, under the eyes of HF Verwoerd's portrait that hung on a wall, Piet Cillié – the big induna of Nasionale Pers – who sat next to me, said with his trademark ironic cynicism: "Do you think he knows that today we're starting with the dismantling of his apartheid system?" His remark was prophetic, in a paradoxical way. The impracticability of the tricameral parliament was a major nail in the coffin for the NP's rigid ideological notion of race-based group rights.

CHAPTER 9

1. At one stage I noticed that some of the students in the residence were shunning us, notably the political activists who had ties with Nusas. It turned out that Mark Behr and some of his Nusas committee members had launched a campaign to cast suspicion on me. Copies of my earlier membership of the Afrikaner Broederbond, as published in a book on this secret organisation from which I had resigned by that time because of sharp differences with some of the members, had also been distributed among the students. I was already aware of Behr's alleged associations as an agent of the security services, and even wondered whether Military Intelligence or the Security Police might be the real inspiration behind the suspicion-mongering. The campus was riddled with agents in those days. De Vries even had to hold a discussion with PW Botha about the matter. Be that as it may, in the end Mark Behr and Nusas did not succeed with their campaign.

2. It is remarkable that the role of the NIS in the transition and negotiation process has not yet received the kind of attention it deserves. The reason for this is presumably that scholars rather focus on "public figures and institutions" and that all kinds of reservations exist about intelligence services as such on account of misconceptions and an inability/unwillingness to rationally examine this extremely important facet of all states. The National Intelligence Service of South Africa was more decisive in the country's transition process than *any* other organisation. A book by a former security agent, Riaan Labuschagne (2002), *On South Africa's Secret Service: An Undercover Agent's Story*, throws an interesting light on matters regarding the NIS and also on Barnard's role in this organisation.

3. Robert Harvey, in his book *The Fall of Apartheid* (2001), grasped very little of the more human facets of the dialogue process. He was not present at the meetings, after all, and his book is based mainly on Michael Young's notes, communications and memories. He also attributes contributions to the dialogue group that are wide of the mark, for instance "messages" that Willem de Klerk

conveyed to his brother FW. De Klerk did forward notes to FW, but whether and how his brother took cognisance of the contents is not as certain as Harvey maintains. He overrates the role of the dialogue project too one-sidedly. It was merely part of a more complex preparatory phase.

CHAPTER 10

1. I watched PW Botha's announcement of his resignation on TV. It reminded me of the resignation of Botha's predecessor BJ Vorster, in which Botha had played a role. I couldn't help thinking that, as in a tragedy, three NP leaders successively had disappeared from the scene in unfortunate cir-cumstances: HF Verwoerd – assassinated; BJ Vorster – resigned as a result of a scandal; PW Botha – resigned as a result of his cabinet's total lack of confidence in his competence. The rebellion of Botha's cabinet (14 August) took place a day before the fourth anniversary of Botha's infamous Rubicon speech of 15 August 1985.

CHAPTER 11

1. Moral issues often surfaced in our discussions, for instance on the part of Mike Louw. To name one example, he was never enthusiastic about South Africa as a military power in the region and in Africa. He and others were increasingly uneasy about South Africa's manufacture of nuclear bombs, at PW Botha's insistence. This was counterproductive, in Louw's view, because it drew unnecessary atten-tion to South Africa, gave rise to more tension in circles where South Africa could not afford it, and created more enemies than was necessary. In March 1984, for instance, relations with Britain were soured when four South Africans were arrested in Britain in terms of British legislation that pro-hibited the export of arms to South Africa. Louw considered all of this morally indefensible.

2. The process of information collection, and the processing and evaluation of the collected infor-mation, are also at the root of the job of an intelligence service not only to provide decision-makers with a strategic capability, but also to keep their eyes on the ball. To this end, when it came to the ANC, government leaders were supplied with information documents, intelligence reports and profiles of the most important ANC leaders. Briefing sessions were held as well. All of this gave De Klerk and his cabinet a certain competitive advantage. Spaarwater was not very positive about this, though. He claimed in *Beeld* (2/11/2010) that government leaders "simply ignored" this information during the settlement process. It provides a possible explanation for the widely held perception that government leaders underestimated the ANC negotiators. Be that as it may, and regardless of what competitive advantage the De Klerk government might have had, the ANC negotiators *did* become increasingly stronger in the formal phases of the process.

CHAPTER 12

1. Lombard, a minister of the Western Cape regional synod of the DRC, was one of the progressive ministers in this region. Another was Willie Jonker, professor of dogmatics at Stellenbosch Uni-versity's faculty of theology. At a church conference in Rustenburg on 6 November 1990, which was also attended by Archbishop Tutu, Jonker made a confession of guilt for apartheid that created a huge stir. It had been preceded by an admission of guilt for apartheid on the part of the DRC's general synod in Bloemfontein some time before. The ANC members were interested in views on civil disobedience within the DRC, as well as in the rethinking within this church with reference to the policy document *Church and Society* that had replaced the apartheid document *Race, Volk and Nation* in 1986. Admittedly, it was a long goodbye.

2. A photo taken at Idasa's Leverkusen conference (in Germany) on which Malan and Terreblanche appeared with Joe Slovo was used ad nauseam by the NP and its supporters as propaganda against

the Democratic Party during the September election. At that stage the anticommunism that Afrikaners had been fed by the propaganda of the Total Onslaught was still a convenient sounding board. Less than a year later FW De Klerk himself appeared on a photo with Slovo, in his red socks, which was taken at Groote Schuur.

3. Niel Barnard was of the view that enough time had to be allowed for very thorough and structured participation in talks about talks. He and his team held talks with Mandela over a period of two years, and not haphazardly either. After all, it was not merely a clarification of fundamental positions, but also a trust-building process. Barnard relates that PW Botha often asked him when he would be able to inform his whole cabinet. Barnard, who wanted to keep the process under wraps until there was greater clarity on the road ahead, reckoned that the cabinet would not have respected the confidential nature of the talks. He even told Botha that Pik Botha was "genetically" incapable of keeping something like this a secret.

4. Both Mbeki and Zuma were opposed to what they called "secret negotiations". At first I did not quite understand what they meant, and only realised later that this pertained to the official, formal process. Included in this position, though, was the concern that the government might enter into a secret agreement with Mandela beforehand. Mbeki was particularly worried about the possibility of an "Abel Muzorewa trap", with reference to the black leader in Zimbabwe who cooperated with Ian Smith, the last white premier of the then Rhodesia. Mbeki and Zuma did not have an objection to a confidential "bargaining process".

5. A storm erupted in the Cape Afrikaans daily newspaper *Die Burger*. Jannie Momberg, an MP of the Democratic Party, wrote a blistering letter to *Die Burger* (4 October 1989) with reference to Dommisse's presence at the talks, in light of the campaign by this newspaper and the NP against Wynand Malan's visits to the ANC. He slated *Die Burger* as "a party-political smear pamphlet". The newspaper responded on the same day with a defence under the heading: "Dialogue with the ANC: What is the position of newsmen who are present?" The gist of the defence was that a "newsman is a communicator and a bearer of information".

CHAPTER 13

1. I was informed on my arrival that the audience was strongly pro-ANC. The AAI, with its headquarters at the United Nations Plaza in New York, focused on solid ties and understanding between the US and Africa's leadership elite. Koos Kruger was convinced that the organisation was an agency of the US's security services. I wondered about this too, apropos of the staff members of the AAI that I met.

2. In the US there was great interest, particularly among a group of intellectuals and academics, in Afrikaners, South Africa's "white tribe" but a "strange" society. At the invitation of the US government under President Carter, I was taken on an extensive trip through this remarkable country. Apartheid had a certain resonance in a country that grappled with segregation and human rights, notably in the South. In Aniston, a village in the South, I had the opportunity to listen for a whole morning to the stories told in the small church of a black minister who had marched with Martin Luther King in protest against racial discrimination in the US. This experience gave me a better understanding of the focus on apartheid.

3. De Klerk also had a "kitchen cabinet", a selected group of expert confidants. They met over weekends. The decisions he made were neither haphazard nor instinctive. They had been thought through and were well planned.

4. This trust was not as remarkable as it may seem at first glance. It had been built over time in the course of the prison talks. Barnard was in my view also correct when he pointed out on one oc-

casion that the confidential nature of the initial talks and the fact that they had escaped the spotlight of the media, was an important reason for the success of the eventual negotiation process.

CHAPTER 14

1.  Thabo Mbeki, together with other high-profile ANC leaders and President Kenneth Kaunda, had of course already met English-speaking business leaders and a few newspaper editors in 1985. One of the editors was Tertius Myburgh of the *Sunday Times*. According to Myburgh, one of the visitors from South Africa had remarked: "I'd rather receive Thabo Mbeki at my home than Ted Kennedy." The business leaders were all very impressed with Mbeki. Gavin Relly, chairman of Anglo American, had to face a barrage of criticism on his return to South Africa, not only from PW Botha and his government but even from Anglo ranks. The ANC was of the view that Relly and his business associates retired into their shells after this, and that nothing substantial had happened in the interaction between South African business leaders and the ANC following the Mfuwe talks. To what extent Mbeki might have intended to play English-speaking and Afrikaner business leaders off against each other, as was sometimes claimed, is not clear. What was clearer, however, was his position that Afrikaner business leaders had a stronger emotional bond with South Africa and Africa. He also believed quite rightly that Afrikaner business leaders had more political influence than the liberal English-speaking ones. After 1990 he had a very good relationship with Sanlam's Marinus Daling in particular, and took special trouble to speak at the memorial service after Daling's death.

CHAPTER 15

1.  The business leaders advanced interesting arguments as to why economic forces helped to sink apartheid. Du Plessis was of the opinion that South Africa had been engaged in an "economic war" with the rest of the world up to February 1990. After all, PW Botha's Rubicon speech (1985) had led to the withdrawal of the country's credit facilities. There was something else as well: the exorbitant costs of South Africa's military action in Angola and the budget expenditure on security. These cost factors, combined with sanctions, had a very negative economic impact. For instance, South Africa had to manufacture sophisticated weapons of its own at great expense. Pretorius concurred with this view and said that sanctions had achieved their intended objectives in South Africa, particularly because of the outflow of capital. It was striking that none of the business leaders, and none of the other Afrikaner participants in the dialogue project either, reckoned that there had been any good reason for South Africa's military involvement in Angola.

2.  In 1990, apropos of De Klerk's 2 February speech, a special initiative was taken: Nedcor and Old Mutual appointed a team to develop post-1990 scenarios for South Africa. Dr Johan Maree, chairman of Nedcor, said at the first meeting: "If this were Switzerland, the exercise would be unnecessary." The "exercise" was one of the most comprehensive of its kind in South Africa up to that point. Willem de Klerk, Oscar Dhlomo and I were responsible for the political section. Mamphela Ramphele, Sheila Sisulu and Maude Motanyana dealt with the social dimension. Others focused on the economic dimension. Between January 1991 and June 1992 the scenarios were presented to more than 45 000 South Africans, including the De Klerk cabinet and the ANC. As early as 1990 we came to a conclusion that I felt very strongly about and stressed repeatedly in discussions with my NIS and ANC contacts: continuing political and criminal violence, along with social disintegration, may scupper the transition process.

CHAPTER 16

1. I experienced something of this during a meeting at the Elsenburg agricultural college where De Klerk had to address a gathering of farmers (27 September 1991). Some farmers walked out of the meeting in protest. At some stage Mandela phoned De Klerk. He wanted to see De Klerk, the president of the country, urgently. And immediately, not tomorrow. Mandela was staying at the Lord Charles Hotel in Somerset West and De Klerk was a guest speaker at the important Elsenburg event. De Klerk, the soul of cooperativeness, agreed to a meeting. I had to assist with the transport arrangements, fetch Mandela and bring him to a safe venue in Stellenbosch. Everything had to be kept highly confidential. De Klerk asked me: "Do you think PW would have done what I'm prepared to do?" I said: "No, but fortunately you're not PW." I realised that day that De Klerk and Mandela were political rivals, both nationally and internationally. That day I also suspected that this was going to cause many political problems in future. My hunch turned out to be correct.

   The Elsenburg event provided some unintentional comedy. I had to pick up Mandela at the Lord Charles, but my BMW was old and decrepit. I arranged with Dawie de Villiers's brother-in-law, Ryno King, to borrow his smart new car. But King's posh car refused to start. When I told Mandela about this, he laughed heartily at my attempt to impress him with someone else's car. That day he wrote me a note in Afrikaans: "To Prof. Esterhuyse, compliments and best wishes. Nelson Mandela." Mandela overwhelmed me once again with his graciousness and his recognition of Afrikaans. Many years later, when he was awarded an honorary doctorate by Stellenbosch University at a special ceremony, he also gave recognition to Afrikaans. He delivered his address in what I called "Mandela Afrikaans".

2. There was another leak, but only on 29 September 1991. The *Sunday Star* blazoned it forth on its front page: "Nats and ANC in secret talks". The subheading was: "Top officials of both parties kept in the dark". The report referred to the talks that had been going on for years (since 1987). Willem de Klerk's presence at the August meeting in question was a particular source of interest. Even Gill Marcus was dragged in. It was reported that she had said the ANC leadership was discussing the matter with those concerned. The two journalists, Ivor Powell and Peta Thornycroft, also stated that Cyril Ramaphosa, the ANC's secretary-general and leader of the ANC's negotiating team, was very surprised at the news of the talks. The ANC's National Working Committee on negotiations, it was claimed, would discuss it within days. Mbeki, unperturbed, reckoned that negotiations were inevitable and that it was necessary to consult informally to get them off the ground.

3. After the election Thabo Mbeki and FW de Klerk were appointed as the two deputy presidents, in the case of Mbeki with a lack of enthusiasm from the ranks of his old opponents from the ANC and the former UDF (which had been integrated with the ANC by then). The relationship between Mbeki and De Klerk was amicable. But I never got the impression that it was collegial and cooperative, particularly not after the ANC started referring to Mbeki as "first deputy" and De Klerk as "second deputy". Issues of a more personal nature also played a role, such as which residence should be allocated to whom. Zanele Mbeki took trouble to build a bridge or two on the informal level, but without success. My own informal attempt to make a contribution in this regard failed as well. The notion of "opponents", which had at least replaced the "enemy construct", was simply too strong on both the formal and the informal, personal level. This also had an impact on the personal relationships between Mandela and the De Klerk couple, for example during the Nobel Peace Prize ceremony in Norway.

CHAPTER 17

1.  Contrary to what is sometimes claimed, Mbeki equated neither the state nor the government with the ANC as party. Luthuli House's bureaucrats and ideologues strove for a form of bureaucratic totalitarianism, for a variety of reasons (for example, an obsession with control by the party; greed; anticapitalism; "redressing" whites' injustices of the past). Their dream was that the state, with its deployed cadres, should control and dictate *all* forms of transformation. In my view, it was this mentality that eventually also led to Van Zyl Slabbert's disillusionment and alienation. The party bureaucrats expected him to join the ANC if he wanted to play a role in future. He was a big fish that they were keen to land. There was *no* interest in these circles in Slabbert as a "mediator", not even after the role he had played in the Johannesburg Metropolitan Chamber to mediate a development partnership between (white) Johannesburg and (black) Soweto. He had sent out "promising signals", as some of my ANC friends put it, but nothing came of it. I suspect that he did not want to join the ANC for the same reason that I did not become a member, namely the ANC's alliance with the SACP and the party's influence on the ANC. To my mind, it was ultimately not Thabo Mbeki who had marginalised Slabbert, as is often alleged. Owing to his exceptional public standing as a leader and thinker, not even a Thabo Mbeki would have been able to promote him to an influential position. For that he would have had to first become a member of the ANC, like Roelf Meyer and Marthinus van Schalkwyk.

2.  De Klerk is quoted in a footnote in Hermann Giliomee's updated version of his book *The Afrikaners* (2003) in which Giliomee also refers to the Afrikaner-ANC dialogue group. In the interview in question (28 May 2009), De Klerk was clearly irritated by what he called the misrepresentations in the film *Endgame*. As an example of the "faction" genre, this film should of course not be seen as a factual documentary. His irritation should also be attributed to the rivalry that existed between him and his brother (Willem) – an intellectual pioneer among Afrikaners – and the impression that is created in the film that he was dictated to by his brother. At least in a certain way the film accords recognition to the crucial role played by the NIS and Neil Barnard. De Klerk emphasised in particular that the Afrikaner-ANC talks were not a parallel channel, nor did they influence him either formally or informally. No one in the dialogue group ever made such claims. His position is also understandable because he was never part of the preparatory processes of which even PW Botha had been aware. Fortunately, De Klerk eventually took over the leadership and finalisation of these processes in an enthusiastic and resourceful manner. It was well deserved that he could open the champagne at a table that taken long to be prepared. His obvious irritation pertains to an important issue that is pointed out in this book: the role of informal and unofficial track-two interactions and the transfer thereof to track-one processes. After he became president, I had a one-on-one meeting with him in his Cape Town office where he was so kind as to say that his door was open to me. Because I got the impression on this occasion that he had not been fully briefed on my Barnard and Mbeki connections, I did not inform him about it. After all, it was not my responsibility and task to do so as my contact regarding this particular matter was not with him but with Mbeki, the NIS and Barnard – strategic midwives of the process. Even today the decisive role of the Coetzee-Mandela-Barnard talks and the role of the former National Intelligence Service with people like Barnard, Louw and Spaarwater are sometimes still underplayed.

    In his brief discussion of the Mells Park talks, Giliomee refers to another important question: the lack of reports on the talks, which Willie Breytenbach has also pointed out. It is a fact that track-two talks, especially when they are private or confidential, should be thoroughly documented in order that "messages" that emanate from them and "positions" that are adopted can be relayed as correctly as possible. It is not the task of the go-between or message-bearer to convey primarily his/her personal views. There were indeed such reports, for instance those which I compiled myself, but which were not submitted to or approved by the dialogue group participants or made public. Summaries of these reports found their way to the NIS, where I discussed them in detail with a small group of members. It is remarkable that no South African researcher or commentator who has written about the Mells Park initiative ever inquired as to whether or not any documentation existed.

Willem de Klerk and I went to a lot of trouble to brief key opinion leaders in Afrikaner ranks. On a few occasions I was criticised sharply because no English-speaking whites had been invited. The easy answer was that the dialogue group had to be kept small. The difficult answer was that it was an exclusive dialogue between Afrikaners and members of the ANC – representatives of the main parties to the conflict. Mbeki did remark occasionally that greater inclusivity could be considered later, depending on progress. Neither he nor I, however, had anticipated that the progress after FW's entry into the process as president of the country would be as rapid as it turned out to be.

3.  As far as this dream is concerned, in certain respects we find ourselves back in the bloody 1980s, with violence still a constant companion of our country and our people. And Thabo Mbeki's "two nations" metaphor (1998), whereby he not only debunked the "rainbow nation" metaphor but also incurred the wrath of many whites, has been "transformed" into a brutal combination of racial and class differences that run like a widening rift valley through our country, its people, its cities, its towns and its institutions. It symbolises what US president Franklin Roosevelt said decades ago in his second inaugural address: "I see one-third of a nation ill-housed, ill-clad, ill-nourished." One "sees" this contrast, only to a worse extent, in South Africa as well, in Johannesburg, in Stellenbosch, in rural towns, and between schools and universities. In the US there is already talk of "two Americas". The post-Polokwane ANC has not only finally shredded the "rainbow nation" metaphor, but also dramatically boosted the "two South Africas" phenomenon. We can "see" this on a daily basis.

EPILOGUE

1.  ANC documents are available at the archives of the University of the Western Cape's Mayibuye Centre. The University of Fort Hare also houses documents in the ANC archives.

2.  Adam and Moodley (in LeMaitre & Savage, 2010) wrote a letter about this to Mbeki. In his reply to their letter, he inter alia expressed his failure to understand why Slabbert had seemingly imprisoned himself "within walls of bitterness". To some of those who had attended the Dakar conference and others close to Slabbert, the Mbeki-Slabbert relationship became an emotional issue after 1994 when Mbeki was the deputy president in Mandela's cabinet and later the president. In 2006, Slabbert attributed the rift between them to something that had occurred about twelve years earlier. In response to a question by Mbeki to Slabbert as to what he (Slabbert) would do if he were in Mbeki's place, Slabbert, according to what he wrote (2006), replied that he would appoint a number of expert committees in key areas to advise him – "to constantly remind me of how much I have to learn and how ignorant I am." This memory of Slabbert's about what had taken place during a visit to Mbeki's home in Johannesburg prompted him to write many years later: "This must have offended him." According to Slabbert, this was the end of their friendship. He even wrote: "He [Mbeki] is the only person I know who has demonstrated to me that friendship was expendable." It is debatable whether the timing of Slabbert's visit, the wording and nature of the suggestion, and ultimately also his version/recollection of Mbeki's reaction were well thought out. The version Mbeki gave me shortly after the conversation in question – as *his* version – was different. In my view, it was a tragic misunderstanding between two exceptionally talented people that could have been prevented through an informal dialogue.

3.  John W McDonald, a former US ambassador, later pointed out multiple tracks: the media, private

individuals, businesspeople and professional conflict-resolution practitioners. The number of possible tracks was increased over time. Among others, they included religion, activism, research, training, education and the donor community (philantrophy). An institute for Multi-Track Diplomacy was even established in Virginia in the US. It developed twelve principles, with number one being "Relationship-building, strong interpersonal and intergroup relations throughout the fabric of society", thereby making the point that the building and sustaining of peace should *never* be monopolised. It is not something for amateurs either.

4. Daniel Lieberfeld, who interpreted the Afrikaner-ANC dialogue project on the basis of the track-two model, conducted several interviews. Apart from me, he spoke to Niel Barnard and Mike Louw of the NIS and Aziz Pahad of the ANC, among others. The conversations and what he wrote about them, as in the case of the film *Endgame*, helped me to understand what the Afrikaner-ANC dialogue group tried to do. His evaluation of the contribution of a track-two approach to conflict resolution in South Africa in his book *Talking with the Enemy: Negotiation and Threat Perception in South Africa and Israel/Palestine* (1999) and in articles and other contributions was particularly helpful. The collection of case studies by Ronald J Fisher, professor in international peace and conflict resolution (American University), in *Paving the Way: Contributions of Interactive Conflict Resolution* (2005), was one of the most valuable works I read afterwards in an effort to gain a better understanding of the Afrikaner-ANC dialogue group's activities and contributions. The book also includes an article by Lieberfeld on the Afrikaner-ANC dialogue group.

5. Pilger's *Hidden Agendas* (1998), which I read afterwards, was also very significant in my retrospective interpretation of the Afrikaner-ANC dialogue group's activities. Hidden agendas cannot be eliminated from the outset. It first requires a dialogue process that explores and gradually fosters the notion of a *common chief agenda*. Access to key role players is a condition in this regard.

6. Lieberfeldt, 2005:21

7. Among the various ways in which I looked at my involvement, there is one that I need to single out on account of Breytenbach's remark in *Rapport*. According to what Pahad told me in 1987, Breytenbach was a committed white militant who was known for his loathing for the ANC communists. Okhela, which had been established as a vehicle for mainly white militants who wanted to support the ANC's infiltration project despite not being communist sympathisers, got Breytenbach to infiltrate South Africa (in disguise) in order to explore the possibility of underground support structures with other activists. Even before his departure from Paris in 1975, I was told, the Security Police knew about the plans. In those days the South African government's project of infiltrating the ANC worked like a dream. Breytenbach was also not popular in the ANC's communist circles that called the tune at the time and wanted to control all forms of infiltration into South Africa. Moreover, in the shadowy world of intelligence and security services there are forms of "quiet co-operation". Breytenbach was captured in South Africa and imprisoned for seven years on a charge of terrorism. When I learned more about the Breytenbach debacle in the 1980s, I accepted the fact that there was no such thing as "indispensable people" in that with which I had become involved. The notion of a principled "rule-bound" ethic is not exactly feasible in an environment of opposing and combative "enemies". "Consequence ethics", in other words, an assessment and value estimate of the consequences of a particular act or deed, tend to be decisive. It was this approach that caused people like Barnard and Maharaj to react very critically and sometimes even negatively to the contributions of intellectuals and academics. To the ANC hotheads in Lusaka Breytenbach was dispensable, like most other people who become involved in a battle for survival *and* power between "enemies". I accepted this, and did not allow myself to be seduced by the illusion of "indispensability". Too many formerly "indispensable individuals" are embittered people today.

# Reading list

| | | |
|---|---|---|
| Adam, H. & Moodley, K. | 1993. | *The Negotiated Revolution and Politics in Post Apartheid South Africa,* Johannesburg. |
| African National Congress | 1986-89. | *Unite for Freedom.* Texts of joint communiqués issued by the ANC and other South African organisations and individuals, Lusaka. |
| African National Congress | 1986-89. | *Unite for Freedom.* Statements by the ANC on the question of unity and anti-apartheid coalition (ANC, DIP), 1985-1990, Lusaka. |
| Atkinson, G. | 1977. | *The Effective Negotiator: A Practical Guide to Strategies and Tactics of Conflict and Bargaining,* London. |
| Boraine, A. | 1987. | *Dakar Report Back.* IDASA Occasional Papers, Cape Town. |
| Boulie, B. | 1996. | *Mediation: Principle, Process, Practice,* London. |
| Carnegie Commission | 1997. | *Preventing Deadly Conflict,* New York. |
| Crocker, C. | 1992. | *High Noon in Southern Africa: Making Peace in a Rough Neighborhood,* Johannesburg. |
| Crocker, C., Fen O. Hampson, & P. Aall (eds) | 2001. | *Turbulent Peace: The Challenges of Managing International Conflict,* Washington. |
| De Klerk, F.W. | 1998. | *The Last Trek – A New Beginning,* London. |
| Diamond, L. & J. McDonald | 1996. | *Multi-Track Diplomacy: A Systems Approach to Peace,* West Hartford. |
| Fisher, R. & W. Ury | 1981. | *Getting to Yes. Negotiating Agreement Without Giving In,* Boston. |
| Fisher, R. & D. Shapiro | 2005. | *Beyond Reason: Using Emotions as You Negotiate,* New York. |
| Fisher, R. & D. Ertel | 1981. | *Getting Ready to Negotiate,* Boston. |
| Gevisser, M. | 2007. | *Thabo Mbeki: The Dream Deferred,* Cape Town. |
| Gharajedaghi, J. | 1999. | *Systems Thinking: Managing Chaos and Complexity,* Boston. |
| Harvey, R. | 2001. | *The Fall of Apartheid: The Inside Story from Smuts to Mbeki,* New York. |
| Heald, G.R. | 2006. | *Learning Amongst Enemies: A Phenomenological Study of the South African Constitutional Negotiations from 1985-1998,* doctoral thesis, University of the Witwatersrand. |
| Kelly, G.A. | 1963. | *A Theory of Personality: The Psychology of Personal Constructs,* New York. |
| LeMaitre, A. & M. Savage | 2010. | *Van Zyl Slabbert – The Passion for Reason: Essays in Honour of an African Afrikaner,* Cape Town. |
| Lieberfeld, D. | 1999. | *Talking with the Enemy: Negotiation and Threat Perception in South Africa and Israel/Palestine,* Westport. |
| Lieberfeld, D. | 2002. | "Evaluating the Contributions of Unofficial Diplomacy to Conflict Termination in South Africa, 1984-1990," *Journal of Peace Research* 39. |

Lieberfeld, D.                         2003.   "Nelson Mandela: Partisan and Peacemaker," *Negotiation Journal*, July, pp 229-250.
Lieberfeld, D.                         2005.   "Contributions of a Semi-Official Prenegotiation Initiative in South Africa: Afrikaner-ANC Meetings in England, 1987-1990", in: Ronald J. Fisher (ed.) *Paving the Way: Contributions of Interactive Conflict Resolution to Peacemaking*, Lanham.
MacDonald, J. & D. Bendahmane                  *Conflict Resolution: Track Two Diplomacy*, US Government
(eds)                                  1987.   Printing Office, Washington DC.
Mandela, N.                            1994.   *Long Walk to Freedom*, Randburg.
Mbeki, T.                              2010.   *Talking to the Enemy*, Fifth Jazeera Annual Forum (May 24), Aljazeera.net.
Mission to South Africa                1986.   The Commonwealth Report, Penguin, Middlesex.
Mitchell, C.                           1989.   *The Structure of International Conflict*, New York.
Montville, J.V. & W.D. Davidson        1981.   "Foreign Policy According to Freud," *Foreign Policy*, Winter 1981-82, p.145-157.
O'Donnell, G. & P.C. Schmitter         1986.   *Transitions from Authoritarian Rule: Tentative Conclusions about Uncertain Democracies*, Baltimore.
Pilger, J.                             1998.   *Hidden Agendas*, London.
Pillar, P.                             1990.   "Ending Limited War, The Psychological Dynamics of the Termination Process," in: Betty Glad (ed.) *Psychological Dynamics of War*, Newbury Park, CA.
Slabbert, F. v. Z.                     2006.   *The Other Side of History*, Johannesburg.
Sparks, A.                             1994.   *Tomorrow is Another Country: The Inside Story of South Africa's Negotiated Revolution*, Sandton.
Stein, G. (ed.)                        1989.   *Getting to the Table: The Processes of International Prenegotiation*, Baltimore.
Stone, D.                              2004.   "Private Authority, Scholarly Legitimacy and Political Credibility: Think Tanks and Informal Diplomacy," in: *Global Governance: Critical Concepts in Political Science* (ed. J. Sinclair), London.
Tucker, B. & B.R. Scott (eds)          1992.   *South Africa: Prospects for Successful Transition*, Cape Town.
Waldmeir, P.                           1997.   *Anatomy of a Miracle. The End of Apartheid and the Birth of the New South Africa*, New York.
Welsh, D.                              2009.   *The Rise and Fall of Apartheid*, Cape Town.
Williams, O. (ed.)                     2008.   *Peace through Commerce. Responsible Corporate Citizenship and the Ideals of the United Nations Global Compact*, Notre Dame.
Zartman, I.W. & M.R. Berman            1982.   *The Practical Negotiator*, London.
Zartman, I.W.                          1985.   *Ripe for Resolution: Conflict and Intervention in Africa*, New York.

# About the author

WILLIE ESTERHUYSE was born in 1936 in Laingsburg, where his father farmed. He studied at the University of Stellenbosch, where after a sabbatical of 2 ½ years in the Netherlands, he obtained a D Phil. His initial qualifications were in theology and philosophy. He started his career as an academic in 1965 as a lecturer at University College, Durban, and in 1967 moved to the then Rand Afrikaans University. In 1974 he joined the university's Philosophy Department as a professor until 2002. From 1999 to 2006 he taught Business Ethics part-time at the University of Stellenbosch Business School, and lectured in management at the University of Cape Town's Graduate School of Business.

He was director of, among others, Murray & Roberts, Metropolitan Holdings, Medi-Clinic, Plexus and Stellenbosch Vineyards and a trustee of the Sanlam Demutualisation Trust. He is currently a trustee of the Thabo Mbeki Foundation, involved in the Thabo Mbeki African Leadership Institute (TMALI), and is non-executive chairman of Barinor Holdings Limited.

Prof Esterhuyse is the recipient of numerous prizes and awards, including the Order of Luthuli (silver) in 2003, the same year that the University of Stellenbosch awarded him an honorary doctorate. He has served as board member and later as chair of Artscape, as board member of the Klein Karoo National Arts Festival and of Freedom Park, and as trustee of the Nations Trust.

His numerous publications include *Apartheid Must Die* and *The ANC and its Leaders*. He was the compiler of Thabo Mbeki's *Africa: The time has come* and *Africa: Define yourself.*

In the movie *Endgame*, which tells the story of the secret negotiations in England, his role is played by William Hurt. Prof. Esterhuyse lives in Stellenbosch.

# Index

The abbreviation 'WE' is used for the author, Willie Esterhuyse.